The Struggle for the Soul of the SBC

Moderate Responses
to the Fundamentalist Movement

Dedicated
to the memory of

Don Harbuck and **Ben Philbeck**

both of whom
died far too soon.

The Struggle for the Soul of the SBC

Moderate Responses
to the Fundamentalist Movement

edited by Walter B. Shurden

Mercer University Press
· 1993 ·

ISBN 0-86554-425-5   MUP/H339
ISBN 0-86554-424-7   MUP/PI0I

The Struggle for the Soul of the SBC:
Moderate Responses to the Fundamentalist Movement.
Copyright ©1993
Mercer University Press, Macon, Georgia 31207
All rights reserved
Printed in the United States of America

The paper used in this publication meets the minimum requirements
of American National Standard for Information Sciences—
Permanence of Paper for Printed Library Materials, ANSI Z39.48-1984

Library of Congress Cataloging-in-Publication Data
The struggle for the soul of the SBC :
Moderate responses to the fundamentalist movement /
edited by Walter B. Shurden
xxvii+318 pages. 6×9" (15×23cm.).
Includes bibliographical references.
ISBN 0-86554-425-5 (alk. paper)
ISBN 0-86554-424-7 (pbk. : alk. paper)
1. Southern Baptist Convention—History.
2. Fundamentalism—History.
3. Southern Baptist Alliance—History.
I. Shurden, Walter B., 1937–
BX6462.3.F86 1993   93-14799
286'.132'09048—dc20   **CIP**

Contents

Abbreviations etc.

The times, as ever, are changing. The names also. Names eventually, even inevitably, beget nicknames—abbreviations, acronyms, a variety of shorthand "handles." Some such nicknames occur on the pages below. This preliminary list of "handles" may help. For non-Baptists and other novices, some older and well-worn "handles" are included.

ABP The Associated Baptist Press (see 169ff.).

Alliance The Alliance of Baptists (originally Southern Baptist Alliance; see 101ff.).

Baptists Originally *SBC Today*, is "a national, autonomous publication ***Today*** [newspaper, tabloid format] of news and opinion for Baptists in the USA" (see 151ff.).

BCMP The Baptist Cooperative Missions Program (see 241ff.).

BJCPA The Baptist Joint Committee on Public Affairs; often just **BJC**.

BP The Baptist Press. SBC news agency (see 169ff.).

BSSB The Baptist Sunday School Board; also simply *the* Sunday School **or just** Board. The SBC publication agency. Designs and provides resourc-**SSB** es for the implementation of a variety of church education and training programs, including especially Bible study (Sunday School) and church training periodical literature; also includes Convention Press and Broadman Press.

CBF The Cooperative Baptist Fellowship (see 253ff.).

CLC The Christian Life Commission of the SBC.

CP The Cooperative Program. The financial plan through which the SBC solicits, collects, and distributes gifts from churches to the many programs, agencies, and institutions through which the SBC works (e.g., FMB, HMB, seminaries, schools and colleges, hospitals, and much more).

CWIM Center for Women in Ministry (Louisville) merged with SBWIM in 1989 (see 129ff.).

FMB The Foreign Mission Board of the SBC.

Formations The basic curriculum series (resources for Sunday School, missions studies, VBS, Winter Bible Study, personal study/devotions, etc.) published by Smyth & Helwys (see 223ff.).

HMB The Home Mission Board of the SBC.

Messenger In *non*-Baptist parlance, a "delegate," is an elected representative of a local church to an assembly of cooperating local churches, either a local association, a state convention, or the Southern Baptist Convention (see SBC, above). Each cooperating (=contributing) local church is allowed a certain number of messengers, and messengers are "registered" to vote in assembly actions upon being certified as an elected messenger from a cooperating local church. (The title is based on the messenger's purpose: to take the local church's "message" to the assembly and in turn to deliver the assembly's "message" back to the local church.)

Missioner One who cares for others in the name of Christ, including but not limited to one who does so professionally ("missionary").

SBC or the Convention The Southern Baptist Convention. *Properly* the annual assembly of messengers from churches, but also the institution (collectively, the officers, committees, boards, agencies, and commissions as elected and authorized by churches at the annual assembly) through which the SBC seeks to accomplish its purposes.

SBWIM Southern Baptist Women in Ministry (originally WIM, SBC; see below, 129ff.).

Smyth & Helwys An autonomous publishing house providing a broad range of curriculum and personal-study resources, both periodical literature and books. Fundamental to the S&H philosophy and purpose is an overarching commitment to contribute to the remembrance and the continuing implementation of the Baptist heritage. The S&H motto is "a free press for Baptists" (see 223ff.).

WMU The Woman's Missionary Union, auxiliary to the SBC.

A Chronology

February 22. *The Christian Index.* Names of those to preach at SBC Pastors' Conference in Houston is released, and reads like a Who's Who of future Fundamentalist leaders of the next decade: Homer Lindsay, Jr., president, Adrian Rogers, W. A. Criswell, Jerry Vines, Charles Stanley, and others.

May 10. *The Christian Index* has article by Toby Druin in which Paige Patterson and Paul Pressler confirm reports that meetings had been held in at least fifteen states to encourage messengers to attend the SBC in Houston to elect a president committed to biblical inerrancy. Patterson said the meetings grew out of a concern that every resolution in recent years aimed at underscoring Southern Baptist belief in biblical inerrancy "has come back toothless." No particular candidate was named but Patterson said Jerry Vines, Richard Jackson, Adrian Rogers, Bailey Smith, Homer Lindsay, and John Bisagno would be acceptable.

May 24. *The Christian Index* reports that Harold Lindsell, president of the Baptist Faith and Message Fellowship, said in an interview with the Memphis *Commercial Appeal* that it is time for Southern Baptists to face the issue of inerrancy even if it meant the loss of 500,000 members. Lindsell also announced he would be speaking in several cities across the nation before the SBC in Houston, promoting sales of his new book entitled *The Bible in the Balance.* Lindsell denied the Baptist Faith and Message Fellowship had been involved in the Pressler-Patterson meetings across the nation.

June 12–14. SBC, Houston, 15,760 messengers, Jimmy Allen presiding.
—At the Pastors' Conference preceding the SBC, Fundamentalist Homer Lindsay, Jr. presides over a parade of preachers who lashed out at alleged "liberals" within the SBC. Moments after Adrian Rogers said "If those liberals will ever come to the cross of Christ, all heaven will break loose," W. A. Criswell endorsed him to be the next president of the SBC. Fundamentalist James T. Draper elected president of the Pastor's Conference.
—Fundamentalist Adrian Rogers elected as president on the first ballot with 51.36% of the vote, over five independent candidates. In a news conference following election, Rogers said he was not part of the Pressler-Patterson

political machine and that he hoped the kind of political organization that led to his election would not be a pattern for future elections of SBC presidents.

—Resolution ironically adopted at the beginning of a twelve-year-long fight "On Disavowing Political Activity in Selecting Officers," read in part as follows: "WHEREAS, There have been numerous public reports of political-type meetings and materials for the purpose of predetermining the election of officers of this Convention; Be it therefore *Resolved*, that this Convention go on record as disavowing overt political activity and organization as a method of selection of its officers; and Be it further *Resolved*, that this Convention urge its messengers and churches to pray for guidance in the priesthood of the believer in all matters of decision and to exercise distinctly Christian actions in all deliberations."

—Paul Pressler, one of the architects of the Fundamentalist Movement, registered as SBC messenger from a church to which he did not belong.

—Wayne Dehoney, former SBC president, drew warm applause when he went to the microphone, pointed to a "sky room" at the top of the convention hall as being campaign headquarters for Paul Pressler. Dehoney also accused Pressler of being an "illegal messenger" who was not properly certified.

—Motion by Wayne Dehoney and approved by convention reaffirming the section of the 1963 Baptist Faith and Message dealing with the Bible.

—A constitutional amendment to prevent ordained women from serving on the home or foreign mission field was defeated.

—Reaffirmed restrained 1976 resolution on abortion.

July 31. Porter W. Routh retires and is succeeded by Harold C. Bennett as executive secretary-treasurer of the SBC executive committee.

• 1980 •

January. SBC president Adrian Rogers, Charles Stanley, and Paige Patterson join with Pat Robertson, Jerry Falwell, Jim Bakker, and others in urging removal of the issue of prayer in schools from jurisdiction of federal courts.

April. Fundamentalist publication *The Southern Baptist Journal* moves from Buchanan GA, where William A. Powell was editor to Columbia SC, where Russell Kaemmerling, Paige Patterson's brother-in-law, becomes editor.

May. Baptist Press reports Paige Patterson and Paul Pressler had revealed a plan for long-range control of SBC.

May 6. SBC president Adrian Rogers announces he will not seek a second one-year term because of local church responsibilities.

May 22. *The Christian Index* reports that W. A. Criswell, pastor, First Baptist, Dallas, had announced that Paige Patterson, president of Criswell Center for Biblical Studies, would withdraw from Fundamentalist effort to control SBC by electing presidents. Criswell said the methods used by Patterson and others are "those of a different world," that Baptists traditionally disdain.

June 10–12. SBC, St. Louis, 13,844 messengers, Adrian Rogers presiding.

—SBC Pastors' Conference elects Jim Henry, pastor of First Baptist Church, Orlando, president.

—Fundamentalist Bailey Smith elected president with 51.67% of the

vote on first ballot over five independent candidates.

—Resolution adopted "On Doctrinal
Integrity" which foretells much of what
was to come for the next decade. In
part it read as follows: "Be it further *Resolved*, That we exhort the trustees of
seminaries and other institutions
affiliated with or supported by the
Southern Baptist Convention to faithfully discharge their responsibility to carefully preserve the doctrinal integrity of
our institutions and to assure that seminaries and other institutions receiving
our support only employ, and continue
the employment of, faculty members
and professional staff who believe in
the divine inspiration of the whole Bible, infallibility of the original manuscripts, and that the Bible is truth without any error."

August. SBC President Bailey Smith
creates a furor with his statement that
"God Almighty does not hear the
prayer of a Jew."

September 1. R. Keith Parks succeeds
Baker James Cauthen as executive director of the Foreign Mission Board.

September 12–13. In a speech at the
Old Forest Road Baptist Church in
Lynchburg VA, Paul Pressler announces that the Fundamentalists "need to go
for the jugular—we need to go for the
trustees." Said Pressler, "We are going
for having knowledgeable, Bible-cen-
tered, Christ-honoring trustees of all of
our institutions who are not going to sit
there like a bunch of dummies and
rubber stamp everything that's presented to them." In answer to a question
about giving to the Cooperative Program, Pressler said, "Work within the
framework of the Cooperative Program." He added, "Give at least enough

to have the maximum number of messengers [to the SBC]."

September 25, 26. Moderate Movement
begins in Gatlinburg TN, when Cecil
Sherman calls together a group of seventeen ministers to counter the Fundamentalist assault on the SBC.

October. James M. Dunn elected as
executive director of the Baptist Joint
Committee on Public Affairs to succeed
James Wood.

• 1981 •

June. Fifteen Southern Baptist historians appeal for defense and protection of
denominational heritage relating to
Baptist distinctives, the purpose of the
SBC, the centrality of the Bible, and
the Baptist aversion to creedalism.

June 9–11. SBC, Los Angeles, 13,529
messengers, Bailey Smith presiding.

—Ed Young, pastor of Second Baptist Church, Houston, elected president
of Pastors' Conference.

—Bailey Smith reelected president
with 60.24% of the vote over Moderate
Abner McCall with 39.30%.

—Motion of Moderates to limit SBC
president's power in the appointment of
the Committee on Committees fails.
The failure of the motion highlights the
power of the presidency in the Fundamentalist strategy to dominate the
boards and agencies of the SBC.

—Motion by Herschel H. Hobbs,
former SBC president and primary
author of the 1963 "Baptist Faith and
Message," that the SBC "reaffirm our
historic Baptist position that the Holy
Bible, which has truth without any mixture of error for its matter, is our adequate rule of faith and practice, and that
we reaffirm our belief in 'The Baptist

Faith and Message' adopted in 1963, including all seventeen articles, plus the preamble which protects the conscience of the individual and guards us from a creedal faith." The apparent intent of Hobbs's motion was to reaffirm the non-creedal and voluntary nature of "The Baptist Faith and Message" while appeasing the Fundamentalist insistence on inerrancy. During later debate on the motion Adrian Rogers asked that some of Hobbs's comments which reflected the inerrantist tendency be read into the record. Later Hobbs's comments would be cited by Fundamentalists as evidence that "The Baptist Faith and Message" article on the Bible was an inerrantist statement. This marks another step in the growing creedalistic usage of the 1963 confessional statement. Fundamentalists used Hobbs's statements which "leaned" toward inerrancy to better effect than Moderates used Hobbs's statement about the noncreedal and voluntary nature of "The Baptist Faith and Message."

• 1982 •

February. Roy L. Honeycutt succeeds Duke K. McCall as president of the Southern Baptist Theological Seminary.

May. Fundamentalist Adrian Rogers stated in an interview with Jack Harwell, editor of The Christian Index, that the point of tension in Southern Baptist life was "the Cooperative Program: we're trying to get everybody to support everything the same way." As Fundamentalists gain increasing power in the SBC, they will affirm the CP; conversely Moderates will echo Rogers's earlier criticism of the way CP is used.

May 27. The Christian Index reports

that Duke K. McCall would be nominated for the presidency of the SBC.

June 15–17. SBC, New Orleans, 20,456 messengers, Bailey Smith presiding.
—Fred Wolfe, Mobile pastor, elected president of the Pastors' Conference.
—Fundamentalist Jimmy Draper elected president on second ballot with 56.97% of the vote over Moderate Duke McCall with 43.03%
—Resolutions approved endorsing scientific creationism, supporting a constitutional amendment prohibiting abortion, and sanctioning an amendment regarding voluntary prayer in public schools. These resolutions mark a deviation from past SBC actions regarding government involvement in religious matters, and mark a sharp turn to the right in SBC life.

November 29. Moderate group meeting at Atlanta airport decides to launch newspaper (SBC Today, later Baptists Today).

• 1983 •

April. First issue of SBC Today.

June. Formation of "Women in Ministry, SBC" (later "Southern Baptist Women in Ministry")

June 14–16. SBC, Pittsburgh, 13,740 messengers, Jimmy Draper presiding.
—Jimmy Draper is unopposed for reelection as president.
—Moderates hold "reception," the forerunner to the SBC Forum.
—Fundamentalist Charles Stanley, who would become the next president of the SBC, became visible at the SBC as the new president of the SBC Pastors' Conference and chair of the Committee on Boards. Previous efforts by

Moderates to challenge nominations from this committee had been successful, but failed in Pittsburgh.

• 1984 •

June 12–14. SBC, Kansas City MO, 17,101 messengers, Jimmy Draper presiding.

—Fundamentalist Charles Stanley elected president with 52.18% of the vote over Moderate Grady Cothen with 26.28% and independent John Sullivan with 21.53%.

—Resolution "On Ordination and the Role of Women in Ministry" adopted 58.03% to 41.97%, and reads in part: "WHEREAS, The Scriptures attest to God's delegated order of authority (God the head of Christ, Christ the head of man, man the head of woman, man and woman dependent one upon the other to the glory of God), distinguishing the roles of men and women in public prayer and prophecy (1 Cor 11:2-5); and WHEREAS, The Scriptures teach that women are not in public worship to assume a role of authority over men lest confusion reign in the local church (1 Cor 14:33-36); and WHEREAS, While Paul commends women and men alike in other roles of ministry and service (Titus 2:1-10), he excludes women from pastoral leadership (1 Tim 2:12) to preserve a submission God requires because the man was first in creation and the woman was first in the Edenic fall (1 Tim 2:13ff.)."

—Motion to eliminate funding for Baptist Joint Committee defeated, but is an indication of what is to come.

—First meeting of the SBC Forum.

—Paul Pressler elected to serve on the executive committee of the Southern Baptist Convention.

June and following. Denominational executives, especially seminary presidents Russell Dilday, Roy L. Honeycutt, Jr., and Randall Lolley, launch all-out attack on Fundamentalists. Dilday preached a fiery sermon at the SBC in Kansas City deploring the political machinations of Pressler and Patterson; Honeycutt used the "Holy War" metaphor from the Old Testament; Randall Lolley defended in a spirited manner the role of women in ministry. All these efforts pointed toward the next SBC (Dallas) and toward unseating incumbent president Stanley.

• 1985 •

June 11-13. SBC, Dallas, 45,519 messengers (largest in SBC history), Charles Stanley presiding.

—Charles Stanley reelected president with 55.3% of the vote over Moderate Winfred Moore with 44.7%.

—Appointment of the "Peace Committee," with Charles Fuller as chair, "to determine the sources of the controversies in our Convention, and make findings and recommendations regarding these controversies."

—Charles Stanley overrules the SBC regarding the Slatton motion. James H. Slatton's motion would have amended the Committee on Committees' report by substituting state convention presidents and state WMU presidents as a more inclusive and representative group to serve Southern Baptists as the Committee on Boards.

December 5. Robert and Julia Crowder of Birmingham and Henry C. Cooper of Windsor MO, file a lawsuit against the denomination and its executive committee because of Charles Stanley's ruling on the Slatton motion.

• 1986 •

May 5. U.S. district judge decides in favor of SBC in the Crowder lawsuit, saying the first amendment of the U.S. Constitution prevents intrusion of secular courts into internal church disputes.

May 5. William G. Tanner, president of the Home Mission Board, elected executive director-treasurer of the Oklahoma Baptist Convention.

May. Foy Valentine, executive director of the SBC Christian Life Commission, requests that a search process be initiated to select his successor. Search Committee appointed.

May. Theologian Clark Pinnock issues apology for fueling controversy over inerrancy, a position he now claims is not "well supported exegetically."

June 10–12. SBC, Atlanta, 40,987 messengers (second largest in SBC history), Charles Stanley presiding.
 —Fundamentalist Adrian Rogers elected president with 54.22% of the vote over Moderate Winfred Moore 45.78%. (Both were members of the SBC Peace Committee.)
 —Fundamentalist motion to deny funding to Baptist Joint Committee on Public Affairs resulted in "Fact Finding Committee" to study relationship of BJCPA to SBC.

June. Paige Patterson, in a statement following the Fundamentalist victory in Atlanta, indicates that Fundamentalists are expected to tie their positions on abortion, euthanasia, school prayer, and federal budget reduction to the hiring of

denominational employees. Speaking of the Fundamentalist social and moral agenda within the SBC, Patterson was quoted as saying, "I think it'll go over nearly as well as the inerrancy thing."

August. Moderate meeting in Macon, where differing strategies for the future surface. Marks the beginning idea of the Southern Baptist Alliance.

August 6. As a result of trustee elections at the Atlanta SBC, Fundamentalists capture the balance of power on the Home Mission Board and force the resignation of a presidential search committee.

October 22. SBC seminary presidents present the "Glorieta Statement," which was affirmed by the Peace Committee and widely interpreted as a capitulation to the growing Fundamentalist power within the SBC. Leading Moderate spokesman Cecil Sherman resigns in protest from the Peace Committee (see appendix 1, below).

October 24. An eight-point peace proposal made by Moderates rejected by Fundamentalist leaders.

December 1–2. Providence Baptist Church, Charlotte. Motion made to organize and incorporate the Southern Baptist Alliance.

• 1987 •

January. Baptist Press reports the beginning of new missions organization by Fundamentalists.

January. Moderate Larry Baker elected to head the SBC Christian Life Commission by a 16–13 vote of the trustees.

Early 1987. "No Lord but Christ, No Creed but the Bible" statement released by Moderates.

February. Patterson-Pressler issue statement to the SBC peace committee lauding developments in the SBC and noting their support for the Glorieta Statement and the Cooperative Program.

February 2–4. Trustees of the Sunday School Board authorize multivolume inerrancy commentary on the Bible.

February 12. Announcement of formation of the Southern Baptist Alliance.

April 10. Fundamentalist Larry L. Lewis elected president of the Home Mission Board.

May 14–15. First Convocation of the Southern Baptist Alliance, Meredith College, Raleigh.

June 16–18. SBC, St. Louis, 25,607 messengers, Adrian Rogers presiding.
—Fundamentalist Adrian Rogers reelected president with 59.97% of the vote over Moderate Richard Jackson with 40.03%.
—Adopted Fundamentalist-dominated Peace Committee Report which takes on creedal nature in Southern Baptist life.

September 15. Moderate Larry Baker, executive-director of the Christian Life Commission of the SBC, avoids dismissal by a 15–15 tie vote. (Fundamentalist trustees sought Baker's dismissal because of displeasure with his views on abortion, capital punishment, and women in ministry.)

November 17. Southeastern Seminary President Randall Lolley and Dean Morris Ashcraft resign their positions rather than implement restrictive hiring policies of Fundamentalist trustees.

December. Bill Moyers's PBS documentary entitled "God and Politics" which highlighted the SBC controversy and brought Daniel Vestal to the forefront of Moderate leadership.

• 1988 •

March. Paige Patterson proposes agency status for WMU.

March 14. Lewis Drummond elected president of Southeastern Seminary by Fundamentalist trustees.

May 15. Moderate Larry Baker, director of Christian Life Commission, accepts pastorate of First Baptist Church, Pineville LA, sixteen months after accepting the CLC post.

June 1. Jack U. Harwell becomes editor of *SBC Today*, succeeding Walker L. Knight.

June 14–16. SBC, San Antonio, 32,727 messengers, Adrian Rogers presiding.
—At SBC Pastors' Conference, W. A. Criswell groups "moderates" with "liberals," saying, "A skunk by any other name still stinks."
—Fundamentalist Jerry Vines elected president with 50.53% of the vote over Moderate candidate Richard Jackson (48.32%) and two other independent candidates.
—Resolution "On the Priesthood of the Believer" adopted by 54.75% to 45.25% of the vote and read in part: "WHEREAS, the doctrine of the priesthood of the believer can be used to justify the undermining of pastoral authority in the local church. . . . Be it

further RESOLVED, That the doctrine of the priesthood of the believer in no way contradicts the biblical understanding of the role, responsibility, and authority of the pastor which is seen in the command to the local church in Hebrews 13:17, 'Obey your leaders, and submit to them; for they watch over your souls, as those who will give an account'; and Be finally RESOLVED, That we affirm the truth that elders, or pastors, are called of God to lead the local church (Acts 20:28).''

July 21. SBC Foreign Mission Board terminates Michael E. Willett, missionary to Venezuela, because of Willett's "doctrinal ambiguity."

September 12, Fundamentalist Richard Land elected head of the SBC Christian Life Commission following Moderate Larry Baker's resignation in the spring.

December 15–16. Continuation of the Moderate political network through the formation of "Baptists Committed to the Southern Baptist Convention."

• 1989 •

January 1. Stan Hastey becomes the first permanent executive-director of the Southern Baptist Alliance.

March 1–3. Third annual convocation of the Southern Baptist Alliance.
—SBA approves opening of Baptist Theological Seminary at Richmond.

April 10-11. Moderate Jimmy Allen resigns as president of the SBC Radio and Television Commission.

June. SBC, Las Vegas, 20,411 messengers, Jerry Vines presiding.

—Fundamentalist Jerry Vines re-elected president with 56.58% of the vote over Daniel Vestal with 43.39%.

July 22. Dellanna W. O'Brien elected WMU national executive director.

June 27. Greg and Katrina Pennington rejected for missionary appointment by the SBC Foreign Mission Board, because she was ordained.

August 7. Baptist Sunday School Board trustees rebuke president Loyd Elder for alleged denominational politics but turn back attempt to fire him.

• 1990 •

June 12-14. SBC, New Orleans, 38,403 messengers, Jerry Vines presiding.
—Fundamentalist Morris Chapman elected president with 57.68% of the vote over Daniel Vestal with 42.32%.
—SBC cuts budget support for BPCPA from $391,000 to $50,000.

July 17. In closed session behind armed security guards, Fundamentalist-dominated SBC executive committee fires Al Shackleford, director of Baptist Press, and Dan Martin, Baptist Press news editor; immediately Nashville attorney Jeff Mobley announces the beginning of Associated Baptist Press.

August. Meetings by concerned Baptist professors, pastors, and laypersons to consider forming an alternative Baptist publishing house (Smyth & Helwys).

August 13-15. Fundamentalist-dominated Sunday School Board trustees vote to destroy all copies but one of a manuscript of that board's centennial history written by Southwestern Seminary church historian Leon McBeth.

August 23–25. Consultation of Concerned Southern Baptists, the Inforum, Atlanta, called by Daniel Vestal, presided over by Jimmy Allen, head of Baptists Committed.

—Formation of the Baptist Cooperative Missions Program, Inc. (BCMP), a funding mechansim for Moderate SBC causes.

—Daniel Vestal elected moderator to lead 60-member interim steering committee.

September 21. BCMP offices open in *SBC Today* facilities in Decatur GA.

September 21. Baylor University amends charter to replace trustees with regents who will have sole governance of the institution. The change established three-fourths of the board of regents as self-perpetuating, with only one-fourth of the regents elected by the Texas Baptist Convention.

September 24–25. Fundamentalist-dominated board of trustees imposes Peace Committee report as new creedal statement for hiring at Southern Seminary.

October 15. Furman University amends charter to give the board of trustees rather than the South Carolina Baptist Convention the power to elect trustees.

November 9. News release announces beginning of Smyth & Helwys Publishing, Inc., a free press for Baptists.

• 1991 •

January 7. Thomas H. Graves elected president of the Baptist Theological Seminary at Richmond.

January 17. Loyd Elder, president of

the Baptist Sunday School Board, forced to retire by Fundamentalist-dominated board of trustees.

February. Smyth & Helwys announces commitment to publish alternative church curriculum resources.

March 14–16. The Southern Baptist Alliance eliminates reference to the Southern Baptist Convention in its statement of purpose.

April 8. Trustees of Southern Seminary adopt a "Covenant Renewal Between Trustees, Faculty, and Administration" which replaces the SBC Peace Committee report as guidelines for hiring faculty but commits faculty and trustees to a document other than the historic "Abstract of Principles."

May 9–11. Cooperative Baptist Fellowship convocation, Omni Coliseum, Atlanta, Daniel Vestal, presiding.

—"An Address to the Public" presented by the Fellowship's interim steering committee (see appendix 2).

—The Fellowship adopts the name "The Cooperative Baptist Fellowship" rather than the recommended "United Baptist Fellowship."

—John H. Hewett, pastor, First Baptist Church, Asheville, elected CBF moderator.

May 20. News release announces Cecil P. Staton, Jr. has become first full-time publisher of Smyth & Helwys.

May. *SBC Today* changes to *Baptists Today*.

May. Meeting held at Woodmont Baptist Church in Nashville, at which was born the Baptist Center for Ethics. (The name "Southern Baptist Center for

Ethics" rejected as too provincial.)

June 4–6. SBC, Atlanta, 23,465 messengers, Morris Chapman presiding.
—Fundamentalist Morris Chapman unopposed for president and reelected by acclamation.
—SBC dropped all financial support for the BJCPA.

July 18. Fundamentalist James T. Draper elected president of the Baptist Sunday School Board.

September. Smyth & Helwys moves to the campus of Mercer University and begins period of cooperation with Mercer University Press; Cecil P. Staton, Jr. becomes publisher of MUP as well as of S&H.

September 10. Baptist Theological Seminary at Richmond begins classes.

October 9. Fundamentalist-dominated Foreign Mission Board trustees vote to delete from budget $365,000 previously promised to the Baptist Theological Seminary in Rüschlikon, Switzerland.

• 1992 •

January 7. FMB Vice-President Isam Ballenger and Area Director for Europe G. Keith Parker announce early retirement in protest of trustees' defunding seminary at Rüschlikon.

January 9. Cooperative Baptist Fellowship coordinating council calls Cecil E. Sherman as first fulltime Coordinator.

February 17. Fundamentalist Morris Chapman elected president of the SBC executive committee.

April 1. Baptist Cooperative Missions Program, Inc. becomes part of the Cooperative Baptist Fellowship.

April 30–May 2. CBF general assembly, Ft. Worth.
—John David and Jo Ann Hopper and Charles and Kathy Thomas resign from SBC Foreign Mission Board to become first missioners for the CBF.

March 5–7. Celebrating its fifth anniversary, the Southern Baptist Alliance dropped "Southern" from its name.

March 20. R. Keith Parks, SBC Foreign Mission Board president, announces retirement on October 31 because of differences with FMB trustees.

May 14. Fundamentalist Paige Patterson elected president of Southeastern Baptist Theological Seminary.

October 9. Formation by Moderates of the William H. Whitsitt Baptist Heritage Society at Mercer University.

November 30. Keith Parks, former president of SBC Foreign Mission Board, announces he will become missions head for Cooperative Baptist Fellowship.

• 1993 •

January 10. Woman's Missionary Union votes to steer a new course and open the door to work with the Cooperative Baptist Fellowship.

January. Former President Jimmy Carter and Rosalyn Carter endorse the Cooperative Baptist Fellowship.

Introduction

Walter B. Shurden

Beginning in 1979 and continuing until 1990, the Southern Baptist Convention (SBC) was torn apart by the most serious controversy in the history of the denomination. Historians and eager graduate students will be exploring for years the roots and the fruits of that conflict. The story will be told and retold from various vantage points, as it should be and as it must be. This book represents an interpretation by one group of the primary contenders in the battle.

Before introducing the papers in the book, I need to sketch in the barest outline the developments of the controversy so the reader, if completely unaware, will have some orientation. Two factions, Fundamentalists and Moderates, polarized the SBC from 1979–1990, and results linger to the present. With numerous antecedents, the conflict began in earnest on June 12-14, 1979, at the annual meeting of the SBC in Houston, Texas. Three Fundamentalist leaders emerged prominently at that meeting and skillfully guided the Fundamentalists to triumph over Moderates for twelve years. Those three were Paige Patterson, then president of Criswell Center for Biblical Studies in Dallas, Texas; Paul Pressler, a layman from Houston, Texas; and Adrian Rogers, pastor of Bellevue Baptist Church in Memphis, Tennessee. Each served a crucial role in the Fundamentalist victory. Patterson, a professor, was the theological architect; Pressler, a judge, was the political strategist; and Rogers, an effective and popular preacher without whom the Fundamentalists may never have won, stirred to action mass SBC audiences.

Beginning in the spring of 1979, Pressler and Patterson designed and announced a ten-year plan whereby Fundamentalists could gain control of the SBC. Garnering a following by proclaiming that "liberalism" had invaded the entire denominational system—seminaries, colleges, universities, publication agencies, denominational press—they discovered they could use the appointive powers of the SBC presidency and thereby dominate the denomination. Following the 1979 election of Adrian Rogers as SBC president, every one of the six presidents through the election in 1990 were Fundamentalists who used presidential powers to achieve the Fundamentalist agenda by stacking the boards of all trustee agencies, something never done in SBC history. By 1990, virtually every SBC agency's board of trustees was dominated by hardline Fundamentalists.

While the political key to the Fundamentalist victory was the election of the SBC president and subsequent trustee appointments, the popular rallying cry was "the inerrancy of the Bible." The popular name of the controversy became "The Inerrancy Controversy." The strife, however, focused on far more than the nature or interpretation of the Bible, so the conflict should be known as "The Fundamentalist-Moderate Controversy."

One issue, generic in character, hung as a colossal canopy over all the contention. That issue was "control versus freedom," no new conflict in Baptist history. Fundamentalists argued for stricter controls in light of what they believed was too much freedom that had issued in false teachings. Moderates, on the other hand, lobbied for freedom in the face of what they thought was a non-Baptistic and paralyzing control. This central issue may also be described as "conformity versus liberty" or "uniformity versus diversity." Fundamentalists were more interested in theological conformity and denominational uniformity, and Moderates were more interested in liberty of conscience and denominational diversity.

The "control versus freedom" war played itself out in numerous smaller battles. Biblically, the two groups disputed the nature and interpretation of the Bible. Fundamentalists argued for biblical inerrancy for nonexistent autographs while Moderates contended for the authority of Scripture "for faith and practice" but not as an inerrant scientific and historical book. Moreover, Moderates took a historical-critical approach to the Bible, allowing, for example, for a symbolic interpretation of Adam and Eve, while Fundamentalists viewed this interpretation as denying the Bible.

Theologically, they wrangled over the role of women and pastoral authority. Fundamentalists insisted on a hierarchical model of male-female relationships and denied a woman's right for ordination to the ministry or diaconate. Moderates advocated equality between women and men and affirmed ordination for women. Regarding pastoral authority in the local church, Fundamentalists asserted it while Moderates countered with the priesthood of all believers and congregational authority.

Educationally, the two parties argued over almost every facet of theological education—content, parameters, personnel, and methodology. Much of the heat of the controversy focused on theological seminaries, especially Southeastern Baptist Theological Seminary at Wake Forest, North Carolina, and Southern Baptist Theological Seminary at Louisville, Kentucky. Ethically, the combatants disagreed over the implications of religious liberty and separation of church and state, particularly as those principles related to prayer in public schools, abortion, and related national issues. Most of the energy in the area of ethics was spent in the Fundamentalist opposition to and Moderate defense of both the SBC Christian Life Commission and the Baptist Joint Committee on Public Affairs, a national agency based in Washington and supported by several Baptist denominations in the United States.

Historically and denominationally, they disputed the place of creedalism in Baptist life, the intent and purpose of the SBC (whether functional or doctrinal), and the freedom/control of the denominational press (Baptist Press) and the denominational publishing agency (Baptist Sunday School Board; Broadman Press). Missiologically, they differed over the theological credentials for missionary appointment and the vocational purposes of missionaries. This particular dimension of the contest focused on the SBC Foreign Mission Board and the Home Mission Board, two of the darling agencies of the denomination. These contrasts could be extended into national politics where Fundamentalists identified with the political far right and Moderates tended to be more centrists. Fundamentalists tended, for example, to support Reagan-Bush Republicans and Moderates identified more with Carter-Clinton Democrats.

The two groups were so divided they could not arrive at mutually acceptable names for the rival parties. Both wanted to be called "conservatives." That term, therefore, has little value in describing the conflict. In fact, both parties wanted the term so much that at one point in the struggle the Baptist Press, the denominational news agency, dubbed the adversaries, in the name of fairness, "The Fundamentalist-Conservatives" and "The Moderate-Conservatives." The most accurate terminology is "Fundamentalists" and "Moderates," though neither party likes its appellation. Fundamentalists are sometimes called "inerrantists," "the takeover group," or "the Pressler-Patterson faction," after the name of two of their founders. Moderates are sometimes called "liberals," "denominational loyalists," "Baptists Committed," or "traditionalists," because they maintained that they were the traditional Baptists.

The results have been: (1) a clear win for the Fundamentalists, with solid control over all SBC agencies; (2) the exclusion of Moderates from all SBC boards and, eventually, elimination from SBC agencies; (3) the establishment by Moderates of new entities such as the Alliance of Baptists in 1987 and the Cooperative Baptist Fellowship in 1990, the latter organization containing all the signs of an emerging denomination; (4) the development by Moderates of new theological seminaries, a publishing agency, a national newspaper, an ethics agency, and other non-SBC enterprises; (5) the removal of the conflict from the SBC to the state convention level; and (6) signs of significant denominational realignment within the SBC.

On the return flight from the meeting of the General Assembly of the Cooperative Baptist Fellowship in Ft. Worth, Texas, on May 3, 1992, I took a pad of yellow notebook paper and sketched out in rough form a conference that I dubbed "The History of the Moderate Movement of the SBC." Like many, I'm sure, both Fundamentalists and Moderates, I had thought long and hard for more than a decade of my life about the history of the Fundamentalist-Moderate Controversy. Moreover, I had thought so very often of how the history of the controversy could get away from us if we did not act with some deliberation to preserve it.

In fact, I have realized from my own bit role in the controversy how the political arena is so much more seductive and enticing than is the call to be a "dull and deadly" historian. It is more fun to "make history" than it is to go to the trouble of preserving, recording, and interpreting history. As a Moderate, I was energized by the religiopolitical cause for which we toiled, but I never abdicated the historical half of my life which prodded the rest of me concerning the urgent and desperate need to preserve, to record, and to interpret the very history we were living through.

I knew, of course, that historians could and would return to the documents—the debris of the battle—and reconstruct the whys, whats, whos, and wherefores of the contest. What historians could not do, however, would be to hear the story of the controversy in the words of "the living documents," those who were principals in the struggle. So after returning home from Ft. Worth and the meeting of the General Assembly, I decided to try to get some of the Moderate mainstays together, asking them to prepare formal historical papers about their particular involvement in the Moderate movement. Some will doubtless ask, "Why not invite Fundamentalists to tell their story at the same time and at the same place as well?" Honest confession. It is not yet time for that. Besides, Fundamentalists now own the news agency, a growing number of the state Baptist editors, and the SBC publishing house. They have no trouble getting their version of the story out.

You will note there are fourteen major papers constituting the body of this book. These are the fourteen papers presented at the conference on the History of the Moderate Movement held at Mercer University in Macon, Georgia, on October 8-9, 1992. The one question most asked of me about the conference was: "How in the world did you get all these busy and important people together on the same conference for this program?" It was absolutely one of the easiest things I have ever done in my life!

What I did was pick up the phone and call them one by one. To each I said, "I don't have a budget; I can't pay your way, not even your lodging; and what I want you to do is to write a twenty-five page research paper on the phase of the Moderate effort of which you are intimately acquainted, and I want you to talk for thirty minutes at this conference on your paper." I called only seventeen people to get the fourteen presenters. Only three people declined this lucrative invitation, and each of those three had schedule problems that precluded their presence. The experience of putting the October 1992 conference together gave new meaning for me to "ask and it shall be given you." I only asked. These busy and talented people responded and created a wonderful conference. This book is one result.

My hope for the conference was simple and twofold. First, I wanted future and contemporary historians to have to come to grips with some of the "primary sources" themselves. I knew then and I know now the risks involved in such an approach to history. We are close—very, very close—to the issues, developments, and raw interpersonal relationships of the controversy. As a result we may very well have a blurred vision of what has happened. But no historian writes or speaks with twenty-twenty vision. All do history from a certain angle. Others operate with "blurred vision," too.

Those "others" include at least three groups: (1) the Fundamentalists who do not agree with Moderate interpretations of what has happened and who are already engaged in revisionist historiography; (2) those contemporary historians—Baptist and otherwise—who think they are the only ones with objectivity enough to tell the public exactly what happened because they were not in the fight and whose view of what happened is flawed, therefore, precisely because they were not in the thick of things; and (3) those historians fifty and a hundred years from now who do not have the advantages of seeing what we see today, even if they may be able to see what we cannot see today.

In editing the papers for publication, I have tried unusually hard to leave them basically as they were originally written. I wanted the flavor of personality as well as the point of view of the individual writers to come through. That is why the book is subtitled "Moderate Responses." The plural is important. You will find, not surprisingly, some differences of interpretation among Moderates themselves about the controversy. Also, I have intentionally left the first person intact where it was originally employed. In fact, in many places, to the dismay of some of the writers, I deliberately changed the style to first person because it reinforced the sense of history being described.

Other than the three pieces I have written or compiled—this introduction to give the background of the book, the chronology to give the reader something of a blow-by-blow date line, and the summary to wrap things up—the fourteen major chapters represent the original conference papers. Because of space limitations we could not include some perceptive and stimulating responses to several of the papers, nor could we include the panel discussion which concluded the conference.

Those who have followed the controversy closely will discern some logic to the order of the individual chapters. The first two papers by E. Glenn Hinson and Cecil E. Sherman are background in nature. Glenn Hinson—among those who do not like the label "Moderate"—interprets the rise of the Moderate movement and the controversy itself as a struggle for the freedom of the Word of God. Now a professor at the Baptist Theological Seminary at Richmond, Hinson was a longtime professor of church history at the Southern Baptist Theological Seminary in Louisville, where he and the seminary were among the chief targets of Fundamentalists.

Cecil E. Sherman, surely one of the two or three most significant Moderates throughout the entire twelve-year bout, provides an autobiographical and historical overview of the Moderate movement and how it interfaced with SBC Fundamentalism. No single person was better equipped to take on this task. Sherman was the person who called for the now-famous Gatlinburg meeting in September 1980 that launched the Moderate effort; he stayed with the resistance endeavor until the SBC in New Orleans in 1990; and in 1992 he was called to be the first national coordinator of the newly formed Cooperative Baptist Fellowship.

After the two background chapters, there are three papers, those by James Slatton, John H. Hewett, and Jimmy Allen, that describe something of the organized political response to Fundamentalism during the controversy. Slatton, respected pastor of the River Road Church in Richmond,

Virginia, like Cecil Sherman, came early, stayed late, and guided much of the Moderate political effort to turn back the Fundamentalists.

John Hewett, now pastor of the First Baptist Church in Asheville, North Carolina, is one of those younger pastors whose first decade of full-time ministry roughly spans the years of the controversy. A remarkable leader, Hewett became influential in the Forum, the Moderate response to the SBC Pastor's Conference, and eventually was elected as the second moderator of the Cooperative Baptist Fellowship. Jimmy Allen, president of the SBC when the Fundamentalists launched their attack, later became the head of the SBC Radio and Television Commission. Allen, along with Daniel Vestal, spearheaded the call for the convocation in the summer of 1990 that evolved into the Cooperative Baptist Fellowship. In November 1989 Allen had become the leader of the Moderate political network, now called "Baptists Committed." It is the Baptists Committed story that Allen describes in his paper.

The next seven papers depict Moderate organizations or institutions that emerged out of the controversy. Each writer has a special relationship with the organization described. Alan Neely, former missionary and longtime professor at Southeastern Seminary and now professor at Princeton Theological Seminary, was one of the founders of the Alliance of Baptists, formerly The Southern Baptist Alliance. He has also written the official history of the Alliance, from which his paper here derives. Libby Bellinger, a chaplain in Waco, Texas, was a president and leader in the Southern Baptist Women in Ministry organization, a particularly crucial ingredient in the entire Moderate movement. Bellinger, one of the best-known woman ministers among Southern Baptists, was especially qualified to tell the story of Women in Ministry.

Walker Knight, one of the most-noted journalists among Southern Baptists in the last thirty-five years, became the first editor and is now publisher of *Baptists Today,* which functions as a kind of national Moderate newspaper. Founded as *SBC Today* in 1983, the newspaper is synonymous with Walker Knight and absolutely no one knows the saga of that paper as does he. Stan Hastey, a former employee of the Baptist Joint Committee and Washington bureau chief for Baptist Press for several years, knows the entangled story of the controversy and the press as well as anyone. On January 1, 1989, Hastey became the first executive-director of the Alliance of Baptists. In that role he has been at the heart of much of the controversy.

Other new Moderate organizations to develop have been a theological seminary, an ethics agency, and a publishing company. Thomas H. Graves, former pastor of St. John's Baptist Church in Charlotte and a former professor at Southeastern Seminary, became the first president of Baptist Theological Seminary that opened for classes in September 1991. He tells the story of the birth and infancy of that institution. Robert Parham, a former staff member of the SBC Christian Life Commission is the executive-director of the Baptist Center for Ethics, which began in May, 1991. Parham describes developments at the Christian Life Commission after the Fundamentalists had a majority of the board members and the subsequent need for a Moderate Baptist voice in the ethics arena. An announcement of the opening of Smyth & Helwys Publishing Incorporated was issued in November 1990. Cecil Staton, the publisher and one of the founders, recounts the background and beginning of that publishing enterprise.

The last two papers depict the beginning of consolidation within the Moderate movement. A new direction came in August 1990 when more than 3,000 Moderate Southern Baptists came together in an Atlanta convocation called by Daniel Vestal, who had been defeated for the SBC presidency in June. Other than the gathering itself, maybe the most significant development to come out of the Convocation was the adoption of the Baptist Cooperative Missions Program, Incorporated, a funding mechanism which opened up new funding options for Moderates. Duke McCall, former president of the Southern Baptist Theological Seminary and Grady Cothen, former president of the Baptist Sunday School Board—both revered Southern Baptist leaders all their lives—spearheaded the new funding mechanism.

Daniel Vestal's paper on the history of the Cooperative Baptist Fellowship (CBF) is indispensable to understanding the closing years of the Fundamentalist-Moderate conflict. Vestal, a theological conservative who was unaligned in the early years of the conflict, became a major voice for Moderates during the latter years of the controversy. Without Vestal, one wonders how the SBC Moderates would have coalesced organizationally. He not only issued the call for the August 1990 convocation, he became the first Moderator of CBF. Skillfully and effectively, he helped to birth the organization that has become *the* stackpole for SBC Moderates.

In spite of the care and precision with which the writers tell their part of the story, the complete story is not told here. Obviously the Fundamentalist side of the story is not presented. We Moderates do not know the details of that story except as it interfaced with us. Beyond that, however, not even the whole Moderate story has been described. For example, much activity was going on at the state level of the Southern Baptist Convention concurrent with and even prior to some of the national developments. Historical accounts of state struggles will have to wait for future volumes, but their stories are no less interesting and necessary if one wants the complete picture.

I said above that I had a twofold hope for the conference. In addition to creating a forum for the presentations of the papers, my second hope for the Mercer conference was that the participants would join in the formation of a new Baptist historical society. Near the end of the conference a committee composed of Loyd Allen, Tom Halbrooks, and Loulie Owens Pettigrew came forward with the recommendation that the group form the William H. Whitsitt Baptist Heritage Society. Whitsitt, president of the Southern Baptist Theological Seminary during the last decade of the nineteenth century, embodied the spirit of honest and courageous intellectual inquiry that Moderates had tried to defend for a decade in the 1980s. Forced from his position at Southern because of his insistence that Baptists began denominationally in seventeenth-century England and not on the banks of the Jordan in first-century Palestine as Landmarkism claimed, Whitsitt lost the battle but won the war of a critical approach to Baptist history. He led, as Loulie Owens Pettigrew said, a Baptist resistance movement long before Moderates came on the scene. So at a conference on the history of the Moderate movement, a bit of history was made in the formation of the Whitsitt Heritage Society. The Moderate movement had berthed yet another offspring, one which would help to preserve and record the Moderate SBC history.

Much gratitude is due many as this book is published. R. Kirby Godsey, president of Mercer University, made it possible for the conference to be held on the campus of Mercer. Margie Evans, assistant to the president at Mercer, took responsibility for all the details of the conference. Due to space limitations, some, who made major contributions to the conference with comments and responses, are not included in this volume. Nancy Ammerman, Oeita Bottorff, Rob James, and Bill Leonard responded to some of the papers when they were presented. Carolyn Cole Bucy, Pat Ayers, and Alan Neely concluded the conference with a stimulating panel discussion. I am especially grateful to the authors of the individual chapters in this volume for working hard to help the rest of us know what they know about this important chapter in Baptist history. I am grateful to Mercer University Press, especially to Edd Rowell and Cecil Staton, for seeing that the book was produced efficiently and professionally.

The Background
of the Moderate Movement

E. Glenn Hinson

To speak intelligently about the background of the Moderate Movement, I need to define how I understand what passes under that rubric. I must confess in doing so that I do not like the designation, for it suggests to me that we came into existence as a divergence from our Baptist tradition when, in fact, I think we are in strict continuity with that tradition. Indeed, I think the continuance of the Baptist tradition is what this "movement" is all about. We are Baptist people trying to conserve an endangered species among Southern Baptists.

I am well aware, of course, that the Fundamentalists who now control the Southern Baptist Convention make a claim of continuity with the Baptist tradition. At one point our claims intersect and thus provide a linkage of both the Fundamentalist and the Moderate positions, that is, in the claim that the Bible stands somewhere at the center of the Baptist tradition and should determine what it is. When it comes to a definition of the exact issue involving the Bible, however, the two groups diverge sharply and critically. For the Fundamentalists the issue is one of *the authority of the Bible and the absolute certainty that an inerrant and infallible authority can supply.* For us, on the other hand, the issue is one of *freedom to discover in the scriptures and to apply to life the Word of God.*

Underneath these vastly different statements of the issue lies another one, whether human beings can have absolute certainty in matters of faith. The Fundamentalists would say, "Yes, in infallible written word." I would say, "No. Only God is infallible, and anything human beings are involved in will partake of their fallibility. To be a believer means to live with uncertainty, trusting the Unseen and Unknowable."

In short, I see here two different understandings of faith as the most basic point of divergence. For Fundamentalists faith is faith in the inerrancy or infallibility of the Bible. For us faith is faith in the living God, the "I AM WHO I AM," who has sought constantly to disclose God's self in nature, in history, and in human experience, but whose majesty no human statements can ever suffice to express. This is why freedom for the Word of God is so crucial. It is blasphemous for human beings to try to put God in a box. Boxes get in the way of God's endless effort to break through with God's Word. They get in the way of real obedience to the Word.

I am not suggesting that early Baptists went through a sophisticated analysis of their prelogical suppositions or underlying presuppositions. I do believe, however, that they grasped instinctively that authenticity of faith depended on its voluntariness. They looked on baptism of infants as a form of coercion, for infants did not voluntarily decide for themselves. They opposed uniformity in following the *Book of Common Prayer* in worship because that left no room for the Word of God to break through. John Bunyan objected even to recitation of the Lord's Prayer because the words would not come from the Inner Prompter, the Holy Spirit, but from recitation by rote. To be authentic and responsible, those early Baptists said, faith must be free.

As I would construe its development, what we are characterizing as "the Moderate Movement" has its background in the effort of Baptists to be faithful to this heritage in voluntary exercise of faith in the conviction that God alone is Lord of the conscience and has left us free to seek the Word of God even as God seeks to communicate that Word. Our Baptist heritage itself should dispel any illusions that everyone even within the Christian fold will understand and applaud this quest. To let scriptures determine our dogma rather than have our dogma determine scriptures will be to follow in the footsteps of many Baptist forebears who, for their audacious unwillingness to relinquish interpretation and application of the scriptures into the hands of ecclesiastical authorities or to stop following its mandates, suffered confiscation of property, imprisonment, fines, beatings, and even death.

I. Freedom for the Word

Forgive me if I dwell on the principle of freedom for the Word of God as the key factor in our background, but I am fearful that the word *freedom* has become so much a part of our culture's cliches that we may not grasp the real issue. To be quite honest with you, I am not sure I got hold of it until I heard a Waldensian, whose forebears anticipated the Baptist tradition by a few centuries, express it with incredible eloquence and clarity. You see, the real issue is not just freedom, our American idea of freedom to do what we please. When we think that way we slide off the end of the scale into what Roman Catholics call autonomism and selfish privatism. And we can find Baptists who have gone that far. No, the real issue is freedom *for* the Word of God, freedom to hear and respond in obedience to God. What propelled early Christians to defy Jewish authorities is what motivated early Baptists in their refusal to stop unlicensed preaching or refusal to pay taxes for support of things they did not believe in.

One thing I want particularly to note here is the integral connection between this freedom and evangelism in the Baptist experience. What authorities would not tolerate among those dissenters in England with whom Baptists originated was precisely what Baptists were convinced the Word of God imposed upon them. Similarly in the American colonies, Baptists found the Word of God commanding and directing them to do exactly what the authorities tried to prevent, and the most evangelistic of them, the Separate Baptists, suffered the most. With the Apostles they declared, against the order to halt their preaching, "We must obey God rather then human beings" (Acts 5:29).

I think it unnecessary to make a roll call of the apologists of religious liberty—Smyth, Helwys, Murton, Bunyan, Leland, Backus, Ireland, and others—but it may not be without value to know what they willingly paid such a high price for. The House of Lords in England holds a handwritten

> supplication of divers poore prisoners and many others the kinges maiesties loyall subiectes ready to testifie it by the oeath of allegeance in all sinceri-tie, whose grievances are lamentable, only for cause of conscience.

Possibly composed by Helwys, the letter complained that

> kept have wee bene by them many yeres in lingering imprisonments devid-ed from wives, children, servants & callinges, not for any other cause but only for conscience towardes God, to the utter undoeing of us, our wives & children.[1]

John Murton, Helwys's successor at the General Baptist helm from 1613 until his death in 1626, expanded on what conscience entailed in *A Discription of What God Hath Predestinated Concerning Man.* He made a full defense of the priesthood of every believer:

---

[1]In Champlin Burrage, *The Early English Dissenters in the Light of Recent Research* (Cambridge: University Press, 1912) 1:242.

> I say it is a meere fixion, there is not the least shew in all the Testament of *Jesus Christ*, that Baptising is peculiar onely to Pastors, which might satisfie any man of reason, neither can it bee proved that ever ordinary Pastor did Baptise. And it is most plaine, converting and Baptising is no part of the Pastors office; his office is, to feed, to watch, to oversee, the flocks of *Christ* already the Church: his charge is to take heede to the flocke, and to feed the Church, and to defend them in the truth against all gainsayers; furthes (sic) then which, no charge is laid upon him by vertue of his office: That hee may Preach, convert and Baptise, I deny not, as another disciple may; but not that either is required, or he doth performe it by vertue of his office; no proofe for that imagination can be shewed: and therefore it remaineth firme stable; every Disciple that hath abilities is authorized, yea commanded to Preach, convert & Baptise, aswell and asmuch (if not more) than a Pastor.[2]

As for the Waldensians, so also these Baptists: ecclesiastical authority is not to put shackles on the Word of God; the Word must be free.

John Bunyan's long imprisonment spoke with equal eloquence about freedom for the Word of God. In Bunyan's *Prison Meditations* he made crystal clear how freedom for the Word of God brought him to this costly decision, one for which he was willing to place his four small children's care in the hands of his young second wife, Elizabeth, and to "leap off the ladder blindfold into Eternity."

> They were no fables that I taught
>   Devis'd by cunning men,
> But God's own word, by which were caught
>   Some sinners now and then.
> Whose souls by it were made to see
>   The evil of their sin;
> And need of Christ to make them free
>   From death, which they were in.
>
> And now those very hearts, that then
>   Were foes unto the Lord,
> Embrace his Christ and truth like men
>   Conquer'd by his word.
> I hear them sigh, and groan, and cry,
>   For grace to God above;
> They loathe their sin, and to it die,
>   'Tis holiness they love.

---

[2]Ibid., 262.

> This was the work I was about,
>> When hands on me were laid,
> 'Twas this from which they pluck'd me out,
>> And vilely to me said:
> You heretic, deceiver, come,
>> To prison you must go,
> You preach abroad, and keep not home,
>> You are the Church's foe.
>
> But having peace within my soul,
>> And truth on every side,
> I could with comfort them control,
>> And at their charge deride.
> Wherefore to prison they me sent,
>> Where to this day I lie,
> And can with very much content
>> For my profession die.

People taken captive by the Word of God also paid a high price for freedom of the Word in the American colonies, but none acted more zealously in its behalf than the Separate Baptists of Virginia and North Carolina, ironically the forebears of the main body of Baptists who constitute the Southern Baptist Convention. (What has happened since the eighteenth century is surely eloquent testimony of the profound difference a transition from minority to majority status makes!) No religious group that I know about took the scriptural mandate to evangelize to heart as did the Separate Baptists. "They cannot meet a man on the road," one lawyer in Virginia charged, "but they must ram a text of Scripture down his throat."[3]

More needs to be said about the lengths to which those early Baptists carried the voluntary principle, precisely because they believed the Word had such power it did not require guardians and defenders. The words of Helwys to King James I in *A Short Declaration of the Mistery of Iniquity* shows how expansive they made it: "Let them be heretikes, Turcks, Jewes or whatsoever it apperteynes not to the earthly power to punish them in the least measure."[4] It echoed again in Roger Williams's *The Bloudy Tenet of Persecution* with an added hint of its motive:

---

[3]In Robert Baylor Semple, *History of the Baptists in Virginia* (Lafayette TN: Church History and Archives Research, 1976) 30.

[4]*Mistery of Iniquity* (1612; rpr. London: Baptist Historical Society, 1935) 69.

> It is the will and command of God that, since the coming of his Son
> the Lord Jesus, a permission of the most Paganish, Jewish, Turkish, or
> antichristian consciences and worships be granted to all men in all nations
> and countries: and they are only to be fought against with that sword
> which is only, in soul matters, able to conquer: to wit, the sword of God's
> spirit, the word of God.[5]

"In soul matters" the Word of God alone can win, for God alone can
command conscience.

Behind this conviction stands a profound belief in the Holy Spirit, the
living God personally present, which came out still more starkly in the
Baptist insistence on the voluntary approach to prayer. John Smyth berated
canonical hours of prayer as human devisings which would stand in the way
of "that libertie wherewith Christ has made us free." Although he would
permit recitation of the Lord's Prayer, he considered it "safer to conceive a
prayer, than to reade a prayer." Better stumbling public prayers than rote
repetition.[6] John Bunyan carried the voluntary principle still further when he
forbade the use even of the Lord's Prayer. Since prayer is, by his definition,
"a sincere, sensible, affectionate pouring out of the heart or soul to God
through Christ, in the strength and assistance of the Holy Spirit," it can be
offered only in the Spirit and set prayers can be described only as "a little
lip labor and bodily exercise."[7]

2. Baptist Education

To turn now to the more direct linkage of the voluntary principle to the ori-
gins of the Moderate Movement, I would like to note its connection with
Baptist education, for it was education and educational institutions that
spawned this movement. You and I both know, of course, that Baptists have
had a mixed record in education. We have produced more than our share of
people who thanked God for their ignorance and had much to be thankful
for. The earliest Baptists often reminded their critics and detractors that degrees from Oxford or Cambridge did not make ministers. Their descendants

---

[5]Roger Williams, *The Bloudy Tenent of Persecution*, ed. Edward Bean Underhill
(London: J. Haddon, 1848) 2.

[6]*The Works of John Smyth*, ed. W. T. Whitley (Cambridge: University Press,
1915) 1:77-78, 81.

[7]See John Bunyan, *I Will Pray with the Spirit*, ed. Richard L. Greaves (Oxford:
Clarendon Press, 1976) 235, 242, 257.

have distinguished themselves by the fact that they would not set education-al requirements for ordination but laid hands on many empty heads. On the American frontier in particular they gloried in lack of formal education.

Such a record as this often obscures the genuine Baptist achievements in education and perhaps clouds the underlying motive for them. What I would argue is that it really gives us a clue to the way in which the volun-tary principle stood behind and gave impetus to the development of Baptist educational institutions. I don't think it would be difficult to establish that the reason Baptists spoke meanly about education early on was not because of hostility to education per se but because they were denied it and yet recognized they could obtain insight through the guidance of the Holy Spirit anyway. Insight did not depend on formal training at Oxford or Cambridge in Old England or Harvard or Yale in New England. It depended on yieldedness to the Spirit before an open Bible.

One is not surprised, therefore, to find Baptists in America very reluc-tant to take their first step toward an institution of higher learning. When Morgan Edwards proposed the founding of the first Baptist college in Amer-ica, he was "laughed at, as the projector of a thing impracticable."[8] Even one of the early agents for the college admitted ambivalence, "lest the purity of the Gospel should suffer, as is very often the case, by men whose learning was their only recommendation for the pulpit."[9] Baptists often re-torted to charges of their ignorance that "the Spirit of God needs none of man's learning."[10] Baptists could also see that Presbyterian and Congrega-tionalist insistence on a trained ministry impeded their outreach to the frontier as people moved westward.

What turned Baptist attitudes around vis-à-vis education was the grow-ing recognition as they increased their ranks that the Spirit of God also needed "none of man's ignorance."[11] Just to read the Bible required some education, but to read it intelligently and to relate it to the needs of people effectively mandated a lot of education. And Baptists established their first colleges to do exactly that. They had to find some way to make their preaching of the Word effective not only among the uneducated and back-

---

[8]Barnas Sears, *Historical Discourse: Celebration of the One Hundredth Anniversary of the Founding of Brown University* (Providence: Sidney S. Rider & Bro., 1865) 12.

[9]Ibid., 8.

[10]Cited by Martin Ross in *Minutes of the Chowan (NC) Association* (1809) 9.

[11]Paraphrase of Ross's retort in ibid.

ward but also among the educated and refined in the cities as America urbanized. Until Rhode Island College opened in 1765 they had no place to do that because Harvard, William and Mary, Yale, and other schools had religious requirements for admission which denied Baptists a place. Remembering their treatment, they chartered Rhode Island College with due concern for freedom of the Word of God, declaring

> That into this liberal and catholic institution shall never be admitted any religious tests: But, on the contrary, all the members hereof shall forever enjoy full, free, absolute and uninterrupted liberty of conscience: And that the places of Professors, Tutors, and all other officers, the President alone excepted, shall be free and open for all denominations of Protestants: And that the youth of all religious denominations shall and may be freely admitted to the equal advantages, emoluments and honors of the College or University.[12]

Furman University's first catalogue likewise boasted that "the College, while under the control of the Baptist Denomination, is, in no way, sectarian in its teaching, and on its student roll are representatives of all the leading Christian bodies."[13]

Granting that Baptists, probably even a majority of those who bear that name, have not known why they have developed institutions of higher learning, I would argue nonetheless that they have done so, above all, to give themselves the most effective voice in espousing freedom for the Word of God. That was exactly the point Barnas Sears, the fourth president of Brown University and noted historian, tried to make about the founding of the first Baptist college:

> It was in this dark hour of adversity that the College was planted, with the express design of unfurling a standard of liberty in matters of religion, around which the sons of freedom might rally, and of raising up a class of men who would loudly proclaim and ably advocate the principles in which the foundations of the College were laid.[14]

It was also what Professor C. R. Henderson of the University of Chicago told the Baptist World Congress in 1905. Baptists, he contended,

> have had an honourable share in securing liberty of thought, expression and worship, over against its enemies in the State and Established Churches;

---

[12]Cited by Sears, *Historical Discourse*, 61-62.
[13]*Annual Catalogue of Furman University, 1903–1904*, 8.
[14]Sears, *Historical Discourse*, 8.

logically, we must advance and secure the vital conditions of liberty for truth within our own Church. The higher and highest education is a necessity. No religious body can live and thrive and influence the minds of men without having a large, strong, independent body of leaders, ministers and laymen. It is for us a question of life and death. We must be aggressive; we must be among the leaders, or we shall lose what our fathers won for us.[15]

Making some allowances for our rhetoric, I would add my signature to the point they were making. Education is the key to the conservation of freedom for the Word of God. In saying that, I am conscious of a role congregations and Baptist congregational polity play in guarding freedom. Congregations are the agencies through which the Baptist voluntary principle comes to expression at the grass roots. But we do not have to reflect long on recent experience among Southern Baptists to discern that people at the grass roots can lose sight of their tradition when (1) cultural forces obscure it, (2) TV evangelists deliberately reinterpret it, (3) means of inculcating it diminish and disappear, (4) congregations become mottled, and (5) a group shifts from minority to majority status. The fact is, concern about freedom for the Word of God is a minority concern, and if it is to survive, education will have to see that it happens.

I am fully conscious that there is an elitist note in what I have just said, and that some criticize educational institutions for being elitist. Against such criticisms I would raise a question as to whether freedom for the Word of God can survive in any other way. The conservation of freedom does not have the support of the majority. It depends, rather, on the minority with strong commitment to its conservation precisely because it is a minority concern, and those who teach are precisely the group who have the greatest stake in freedom for the Word of God.

3. Training for Ministry

You may think I have wandered rather far afield to get here, but I would see the next factor in the background of the Moderate Movement in training for ministry. Nowhere is freedom for the Word of God more important nor more threatened than in education for ministry, judging by the history of

---

[15]Henderson, "The Place of Denominational Academies, Colleges, Universities, and Theological Seminaries," *The Baptist World Congress: London* (11-19 July 1905) 226-32.

Baptist theological schools. Given the centrality of the scriptures in Baptist faith and life, training of ministers for "rightly dividing the word of truth" would seem to be the most important activity going, for what ministers do will impact others directly. Of all religious groups Baptists would seem to have the biggest stake in open Bibles and unrestricted efforts to search out the truth found in them. But, alas, if that is true of some Baptist groups, it has not been true among Southern Baptists and the sad tale of denial of freedom is the immediate reason why we have a Moderate Movement today. Instances of constriction of freedom run from the beginning of the Southern Baptist Convention to the present moment. A look at the story of education in the oldest Southern Baptist seminary should make the point fairly well, just by itself, but the expansion of Southern Baptist theological seminaries has multiplied the problem many times. Basically what the whole story shows is that the exercise of freedom for the Word of God is still a costly venture for those courageous enough to undertake it.

The objectives of James Petigru Boyce in founding Southern Seminary may have been what ultimately generated the greatest danger for freedom of the Word in training of ministers. Boyce wanted a seminary that would do its very best to equip persons of diverse abilities and equipment at diverse levels and in diverse ways to serve a diverse constituency and thus to unite the denomination. Admitting persons of limited general education along with college graduates necessitated a goodly measure of "doublespeak"[16] in the classrooms, in representing the seminary to the denomination, and in general style. Boyce clearly had an eye on the denominational constituency and not on the cherished Baptist principle of freedom for the Word of God when he insisted that each professor sign the "Abstract of Principles" "so as to guard against the rise of erroneous and injurious instruction in such a seat of sacred learning."[17]

Desire to cater to such a broad constituency constantly strained the Seminary's effort to exercise freedom for the Word of God and the problem has increased as the Seminary has received more and more of its funding from the denomination and less from churches or individual subscribers. William

---

[16][Editor's note: For an account of more contemporary "doublespeak," see the work by Ralph H. Elliott to which Hinson refers later: *The "Genesis Controversy" and Continutiy in Southern Baptist Chaos: A Eulogy for a Great Tradition* (Macon: Mercer University Press, 1992).]

[17]John A. Broadus, *Memoir of James Petigru Boyce* (New York: Armstrong & Son, 1893) 121.

Williams, who taught church history, government, and pastoral duties, aroused the ire of many of the Seminary's constituents by suggesting that "alien immersions" were valid. Boyce handled that problem by assigning Williams's course in church government to another faculty member. When hostility to Williams persisted, Boyce counted on commitment of Baptists to "soul liberty" to help. "If they should treat him badly," he wrote John Broadus, "I shall be sorry on his account and theirs, but it will help us. Soul liberty is worth more than alien immersion, even with Landmarkers."[18] The issue was not one of academic freedom so much as commitment to one of the deepest of Baptist principles against the Baptist high churchism of J. R. Graves.

Freedom of the Word did not fare so well, however, in the case of C. H. Toy. Although Toy launched his career in 1869 with both a clear conviction that "the Bible, its real assertions being known, is in every iota of its substance absolutely and infallibly true" and an enthusiasm for the historical method,[19] acceptance of Darwinian evolutionary theory and the Kuenen-Wellhausen theory of Pentateuchal criticism shoved him beyond the comfort range of the principles laid down by Boyce. Toy himself did not sense any danger here, for, as Broadus remarked, "He was satisfied that his views would promote truth and piety." But Boyce thought otherwise and tried to dissuade him from teaching historical-critical theory, convinced that "nothing of that kind could be taught in the Seminary without doing violence to its aims and objects, and giving the gravest offence to its supporters in general."[20] Though Toy assured the trustees that he could do much good by teaching what historical method led him to teach, when he submitted his resignation in May 1879, the trustees accepted it. After Toy a little historical criticism sneaked in, but John A. Broadus, during his tenure as president, banished it to the senior year of studies.[21]

The cherished Baptist principle of "soul liberty" also did not fare well in the case of William H. Whitsitt, the third president and a church historian at Southern. Whitsitt's conclusion from historical study that Baptists origina-

---

[18]In A. T. Robertson, *Life and Letters of John Albert Broadus* (Philadelphia: American Baptist Publication Society, 1901) 290.

[19]C. H. Toy, *The Claims of Biblical Interpretation on Baptists* (New York: Lange & Hillman, 1869) 13.

[20]Broadus, *Memoir of Boyce*, 261.

[21]William A. Mueller, *A History of Southern Baptist Theological Seminary* (Nashville: Broadman, 1959) 149-50.

ted in England around 1641 and could not trace their succession from John the Baptist by way of early and medieval sects caused an explosion in 1896, the year after he became president. Of particular moment here was the fact that one of his chief antagonists was B. H. Carroll, then a Southern Seminary trustee but later the first president of Southwestern Seminary. What was already a critical situation for the exercise of freedom for the Word was heading toward a still more dangerous point with the creation of a competing institution that would approach training of ministers from a radically different perspective, one far more pragmatic. I do not want to appear to make invidious comparisons, but I believe the ethos of education shifted in the founding of Southwestern, and the more pragmatic ethos of the latter is what has come gradually to prevail in the Southern Baptist Convention.

One of the ironies of the Fundamentalist attacks in the past several decades has been that they were directed at the institutions which took the Bible with the greatest seriousness. From the first, Southern Seminary accentuated biblical studies, rooted everything in the Bible, even if it was not always able to exercise fully the freedom for the Word of God. Early professors such as John A. Broadus, C. H. Toy, and A. T. Robertson did distinguished work. John R. Sampey chaired the Old Testament section of the American Standard Bible Revision Committee from 1930 to 1938. But others injected biblical insights into their special areas. W. O. Carver, for instance, helped to erect the world mission program of Southern Baptists on a biblical foundation in his influential book devoted to *Missions in the Plan of the Ages*. Gaines S. Dobbins sought to do the same for religious education, evangelism, and church administration. Wayne E. Oates has informed his vast writing in pastoral care with a biblical perspective, devoting some of his writings explicitly to this connection. Southern Seminary's theologians, from Boyce and Manly and Mullins to Rust and Moody, have written essentially biblical theology. Dale Moody's *Word of Truth*, which systematizes Bible doctrines, probably epitomizes the tradition of training for ministry at Southern Seminary.

This same tradition persisted in the institutions that bore most closely the stamp of Southern Seminary—Southeastern and, at first, Midwestern. Before these came into existence, however, a massive change of ethos which would cast a dark cloud over the exercise of freedom for the Word of God in training of ministers was taking place in Southern Baptist life. I am speaking about the development of the corporation motif and mentality. Those who began as a people associating voluntarily to seek truth in the Word under guidance of the Holy Spirit were gradually being taken over by the prevailing social model in America, the corporation, which had very different views about freedom for the Word. The corporation's concern is conformity that can assure success of the corporation. The more the Southern Baptist corporation dominated in the southland, the more it demanded conformity which would comfort the people in the pew.

I am saddened to say that Southern Seminary, despite its grounding of everything in the scriptures, had a part in promoting the corporation motif. In 1923 Gaines Dobbins wrote a work entitled *The Efficient Church*, in which he prodded the churches to apply business methods. But he was not the initiator of this development. A stream was already flowing and growing wider and wider. In 1917 the executive committee, from 1919 to 1924 the "75 Million Campaign," after 1925 the Cooperative Program, in 1927 an executive secretary—all gave indisputable evidence of the widening stream. And that stream has swept everything in its path. In 1956 the executive committee hired Booz, Allen, Hamilton to study the efficiency of the whole corporation and to make proposals that would help to bring the entire operation into a more cohesive and effective unit. James L. Sullivan, longtime head of the Sunday School Board, has indicated very clearly what this means when it comes to exercise of freedom for the Word of God and why we are involved in what we call the Moderate Movement.

> The institution, unlike the convention, is a corporation. It must operate under a system of management to produce accomplishments for the churches, to fulfill the purposes for which the institution is brought into being. For that reason, an institution is not a democracy. Matters are not to be taken under consideration by employees to see whether they will carry out orders or not. In a corporate structure, like a Southern Baptist institution, the worker must either carry out the directives or seek employment elsewhere. It is just that simple. All democratic processes are taking place in the chart above the executive officer, none below him. Above him the question is "Wilt thou"? Below him the directive is, "Thou shalt." That is the difference between a democratic process and the operation of a corporate structure. For this reason some people are temperamentally unqualified to serve Southern Baptist institutions because they want to work as if the institution were a democracy. Such is impossible for Baptist agencies if the mission of the institution or agency is to be fulfilled.[22]

Theologically, please note, this means that the Holy Spirit can function only above the level of the executive. Because local congregations have taken on

---

[22]Sullivan, *Baptist Polity As I See It* (Nashville: Broadman, 1983) 172-73.

the corporate model, you would not expect to find the Spirit operative there except in the executive hired to run the corporation or the board of deacons or some executive committee. Because seminaries are institutions, no one could expect to find the Spirit operating in any except the president or the board of trustees. So also all the rest of the gigantic corporation. There can be no freedom for the Word of God except among the select few.

4. The "Genesis Controversy"

I could document the telling impact of the corporation mentality in numerous instances, but we have a carefully documented case in what most know as the "Elliott Controversy" but which Ralph Elliott himself prefers to call the "Genesis Controversy." What Ralph Elliott has established very well in his recent book by that title is how readily Southern Baptist leaders have come to resort to "doublespeak" and political juggling and dancing to save the institution at the price of truth, human well-being, integrity, and decency. In his case, Elliott is careful to point out, most did so without malice in most instances, thinking they did the best they could in the circumstances, although a few waited to see which way the wind was blowing to decide how they would act. The major casualty of the whole affair was not Ralph Elliott, who survived and grew stronger, but the central Baptist principle of freedom for the Word of God.

Ralph Elliott went to Midwestern Seminary as the first faculty member on the heels of the crisis at Southern in 1958.[23] Before going to Midwestern, he had already begun preparation of *The Message of Genesis* at the behest of Broadman Press and with the encouragement of his major professor Clyde T. Francisco. The book, a *conservative* approach to Genesis, created a storm almost immediately after its appearance in July 1961. The first thunder came from John F. Havlik, then Director of Evangelism for the Baptist State Convention of Kansas; the next came from Earl Pounds, pastor of Mary Ann Baptist Church in St. Louis. Fundamentalists soon turned these first booms into a terrific storm.

There is not enough space here to recount the story in detail, but the main point of the whole should not escape us, for that is precisely what has

---

[23][Editor's note: Hinson refers here to the conflict between the president and some of the faculty at Southern Seminary, resulting in the dismissal of 13 faculty members. For the story, see Hinson, "Southern Baptist Theological Seminary," *Encyclopedia of Southern Baptists* (Nashville: Broadman, 1971) 3:1978-83.]

brought us to this occasion and place. In the entire saga you will have to look hard to find people in positions of influence or power who were willing to stand by Ralph Elliott—President Berquist, some colleagues at Midwestern, some students, editors of the book at Broadman. Millard Berquist strongly backed publication of *The Message of Genesis* and he stayed with Ralph Elliott up to the point where Herschel Hobbs persuaded him that the solution lay in knuckling under for the sake of saving the institution. Hobbs was then president of the Southern Baptist Convention. (Recently we have heard Hobbs issuing further pleas to sacrifice for the sake of an institution.) Heber Peacock, Bill Morton, Hugh Wamble, and especially Morris Ashcraft offered major support. Bill Fallis and Joe Green at Broadman never backed away from the decision to publish the book; Fallis assisted Elliott in getting it reprinted. Far more numerous were those who, though admitting agreement with the book, used the occasion to enhance their own standing at Ralph Elliott's expense. Especially painful to Elliott was what he felt was abandonment of him by the mother seminary, Southern Seminary, and the "doublespeak" of his supervisory professor, who at one point evidently fanned the flames of hostility to Elliott and *The Message of Genesis*. The trustees at Midwestern indicated support early on, but after the changing of several trustees at the annual convention they were no longer ready to stand by him. They did not want to be charged with book banning and thus tried to put the matter in such a way that he rather than they would have to take the blame. They fired him for insubordination.

I agree with Ralph Elliott that what has taken place in the Southern Baptist Convention in the last thirteen years is only an extension of what he went through in 1961–1962. He may be right also in wondering whether, had Southern Baptist leaders acted with integrity and stood fast against the Fundamentalist agitation, we would be where we are today. An editor for *The Christian Century* showed a lot of insight into the issue when he noted that it was much vaster than the right of a professor to teach a mild form of biblical criticism. It was, rather, one of "control of the Southern Baptist Convention's academic institutions and, through this, of the training of the ministry." The editor went on to note that Elliott's dismissal was "a warning that [faculties] will have a fight on their hands if they want to preserve academic freedom, intellectual integrity, and creditable scholarship in the institutions they love and serve" and "bad news for the Southern Baptist Convention, whose unity is now gravely imperiled by a desecration of the religious liberty whose defense is the special pride of Baptists."[24] Now we can see that those who cherish freedom for the Word of God have lost the fight and find themselves in a new phase of the Moderate Movement.

Yes, we are at a new phase, but I don't think our task has changed despite the fact that we have lost the battle for control of the seminaries and thence of the training of ministers. Ralph Elliott is a prime example of what the Moderate Movement is about. He loves the Bible. It holds such authority for him that he would sacrifice a job he loved and a career to remain faithful to the search for truth he is convinced will be found there. Dale Moody is another prime example. No one who ever heard Dale Moody preach or teach could come away with any impression but that Moody walked with at least one if not both feet on the bibliolatry side of the line that separates it from appreciation for biblical authority. So greatly did he revere the scriptures that he was willing to risk dismissal from Southern Seminary rather than subscribe to an article of the Abstract of Principles he thought conflicted with them. If I have not wrongly perceived the many smaller stories within the larger story, the background of the Moderate Movement lies in the efforts of all of these who paid the high price for exercising freedom of the Word of God. If in the future we intend to be faithful to our forebears, we will need now to count the cost and see whether we are prepared to go on paying such a price, indeed whether we will create programs and institutions through which the Word of God need never be shackled and in which persons can exercise freedom for the Word.

---

[24]*The Christian Century*, 14 Nov 1962, 1376.

An Overview
of the Moderate Movement

Cecil E. Sherman

It was June 1980. The place was St. Louis. The Southern Baptist Convention was in session. My wife and I were sitting in the hall taking in the first SBC ever presided over by the new regime of Fundamentalists. Adrian Rogers was in the chair. Believe me, it was different. Speakers seemed compelled to identify themselves as biblical inerrantists. Speeches and business sessions were filled with digressions so the house could be evangelized to the new orthodoxy. My wife and I had not heard it this way before in our three decades of attending the SBC.

My wife leaned over and whispered in my ear: "Honey, did we come the wrong week? This must be a political convention, not the Southern Baptist Convention. Maybe we made a mistake." My wife felt the change. Our convention was redirecting its energy. Before 1980, the SBC was outer-directed in mission and ministry to the world. After 1980, the SBC would be turned inward. We would fight against not "the world, the flesh, and the devil"; we preferred to fight each other. The needy world could wait.

My wife Dot and I sat with a number of friends through the 1980 convention. Of course, we talked of what might be done to bring some balance, to resist the steamroller of Fundamentalism that threatened to run over us. It was in St. Louis that I saw our predicament clearly. If we did nothing, the SBC would fall to the Fundamentalists. They were organized; we were not. They had one candidate for the presidency of the Convention; we had several. Their votes were directed; ours were scattered. They had a plan; we had none. They had leadership; we were loathe to give leadership or, as later history would demonstrate, to discipline ourselves to "followship."

The results were clear for all to see. In 1979, the Fundamentalists had direction and political organization. Adrian Rogers, Fundamentalist pastor of Bellevue Baptist Church in Memphis, was elected on the first ballot by a political organization put together that spring by Paul Pressler and Paige Patterson. He defeated good candidates who had no organized structure to support them.

Then it happened again. In 1980 three good non-Fundamentalist pastors were offered to the convention: Richard Jackson, James Pleitz, and Frank Pollard. All would have made good presidents; all had "paid their dues" to the SBC. They had led strong churches to support the convention, but, by now, qualifications did not elect. Political structure did. Bailey Smith, then pastor in Del City, Oklahoma, who was not truly qualified to serve as president, was elected on the first ballot by the Fundamentalist machinery. He had an organization behind him.

I had some idea what was at stake. The SBC was losing its innocence. It had become too big and too rich. It was ripe for the plucking. Fundamentalists rallied their troops behind the battle cry of biblical inerrancy. They were organized. Baptist ideas were forgotten in the zeal to "save the Bible." I was not the only one to see the predicament: if we create a counter organization, we do battle with brothers and sisters in Christ. We divert the SBC from her mission task. Our reactions to the Fundamentalist agenda to take over the SBC would set in motion something that would be irreversible. If we don't create a counter politic, however, we concede a contest with serious consequences for serious Baptists.

After the St. Louis convention I went back to Asheville, North Carolina, where I then served as pastor to think about the confusion of the non-Fundamentalist side of the SBC. I corresponded with Duke McCall, longtime president of The Southern Baptist Theological Seminary, and, by any measure, one of Southern Baptists' most revered patriarchs. He encouraged some political organization. Telephone conversations with others across the SBC supported the idea that something had to be done if the SBC were to be saved from Fundamentalism. I wrote a letter to twenty-five friends. All were pastors. I invited them to the Holiday Inn in Gatlinburg, Tennessee. It was the last week in September 1980. Seventeen persons accepted the invitation. The "Moderate Movement" of the SBC was born in Gatlinburg in September 1980.[1]

---

[1][Editor's note: To specify the date of the beginning of the Moderate Movement is extremely important. The Moderate political movement came into existence, as

I. Gatlinburg and the Birth of the Moderate Movement

When we assembled in Gatlinburg, we had something to talk about. Just a few days before in Lynchburg, Virginia, Paul Pressler of Houston, Texas, one of the architects of the Fundamentalist takeover, had made what would be one of the most infamous speeches of the entire controversy. He said

---

the SBC Peace Committee Report rightly says, as a *reaction* to the Fundamentalist attack beginning in Houston in 1979. There was no "Moderate Movement" prior to 1980. As the controversy developed into the decade of the eighties, Fundamentalists often tried to justify their takeover of the SBC by saying that "Moderates" had been doing "the same thing for years." By "doing the same thing for years," Fundamentalists meant organizing politically to elect the president of the SBC and then urging that president to "stack" the committees with only one kind of Southern Baptist.

Regarding this interpretation of the controversy, several points need underscoring. One, *no* president of the SBC, regardless of theological orientation, had ever used presidential powers in a tyrannical fashion, as did the Fundamentalists of the 1980s to exclude some Southern Baptists from serving on agencies of the convention. W. A. Criswell, the grandfather of the 1980s SBC Fundamentalists, admitted such in the midst of the controversy. Second, it needs to be repeated that "Moderates" as an identifiable movement within the SBC began in 1980, just as the new "Fundamentalist" coalition spearheaded by Pressler and Patterson began in the spring of 1979. The Fundamentalist and Moderate parties of the 1980s simply did not exist as sharply defined branches of Southern Baptist life prior to this point. To equate pre-1979 presidents of the SBC with the Moderate movement, as Fundamentalist interpretations tried to do, is simply to distort history. The following SBC presidents could not be remotely categorized as "Moderates" at the time of their election and as the term came to be used later: R. G. Lee (1949–1951), J. D. Grey (1952–1953), J. W. Storer (1954–1955), C. C. Warren (1956–1957), Ramsey Pollard (1960–1961), K. Owen White (1964), Wayne Dehoney (1965–1966), H. Franklin Paschall (1967–1968), W. A. Criswell (1969–1970), and Jaroy Weber (1975–1976). From 1950 through 1979 only a handful of SBC presidents (Brooks Hays 1958–1959, Herschel Hobbs 1962–1963, Carl Bates 1971–1972, James Sullivan 1977, and Jimmy Allen 1978–1979) could be interpreted as "Moderates." But the point that deserves repetition is that not a single SBC president from 1950 to 1979 was ever elected by a "Moderate" political machine. No such machine existed. What the pre-1979 SBC presidents had in common, and this includes presidents as different as R. G. Lee and Brooks Hayes, was their commitment to the denomination, not their similar theological point of views. None of these presidents owed their election to a "Moderate" political machine.]

Fundamentalists would "go for the jugular." He also said his new trustees would not be of the "rubber stamp" variety. But more revealing than the violence of his rhetoric was the plan Pressler outlined. The design was this: elect presidents of the SBC who would make appointments from the Fundamentalist party faithful. The party faithful would pack the Committee on Boards. There the faithful would appoint to places of trust people who would carry out what would amount to a theological purge of the Southern Baptist Convention. All would bow before the new Fundamentalist orthodoxy or they would risk losing place in the SBC. Happily, the *Religious Herald,* the Virginia Baptist state paper, carried an excellent story on Pressler's Lynchburg speech.[2] The design the Fundamentalists would use to takeover the SBC was out. Only those who did not want to understand—and there seemed to be many—remained unaware. Certainly those who came to Gatlinburg took Fundamentalism seriously. The Lynchburg meeting and Pressler's incendiary quote focused the Gatlinburg meeting.

I've met a number of people who say they were at Gatlinburg. The following, listed in alphabetical order, are the names of those present: Carl Bates, pastor, First Baptist Church, Charlotte, North Carolina; Lavonn Brown, pastor, First Baptist Church, Norman, Oklahoma; Frank Campbell, pastor, First Baptist Church, Statesville, North Carolina; Kenneth Chafin, pastor, South Main Baptist Church, Houston, Texas; Henry Crouch, pastor, Providence Baptist Church, Charlotte, North Carolina; Earl Davis, pastor, First Baptist Church, Memphis, Tennessee; Vernon Davis, pastor, First Baptist Church, Alexandria, Virginia; Clyde Fant, pastor, First Baptist

---

[2][Editor's note: See *Religious Herald,* 18 Sept 1980, 8. Pressler, speaking at the Old Forest Road Baptist Church in Lynchburg, Virginia, said, "We have been fighting battles without knowing what the war is all about. We have not been effective because we have not gotten to the root of the problem." He then added, "The lifeblood of the Southern Baptist Convention is the trustees. We need to go for the jugular—we need to go for trustees." The political way to "go for the jugular" in Southern Baptist life is spelled out below (61n.19) as a four-step process. In summary, the agenda was to *elect* a Fundamentalist president who *appoints* a Fundamentalist Committee on Committees, which *nominates* (to the SBC) a Committee on Nominations (previously known as Committee on Boards), which *nominates* (to the SBC) Fundamentalist trustees of all the agencies and institutions. In turn, the trustees transform the agencies and institutions according to the Fundamentalist agenda. For an example of trustee action in SBC agencies, see Roger Parham's article in this volume.]

Church, Richardson, Texas; C. Welton Gaddy, pastor, Broadway Baptist Church, Ft. Worth, Texas; T. L. McSwain, pastor, Hurstbourne Baptist Church, Louisville, Kentucky; Bill O'Connor, pastor, First Baptist Church, Jackson, Georgia; Ed Perry, pastor, Broadway Baptist Church, Louisville, Kentucky; Carman Sharp, pastor, Deer Park Baptist Church, Louisville, Kentucky; Bill Sherman, pastor, Woodmont Baptist Church, Nashville, Tennessee; Cecil Sherman, pastor, First Baptist Church, Asheville, North Carolina; Jim Slatton, pastor, River Road Church, Richmond, Virginia; Ches Smith, pastor, First Baptist Church, Tifton, Georgia.

Because of later charges made during the controversy, a question must be answered at this point: were these the people who had been running the SBC with a "good ole boy politic" for years? Not really. Not at all. When I think of the "good ole boy network," names like these come to mind: Porter Routh and Albert McClellan, Herschel Hobbs and J. D. Grey, Ramsey Pollard and Louie Newton. In a real sense, these men had had a disproportionate influence on the SBC, but they were not part of an organized "Moderate" political movement. The people who met in Gatlinburg were not opposed to these "good ole boys." Neither were we *of* them.

The reasons we came to Gatlinburg were clear in our minds:

1. We had seen the futility of disorder when pitted against an organized politic. We could not beat back the Fundamentalists unless we were ready to do serious politic.

2. We disagreed with Paul Pressler's first premise: that the Southern Baptist Convention was "drifting into liberalism." None of us thought the SBC too liberal. We might have thought it too closed or sometimes too conservative. But we surely disagreed with Pressler's first premise.

3. We were happy with the stewardship of the administrators and presidents of our agencies. We thought the SBC was doing what the New Testament required. So, we spoke of ourselves as "the friends of missions." We saw ourselves as "loyalists."[3] We were happy with the system and came

---

[3][Editor's note: A number of terms came to be used to describe those involved in the "Moderate Movement." Those in attendance at Gatlinburg came to be known somewhat humorously and facetiously, and from the Fundamentalist point of view derogatorily, as "The Gatlinburg Gang." The earliest general term for those who opposed the Fundamentalists was "Denominational Loyalists." In different states they were known under different names, e.g., in North Carolina as "Friends of Missions" and in Georgia as "Concerned Southern Baptists." Later the Moderate Movement would travel under the rubric of "Baptists Committed." Ultimately, the

to the meeting to set in motion something that would save the SBC from a militant, intolerant, judgmental Fundamentalism.

4. We were invested in the Southern Baptist Convention. We were products of the denominational educational system, the colleges and seminaries. We had led the churches we served to fund the denomination. It was an offense to us that people were being put forward to lead the Fundamentalist party who had little investment in the SBC. Several of us had been or were presidents of state conventions. Carl Bates had been a president of the SBC. We were invested.

5. We had some sense of Baptist history and polity. The group was unusually well educated. Half had earned doctorates. Several had been teachers. We knew who Baptists were and what Baptist principles were. When Fundamentalists designed to take Baptists where no Baptist should ever go, someone with some sense of history had to rise up and say this was not a route a Baptist ought to take. The people at Gatlinburg knew where Baptist benchmarks were. Further, the people at Gatlinburg knew something of American Fundamentalism. Frank Norris was more than a name to us. We recognized where he differed with Baptists on critical matters of doctrine and polity. Some in the room had grown up in the shadow of Frank Norris. That the Fundamentalists who were now leading the SBC were more akin to Frank Norris than to John Leland and Isaac Backus was not lost on us.[4]

And so it was agreed at Gatlinburg that we would return to our home states and begin putting together a network. This network would become a politic to counter Fundamentalism in Southern Baptist life. We would meet again in February 1981. We would find others to join us. We would find a presidential candidate to carry our banner at the next meeting of the SBC in Los Angeles 1981. If asked about our meeting, we would truthfully answer; if not asked, we would remain silent. And so we left Gatlinburg.

Not everyone at Gatlinburg remained active in the Moderate politic. Most did. Since I had called the group together, they left me in the chair of

---

movement would coalesce into the Cooperative Baptist Fellowship.]

[4][Editor's note: J. Frank Norris led the Fundamentalist attack on the Southern Baptist Convention during the 1920s. Censorious and inflexible, Norris was disowned by Southern Baptists. For a brief introduction see Walter B. Shurden, *Not A Silent People* (Nashville: Broadman Press, 1972) 83-103. John Leland and Isaac Backus both died in the 19th century and are viewed as in the mainstream of the Baptist tradition in America.]

leadership. I would remain in that capacity (with a brief hiatus) until after the 1985 SBC in Dallas.

2. The Way the Moderate Politic Worked

Some states were not represented at Gatlinburg. Those states required some special attention. I had the task of going about from state to state with the mission of finding people who would do networking. Sometimes these people were easy to find. South Carolina comes to mind.

When I asked Henry Finch, David Matthews, Posey Belcher, and Bob Whaley to organize South Carolina, all said yes. And they meant it. They did what they said they would do. They were mainline South Carolina Baptists. They were in contact with many churches. Harold Cole, executive secretary of the state convention, understood what we were about and was supportive. South Carolina is an illustration of an easy state to enlist.

Alabama was more difficult. Two good men would not do the work. They were qualified and had the relationships in place but they would not put themselves to the work of doing politic. Dotson Nelson said he would not become chairman of Alabama. He, like too many others at that time, thought our Moderate efforts unnecessary. In his slow drawl Dotson told me, "Cecil, there have always been little groups who have arisen with grand schemes, but they will come to nothing." He thought doing Moderate politics was only going to make bad matters worse. He thought we would do better to go home and wait for "the pendulum to swing back."

Drew Gunnells was another I tried to enlist in Alabama. He was president of the Alabama Baptist Convention at the time. Drew did not feel he could take a firm Moderate position and remain president of Alabama Baptists. He declined. I tried to persuade him by saying that I was at that time also president of the North Carolina Convention (1979–1981). But that did not move him. He suspected we were intemperate and suggested that a waiting approach and Christian charity would serve our cause better than an organized politic. Finally some leaders surfaced in Alabama. Nelson and Gunnells, doubtless sincere in their convictions, are mentioned to illustrate what Moderates were up against in trying to organize. Among some of the non-Fundamentalist wing of the SBC there was a fear of politics.

Some states were harder to organize than others. As a general rule, the farther East one went, the easier the organization was. People in Maryland, Virginia, and North Carolina saw Fundamentalism as a clear threat to a Baptist body. They were ready to be organized, and they rallied to the Moderate cause early.

The West was another matter. Not until 1985 was there an effective organization in Texas. Oklahoma was organized as best it could be. The climate in Oklahoma has been and remains friendly to Fundamentalism; Fundamentalism is the majority party there. So, our work was spotty. Lavonn Brown of First Baptist Norman and Gene Garrison of First Baptist Oklahoma City put their reputations on the line and did the best that could be done in Oklahoma. Don Harbuck did the same in Arkansas. It was not a case of no one doing anything. It was a case of trying to grow Moderates in stony soil. We got what was there; there weren't many there. All of this is only to prove the contention that Moderates had not been running the Southern Baptist Convention.

East Tennessee was friendly and organized quickly. Bill Bruster, Knoxville pastor, led in that region. Middle Tennessee was harder; Bill Sherman, pastor of Woodmont in Nashville, did what could be done. West Tennessee was tough. Earl Davis of First Baptist Memphis labored hard, but there were few to count. And so it went from state to state. Florida was slow to get together. Missouri was surprisingly well led. Mississippi and Louisiana never fully mobilized to the Moderate or the Fundamentalist cause early on. Strength and weakness; good leadership and careless leadership: this was the story. Some people would work, some would not.

We would gather state and regional captains at each meeting of the SBC. Then there would be meetings about twice a year that were gathered as far West as Texas. Memphis, Knoxville, and Atlanta were other meeting locations. The purpose of our meetings was to build our network, encourage our state leadership, and make group decisions.

Decision making was democratic. Whatever number of people came to a meeting, each had a vote. Issues were discussed, sometimes argued. Then they were put to a vote. The majority ruled. The selection of candidates for the SBC presidency and vice presidencies is an illustration. The names of the people being considered were listed on a board. Each was discussed. Then a vote was taken. The name that received the most votes was our first choice. Then people were chosen to enlist the candidates. Nominators were chosen. Sometimes other strategies for the upcoming SBC were lined out.

On occasion this democratic method was called into question. For example, we voted on whether or not to oppose Jimmy Draper for the SBC presidency in Pittsburgh in 1983. Although a devout member of the Fundamentalist party, Draper had put forward a smiling face in his first year as SBC president. He had posed as a peacemaker and hosted a meeting of reconciliation at the Dallas/Fort Worth airport. This created the impression in the press that Draper was really trying to resolve the differences between the opposing sides. This favorable impression caused most of our people to think Jimmy Draper unbeatable in his bid for a second term. When put to a vote, nineteen of our captains voted not to oppose Draper. Only six were of the opinion we should choose a candidate and go against him. That nineteen to six vote stood. We ran no candidate in Pittsburgh. Only representatives from Virginia and North Carolina were of the opinion we would have a chance in a contest with Draper in Pittsburgh.

And that led to another turn in the road. Foy Valentine, Executive Secretary of the Christian Life Commission of the SBC, was especially unhappy that we did not run someone against Draper. He was so displeased that he said he would take care of the politic in Kansas City in 1984. In 1984 the Moderate politic born in Gatlinburg did not function. Foy valentine and some others hired a man to make telephone calls. His office was in the Dallas/Fort Worth area. From those calls, he built a base for Grady Cothen, recently retired president of the Baptist Sunday School Board, to run as SBC president against the Fundamentalist candidate, who was to be Charles Stanley, pastor of the First Baptist Church in Atlanta. The effort was not successful, and by 1985, the Moderate politic was back on track and working to elect Winfred Moore, pastor of the First Baptist Church of Amarillo, Texas, at the Dallas meeting of the SBC.

The Kansas City convention (1984) was an eye-opener to the presidents of the seminaries. They decided they could be in trouble. After Kansas City, they banded together, chose Winfred Moore to be their candidate, and then came to us to ask if we would put our network back on line and elect Moore. Roy Honeycutt, president of Southern Seminary in Louisville, called me about September 1, 1984. He asked if he and June could take Dot and me to lunch. We met at the Hilton Hotel in Asheville, and he presented the wishes of the seminary presidents. Would we help them elect Moore? He especially wanted to know if we would organize the Southeast. And since that was the region where we had functioned best, we really were the presidents' best resource.

The leaders of the Moderate political network gathered in the Atlanta airport in October 1984. Roy Honeycutt of Southern and Randall Lolley, president of Southeastern Seminary in Wake Forest, North Carolina, were present. They made their statement and asked our help. The group voted unanimously to pull together and support Winfred Moore in his presidential race against Charles Stanley in Dallas, June 1985. This was really the sense of the Moderate movement. We were trying to help the people in power keep their posts and be free in the exercise of their responsibilities. Far more painful to us than defeat was the fickle way in which we were treated by some of the people we were trying to help. First they thought we were "too hot" in our opposition to Fundamentalism. They could handle them. Then they asked our help. And ultimately they threw us away and made an uneasy peace with the very people who accused them of liberalism.

The Moderate way of doing business was hardly an executive model. At each meeting a new face would surface. That new face had to be brought up to date. Often these new people urged upon us ideas already tried and failed. It was a delicate process to "let them down easy." If we smashed their ideas, we lost them to our cause. If we gave heed to their ideas, often we were courting one mistake after another.

Not all people who took responsibility were willing to perform. They enjoyed our meetings, but when they returned home, they sometimes did little work. For example, we tried hard to get some idea of how many votes we would have at an upcoming convention. Sometimes I was given numerical reports that were obviously out of touch with reality. Such were the perils of Moderate politics.

Other times, however, we counted very well. For the 1981 SBC in Los Angeles I predicted we would have 4,500 Moderate votes for Abner McCall, retired president of Baylor University. We voted 4,524, but that was not enough. After some of our group urged Duke McCall to be our presidential candidate at the 1982 SBC in New Orleans, McCall asked me if we could find 6,000 votes for him in New Orleans; we came up with 6,190 on the first ballot. Again, not enough. In 1985 in Dallas, the convention was a madhouse—there were 45,000 messengers registered. To figure how many would be Moderate and vote for Winfred Moore was very hard. But Larry McSwain, faculty member at Southern Seminary, and I came up with at least 16,000 votes we could identify on Friday before the convention. We voted exactly 19,795 for Moore on the following Tuesday.

The way it worked was quite simple. Precinct leadership was at the associational level. These people would report the number to state captains. When all the precinct leaders had their totals in, the state leadership would adjust the numbers (for they had a kind of knowledge that made this adjustment necessary), and then call it to me. Larry McSwain and I would pore over the totals and make further revisions. From this kind of data and from careful study of past conventions held in the host city, we would make our predictions. While this process was in motion, we had absolutely no idea what the "other side" was doing. We worked but one side of the street.

A meeting of importance took place in August 1986. The SBC in Atlanta was finished. The Moderate candidate Winfred Moore was defeated by the Fundamentalist candidate Adrian Rogers. The state leadership of the Moderate Movement was invited to gather at Mercer University, Macon, Georgia.[5] The meeting was larger than most. There were about forty present. And the group was divided over strategy.

One part of the Moderates had had enough politics. They were mostly from the East (Georgia, North Carolina, and Virginia), and they wanted to expend their energies in different directions. Struggling to get a larger number of people to a convention to "save the SBC" was something they were no longer willing to make a top priority. Others, especially from the West, were of a different mind. They thought there was still hope that the SBC could be turned back to a more open, wholesome direction. So after considerable discussion, the group voted. Blessing was given some people from the East to drop out of the active politic and give birth to something else. What came of that vote was the formation of the Southern Baptist Alliance, popularly called the "Alliance." And though birth would not come until February 1987, the decision for a new and different venture was marked out in Macon, Georgia, in August 1986. When Alliance people came to the SBC annual meeting, they uniformly voted with the Moderates, but no longer were some Moderates willing to do politic with the same enthusiasm as before.

Throughout this paper there has been an autobiographic flavor. For those who come after, a mark needs to be drawn. From September 1980 (the Gatlinburg meeting) until June 1985, I chaired the Moderate politic, except for a very brief period when Don Harbuck, pastor of First Baptist Church El Dorado, Arkansas, was the designated leader. At the Dallas convention in 1985, I was placed on the recently appointed SBC Peace Committee. Those who served on the Peace Committee were supposed to drop out of organized politics. So the leadership of the Moderate group passed to Jim Slatton, pastor of the River Road Church in Richmond, Virginia. Slatton had been involved since 1980; he knew the Moderate organization as well as anyone. And he had heart for what we were about. He was trusted, and he did a very good job. In fact, Jim Slatton gathered some political expertise to the Moderate cause, and by 1988 the Moderate movement would make

---

[5][Editor's note: See p. 105 of Allen Neely's paper on "The Alliance of Baptists" for another brief account of this meeting.]

their best political showing with more than forty-eight percent of the vote for Richard Jackson in San Antonio.[6]

When the Alliance came into being, the old Moderate political group came forward with a new name. They came to be known as "Baptists Committed." Leadership for Baptists Committed came mostly from the West, especially Texas. After two years Jim Slatton gave the leadership to Winfred Moore, and finally Winfred gave way to Jimmy Allen, retired president of the SBC Radio and Television Commission. These people did good work. They kept the Moderate forces in the West alert and thinking. At a later time Baylor University was threatened, and the Baptists Committed network came forward to help. They worked effectively. Baylor was saved for Baptists and for freedom and quality education. One important part in the defense of Baylor was Baptists Committed. There were other places where that group came forward to do good.

In fact, all sorts of good things and good special interest groups have come of the Moderate movement. The movement was quite fertile in reproducing itself: Baptists Today, the Forum, the Baptist Alliance, Associated Baptist Press, and on and on—these are some of the children of the larger Moderate movement. They continue, and until this day they hold high Baptist ideas.

We've been criticized for our democratic style of doing politic. And because we always lost, we have often been second-guessed. If we had done this or that, we would have won—so we were told. Later in this paper I will comment on this process as weakness, but this is not the place. In fact, two comments are appropriate.

1. We did politic with Moderates the only way it could be done. Had we been more authoritarian, we would have had no one to lead.

2. I can't say enough good about some of the people who came early to the Moderate politic and stayed late. Henry Crouch, pastor of Providence Baptist Church in Charlotte, caught nothing but grief for his participation in our cause, but he stayed because he thought we were right. Bill Sherman was in a company town—for that is what Nashville is. But he took the criticism and stayed. Lavonn Brown of Norman, Oklahoma, and Gene Garrison of Oklahoma City also come to mind. They worked stony ground and never backed off during the height of the political war. They are my heroes.

---

[6][Editor's note: For an account of the Moderate political movement under Slatton, see James Slatton's article in this volume.]

The truth of the matter is that there are a sizable number of very principled pastors out there—Jim Slatton and Ken Chafin come to mind. They saw Fundamentalism as the very opposite of anything a Baptist ought to touch. Early they declared themselves and risked themselves professionally. And a number of them paid a professional price. Invitations were canceled. Other invitations that would have come never came. Some of these involved promotions and advancement in our profession; other times they suffered the abuse of being ignored by people who once were friends; or they were called liberals. Some people took the titles and the advancement while others were trashed by the convention they sought to save. I don't know any advantage gained by these people I've mentioned for their service to the Moderate movement. They did it because they thought it right. They have yet to be appreciated. Other names have been left out of this comment who are worthy. We lost. But our losing was the noblest act of our professional lives.

3. Issues That Defined Moderates

Again and again it was said, "This is just a political spat between two contending groups." Nothing could be further from the truth. Two groups did politic because they disagreed on basic theology and polity. Where the Fundamentalists are going to take the Southern Baptist Convention is to *their* theology. Where the Moderates would have taken the Southern Baptist Convention is to *their* theology. And the theology of the two groups was, is, and will be quite different. Let me list some of the defining points of theology of the Moderates.

1. *The Bible.* I do not know an irreverent Moderate. A part of their reverence is in the Moderate attitude toward the Bible. The Bible is a witness to Jesus Christ. The Bible is not all of revelation; actually the Bible is a "true sample" of God's *ongoing* revelation. All of the Bible is culturally conditioned. Parts of the Bible are so trapped in time and culture that they have been bypassed in God's continuing stream of self-revelation. So slavery allowed in the Bible is no longer consistent with our understanding of the character of God. Jesus laid aside whole sections of the Old Testament. Those parts of the Bible no longer inform our Christian walk. But always we Moderates are in touch with and are serious students of the Bible.

But such a statement about the Bible was not good enough. Moderates were said to "not believe the Bible" because we would not say we were biblical inerrantists. Early on in the political contest Moderates debated whether or not we should take up the subject of inerrancy, criticize it, and make our case before Southern Baptists. The people best qualified to make the case were teachers. If they made our case against inerrancy, they could lose their jobs. Most pastors were afraid to touch the subject. Their laity might think they did not "believe the Bible." The Bible issue was a "gotcha." If we were silent, we were soft on the Bible. If we spoke or wrote our case, to the half-learned we proved we did not believe the Bible.

How the Bible is handled and interpreted remains a major point of difference between Moderates and Fundamentalists. Modern scholarship cannot be ignored. We cannot read the Bible as if the date were 1650. Too much has happened in Bible studies. We are post-Enlightenment people whether we want to be or not. New science and new history instruct the way we read our Bibles. Newfound manuscripts cannot be ignored. None of this new data steals power from the Bible. But accommodations do have to be made. God's moving revelation has to be factored into the equation. A position on the Bible that is different from the glib "biblical-inerrancy" stuff of Fundamentalism defines us.

And then there is the one who can't leave the magic words. This person just has to say "inerrancy" though the term is qualified in such ways that causes this one to teach the Bible like I do, while keeping the inerrancy label. This is politically safe. But words have meaning. If I qualify and condition the statement "I am faithful to my wife" enough, I come to mean exactly the opposite of what the statement means. I think this is what some of our latter-day Protestant scholastics are doing in their rush to become biblical inerrantists. They still believe about the Bible and study the Bible just as we do, but now they get to say they are "biblical inerrantists." If terms are elastic enough, they come to lose all meaning. I don't believe in biblical inerrancy because the biblical text will not support the assertion. *Inerrancy is not the truth.*

That's the Moderate position. We ought to tell the truth about the Bible. Our religion does not have to be propped up to survive. The Bible is not the centerpiece anyway. The Bible is a witness to Jesus. Not only is Fundamentalism wrong about what the Bible is, Fundamentalism in a rush to defend the Bible has shifted the focus from Jesus to the Bible. This shift is not good.

2. *Education.* Listen carefully to the tapes of early Fundamentalist speeches in this SBC controversy. The heretics were the teachers; they were liberals. They were in our seminaries and colleges. By electing Fundamentalist candidates, this liberalism would be rooted out. That was the Fundamentalist line.

Fundamentalists have been elected, and in no place have they laid a heavier hand than on our schools. Some, such as Southeastern Seminary in Wake Forest, North Carolina, they have redone. And historic Southern Seminary in Louisville is in the process of a Fundamentalist renovation. Other seminaries have been intimidated. They are no longer free to probe and push, to change and shift. In fact, such movements of exploration in education are deplored by Fundamentalists. Two different visions of education are at work. The two will not be reconciled. The Fundamentalist one requires much control; the Moderate one, a considerable degree of freedom. No wonder the Fundamentalists reached for the schools as soon as they were in power. We disagree about education.

3. *Church Growth.* I think the bottom line for Southern Baptist Fundamentalists is growth. It is more important to them than the Bible. I doubt they know it or would admit it if they did. But think about it. No person has been put forward by the Fundamentalist party to be president of the SBC except a pastor of a very, very large church. The size legitimizes him. That they have grown large is proof to them that God is blessing. (Strange they don't apply this same logic to the growth of the Mormons and Jehovah's Witnesses.)

While Fundamentalism is so traditional in some ways, in this particular it is as modern as American capitalism. The bottom line matters. And with Fundamentalism the bottom line is what matters most. Buried in the rhetoric of the Fundamental stump speech is a line that will run something like this: "You don't want Southern Baptists to go the route of all those denominations that have gone liberal, do you? Of course not. Look at the Presbyterians and the Methodists, look at the Disciples and the Episcopalians. They went liberal and now they are losing, shrinking, fading. God has withdrawn his hand from them." That is the Fundamentalist party line.

There is some truth in the comment. And there is much more that is left unsaid. Actually, the difference in Moderates and Fundamentalists is profound at the point of evangelism and church growth. It is theological. If getting bigger becomes the end-all, the operating principle in doing church, then entertainment will be allowed. Entertainment will pack them in. Worship will become show business.

A leader in the Fundamentalist movement hired two men to produce two professions of faith a Sunday at their church. That would be a guaranteed growth in baptisms of four per Sunday. I asked this pastor if he did not fear what this practice would do to the doctrine of evangelism, and the pastor said this was not a concern. And so it should not be a surprise that evangelism has become the most mangled doctrine of all in this contest. To get bigger is the goal, and it seems whatever will get there is fair game.

Moderates have been criticized for not being able to produce growing churches. Some Moderates have been careless at this point. But not all. A number of Moderate pastors have served the Church well and enlarged the Church of Christ. And all the while they have gone no further than anyone ought to go. People are not saved by our methods or witness. They are saved by the Spirit of God. To go too far in "managing" people to grace is to put ourselves in God's place. And that is our "original sin."

4. *Role of the Pastor*. Fortunately the Fundamentalists have been open about their theology. It is put into resolutions for all to see. In 1988 in San Antonio a resolution was put to the SBC and adopted. It stated that the role of the pastor was to be "the ruler of the church." Moderates, as most Baptists around the world, disagree.

We believe the pastor is to be interpreter of the Bible and the servant of the congregation. And further, we believe this idea we have about the role of the pastor to be in keeping with the radical reinterpretation Baptists made in the seventeenth century.

One of the ways to "do church" modeled in the New Testament is the model used by Catholics and Episcopalians. The pastors/bishops are the leaders and rulers of the church. Paul and the apostles functioned this way. It is in the Bible; it is one legitimate model for the way to do church.

But early Baptists suffered much of this system. And in an age when democratic ideas were surfacing in the political arena, there arose alongside a democratic politic a democratic way of doing church. Common people were empowered. They were trusted with the vote and the interpretation of the Bible. Theology would no longer be done in the councils of bishops; now theology would be done in the congregation. Lay people would think, pray, study, and under the guidance of the Spirit, lay people would do theology. They would decide what the Bible means, who can be a member of the congregation, and who will be pastor of the church.

And who is the pastor in this new arrangement? The pastor is an interpreter with more biblical educational opportunity than most of the laity. With that opportunity, it was understood that the Spirit spoke through the voice of the congregation in session. The pastor helped form the mind of the people; the people decided the mind of the Spirit. Moderates still accept this radical reinterpretation of the New Testament. That is one reason we are called Baptists.

5. *Role of Women.* In Kansas City in 1984, a Fundamentalist resolution was put forward at the Southern Baptist Convention defining the role of women. In theory it was the opinion of the body at that particular time and was not binding on the churches or the agencies and institutions. In fact, it was the new orthodoxy of Fundamentalism on women. Women were "first in the Edenic fall." Therefore, women would have a proscribed, limited place in the life of the congregation/denomination. It passed. And since then there is a body of evidence that the denomination is abiding by the wishes of the national body.

Not all Moderates agree on the role of women in the Church. Some Moderate churches have women pastors (there are only a few.) More Moderate churches have women deacons. But all Moderate churches agree that this issue ought to be left to the local congregation and is not the province of the denomination.

God gets to be God. If God chooses to call a woman and the life of the woman called seems to bear witness to this call, who are we to deny that God has called her? W. A. Criswell, pastor of the First Baptist Church of Dallas, does not agree. David Frost put to Criswell this question: "What if a woman believes she has been called to be a minister?" Criswell replied, "Well, she has made a mistake."

In stolid, woodenheaded fashion, the Fundamentalist goes to the Bible and comes forward with texts to back a rigid position. Ephesians 5:21-33 and Colossians 3:18 and 1 Peter 3:1-7 are offered as support for the Fundamentalist position. But few of the same people are prepared to defend slavery by using the same texts. They are ready to interpret one paragraph one way and the next paragraph another. Some hermeneutic!

Rather than the literalism that trapped Pharisees and monks, scholastics and Fundamentalists, let us let the text roam free. Perhaps Galatians 3:28 should be taken literally. God is calling wonderful people to do amazing things; some of them are women. Let us give thanks.

6. *Role of the Denomination.* In very few interpretations of the debate in Southern Baptist life has this one been cited. I think this is an oversight. The Fundamentalist has a reason for reaching for the machinery that is the Southern Baptist Convention. Schools shape opinion. Sunday School literature shapes opinion. Who speaks on the Evangelism Conference program shapes opinion. Both the words spoken and the person modeled shape minds. If you put an idea forward often enough by example, speech, and written word, that idea becomes normative for the body. That is what

Fundamentalists are doing with the Southern Baptist Convention. They are using the national body to remake the churches.

This is a novelty for Baptists. Always Baptists have said the national body was a servant to the churches and implementor of the wishes of the churches. So in the beginning of Southern Baptist life the operative sentence in the constitution was "to elicit, combine, and direct." Missions pulled us together. The denomination would "elicit, combine, and direct" the energies of the churches to the task of missions.

No one has said the role of the denomination has been changed. No one is prepared to argue that the denomination has come to be the thinker, interpreter, and model for what is good and correct for the churches. But when the Home Mission Board favors one person and rejects another, what has this said to the churches? When one kind of missionary is appointed and another is rejected, what does this say to the churches? When one kind of teacher is advanced and another kind is put down, what does this say to the churches?

The Fundamentalist would plead majoritarianism: "The largest part of Southern Baptists have voted for this idea; we are just carrying out their wishes." That there might be a plurality of ideas creating the wealth of the SBC and that those several ideas have a right to find expression in the appointments and programs of the SBC—this kind of thinking has escaped the Fundamentalists. The denomination is a tool to reconstruct the collective mind of Southern Baptists. And that is why they wanted to gain power. The denomination is a means to an end. It spreads their ideas, normalizes their ideas, and it does so exclusively. This is foreign to the purpose of a Baptist mission-delivery system—for that is all a denomination ought ever to be to Baptists.

7. *Church and State.* From Baptist beginnings in seventeenth-century England there has been in place a church and state attitude. We emerged in a climate where the orthodoxy pressed down upon our ancestors was enforced by the arm of the state. So, in order to save themselves pain and to gain freedom, our Baptist forebears came forward with the separation doctrine. In matters of conscience, the state has no place. In matters pertaining to the first table of the Law (the first part of the Ten Commandments), the state was out of bounds. This was the message of Roger Williams, John Leland, and Isaac Backus.

In these days some Fundamentalists who wear the name Baptist are snuggling up to the state. They have given up on Baptist ideas. They say our society will go to wrack and ruin unless we create laws that will compel goodness and punish badness. That this is outside the Baptist pattern is lost on the Fundamentalists. So, leaders of the Southern Baptist Convention are now regularly seen with leaders of the Republican party. W. A. Criswell spoke clearly their doctrine when he suggested that the separation of church and state is the product of the imagination of an infidel.

That Morris Chapman, present Fundamentalist head of the SBC Executive Committee, should be in the company of the vice president of the United States, should invite the Republican vice president to address the SBC in session in Indianapolis (1992), should be a part of rallies to reelect George Bush and Dan Quayle—these things are not bad, they are good, according to Fundamentalists.

Further, in a systematic way that extended over a number of years, an effort was made to disassociate the SBC from the Baptist Joint Committee on Public Affairs. For more than fifty years this honored committee had represented a number of Baptist bodies in Washington particularly in the area of church-state separation. No longer. The funding from the SBC to the Baptist Joint Committee was stopped. The money previously given to the BJC is today invested in the now-Fundamentalist Christian Life Commission of the SBC. The CLC under Richard Land's stewardship is committed to right-wing causes and a further breakdown of the wall of separation between church and state.

Over the years the Moderates have carried the torch for the Baptist Joint Committee. It is not a matter of agreeing on each issue. It is the principle of church and state. And there the Moderates are rock solid. We are for the first Baptist position of church and state. It defines us. And today the Cooperative Baptist Fellowship has replaced the SBC as the leading supporter of the Baptist Joint Committee.

The above list does not constitute all that defines Moderates, but it is a good start. Further illustrations of what separates us from Fundamentalism are, for example, their single-issue politics on abortion and their negative attitude toward ecumenism and the rest of the larger Church of Jesus Christ. In profound and substantive ways, we are different.

After all the above illustrations have been given, some old and tried Baptist language has not appeared. I've not mentioned soul competency and the priesthood of the believers. These ideas have already been spoken. They have just been put in their twentieth-century setting and language. The issue of the priesthood of the believers is being fought out over the role of the pastor in the local congregation. Lose the role-of-the-pastor fight and you have lost the priesthood-of-the-believers issue. Lose the battle over the role of the denomination in our common affairs and you will lose the fight on local church autonomy.

Defining the Moderates' mind in contrast to the Fundamentalists' mind is not easy. The Fundamentalist has a pre-Enlightenment view of the world; the Moderate has a post-Enlightenment view. The Fundamentalist is working from the Old Testament much more than the Moderate. But that can be turned around. The Moderate is trying to find the sense of the New Testament much more than the Fundamentalist. The radical teachings of Jesus are lost on the Fundamentalist.

No amount of my best thought can really communicate the mind of the Fundamentalist. I believed I was conversant with all the parts of Southern Baptist life and thought when I went on the Peace Committee in 1985. I was in for a surprise. The Fundamentalists on the Peace Committee were led by Adrian Rogers, pastor of Bellevue Baptist Church in Memphis. Others spoke often and well, but he was the unquestioned leader. Watching his mind work was a revelation to me. He has a good mind, but there is a bent to that mind that is beyond my comprehension.

Adrian Rogers told us that as often as he could he took the Bible literally. He illustrated by saying he believed the world was created in six twenty-four-hour days. And he repeated this to make an impression upon us. In private (Jerry Vines was present with us), I asked Rogers what he did with the slavery passages of the New Testament. Did he take them literally? He paused, then said, "Well, I believe slavery is a much-maligned institution. If we had slavery today, we would not have this welfare mess." Moderates are *different* from Fundamentalists.

Beneath all the particulars of the way Moderates are different from Fundamentalists lies a different vision of God. Their vision is different from ours, and the vision of God orders all.

A caveat is required. Not all Moderates have thought about these things. Not all Moderates are comfortable with the broad outline I've given about Moderate thought. There are numbers of people who are between us and the Fundamentalists. They have not sorted it out. Other Moderates have thought their way through. The leadership of Fundamentalism has thought about these things. They know we are different. And while they might not agree with some of the ways I've described them, they would agree to the full that we are different in ways that cannot be papered over. So though a Sadducee bureaucracy may try to hold us together, they will fail. It is hard to paper over the Grand Canyon.

4. Why Moderates Failed

All who study us will try to sort out why Moderates failed. My opinion on the subject is no better than any other, but I've given this some thought. Here are my reasons for our failure:

1. *Ambivalence about doing politic.* From the beginning there were Moderates who had a question about the morality of doing politic. For them it did not seem right. This moral hesitation limited us.

The Fundamentalists were of another mind. Early on they saw doing politic as a way to attain what they believed to be godly goals. They could "save the Bible" if they could get more people to the Tuesday afternoon session of the annual meeting of the SBC when the president was elected. And some cheating did occur. I saw a couple voting their children; the children were quite young, maybe five or six years old. But evidently the couple reasoned that the small problem of children voting who are too young to understand the issues seemed small compared to the good that could be done were the right people elected.

So, Fundamentalists went to the annual meeting, packed the section right in front of the platform, took orders willingly, and voted on cue. They were acting out what they often sang. "Onward Christian Soldiers" described them. They were, so they thought, doing God a service when they got in step and defeated the people who did not believe the Bible the way they did.

The attitude of the Moderates toward hardnosed politic was altogether different. A few relished the work; most despised it. It was sub-Christian. We were supposed to love our brothers and sisters, not beat up on them. The entire exercise was repugnant. Not a few Moderates came to hold that our system was open to question. When did God work through a majority bused to the meeting? Did not God work through prophets and apostles who were uniformly outnumbered? And so these Moderates pondered what we were about. Other Moderates came and held their noses. Some could hardly abide the meeting. It was nauseous and offensive. After an annual meeting of the SBC, some Moderates had to recover from the meeting. With attitudes as I've described, it should be apparent that Moderates did not look forward to the political exercise.

2. *Changing Leadership, Inexperienced Leadership.* Since I was one of the Moderate leaders in politic, I was in a place to know our leadership was amateur. We had little experience in politics, though I am not convinced we would have prevailed had we had seasoned professionals. Moderates did not follow well; we did not lead well.

More important than our amateur politic was our changing leadership. I led for a time. Jim Slatton led for a time. Don Harbuck led for a few months. We were not really in control of our own people. When Foy Valentine did not approve of our group decision to oppose Jimmy Draper in Pittsburgh in 1984, he pushed us aside and put his own program in place. When that failed, the seminary presidents tried their hand for a little. Early on they learned that it was a game where one could get hurt. Then they were out. Losing makes a restlessness that would not have been present had we won even occasionally. But we didn't.

Fundamentalists were not burdened with changing leadership. The same leadership has been in place with Southern Baptist Fundamentalists since before 1979. It is a small cadre of pastors. They command; their people obey. If they obey, they are rewarded, for the spoils of winning have been available to them for a long time. This has not been lost on some people who started in the middle of this mess. I suspect the leadership of the Fundamentalist politic could comfortably ride in a minivan. A few designed their strategy and still do. We have had several leaders.

3. *Moderates might be liberal.* When compared to Fundamentalists, Moderates are to the left. This was a given in the contest. We had to live with it.

As obvious as the statement about right and left, conservative and liberal, Southern Baptists are not comfortable with anything that is left. It is suspect. But by definition, Moderates were left of Paul Pressler and Adrian Rogers. It was the honorable place to stand in this face-off. But honorable or no, the place where we fought was the South. The time we fought was during the Reagan/Bush era. Political ads in Dallas/Fort Worth freely described anything bad as "liberal." That the word might or could have a positive meaning has not occurred to most of the electorate. So, the ads run. Liberal is of the devil, and if anyone or any cause can be stuck with the liberal label, then those people and that cause are in big trouble.

Were Southern Baptist Moderates liberal? It depends upon what you are comparing to them. When compared to Adrian Rogers, I am more liberal theologically than he. By any reasonable standard of theological measurement, however, I am a fairly conservative Christian.

The pity of all this was that it was argued out before an unsophisticated people. If you believed in inerrancy, you believed the Bible. If you did not believe in inerrancy, you did not believe the Bible. It was as simple as that. That a person might not believe in inerrancy and still be a quite conservative Christian—well that was impossible. The inerrancy rallying cry defined all.

If you would say inerrancy, you were okay. If you could not, you were suspect. The Moderate cause came to push forward people, especially SBC presidential candidates, who said they were inerrantists. This was done to blunt the charge of liberalism. It did not succeed. Most of us who led Moderates would not use the word. I don't use it because it does not describe anything we have in the Bible.

At this point I think the Baptist system failed us. We are the Christians who have great faith in common people. We trust them to sort out complicated theology, do complex interpretation. It will work if the pastor/teacher will do his/her job. But too many had not. And by the time this contest was joined, all the preachers were in a bind. If they said they did not believe in inerrancy, they might arouse the Conservative/Fundamental members of their congregation. "It just could be the preacher does not believe the Bible!" And so the preachers did not do their job. And the Baptist lay people were left to work through a complicated set of issues. All the help the laity received was slogans from Fundamentalist preachers and a press that only occasionally tried to help them. Much misinformation was allowed to stand. And many good people were tarred with the taint of liberalism. Good reputations were damaged and careers cut short or redirected. The taint of liberalism was a powerful political tool used by the Fundamentalists against Moderates.

Our scholars knew Moderates were not liberal. And personal friends knew Moderates were not liberal. But the Southern Baptist family is big. Most people "got the word" at the Evangelism Conferences or at the Pastors' Conference. There the lie was told: "Moderates don't believe the Bible. They believe the Bible has errors." Undecided people were swayed, for no Southern Baptist wants to put "liberals" in a responsible place in the SBC. And so the people voted for the safe candidate, the one who *really* believed the Bible.

4. *The people we set out to save would not own us.* The Moderate Movement was out to protect and defend presidents and heads of SBC institutions: Russell Dilday (Southwestern Seminary), Randall Lolley (Southeastern Seminary), Roy Honeycutt (Southern Seminary), Keith Parks (Foreign Mission Board), Grady Cothen and later Lloyd Elder (Baptist Sunday School Board), Foy Valentine (Christian Life Commission), Jimmy Allen (Radio and Television Commission), and W. C. Fields, Dan Martin, and Al Shackleford (Baptist Press). We believed in them. We were the people who had led mainline Baptist churches to send a sizable part of their treasure to fund them.

When militant Fundamentalists described the SBC as "drifting into liberalism," the Fundamentalists were talking about people Moderates knew well. They were our friends. We did not believe the charge. We thought our friends were being unfairly treated, and we rose up to defend our friends. Everywhere Paul Pressler spoke, he raised a question about the theological soundness of Southern and Southeastern Seminaries. The intent of the Fundamentalist movement was to replace good people, which they now have done. Moderates disagreed with the first premise of the Fundamentalists and we set out to help our friends by creating a politic that might save them.

We organized to save the agency heads, but some of those agency heads were hesitant about owning us. In fact, agency heads had varying opinions about Moderates.

a. *Uncertainty.* I suppose we looked as troublesome to Porter Routh, the head of the SBC Executive Committee, as the Fundamentalists did. In 1981 in Los Angeles, Routh told me, "Stop what you are doing, Cecil. We can handle these people. The pendulum will swing back." When I told him he was wrong about Paul Pressler, Paige Patterson, and Adrian Rogers, he said I was a novice; I should trust him.

Russell Dilday, president of Southwestern Seminary in Ft. Worth, said the same. I was speaking for Music Workshop at Southwestern Seminary in February 1982. Dilday said, "We can handle these people." In a decent way, I told him I thought he was underestimating Fundamentalist leadership.

The first response of the agency heads was mixed. While Routh and Dilday were urging Moderates to stand down, Valentine (Christian Life Commission) and Allen (Radio and Television Commission), Morgan (Annuity Board), and McCall (Southern Seminary) were quietly urging us forward. There was no certain message from agency heads in the beginning.

b. *In Concert.* The Kansas City convention in 1984 cleared the minds of some people. After that meeting seminary presidents and some people in Texas who to that point had been passive, grabbed leadership. They did not consult with the Moderate leadership. They chose Winfred Moore to be a candidate. And after all was settled, Roy Honeycutt, now having succeeded Duke McCall as president at Southern, came to me and asked if the Moderate network in the Southeast would come back on line and help elect Moore.

And that was the year. In 1985 we came as near as ever we came to getting all the parts in place. We had the West organizing. The East was still in the fight. The agency heads were publicly, effectively speaking for us. The Moderate parts were working together. But we fell short. After 1985 and the convention in Dallas the agency heads scattered. Some still supported us. Some, however, began trying to find a safe port in the Fundamentalist storm.

c. _Rejection._ The Peace Committee, which worked from 1985 to 1987 and was weighted toward Fundamentalists, in my judgment frightened agency heads. In the development of the Peace Committee, each agency was visited by members of the Peace Committee and asked to give an account of any questions that had been raised about their orthodoxy. I, along with others, called on Southern and New Orleans Seminaries. If agency heads did not give the right answers to the visiting members of the Peace Committee, then that school could be found to be working outside the bounds of our confessional statement ("The Baptist Faith and Message" statement). So, agency heads were keen to please the Peace Committee. If they did not, the Peace Committee might find them liberal. The report would be given to a convention that had been controlled by Fundamentalists for several years. So the agency heads had to get the Peace Committee off their backs. This is the background of the Glorieta Statement which the six seminary presidents gave to the Peace Committee in October 1986.

The Glorieta Statement was shameful.[7] It was not the truth, and the people who wrote the statement knew it. The presidents said what they thought they had to say to "save" their schools, but in so doing, they gutted serious theological education among Southern Baptists for at least a generation. Well-placed people will deny my assessment of the effects of the Glorieta Statement, but the exodus of good teachers from our seminaries, the rape of Southeastern Seminary, the exodus of top-notch faculty members, such as Glenn Hinson, Alan Culpepper, Andrew Lester, John Jonsson, Page Kelley, and Paul Simmons, from Southern Seminary and the resulting transformation of that historic school, and the climate of fear and intimidation that now exists at places that once were free makes my point.

Regularly I returned from Peace Committee meetings and called Russell Dilday to report on the happenings, particularly as those happenings impacted the seminaries. Russell seemed to appreciate my concern for the schools. I had been put on the Peace Committee at the suggestion of Roy Honeycutt. Roy said, "Put Cecil Sherman on the committee; he won't give away the key to the store." I knew the schools needed friends. I heard the charges made by Ed Young and Jerry Vines and Adrian Rogers about the liberalism taught in our schools. Those charges are on the tapes of the Peace

---

[7][Editor's note: See appendix 1 for a copy of "The Glorieta Statement."]

Committee and will be public property beginning in 1995. I was on the Peace Committee to represent a constituency. I took that responsibility seriously.

Imagine my surprise when Milton Ferguson, president of Midwestern Seminary, stood at Glorieta to read the Glorieta Statement on behalf of the other seminary presidents. I did not know it was coming. I didn't have a clue. For me it was a betrayal. And it was gutting the Moderate movement. If the seminary presidents could live with Fundamentalism, then the Moderates had no reason for being. Much more than the mission boards and the seminaries were under attack. Now the people under attack were coming to terms with their attackers. And they were abandoning their Moderate friends.

I resisted the Glorieta Statement. I had no support. At a break in the proceedings, I was saying my mind to Russell Dilday, Southwestern Seminary president. He had no sympathy for what I was saying and dismissed me with this comment, "Cecil, you are more trouble to us than they are" as he nodded toward a cluster of people that included Adrian Rogers, Ed Young, and Jerry Vines, Fundamentalist leaders.

I did not sleep that night. I thought I was helping the schools. They did not want me and had come to count our efforts as trouble. The next day I resigned from the Peace Committee. There was no point in further struggle. The people we were trying to save no longer wanted our help. They had turned to make some accommodation with the people who had accused them of liberalism in the first place.

I've had more trouble with the seminary presidents than I've had with the Fundamentalists. Some very good people went out on a limb to help embattled agency heads, especially some seminary presidents. The presidents were hesitant to embrace us. Then they used us. And then they threw us away. The vacillation of key agency heads did us much harm and had much to do with Moderate failure.

This point needs a postscript. Some agency heads were absolutely heroic. Duke McCall came early and stayed late in resisting the Fundamentalists. He and Grady Cothen would both offer themselves as sacrifices as Moderate presidential candidates. What Randall Lolley did at a later time in resisting Fundamentalism at Southeastern Seminary was a "profile in courage." What W. C. Fields of Baptist Press did for a free press was raw courage. And what Keith Parks has done in 1992 to resist the onslaught of Fundamentalism at the Foreign Mission Board stands tall. He is a principled man. These and others were a grace note for me.

I doubt I will ever forget the kindness of Foy Valentine in 1981. I had tried so hard to come up with a respectable showing for Abner McCall against Bailey Smith. We had done better than any expected, but we lost. Foy and Mary Louise Valentine asked Dot and me to dinner after that election. I was down and very tired. Foy said we had done well. He pastored me and encouraged. I will remember. It was great to be appreciated by the people we were trying to help.

And Darold Morgan (the Annuity Board) and Jimmy Allen (Radio and Television Commission), James Dunn (Baptist Joint Committee) and Carolyn Weatherford (Woman's Missionary Union)—these people were gracious and helpful and steadying. I remember these friends fondly.

But it is galling until this day. The seminaries that taught us that Fundamentalism was a misrepresentation of the gospel of Jesus Christ found a way in the end to make accommodation with Fundamentalists and with Fundamentalism. Moderates never expected favors from Fundamentalists. We did expect steady support and appreciation from the people we set out to save. We did not get it.[8]

5. *Too many influential preachers were silent.* The people we set out to save were within the SBC system. The people who were free to do the political work were preachers. If we were well received in our churches, we were free. I was well established in my church in Asheville, North Carolina. The people in my church trusted me. My years of service earned for me the freedom to do Moderate politic.

I was not alone. Jim Slatton had been at River Road in Richmond for a long time. Bill Sherman, my brother, had been at Woodmont in Nashville for years. Lavonn Brown had long tenure in Norman, Oklahoma. And the same could be said of Bill Bruster of Knoxville and Ken Chafin of Houston. These pastors were the backbone of the Moderate politic. They went to friends. They could get honest answers and give accurate estimates of the votes we were likely to receive in their territories. Already I've written of my admiration for these people. I've not named all, but these and unnamed people just like them did the work, took the heat, and kept on.

But for every one who stepped forward to work, there were two who stood down. They took a pass on this fight. They would not identify with

---

[8][Editor's note: Sherman's point here only echoes Ralph Elliott's chagrin concerning an earlier controversy. See Ralph H. Elliott, *The "Genesis Controversy" and Continuity in Southern Baptist Chaos: A Eulogy for a Great Tradition* (Macon: Mercer University Press, 1992).]

us. I've no doubt these quiet friends voted with us, but they would not go public with their support. The refusal of these people to work with us was very hurtful to our cause.

Even naming these people would not damn them. They know who they are. Doing Moderate politic was risky. One could lose some significant invitations for speaking and leadership, perhaps some churches might not call if one were involved. So, they took the high road. They sat out the public part of the fight.

I think our cause was right and moral. To take a pass on a moral fight does not become a prophetic preacher. As I write these words, I know that the people who sat out the fight are good. They are of the opinion that our politic was a dirty exercise, and they are right. But Moderates were trapped. If we fought to save the SBC, we were bad for fighting. If we did not fight, we let the SBC pass into the hands of Fundamentalists without raising our hands. To resist was right. It was the best option we had.

That brings me to the conclusion of why we lost. This point about the people who excused themselves from the Moderate politic makes my point. Moderates did not have enough moral energy to win. We could not bring ourselves to use moral language to describe our cause. Truth was butchered. We said nothing. Good people were defamed. We were silent. Baptist principles were mangled and Baptist history was replaced, rewritten. All the while, teachers who could have written about the problems in calling the Bible inerrant, did not. And preachers who could have called us to arms said nothing. The want of moral energy was the undoing of the Moderate movement.

5. What Does the Future Hold for Moderates?

Moderates will not go into the future as one, completely together. We have scattered. So to speculate about the future for Moderates requires that I write of several groups of people.

1. *Some Moderates have already left Baptists.* The bickering and the ugliness have left their mark. Some will have no more of it. They are gone. Most of these people are not out of the faith; they still practice their profession. But no longer will they be Baptists. This is a loss. Some of these people are among our brightest.

Particularly is this true of women. The heavy-handed doctrine of Fundamentalism about women gives them small place to exercise their gifts or their calling. They have chosen to leave us and go where they can be all God has called them to be.

2. *Some Moderates will continue in the SBC.* I suspect this will be a sizeable group. These will not be happy. They will privately groan under the weight of triumphal Fundamentalism. Many of these people will not even attend the annual convention; it will be too painful. They have memories of a happier past, and they find solace in those memories.

What Stan Hastey has called "mother church" will be overpowering for these people. They were reared Southern Baptists. It has been the defining family; the SBC in all her entangling parts constitutes home. And these people will not be able to leave home.

These are not bad people. Though they know our history has been reinterpreted and though they know good people have been harried from the house, these still will stay in the house. The Annuity Board and security, the web of friendships formed in college and seminary, the prospects for advancement in the SBC, the expectations of friends who would never understand if they left—these and other reasons will hold them. Some Southern Baptist Moderates will stay in the SBC.

3. *A few Moderates will join the American Baptist Churches.* Around the edges of the SBC are individuals and churches who will find their way into the ABC. The ABC is very Baptist. And they give great freedom to both congregations and individuals. This will appeal and some will go this route. Should the Cooperative Baptist Fellowship flounder, the ABC option will loom larger still and will be the preferred route for more Moderates.

4. *Most Moderates are watching the Cooperative Baptist Fellowship.* At this point, the reader should beware. I am the coordinator of the CBF and hardly unbiased in my estimate of it.

After the 1990 meeting of the SBC, Daniel Vestal, the defeated Moderate candidate, called Moderates to Atlanta. Surprisingly, with almost no notice, 3,100 people came. Out of that meeting and out of the Moderate movement, came "The Fellowship." Now the name is the Cooperative Baptist Fellowship (CBF). In the CBF is the heart of the old Moderate movement. And if CBF performs well, many, many Moderates will come out of the SBC and "do church" with the CBF. It is too early to tell what CBF will become. In all probability, CBF will become a convention of free Baptists. I am hopeful for CBF. I think that fragile infant carries Baptist ideas. Of course CBF is not alone in bearing the standard for Baptist ideas.

But out of the old SBC and out of the Moderate movement, it is CBF that now is our best hope.[9]

Conclusion

There is more to the story than I've told. And it is quite possible important events have been left out of this chronicle. But this paper is an overview. I've purposely tried to avoid minutia. Others will tell detailed stories of particular parts of the Moderate effort, for we did spin off several significant and continuing organizations.

Are there regrets? Not at all. There has been pain. When it finally hit me that we had lost it, that the SBC was beyond anything I could retrieve, I wept. I am a child of the SBC. But I did what I could. And several hundred other good people could rise to say the same. We did not win. But we were right. And we did all we could at the time when it could have made a difference. It was an honorable exercise. We made the right choice. As I said, it is one of the few noble things I've done in my life. No regrets. Though Fundamentalists now control and guide the old SBC, Baptist ideas, largely forgotten there, are alive and well among Moderate Baptists.

---

[9]Since this paper was delivered on 8 Oct 1992, a number of very encouraging developments have occurred for the CBF. First, Keith Parks, embattled and recently retired president of the SBC Foreign Mission Board, has joined the CBF to lead its missionary efforts. Second, former President of the United States Jimmy Carter has come out in support of the CBF. Third, the Woman's Missionary Union of the SBC has announced that it will broaden its missionary support system to include efforts of the CBF. The story continues.

The History
of the Political Network
of the Moderate Movement

James H. Slatton

Beginnings

Could you come to Gatlinburg, Tennessee, Thursday, September 25, and Friday, September 26, and we could talk about important things in the life of our convention?

With these cryptic words of invitation in 1980 sent to a score of friends, Cecil Sherman initiated what was to become the Moderate "political network" in the Southern Baptist Convention. The situation in the fall of 1980 was ripe for reaction to the Fundamentalist movement that had emerged to dominate the last two national SBC meetings. Anyone might have begun the reaction. No other person or group did.

Cecil Sherman was pastor of the First Baptist Church of Asheville and president of the North Carolina Baptist Convention. He had served Southern Baptist churches in Texas, Georgia, and North Carolina, and had worked on the evangelism staff of the Baptist General Convention of Texas. A little circle of Th.D.s from Southwestern Seminary, former students of T. B. Maston, people involved in Christian social ethics, and Sherman's professional friends made up his own informal network upon which he called in this endeavor.[1]

---

[1]For a list of those present, see Sherman's "An Overview of the Moderate Movement," above, 20-21.

Out of the meeting came a common resolve to try to derail the Fundamentalist takeover. Our role was envisioned originally as a low profile one. The obvious means was to cultivate a network of support for a SBC presidential candidate who would appeal to the widest possible constituency in the convention and work hard behind the scenes to elect that person. A goal of 6,600 Moderate messengers from seventeen states was set for the Los Angeles convention in 1981. A goal was set to get regional and state groups started by Thanksgiving.

The people who came together in response to Sherman's invitation formed the nucleus of a national steering committee. The steering committee in turn reached out to friends and acquaintances across the denomination and built what was to become the national Moderate network. By the end of 1980 organizational meetings had taken place in a number of the states and additional state leaders had joined the "Gatlinburg Gang" as the Fundamentalists dubbed us. Pat Harrison began work in Alabama, Henry Finch took leadership in South Carolina. Bill Bruster of Knoxville joined Bill Sherman and Earl Davis in working with Tennessee people. In Arkansas there was Don Harbuck, John McClannahan, and Nathan Porter. These are only illustrative of the network.

Some basic facts are important to understanding the network that developed. The network lived by telephone calls, letters, and occasional meetings in airports, hotels, churches, and church camp grounds. It was to some degree a come-and-go affair. There were new faces and missing faces at every meeting. Typically, in an airport club room, members of the group would arrive early and late, and depart while heated discussion was still in progress. Though everchanging in personnel, the group that began at Gatlinburg continued to function as an organization until Baptists Committed closed their national office in May 1992 and their national executive committee ceased to function. All the major decisions about candidates, plans, and strategy were made or ratified in this national committee.

We on the national steering committee were self-appointed volunteers. As state networks were developed and as the local and state organizers met, a vote was usually taken on the person to serve on the national committee. More often than not the conference would confirm those who were already serving. Most who came to the Gatlinburg meeting paid their own expenses as we would in attending so many meetings in the years to come. There were no funds to draw upon as the 1981–1982 campaign began, and there would be no systematic effort to raise funds. There would be no paid staff. All of the first group were pastors or spouses of pastors who had full-time jobs with strong churches. Networking was done on a part-time basis and at personal expense, except where local churches afforded funds or office support.

The network was predominantly a network of ministers, and not only because it was begun by such. The importance of lay involvement was evident from the first. However, ministers simply provided the best and most easily accessible group for creating a political network among churches. This was because the clergy already had the most extensive web of connections across the denomination. Attendance at numberless conferences, state and national conventions, and associational meetings accounted for this. School friendships contributed. The clergy were the most visible members of the congregations and the best source of contact with a church's messengers.

The Moderate Political Network was often critiqued by other Moderates from a couple of perspectives. One was the lack of laypeople involved. To fault the network as too much centered in the clergy leadership is to utterly misunderstand the situation. Those of us involved in the movement sought earnestly for support from every quarter and tried with more or less success to engage everyone we could think of in the effort. The network effort has been criticized, secondly, as too loose-knit, too open to those who came and went, too poorly disciplined. It seems to me one cannot have it both ways.[2]

A network approach was important as a means of increasing the number of messengers and as a counter to the Fundamentalist effort, which already had such an organization. The person-to-person approach was essential also as a means of coping with the difficulty of waging a public campaign. It must be remembered that in 1980 and 1981 the mood in the convention was still one of denial. News stories spoke not only of a controversy but gave evidence of organized campaigning. The sky box at the Houston convention[3] and Pressler's "go for the jugular" comment at Lynchburg had been

---

[2][Editor's note: Cecil Sherman speaks to this same issue in his paper, above.]

[3][Editor's note: At the 1979 Houston SBC meeting Paul Pressler had reserved a booth above the meeting hall where he, Patterson and other Fundamentalists could "oversee" the actions. At one point in the proceedings Wayne Dehoney, former SBC president, rose to speak, calling in question Pressler's false credentials as a messenger to the convention. Pressler had come as a "messenger" to the convention from a church where he was not a member, a clear violation of the SBC constitution. In the process of his remarks, Dehoney waved toward the "sky box" where sat Pressler and his cohorts. It was a dramatic moment at the Houston Convention.]

reported. The grapevine had been humming with stories of Fundamentalist messengers bussed in, complimentary hotel rooms, floor-management tactics, and printed instructions on how to vote at St. Louis.

At the same time many were reluctant to credit the stories of hardball politics. Many of those who did still refused to put a sinister construction on the situation. What could be so bad about a spontaneous wave of conservative sentiment in a denomination everyone knew to be archconservative? Fundamentalist operatives added to the obfuscation. They had "prayer meetings," not political rallies, and they were "led of the spirit" to nominate "godly" men for office. Denominational officials, state and national, refused to stir. They remained convinced that overt and active resistance would only anger Fundamentalists and harden their resolve. They feared further division and polarization would follow such an effort. In imagery that would remain compelling to so many for years to come, it was argued that the pendulum would eventually swing back from right toward center.

Los Angeles and 1981

The problem for Moderates at this point was to rally opposition without sounding shrill and meanspirited and without presenting the image of a political machine ourselves. (We still assumed at that time that if the Fundamentalist political plot could be sufficiently documented and publicized the convention would react by voting them down.) In this environment the one-to-one approach of the network was the method of choice.

The really remarkable thing about the Moderate movement was not that it failed throughout ten years to defeat the Fundamentalist presidential candidates, but that so many people were mobilized by so few with so limited resources. In the words of the late Donald Harbuck at the Los Angeles SBC, "I've never lost in such great numbers before."

In the spring of 1981, SBC president Bailey Smith, entitled by tradition to a second term, was conducting himself in a conciliatory fashion, something Moderates came to expect from first-term Fundamentalist presidents. At the SBC Executive Committee that spring, people were so relieved by his smoke screen that they acted as if a threatening war had been called off,[4] and agency chiefs friendly to us were advising us that Smith would be invincible in Los Angeles.[5] In private conversation Presnall Wood, editor of

---

[4]Cecil Sherman, unpublished letter to moderate network, 4 March 1981.
[5]Telephone conversation between Jim Slatton and Jimmy Allen, March 1981,

the *Texas Baptist Standard*, thought we should not oppose Smith. He claimed Smith was so completely on the record with a promise to make inclusive appointments that he would have to do so. "If he doesn't," said Wood, "the Convention will rise up in righteous indignation and vote the Fundamentalists down."[6] Baptist Press reported us as "watching and waiting on key appointments before deciding whether to oppose a second term for . . . Bailey Smith."[7]

In April, the Moderate Network leadership met at the First Baptist Church of Memphis, hosted by pastor Earl Davis. In early May, President Abner McCall of Baylor was announced as the Moderate candidate for SBC president. McCall's candidacy engaged the Baylor network, with staff and alumni working with us. One of my assignments was to call Joel Gregory and ask him to nominate a candidate in Los Angeles. I don't remember the proposed candidate, but I do remember Gregory seemed very nervous and troubled that I should ask him. He refused.

In Los Angeles, Abner McCall received 4,524 votes (39.30% of those voting) against Bailey Smith's 6,934. Moderates succeeded in electing Christine Gregory as first vice-president. A less noticed, but perhaps fateful, loss was that Clyde Fant narrowly missed election at the pastor's conference on a standing vote to Ed Young.[8] Many who observed thought Fant had the majority of the votes. Because the Pastors' Conference was consistently used to draw the Fundamentalist crowd and prime them for the convention, one can only speculate on the difference a Fant victory might have made.

The events at the Los Angeles convention were not lost on a recently returned missionary, Bob Perry. He found Kenneth Chafin, a significant Moderate pastor from Houston, and asked what he could do to help. Chafin said, "You can help us with the network when you get back to Missouri."

---

and between Jim Slatton and James Dunn, 18 March 1981. [Editor's note: Allen was then president of the SBC Radio and Television Commission and Dunn was head of the Baptist Joint Committee on Public Affairs.]

[6]Private conversation between Jim Slatton and Presnall Wood, Spring 1981.

[7]Dan Martin, Baptist Press in "Sherman's Group May Offer Alternate Candidate," *Religious Herald,* 5 March 1981, 8-9.

[8][Editor's note: At this early point in the controversy Ed Young feigned neutrality in the conflict, but, as many others would do when it was obvious that the future politics of the SBC lay with the Fundamentalists, he clearly moved into the Fundamentalist segment of the SBC later. He would become SBC president in 1992.]

Bob Perry became a key person in Missouri, along with Pete Hill whom he helped recruit.

New Orleans and 1982

For the 1981–1982 campaign, Don Harbuck of Arkansas initially agreed to serve as chair, replacing Cecil Sherman. The principal reason for the change was an attempt to shift the overwhelming burden of leadership that would have taxed a full-time executive. Also, Arkansas was closer to the site of the upcoming New Orleans convention. After a short while, however, Harbuck withdrew as chair because he felt obligated to John Sullivan, at that time pastor in Shreveport, who was planning to run independently. At the urging of the group, Cecil Sherman resumed leadership of the network.

Despite the discouragement of the Los Angeles defeat in 1981, prospects for the New Orleans convention the following year seemed somewhat brighter. The California vote had been a factor in defeating the Moderate candidate in Los Angeles. California Baptists were known to have conservative sympathies and were trying to hold themselves aloof from the controversy. Fundamentalists had a much better organization in California than did we. New Orleans was closer to the East Coast and nearer the geographical center of traditional Southern Baptist strength.[9] Nor would we be bucking tradition by opposing an incumbent.

---

[9][Editor's note: The issue of "geography" has played an important part in interpreting Southern Baptists throughout the years, and it played a prominent role in the interpretation and speculation about the controversy. The "orthodox" geographical interpretation about the SBC is that the further west you move from the Mississippi River, the more conservative Southern Baptists are, while the further east you move from the Mississippi, the more liberal they are. There is some obvious truth to this. Virginia, e.g., is by any count the most liberal of all Southern Baptist states. Whether a rigid imposition of this scenario is accurate is difficult to prove. E.g., Texas Fundamentalists have had few victories in the Texas Baptist Convention. While the "geographical thesis" cannot be rigidly imposed on the controversy, it is revealing to note in what cities the SBC met from 1979 to 1990. During those twelve years, the convention met twice *on* the Mississippi, in New Orleans (1982 and 1990), eight times *west* of the Mississippi (Houston, 1979; St. Louis, 1980, 1987; Los Angeles, 1981; Kansas City, 1984; Dallas, 1985; San Antonio, 1988; Las Vegas, 1989), and only two times *east* of the Mississippi (Pittsburgh, 1984—at which convention the Moderates had no SBC presidential candidate; Atlanta, 1986). See also below, 65.]

The New Orleans effort, however, was marked by a failure to unify the people who were not solidly of the Pressler-Patterson network. At a January meeting at the First Baptist Church, Memphis, Clyde Fant, then pastor of First Baptist Church of Richardson, Texas, came with a brown golf shirt for everyone, the pocket emblazoned with a logo: a bull's-eye with a bullet hole off-center, and the legend "The Gatlinburg Gang." A confectioner and member of First Baptist Memphis supplied each of us with never-to-be-forgotten chocolates. A fairly substantial list of potential candidates was discussed.

Throughout the winter and spring of 1981–1982 appeals were made to people with name recognition and wide appeal in the convention, including people who were well on the right theologically, but not openly linked to the Fundamentalist movement.[10] The prospect of opposing a Fundamentalist candidate, and of being identified as Moderate candidates proved not to appeal to those best positioned to be of help.

Eventually, Duke McCall, past-president of Southern Seminary, agreed to be the Moderate standard bearer. Dr. McCall had some baggage from years of public service in the denomination, especially the rift in the Southern faculty in the late 1950s, and he was well of aware of that. But he also had no illusions as to the consequences of an unchecked Fundamentalist agenda for the denomination, and he was willing to take up the Moderate standard if others would not. In a conference telephone call that spring an executive committee of the Moderate network decided unanimously on Duke McCall as the candidate.[11]

---

[10][Editor's note: That Moderates were willing and, in fact, did sponsor candidates who were very conservative in theology should not be lost on those who want to understand the essence of this controversy. The issue for most Moderates throughout most of the controversy was not primarily "theological" but "denominational." That is, Moderates did not object to very conservative people being elected to positions within the SBC as long as those people would honor the diversity of the convention with their appointments and approach to denominational life. The objectional feature of the Pressler-Patterson-Rogers Fundamentalist-led party was its exclusionary approach to denominational life. These Fundamentalists wanted "control" in order to "exclude."]

[11][Editor's note: In the spring of 1982 I was serving as dean of the School of Theology at The Southern Baptist Theological Seminary in Louisville, where McCall had recently retired as president. Don Harbuck called me on behalf of the Moderate Network and asked me if I would ask Dr. McCall to allow his name to be nominated for SBC president. I invited Dr. McCall for breakfast to the Browns-

The belief in the potential residing within a great uncommitted middle in the denomination was quite strong at this time in the struggle. Perry Sanders and John Sullivan, both prominent Louisiana pastors, offered themselves as candidates for the New Orleans convention, and independent of the Moderate network. On the first ballot Perry Sanders drew 1,725 votes, John Sullivan 1,625. Duke McCall with network backing received 6,124 votes and Jimmy Draper, the Pressler-Patterson man, 8,081. In the runoff that followed, Draper was elected with 8,331 votes (56.97%) to Duke McCall's 6,282 (43.03%). The idea that the SBC presidency was an impromptu popularity contest or that one could "run" as an SBC presidential candidate, independent of the Fundamentalist and Moderate political networks, clearly was no more in Southern Baptist life. Nationwide political organization was the order of the day in the SBC.

The SBC Pastor's Conference, meeting the day before the SBC, had become a staging ground for SBC Fundamentalism. That year the conference hosted George Bush who came to bring a message of affirmation and encouragement to the religious right. The SBC Resolutions Committee, dominated by people in line with the new Fundamentalist leadership, pushed through resolutions in keeping with the agenda of the religious right, principally an affirmation of prayer in the public schools and a strong pro-Israel statement which was driven by the millennialist sentiment. Afterwards I telephoned the White House and talked to President Reagan's assistant for religious affairs, a Mr. Blackwell at that time. He denied that the White House staff had been involved in the machinations of the Committee on Resolutions. He made clear, however, that he believed that promoting religion in general and the Christian faith in particular was a legitimate agenda of the federal government and of his office.

---

boro Road Holiday Inn one morning and made the request. He resisted, conscientiously so, arguing that he did not think that he was our best candidate. I applied as much pressure as I thought possible for a dean to exert on a former president. He was at that very time serving as the president of the Baptist World Alliance (1980–1985), had just retired after the longest presidency in the history of Southern Seminary (15 Sept 1951–31 Jan 1982), and deserved relief from denominational service, which had been his life. I pushed—gently—and he promised only that he would discuss the possibility with his family. A few days later, he called and said, "I really shouldn't, and I really think you folks can find a better person for the job, but if this is what is wanted, I'll do it."]

As sorely disappointing as the New Orleans loss was, there were certain signs of hope as we departed. Word was reaching us that some denominational agency heads were now convinced of the necessity of the Moderate network, believed it needed help if some balance were to be restored in the convention, and were determined to give assistance and encouragement to Moderates. This was a welcome change to those leading the effort, because it was our reading that all but one or two agency heads were holding us at a chilly distance and regarded our organizational efforts and public statements as troublesome to the peace of the body.

Looking back, the little group that started at Gatlinburg could well think of itself as a network that held together the mainstream of the denomination. Thousands had supported our candidate in New Orleans even though he lost. We had begun to provide an alternative voice in the denomination signaling the formidable presence of a more traditional kind of Baptist.[12]

Pittsburgh and 1983

Perhaps the most hopeful factor after the New Orleans defeat was that the next convention would be in Pittsburgh, in the Northeast, border territory, far from the more conservative West, not only nearer Moderate strongholds, but outside the deep South. We hoped far fewer Fundamentalists would go.

In North Carolina Henry Crouch continued to work as state chairperson. The state was divided into three areas with Harold Shirley, Lamar King, and Dewey Hobbs as area captains. Eight regions comprised the three areas, each with a captain. Virginia was organized along associational lines with an associational organizer in most of the district associations.

At first Vernon Davis and I each took responsibility for twenty or so of Virginia's associations and recruited leaders for each association. We jointly represented Virginia in the national meetings. For New Orleans, we were responsible for Maryland, the District of Columbia, and Virginia, and were asked to find 600 votes. In late May, our associational organizers turned in a vote count of 729.

After Vernon Davis's move to Midwestern Seminary in 1983, a group of three Richmond pastors, Tim Norman, Sherrill Stevens, and David White, shared with me the coordination of the state network by working with the associational coordinators. As career moves occurred, others like Ronald

---

[12]Cecil Sherman, paper read to the national committee at Knoxville, Tennessee, 6 Sept 1982.

Crawford, Edward Freeman, and Bill Wilson filled the ranks. I continued to work with the national committee, Tim Norman became chair of the state network, followed later by Ron Crawford.

By this time skirmishes were taking place between Fundamentalists and Moderates in state conventions. Yet most Moderate state networks had not begun to organize for state convention meetings. By no means had all of the states organized Moderate networks, and not all state networks were organized equally well. Eventually, it became transparent that good organizers were able to find a lot more votes for us than poor ones. Someone said that the motto of the Moderate movement was "Don't be unpleasant, and don't make me late for lunch." We always worked with the disadvantage that Moderates were, by definition, *moderate.* Many people over the years worked tirelessly and sacrificed not only time but money and careers. Too many others were simply unwilling to go to extraordinary lengths. That was a key difference. We were pitted against people who were willing to go to the lengths necessary to prevail.

Immediately following his election, Draper began running for president. He promised to be the president of all Southern Baptists. In the wake of such soothing talk, state papers struck hopeful tones. I was told with the greatest conviction by a Virginia Baptist agency official that Draper was not the problem we thought he was. He had visited with Draper on a trip to Texas and had been assured that his presidency would be evenhanded and that he would not be pushing the Pressler-Patterson agenda of stacking boards and committees with Fundamentalists.[13]

The charges of takeover and a confrontational approach against Draper in this environment sounded meanspirited and divisive. The dilemma for Moderates remained. What was needed was a focus, a rallying cry, a statement of purpose that was both compelling enough to mobilize the multitudes and positive at the same time. This was tantalizingly difficult to those of us all too conscious of the relentless and retrograde alterations the Fundamentalists were already wreaking and all they had yet in store for the denomination's agencies. It was like being on a ship that was already grinding into an iceberg and being forbidden to shout a warning. We must not be as confrontational about the takeover, we were lectured, but rather positive about what we advocated. Inclusiveness, freedom of conscience, the priesthood of believers, academic freedom, and the fine points of church-state separation,

---

[13]Private conversation with Bill Jenkins, sometime during 1983.

were clearly issues critical to the moment, but somehow they did not ignite passion. Nor did the group yet hit upon an effective way to thwart the Fundamentalists from posturing on the Bible with the inerrancy slogan.

In preparation for the 1983 Pittsburgh convention, network organization was pursued as before. A national network meeting was convened at a church campground near Knoxville, Tennessee. There was a feeling of momentum derived from the fact that so many new people showed up that we ran short on food. As on other occasions, the group hashed through everything that had ever been decided before.[14] State and regional networks were reassigned. A small delegation from the network met twice with Draper to press the concerns of Moderates. Harold Bennett, executive secretary of the SBC Executive Committee, was present for these two discussions which proved fruitless.

There was better coordination in getting Moderates to enter the "hotel sweepstakes" by applying to the convention housing bureau for blocks of rooms. Travel agencies were better used than ever to reserve blocks of rooms—as the Fundamentalists had been doing for years. Still, when Moderate messenger counts were tallied in May, the results were discouraging. After much discussion it was decided not to offer a candidate against Draper in Pittsburgh.

Those committed still went to Pittsburgh. For the first time, there was a public rallying point for Moderates. A reception was held in a downtown office building on Monday evening under the name of "Friends of Missions," and hundreds came, including a number of agency officials and seminary presidents. While the Pittsburgh convention was in progress, Foy Valentine, head of the Christian Life Commission, was already notifying us that whatever anyone else did, he already had a candidate, Grady Cothen, retired Sunday School Board president, and that he was going to pull out every stop to get him elected. This had the effect of removing the decision from the Moderate leadership and the network, which was already demoralized by the decision to stand down before Pittsburgh.

---

[14][Editor's note: Cecil Sherman makes this same point, an issue of no little frustration for those who had been persistent in their labors on behalf of the Moderate movement. See above, 26.]

Kansas City and 1984

Although the network was actively worked in 1983–1984, it proved to be ineffective in bringing a unified and adequate body of Moderate messengers to the convention in Kansas City. In part this was believed to be fallout from the failure to offer a candidate in Pittsburgh. Clifford Johnston was employed to organize messenger support and was supplied with funding through the efforts of Foy Valentine. Unfortunately, some of the key states nearer Kansas City were without networks capable of producing strong Moderate turnouts.

Once again John Sullivan tried to run as an independent candidate. Charles Stanley, pastor of First Baptist, Atlanta, defeated both Sullivan and Grady Cothen on the first ballot.

At the Moderate committee meeting in Pittsburgh the decision had been made to organize an alternative to the SBC Pastor's Conference. The effort to promote a sufficient Moderate attendance at the SBC Pastor's Conference had failed badly at New Orleans and Pittsburgh. It was hoped that a more attractive program would motivate Moderates to attend a preconvention meeting and provide inspiration and encouragement. The first meeting of the SBC Forum was held in Kansas City the following year.

Ironically, the Kansas City convention provided capital to the Moderate cause and helped revitalize the network. Charles Wade of Texas acquitted himself well on the platform in debate and emerged as a significant leader in the network. Russell Dilday's convention sermon, a denunciation of the politics of takeover, gave legitimacy to the Moderate case. The convention's resolution subordinating women to men in church and society sent shock waves throughout the SBC and brought many to the Moderate cause. Winfred Moore of the First Baptist Church of Amarillo, while not opposing the Fundamentalists on biblical inspiration, was determined their movement must be stopped and consented to oppose Stanley for the presidency in Dallas in 1985.

Following the Kansas City convention, agency chiefs, especially seminary presidents, including Lolley at Southeastern, Honeycutt at Southern, and Dilday at Southwestern talked among themselves about the need to assist Moderate elements in the convention to thwart the Fundamentalist agenda. Subsequently, some staff and friends of the schools and their administrators began to do valuable volunteer work in the fall of 1984.[15]

At Southeastern Seminary, Tom Graves became involved. When the administrative chiefs agreed, Lolley asked Tom to assist. He began working with two North Carolina pastors: Bill Stillerman and Tom McDearis. Seeking advice on doing political work, Tom met with former U.S. Senator Robert Morgan of North Carolina. At a luncheon meeting Morgan introduced him to a professional political consultant named Randolph Cloud who was immediately employed as consultant to the network which became known as the North Carolina Friends of Missions. At this point the state network went public, organized under ten regional heads which were subdivided under associational leaders. Bill Puckett and George McCotter became state leaders of Friends of Missions. Cloud began almost immediately to publish a newsletter.[16]

On the Fundamentalist side, a protege of Senator Jesse Helms, Sam Curran, a U.S. attorney, became involved in denominational politics as did three other individuals out of his office. Helms was reported to be supporting changes at Southeastern Seminary.[17]

Within a year, North Carolina Friends of Missions turned their network organization to Baptist state convention politics, supporting Bill Poe, a Charlotte attorney, for state convention president. At the 1986 North Carolina Baptist Convention they appeared wearing badges and handing out campaign cards with candidates pictures. Public campaigning worked in Carolina, and Moderates elected their slates from 1986 forward.

Dallas and 1985

The 1985 SBC meeting in Dallas proved to be the most dramatic and tumultuous of all. On the eve of the convention, in the downtown Hyatt Hotel there was guarded optimism among Moderates as state coordinators reported large numbers of messengers. Another large public reception was held by Moderates in one of the hotel ballrooms. There were Moderate travel services offering convention accommodations so the Fundamentalist network did not have a lock on hotel rooms.[18]

---

[15]Personal conversation with Jim Slatton, 6 Oct 1992, reported by Tom Graves.
[16]Ibid.
[17]Ibid.
[18]Marse Grant had been offering convention packages in North Carolina for

The Moderate network leadership was told the night before the election that Winfred Moore would not agree to his nomination for vice-president should he fail to win the presidency the next day. When Stanley was declared the winner, Ray Allen, a messenger from Virginia, unaware of the prepared strategy, called for Moore's election to vice-president as a gesture of generosity. Moore's quickness of wit in the situation forced Stanley to appear to accept this arrangement, perhaps confusing some of his own supporters. Moore's subsequent election as vice-president gave Moderates a standard bearer for Atlanta, a year in which the incumbent president, Charles Stanley, would serve out his term and a new president would be elected.

The creation of the Peace Committee at the 1985 convention—seemingly inclusive, but actually giving Fundamentalists a clear edge of committed representatives—placed a powerful weapon in the hands of Fundamentalists. Calls for peace and hopes that the crisis was being managed within and by the Peace Committee served Fundamentalists' purposes. They were the party in office. Challenges and criticisms of their activities were made to seem disruptive and harsh. Elected to the Peace Committee, Cecil Sherman gave up leadership of the Moderate network; at a national committee meeting during the convention, I was elected to replace him.

The strategy of offering a substitute slate for the Committee on Boards[19]

---

years and they were used by both sides. In Virginia, Jim Slatton, David White, and others formed a nonprofit corporation called Baptist Travel, which had a large selection of rooms for the Dallas Convention. David White proved effective in negotiating with the Fairmont Hotel when it overbooked and turned away numbers of Baptist Travel clients. Through 1990, travel packages, including bus tours, were arranged by agents working with Moderates.

[19][Editor's note: The Fundamentalist attempt to "go for the jugular" and to dominate and control the denominational boards and agencies appeared complicated to many, but it was actually a rather simple four-step process. First and foremost was the election of a Fundamentalist president. Second, the Fundamentalist president would "appoint" (according to the SBC constitution) a Fundamentalist Committee on Committees. Third, the Fundamentalist Committee on Committees would "nominate" to the SBC a Fundamentalist "Committee on Boards." Fourth, the Fundamentalist "Committee on Boards" would "nominate" to the SBC Fundamentalist Trustees to control the SBC agencies and institutions. Slatton's motion had to do with the third step in this process. If Moderates could not elect the SBC president who would be fair and inclusive in appointing a Committee on Committees, their next available step in the process was to try to make the Committee on Boards a fair and representative selection of Southern Baptists. This was what Slatton was

made up of presidents of the W.M.U. and presidents of the state conventions had been agreed upon by the group, and a list of the substitute slate had been prepared for the occasion. I was designated by Cecil Sherman to bring the motion, and appealed the decision of the chair when Stanley ruled that I could not offer the entire slate as a substitute slate. He ruled that I must nominate each person individually. When the house sustained my right to offer the entire slate, Stanley's overruling of the house and his manner of presiding afterwards impressed many in and out of the hall as extremely undemocratic and high-handed.[20]

The Fundamentalists were also accused of voting irregularities. The attempt to use the peace appeal to muffle criticism of the ongoing takeover was substantially thwarted by the dispute over Stanley's presiding.

The class-action lawsuit to obtain redress from Stanley's handling of the substitute slate issue was an independent action on the part of Robert Crowder and others and was not of the Moderate network. I personally asked Crowder not to pursue it, and I believe it prevented Moderates from making as much capital as we might have from Stanley's abuse of the chair.

Between 1980 and 1985 the Moderate network was without certain basic elements of a sophisticated and thoroughgoing political effort. There had been no paid staff or manager in the Moderate effort except in the brief instance of Clifford Johnson who worked at the behest of Foy Valentine and in behalf of Grady Cothen's presidential candidacy in 1983–1984. There had been no systematic fund-raising program. Funds for the Forum as well as start-up money for *SBC Today* had been collected for the most part from the churches whose pastors were working actively in the network. Some state network coordinators had put out the word to their network and small gifts came back from the pastors and a few laypeople. Political and public relations consultants had not been utilized.

Atlanta and 1986

That began to change in the summer of 1985. I presided at a meeting of perhaps forty Moderate leaders and state coordinators at Mercer University in Macon, Georgia. Winfred Moore, pastor of First Baptist Church, Amarillo, brought new support and energies from Texas. Some of the Baptist universities had people there, including two presidents. SBC agencies were

---

trying to do with his motion.]

[20][Editor's note: See *SBC Annual 1985,* 78-79, 81.]

also represented. Out of that meeting came not only the usual formation of new committees and division of assignments but the decision to employ a professional to manage the overall campaign.[21]

In the short time available, we were unable to settle on a person who combined professional political skills, immediate availability, and an insider's grasp of the SBC situation. No one we found could leave a good position immediately and work for us. We were able, however, to find someone with those qualities inside an SBC agency. This person worked with the knowledge of the agency chief, part time, although there were many months when the work was all consuming. A stipend was promised and expenses provided by the Moderate organization.

For the Atlanta campaign, our manager provided a game plan. The steering committee that year was Larry McSwain, Kentucky; Dewey Presley, Texas; Norman Cavender, Georgia; Bill Sherman, Tennessee; Henry Crouch, North Carolina; Larry Eason, a Fort Worth layman; Welton Gaddy, Georgia; Gene Garrison, Oklahoma City; Lavonn Brown, Oklahoma; Richard Maples, Texas; and our new manager and I. There were eight task groups: (1) Get out the vote; (2) Finance; (3) Housing and Transportation; (4) Floor Strategy; (5) Information and Public Relations; (6) Denominational Relations; (7) Forum; and (8) Trustees. Fourteen states were identified as essential to the Atlanta convention and a goal was set to have someone from each of those states on the eight task groups.

In addition to a part-time consultant/manager, an office was opened in Dallas. Claudia Barner of Dallas was employed to run the office and coordinate communications. Polling information secured by Wilkerson and Associates prior to the Atlanta meeting found in a ten-state sample that fifty-four percent of rank-and-file Baptists preferred to identify themselves as Moderate, progressive, or liberal. Thirteen percent chose liberal; less than ten percent preferred Fundamentalist; eighty-eight percent thought Baptists should work together without having to agree on the interpretation of the Bible or on a position regarding the nature of biblical authority.[22] A *Florida Baptist Witness* poll released June 1, 1986, found that of laypersons aware of the

---

[21][Editor's note: This is not the same meeting at which the emerging differences in the Moderate political strategy emerged. Two meetings were held at Mercer, one during the summer of 1985 following the Dallas convention and one in the summer of 1986 after the Atlanta convention.]

[22]Poll commissioned by Wilkerson Associates, Laymen for the Cooperative Program, Kentucky, 1986.

controversy fifty-five percent chose to identify themselves as moderate-conservative versus fundamental-conservative.

A campaign budget was adopted, and efforts were fostered in the state networks to obtain funds both from churches and from interested individuals. Winfred Moore, Dewey Presley, former president of the First National Bank of Dallas and a Baylor trustee, and Larry Eason, a Ft. Worth businessman, proved effective in raising funds. However, sufficient funds were never raised to fund a projected campaign budget. It is both my opinion and that of our campaign manager that Moderates lost the struggle for the SBC for one reason above all others: we never had enough money to operate a winning campaign. This, of course, reflected an even more basic factor: Moderates in general lacked the willingness to do what had to be done to prevail. Individual Moderates made great efforts; some, great sacrifices. The people who had the influence and the means to make the vital difference came to understand the consequences of the Fundamentalist takeover too late, and they did not come in time or at all to a willingness to make the extraordinary efforts in money, in speaking out, and in action that were necessary. This is a very great irony, but people who had poured treasure and energy into the Southern Baptist Convention—and who did not want the transformation that has come upon it—would not make the same sort of effort to save it.

Winfred Moore received funds from friends and from the network to travel about. A concerted effort was made by Moderates to have him on state convention platforms and in gatherings at local churches. Moore was put forward, but the existence of a national office with paid staff and an extensive network was not. There were two opinions about this among us. Two states had gone public with state offices. North Carolina has already been mentioned. Georgia also published the existence of a state organization and the names of its leaders. Jo Ellen Witt was active in the Missouri organization which publicized the existence of a Moderate organization and began publishing a newsletter. In Virginia, Texas, and other states, it was thought there was nothing to be gained by publicly opening an office or announcing the existence of a new state Baptist organization. At the Atlanta SBC in 1986, Richard Jackson, prominent conservative pastor from Arizona, identified himself with Moderates by nominating Winfred Moore for the presidency. Moore polled the largest percentage of the vote a Moderate had received since the network began, 45.78%.

Winfred Moore, Norman Cavender, a layman from Georgia, and I were identified to the Peace Committee as leaders of the Moderate network. We were invited to meet with subgroups of the Peace Committee. The Fundamentalists had been stung by accusations of voter fraud in Dallas, and the real purpose of the meeting was to challenge us for the evidence for the charges. Uninformed as to the purpose of the meeting, we were unprepared to present such evidence. It is indicative of the situation at the time that we really thought the purpose of the committee would be to grill us regarding Moderate organizational efforts.

A second meeting with the Peace Committee took place in Dallas in July 1986. The ostensible purpose of that meeting was to ask both Moderates and Fundamentalists to desist from their efforts. Charles W. Pickering, a layman of Mississippi on the committee, was especially interested in the cessation of political activities. Norman Cavender, Winfred Moore, and I were brought face to face with Paige Patterson, Paul Pressler, and Adrian Rogers in the presence of Pickering and Charles Fuller, the chair of the committee. We challenged the Fundamentalist leaders to dismantle their war machine, and we agreed to do exactly as much as they would do by way of standing down. There was much talk, but Patterson, Pressler, and Rogers offered not a single concession. At midnight, I said that I had brought a note pad to write down everything that had been offered by way of standing down on political effort in the SBC. I noted that my pad was totally blank, and said, "We will be glad to meet with you as long as you wish tomorrow, but nothing has been agreed to, and I am tired and need to go to bed." With that the conference ended.

The Fundamentalists were winning and felt no need to compromise. But the meeting had been, perhaps inadvertently, a gesture in the right direction. We urged upon Charles Fuller the concept of the Peace Committee acting not as a court of high commission to decide and then attempt to impose its findings, but rather as an agent to bring the two parties into direct negotiation. We even suggested the use of a professional mediating service which would be impartial, and expressed willingness to participate in such a process.[23]

St. Louis and 1987

In the summer of 1986 the national leadership of the network met a second time in Macon. Opinion at this meeting was seriously divided. Amateurs at politics, from the beginning we had thought only in terms of the convention

---

[23]Telephone conversation between Jim Slatton and Charles Fuller in Richmond, summer 1986.

immediately ahead. We were being coached by our campaign manager to think in terms of a long-term effort and to look for incremental gains, not to see the next convention as the whole story, a once-for-all, do-or-die effort. To church people who thought politics was sub-Christian anyway, this long look was hard to sell. The Atlanta convention of 1986, in the face of repeated losses and of the ongoing encroachments the Fundamentalists were achieving in the agencies, took on the character of a last best chance. The loss in Atlanta was consequently very demoralizing.

At Macon some of the group said the time had come to accept the fact that the Fundamentalists had prevailed. They wished to put energy into joint ministries that were positive, not political, that promoted Baptist principles rather than just fighting the Fundamentalist political machine. Walter Shurden, Henry Crouch, and Jim Strickland were among those who voiced these sentiments. Others present voiced a determination to go on with the political struggle. The group as a whole committed itself to continue and proceeded with planning for the St. Louis campaign, but blessed those who might wish to begin something new and different.

To some degree the tension within the group was between East and West. The eastern states like Carolina, Virginia, and Georgia had organized sooner and had been in the fight longer. The western states like Texas had, for the most part, come later to the fight in any organized way. The challenge was to hold East and West, new people and veterans together.[24] The Macon meeting marked the beginning of the movement that became the Southern Baptist Alliance and the continued development of the Moderate political network as well.

As had been the case the previous year, representatives of denominational agencies were present whose leadership was increasingly invested in the Moderate effort. For the first time at this meeting a significant single donation of money was promised to the effort. State organizations were asked to caucus and elect representatives to the steering committee for the year to come. State steering committee members were Fred Andrea, South Carolina; Charles Wade, Texas; Bill Scarborough, Georgia; Sherrill Stevens, Virginia; John Roberts, Maryland and New York; David Gasperson, Florida; John Jeffers, Alabama; Joe Brown, Oklahoma; Billy White, Arkansas; John Harris, Louisiana; Leonard Markham with Jack Prince, Tennessee; Dan

---

[24]Letter, Sherman to Cavender, Slatton, and campaign manager, 22 Aug 1986; circular letter, Slatton to Macon conference attenders, 1988. See also n. 9 above.

Cooper, Kentucky; Jerry Barnes, Kansas; Lee Stephens, Missouri; Lee Coleman, Illinois; and Ray Lloyd and Charles Myers, Mississippi.

A smaller oversight committee made up of the campaign manager, Winfred Moore, Norman Cavender, and me was empowered to act in behalf of the body between sessions. A plan of organization was adopted for a year-long campaign. It was agreed to continue the search for a paid national coordinator.[25]

On the heels of the Atlanta loss, the Peace Committee, by conveying the false impression that the denominational crisis was being dealt with and that partisan activity was disruptive, continued to prove a powerful obstacle to Moderate efforts. This was, of course, favorable to the incumbent party.

A nearly fatal stroke was forthcoming from our friends, the presidents of the theological seminaries. The "Glorieta Statement" in which the six seminary presidents affirmed inerrancy potentially cut the ground out from under the St. Louis campaign. If the seminaries were prepared to embrace inerrancy, as the statement could be read to mean, what reason remained for fighting? If a settlement had taken place at the top, among duly constituted authorities—Peace Committee, seminary presidents—why should those of us without portfolio continue a struggle already officially resolved?

The settlement of the Glorieta statement was, of course, no real settlement of anything. A way of making that reality publicly clear was vital. To put Pressler, Patterson, and Rogers in a position of having to admit that they would continue the takeover, we hit upon the notion of making a highly publicized peace offer. Such a proposal would make clear what a real settlement would be. Should they reject it, their real position would be exposed.

The result was the eight-point peace proposal that Winfred Moore, Norman Cavender, and I put to the three Fundamentalist leaders on October 24, 1986. The proposals challenged Adrian Rogers, now SBC president again, since he was satisfied with the Glorieta settlement, to appoint the presidents of the state conventions and WMU chapters as the Committee on Committees for the next two years. This we thought would make for representative rather than political appointments. Additional points in the proposal were (2) that a joint committee of Moderates and Fundamentalists select the program people for a joint Pastor's Conference/Forum with the proviso no one could speak on the points at issue between us; and (3) that a joint committee made up of an equal number of elected representatives

---

[25]Circular letter, Slatton to steering committee, 7 Oct 1986.

from each side make a joint nomination of a president for San Antonio in 1988, with the understanding that both sides would support the common candidate. Additional proposals dealt with halting the activities of itinerating network agents and the *Southern Baptist Advocate*, and called upon the Peace Committee to facilitate a peace meeting of the two sides and join the seminary presidents in endorsing the peace plan.[26]

The three Fundamentalist leaders accommodated us by rejecting the entire plan, and by doing so in personal letters, allowing us to break their refusals to the press and to make it our story instead of theirs. It was our feeling that the peace offer and its rejection, along with the story that followed Cecil Sherman's resignation from the peace committee, was an effective counter stroke to the damage of the Glorieta statement. This incident illustrates the enormous amount of work that fell on the network chair. I had to work with the campaign coordinator in developing the statement, checking with Cavender and Moore, and getting the material to the press. An adequate paid staff would have done almost all of the work. As it was, I had to do most of it.

Another major problem was that Moderates had never hit the Bible issue head on. During year's end 1986 and early 1987, I wrote a statement on the Bible intended to deprive the Fundamentalists of the issue. The fact was, the Fundamentalist movement stood foursquare not on the Bible at all but upon a human construct about biblical inspiration, namely the inerrancy doctrine. More than 30,000 copies of "No Lord but Christ, No Creed but the Bible" were sent out to pastors in the denomination over the endorsement of a list of known pastors from all over the convention. Whatever the impact of that one piece, I still believe we were on the right track with the argument it made, and that we should have aggressively dealt with the Bible issue in such a way from the beginning. The better, but insufficient, job we were doing raising money made that and other such publications possible.

Another important item on the public side of the campaign was the first systematic attempt to analyze the appointments of a president. Adrian Rogers's appointments to the Committee on Committees were rated by

---

[26]"Statement and Proposal for Peace in the Southern Baptist Convention, Offered in Behalf of Those Called Moderate Southern Baptists on the Occasion of the Report of the Presidents of the Six Theological Seminaries and the Acceptance of the Report by the Peace Committee of the Southern Baptist Convention," by Winfred Moore, James H. Slatton, and Norman Cavender, Richmond, Virginia, 24 Oct 1986.

asking state convention insiders in each state for an assessment of the appointments from their states. In a release to the newspapers in May, we reported that

> We received reports from thirty states on sixty of the appointments out of a total of thirty-three states and sixty-six appointments. As to political alignment, we could identify only one of the sixty as Moderate. Eleven . . . are people considered neutral or unaligned. Forty-three of the sixty (72%) are clearly identified Fundamentalists. . . . of the total . . . only five were persons whose political identity we were unable to determine.[27]

Based upon the known level of participation in Baptist life in their home states we found that fifty-five percent of Rogers's appointees were either unqualified or marginally qualified.

John Jeffers, retired pastor of First Baptist Church, Auburn, Alabama, had been employed in January 1987, for a modest stipend and travel expenses, to work for the network in getting out the vote for the St. Louis convention (1987) and subsequently for the San Antonio (1988) convention. One of Jeffers's first contacts was in Charlotte, on February 12, 1987, only to be greeted by the news in the *Charlotte Observer* of the formation of the Southern Baptist Alliance. This development, in Jeffers's opinion, became a discouraging factor in the networking effort.

Richard Jackson, pastor of North Phoenix Baptist Church in Arizona, agreed to be nominated in St. Louis in 1987. In connection with the Jackson campaign Mary Myrick worked with the network as a political consultant. In St. Louis Adrian Rogers was elected to a third term as president, winning by 13,980 votes (59.97%) to Jackson's 9,331 (40.03%). At the meeting of the steering committee at Kirkwood Baptist Church before the opening of the convention, I gave up the chair of the group, and Winfred Moore became national chairperson. Our part-time campaign manager/consultant continued to work with the network, as did Claudia Barner.

San Antonio and 1988

As the network turned toward San Antonio there were new assets and old problems. There was still no full-time campaign manager. However, in addition to our part-time coordinator, our office person Claudia Barner, and John Jeffers, who was performing yeoman's service, we added David Currie

---

[27]John Jeffers, Norman Cavender, and James Slatton press statement, 18 May 1987.

in the western part of the convention. John Baugh, a Baptist businessman and philanthropist from Houston, had started the *Laity Journal*. Working for John Baugh was Dr. Neal Rodgers. Baugh, a dedicated opponent of the Fundamentalist takeover, was devoting funds, his own efforts, and those of the *Journal* to assisting the network, although he and the *Journal* remained essentially independent of the Moderate network.

The steering committee remained large. Its membership tended to fluctuate as individuals came and went, and its meetings were characterized by much reprocessing of ideas and strategies. The campaign plans were not executed efficiently by a number of the members.

Illustrative of how the Moderate network was often transferred to work in state convention struggles is the case in Virginia. In the fall of 1987, the Virginia Baptist network voted to use its organization for the first time to enlist messengers and support an agenda for the state Baptist convention. Until that time the network was used only to organize for national conventions. General T. C. Pinckney, a retired Air Force officer, had been working for some time with Fundamentalists in the state. General Pinckney had sent a circular letter to Fundamentalist pastors revealing a computerized operation to track the politics of every pastor in the state, and to identify all vacant pastorates so that Fundamentalist candidates could be recommended. This candid letter revealing the Fundamentalist game plan for Virginia was a "smoking pistol." Moderates mailed a copy of Pinckney's insider letter to every church in Virginia. It was accompanied by an explanatory cover letter from a well-known Virginia Baptist minister, Fred Skaggs. The publication of the Pinckney letter proved to be the most effective single action by Moderates in Virginia. The convention meeting in Williamsburg afterwards had a record attendance and won a crushing victory over Fundamentalists in every vote taken and elected a complete slate of Moderate state officers.

Due to a number of factors, not the least of which was the work of Jeffers, Currie, and many others, the San Antonio SBC of 1988 marked the peak of the Moderate networking effort. Many suspect that Moderates actually had more people there than the Fundamentalists. The absolute control of the platform by Fundamentalists and the disciplined behavior of Fundamentalist messengers in arriving early and packing all the seats around the platform and in the main hall proved devastatingly effective, as did an electronic microphone system used to control speech from any part of the house. Moderate candidate Richard Jackson's 15,112 votes were 48.32% of the house against Fundamentalist Jerry Vines's 15,894 for 50.53%.

Las Vegas and 1989

For the 1988–1989 campaign a comprehensive plan of operation was put to Baptists Committed leadership by the campaign manager. An executive committee succeeding the oversight committee was formed made up of Winfred Moore, chair, Norman Cavender, Randall Lolley, Cecil Sherman, John Baugh, and me. Richard Jackson attended the executive committee by invitation.[28] The steering committee continued to be made up of state representatives. A complete action calendar for the year-long effort was adopted as well as a proposed budget of at least $358,000, preferably $437,000. As in previous years the proposed budget was not fully met.

In the press release from the December 15-16 meeting, Baptists Committed was styled as a centrist coalition seeking to bring an end to the controversy. David Currie was named as a coordinator. Oeita Bottorff was named project coordinator and brought to the group her exceptional organizational skills. An office was opened in the South Main Baptist Church of Houston, and office equipment loaned and donated to the network. Oeita Bottorff became the key person in communicating with Moderate network leadership around the nation until the middle of 1992.

To focus attention on the issues at stake leading into the 1989 Las Vegas convention, a press conference was held in February in Nashville in connection with a meeting of the SBC Executive Committee. Persons speaking at the press conference were Winfred Moore, Richard Jackson, Daniel Vestal, John Baugh, Steve Tondera, George McCotter, and I. Later in the year a symposium was held in Nashville for the same purpose and with a somewhat larger group of speakers addressing issues of concern: Winfred Moore, Daniel Vestal, Russell Dilday, Bill Sherman, John Baugh, Brian Harbour, James Dunn, and Leon Smith.

Daniel Vestal proved to be a superb campaigner as the Baptist Committed presidential candidate both for Las Vegas (1989) and for New Orleans (1990). Traveling about the country, more at the expense of private donors than of the network, his personal testimonial and conviction were compelling. He succeeded in stating the issues in a way that effectively deprived Fundamentalists of the Bible issue for any who were open to hear him. His defeat was a function of the greater discipline on the part of the Fundamentalist movement in carrying out the agenda of its leadership. The Las Vegas

---

[28]Report of Baptists Committed meeting, 15-16 Dec 1988.

convention marked the close of Winfred Moore's chairmanship of the political network. I again became acting chairman until the executive committee could elect another.

New Orleans and 1990

After Las Vegas, the executive committee was enlarged to include for the next year's campaign Winfred Moore, Texas; Marian Aldridge, South Carolina; Alfred Ayscue, North Carolina; John Baugh, Texas; Norman Cavender, Georgia; Steve Graham, Oklahoma; Charles Horton, Florida; John Hughes, Missouri; Randall Lolley, North Carolina; Howard Olive, Tennessee; David Sapp, Georgia; Cecil Sherman, Texas; Steve Tondera, Alabama; Charles Wade, Texas; Jim Yates, Mississippi; and Jim Slatton, Virginia. Once again a comprehensive plan of operation was presented by the campaign manager who had been serving with us since 1985. An advisory board was planned to consist of 192 members from seventeen states. A board of directors was planned to be made up of 100 persons recommended by state leaders. A process was approved to permit the chair, vice-chair, and project coordinator to act between meetings of the executive committee. By 1989 it was standard to hold telephone conferences rather than the more cumbersome, expensive, and exhausting one- and two-day meetings. A total budget of $805,000 was projected. An actual budget of $400,000 was accepted as needed for the basic essentials of a campaign. As in the case of previous budgets, funds actually raised did not come close to the needs of an effective campaign.[29]

Jimmy Allen consented to serve as chair of the executive committee for the network. Daniel Vestal proved to be a game and effective campaigner once again. A newsletter was issued periodically, and state coordinators were publicly named. With the endorsement of prominent ministers who were supposed to have been previously neutral, Fundamentalists countered with a promise to widen the leadership tent in the SBC. By the end of May, Baptists Committed had received for the five months of 1990 a total of $138,107 toward the needed campaign funds. Despite guarded hopes, Daniel Vestal was defeated by Morris Chapman in New Orleans by 21,471 (57.68%) to 15,753 (42.32%).

---

[29]Baptists Committed "Plan of Operation, 1990 Convention," New Orleans, 19 Sept 1989; minutes of the executive committee, Nashville, Tennessee, 19 Sept 1989.

With the New Orleans convention of 1990, the will to continue a struggle for the presidency of the SBC faded among Moderates. The network did not dissolve. State conventions had their own Moderate-Fundamentalist struggles, and the state networks found it necessary to transfer their full attention to state conventions. On the day following the election in New Orleans, at a meeting of the network executive committee it was decided to set July 12 and 13 as the dates for a meeting to plan a convocation for Moderates. Members of the executive committee of Baptists Committed subsequently met in Dallas in July, along with the leaders of other Moderate groups whom they had invited and planned the convocation that became the Cooperative Baptist Fellowship. Persons currently involved in state networks are also the principal people who are helping move their own churches toward the Fellowship.

The History
of the SBC Forum

John H. Hewett

It all started in Atlanta, January 1984, in the pastor's study at Wieuca Road Baptist Church in suburban Buckhead. Some of the ministers attending one of Pastor Bill Self's "Doing Church in the Eighties" conferences were commiserating with each other over their growing discontent in a denomination lurching toward militant Fundamentalism. They had lost four consecutive presidential elections and been made to appear foolish at the fifth, the summer before in Pittsburgh, when SBC Moderates, for the sake of "peace," stood down from running a candidate against incumbent Jimmy Draper. It was increasingly clear the Moderate strategy for restoring the Southern Baptist Convention to its heritage was not working. If Moderates ever hoped to elect a convention president who would respect the diversity of Southern Baptist churches and individuals, Moderates needed to do more, and quickly. The pivotal Kansas city Convention was less than six months away.

For five years Fundamentalists had effectively used the preconvention Pastor's Conference, which they also controlled, as an orchestrated political rally for their movement. These annual programs paraded Fundamentalist pastors, evangelists, and politicians across the platform to preach old-time religion, bash "liberals," and enlist new converts to the takeover cause. Since 1979, when, from the platform in Houston, Fundamentalist patriarch W. A. Criswell endorsed Memphis pastor and Criswell's heir apparent Adrian Rogers, the Fundamentalists' handpicked presidential candidate had been publicly anointed at every Pastor's Conference and granted prime time to exhort the faithful the night before the election. It worked. *They elected every one.*

Attending these meetings was dispiriting for Moderates. They were excluded from the program. They'd grown weary of being personally reviled from the platform and berated in the halls. They were tired of having their theology, ecclesiology, preaching, and worship styles attacked by angry men who called them "snakes," "cancers,"[1] and "skunks."[2]

Moderate leaders had tried to open up the Pastor's Conference to their kind of Baptists. Cecil Sherman wrote Pastor's Conference presidents Fred Wolfe in 1982 and Charles Stanley in 1983, suggesting the names of Moderates who could balance the Pastor's Conference program and strengthen its appeal. Both replied with polite letters, thanking him for his suggestions, and assuring him of their prayerful consideration.[3] None of the names Sherman suggested would ever appear on a Pastor's Conference program.

So most Moderate pastors simply stopped going. Some chose to attend other preconvention meetings sponsored by church musicians, religious educators, directors of missions, campus ministers, and Woman's Missionary Union. This exodus from the Pastor's Conference did not help the Moderate resistance. Without a central place to gather before the convention opened, pastors opposed to the Pressler-Patterson agenda had no opportunity for worship, fellowship, or strategy planning. They had no platform from which they could present alternative perspectives on current Baptist issues or articulate different visions of the Baptist future. They had no place to hear preachers who didn't scream, musicians who didn't croon, and evangelists who did not practice ventriloquism.

A first step to remedy this situation had already been taken. At the 1983 convention in Pittsburgh, Moderate leaders, especially Cecil Sherman, had quietly reserved a banquet room atop the U. S. Steel building and invited others of like mind to gather Monday evening for a drop-in reception. They were astounded by the size of the crowd that found its way to the fellowship. Messengers came off the elevators like exiles disembarking at Ellis Island. It was clear the leaders had tapped into an urgent need.

By the time the group left Wieuca Road the following January, they had committed themselves to take the next step. With admittedly high hopes, they planned to hold the first SBC Forum at the Kansas City Convention

---

[1]The terms "snakes" and "cancers" were widely used by Texas evangelist James Robison to refer to those he considered theological liberals.

[2]The term is W. A. Criswell's, who said on occasions: "They don't like to be called liberals, but I say a skunk by any other name still stinks."

[3]Telephone interview with Cecil Sherman, Sept 1992.

that June, and follow it with a Monday night party for anyone who would come.

The name implies the original intent for the meeting: it was supposed to be a forum. (The title was not new to the Moderate leadership: they had proposed the name "Forum" in 1982 for a new Moderate newspaper they were working to get started.)[4] The idea, proposed by Bill Bruster, was to invite thoughtful, convictional Southern Baptists to debate current issues of importance to Baptists from differing points of view.

The first issue was to be the ordination of women in ministry. Moderates wanted the SBC Forum to make a contribution to a restored dialogue in the convention by giving Southern Baptists an opportunity to disagree openly yet agreeably on a subject that already was threatening to permanently divide the house.

It was a terrific idea, or so they thought, until they tried to recruit a convictional Fundamentalist to participate. The first refusal came from Adrian Rogers, who told Cecil Sherman flatly, "No. And I am not going to help you gather a crowd."[5] They then asked Paige Patterson, Mark Corts, and finally Morris Chapman. All declined.[6]

When it became apparent dialogue with Fundamentalist leaders was impossible, organizers shifted gears. Instead of a pro-and-con discussion of current issues, the Forum would be an alternative preconvention meeting for Moderates who had no place to go. They would put on their kind of program, showcase their brightest and best preachers and musicians, and give Southern Baptists a clear choice. In keeping with their original commitment to address the issue of women in ministry, they would invite Sara Ann Hobbs, missions division director of the Baptist State Convention of North Carolina, to address the Forum on the topic.

On February 29 the organizers went public. Bill Bruster, pastor of Central Baptist Church–Bearden in Knoxville, Tennessee, and publicity chairperson for the first meeting, announced the meeting. Refusing to cast the Forum as competing with the Pastor's Conference, he labeled it "another option" for messengers "not attending any other preconvention meeting."[7] Bruster said that

---

[4]Letter from Cecil E. Sherman, 2 Dec 1982.

[5]Letter from Cecil E. Sherman to Peter Rhea Jones, 25 July 1989.

[6]"Women's Discussion Cut," Baptist Press news release, May 1984, corroborated in telephone interview with Bill Bruster, 25 Sept 1992.

[7]" 'SBC Forum' To Offer Preconvention Option," Baptist Press, 29 Feb 1984.

The SBC annual meeting is like the church and the preconvention meetings are like Sunday School classes. Many church members (messengers) are not coming to Sunday School (the preconvention meetings). The Forum is simply starting another Sunday School class for those who are not attending.[8]

Bruster added that the Forum would

not be political, and underline the "not." It is not designed to get anyone elected to anything. Not one of the speakers is running for SBC office. It is simply designed to help contemporary Christians deal with the issues of the day.[9]

Gene Garrison, pastor, First Baptist Church, Oklahoma City, was invited to preside at the first meeting. Garrison described his hopes for SBC Forum:

I remember the day when I looked forward to the annual pastor's conference as a place for inspiration and affirmation. Recent years . . . have seen the conference become merely a revivalistic religiopolitical platform. Our program will be entirely nonpolitical and completely positive. It will provide a clear alternative for those who come to Kansas City seeking this kind of fellowship and proclamation. . . . It will not be a lot of pulpit-pounding harangue, but substantive preaching.[10]

At the time I was pastor of the Kirkwood Baptist Church in St. Louis, and chairperson of local arrangements for the meeting. I spoke to Jimmy Draper's criticism that the Forum was a "rump session" of the convention. "When the Forum is over," I said, "we will go to the convention and participate as loyal messengers from loyal churches."[11]

Six months later, on Monday, June 11, 1984, at 1:30 p.m., SBC Forum was born. For the next seven years Moderates would gather at the Forum each June to worship, pray, laugh, and weep, in hopes that a return from denominational exile might be in sight. Return from exile was not to be.

Putting on the first Forum was an exercise in great faith. Obstacles abounded. Through their master contract with the Roe Bartle Convention Center in Kansas City, the SBC retained authority over all convention facilities, including the 2,400-seat Music Hall. Even though they had no plans to use the room, the Committee on Order of Business still had to

---

[8] As cited in Ibid.
[9] As cited in Ibid.
[10] As cited in Ibid.
[11] As cited in Ibid.

release it officially before Forum planners could book it. Convention executives Harold Bennett and Tim Hedquist were extremely reluctant to allow a group competing with the Pastor's Conference to have use of the room at all. They dragged their heels.

The Committee on Order of Business, still with a Moderate majority, finally met and voted to release the space. A contract was signed. Public announcements were made. SBC Forum was going to happen.

But not without money. Cecil Sherman wrote his informal Moderate network in early March, asking them to send $100 each to me, chairperson for local arrangements, for start-up expenses.[12] All that spring funds trickled in to my office. By June 11 more than $2,000 had been raised. That $2,000 and the anticipated offering to be taken at the Forum meeting was all organizers had to cover the expected costs of the meeting.

And not without opposition. Those in positions to bring pressure to bear on program planners and participants did so persistently, and often effectively. Bobby Terry, editor of *Word and Way,* the Missouri state paper, repeatedly expressed to Forum organizers in Missouri his opinion that the meeting was unnecessary, that the Pastor's Conference presidency was winnable, and that the Forum would be counterproductive to winning the SBC presidency in Kansas City. William Jewell College president J. Gordon Kingsley, previously announced as a Forum speaker, withdrew from the program under intense pressure from Missouri Baptist Convention executive director Rheubin South.

Several other denominational executives and state paper editors warned Forum organizers they were going to "split the convention." In a letter to Moderate leaders dated March 9, 1984, Cecil Sherman described his talks with these men:

> The sense of these conversations is fear. They are afraid of us. They are afraid that we are going to be divisive, be troublesome. That we are just a group of Baptist pastors who want to get together and hear our kind of preachers is more than they can take in.[13]

Sherman concluded his letter with this prophetic note:

> I believe we can make a success of Southern Baptist Forum and the social hour. Ten years from now the very people who opposed will be attending. They will wonder why it was not always so. But in the meantime we have

---

[12]Letter from Cecil E. Sherman, 9 March 1984.
[13]Letter from Cecil Sherman, 9 March 1984.

a job to do. If we do the job well, the Moderate side of the SBC will stay in place. If we fail, they will quietly drift off, stop attending conventions, and the victory of the right wing will then be complete. Let's do a good job.[14]

Few Fundamentalists had much to say about the Forum. SBC president Jimmy Draper called the meeting "unnecessary" and warned it could set "a potentially dangerous precedent."[15]

> I would not oppose their meeting, but I don't see the need of it. We have gone to the pastor's conference and haven't found it necessary to hold any rump caucuses or out-of-the-ordinary meetings.[16]

Adrian Rogers predicted the meeting would have little impact. "They have every right to have a meeting," Rogers said. "I am sorry that they feel they have to run in competition with the pastor's conference."[17]

Thus Moderates came to Kansas City with a mixture of high hopes and gnawing fears. At breakfast Monday morning Cecil Sherman related an eerie dream that had kept him awake the night before: the Forum had happened and only 110 people had showed up! Those at the table quickly and loudly assured each other that a crowd would come. Privately, they wondered if Sherman's dream were an omen.

They quickly adjourned and went to work. The Music Hall was hard to find, so some went to post signs, directing messengers to the Forum. Others took programs to distribute throughout the halls. Ushers had to be trained, music rehearsed, and speakers tracked down. The Forum was to begin at 1:30; much remained to be done.

Meanwhile, Harold Bennett and Tim Hedquist were doing their best to dissuade messengers from even finding the Forum. They refused to allow signs to be posted directing messengers to the Music Hall, and they resisted the requests of Forum planners to distribute their programs at convention information desks. A flurry of last-minute negotiations ensued. Finally, under pressure, Bennett and Hedquist relented. The signs went up. A few minutes after 1:00 people began to trickle into the Music Hall. By 1:30 a healthy crowd had gathered. Excitement was in the air.

---

[14]Ibid.

[15]"Moderate Baptist Ministers Planning Splinter Meeting," *Tyler Morning Telegraph*, 10 March 1984, sec. 4, p. 7. (This was an Associated Press wire-service story carried throughout the nation.)

[16]As cited in ibid.

[17]As cited in Ibid.

Gene Garrison, pastor, First Baptist Church, Oklahoma City, welcomed the crowd and presided over the meeting.[18] Featured speakers for the afternoon included David Matthews, pastor of First Baptist Church, Greenville, South Carolina ("Preaching and the Sovereignty of God"); Kirby Godsey, president of Mercer University, Macon, Georgia ("The Spirit of Learning and Learning of the Spirit"); Sara Ann Hobbs ("Women As Ministers"); Duke McCall, president of Baptist World Alliance and chancellor of The Southern Baptist Theological Seminary, Louisville, Kentucky ("The Revelation We Proclaim"); and Kenneth Chafin, Carl Bates professor of preaching at Southern Seminary ("An Encouraging Word").

Dean Wilder, professor of voice at William Jewell College, Liberty, Missouri, was featured soloist for the afternoon. Lowell Dotson, minister of music at Providence Baptist Church, Charlotte, North Carolina, also sang and served as music leader.

Leading scripture readings and prayers that afternoon were Charles Wade of Texas, Raymond Langlois of Tennessee, and I of Missouri.

Program planners had planned to host a drop-in reception following the Forum at the adjacent Radisson Muehlebach Hotel, similar to the Monday evening fellowship so successful the year before in Pittsburgh. They had already reserved the Radisson's Trianon Room, one of the hotel's smaller banquet areas. Light refreshments were ordered. It was all they could afford.

By 3:00 more than 2,000 people had filled the main floor of the Music Hall and spilled over into the balconies. As Dean Wilder sang and Duke McCall preached, I and North Carolina pastors Lamar King and Keithen Tucker sat in a stairwell outside the hall, counting the offering. When we finished, we filled my briefcase with $3,000 in small bills, ran next door to the Radisson, and reserved the Grand Ballroom for that evening's reception. It was an act of radical faith!

By seven that evening the Grand Ballroom was filled to overflowing. Baptist leaders afraid to be seen earlier at the Forum flocked to the reception that night. A spirit of euphoria pervaded the room. Moderates were not as fragmented as some had suspected. People had come after all. At last we Moderates had done something right! Duke McCall called it "the biggest baby ever born at a Southern Baptist Convention."[19]

---

[18]Garrison presided at the 1984, 1985, 1986, 1987, and 1988 meetings of SBC Forum. He preached at the 1990 Forum in New Orleans.

[19]"Forum Addresses Variety of Issues," *Baptist and Reflector*, June 1984. (This was a Baptist Press story that circulated widely in state papers following the

An informal network of those behind the Kansas City meeting began immediately to plan the next Forum in Dallas. It was not long before Moderates began organizing a full-scale political challenge to convention president Charles Stanley. The Forum would be crucial to that effort. James Slatton, pastor of River Road Church, Richmond, Virginia, served as general chair for the informal steering committee. Henry Crouch, Bill Bruster, and I set to work planning the program, with Charles Wade coordinating local arrangements in Dallas.

1985

The 1985 SBC Forum was held in the West Hall of Reunion Arena, downtown Dallas. Anticipation surrounding the presidential election drew more than 40,000 messengers to the Dallas convention, and more than 5,000 to the Forum. In those days Moderates often went by the label of "denominational loyalists." As publicity chairperson for the Dallas meeting, I described the upcoming program as "pro-convention, pro-missions, pro-Cooperative Program, pro-Baptist colleges, pro-seminaries, and pro-local church."[20]

Gene Garrison, declaring he was "flattered" to be asked,[21] presided for the second time. Featured speakers included W. Randall Lolley, president, Southeastern Baptist Theological Seminary, Wake Forest, North Carolina ("Integrity in Proclaiming the Gospel"); Cecil Sherman, pastor, Broadway Baptist Church, Fort Worth, Texas ("To Trust Again"); Bill Self, pastor, Wieuca Road Baptist Church, Atlanta, Georgia ("What They Don't Teach You at a Baptist Preacher School"); and Catherine Allen, associate executive director, Woman's Missionary Union, Birmingham, Alabama ("The Doctrine of First Things"); and Walter B. Shurden, professor, Mercer University, Macon, Georgia ("The Priesthood of Believers"). Bill James of Dallas served as music director for the meeting. Guest soloists were Darrell Adams, Bill O'Brien, Cynthia Clawson, Bob Bailey, and Ken Medema.

Program planners had hoped to get CBS television news analyst Bill Moyers to speak, but his schedule prohibited. Another previously scheduled speaker was Don Harbuck, pastor of Chattanooga's First Baptist Church. His

---

convention.)

[20]News release picked up by Baptist Press and run in several state papers in the spring of 1985.

[21]"Garrison to Preside Again at Forum," *Oklahoma Baptist Messenger*, May 1985, 5.

sudden illness and untimely death caused by a brain tumor robbed the Moderate movement of one of its most insightful spokespersons and leaders.

Leading scripture readings and prayers at the Dallas meeting were E. W. McCall of California, Billy Daniels of Kentucky, and Joy Steincross of Missouri.

The successful tradition of Monday evening receptions was continued in Dallas. Moderates gathered from 7:00–10:00 in the Reunion Ballroom of the Hyatt Regency Hotel. The renewal of friendship at such receptions was an important factor in helping the Moderate movement to congeal.

Because of the intense national interest generated by the Dallas Convention, ABC News assigned correspondent Jeff Greenfield to cover the Forum for its "Nightline" broadcast. At a loss for words to describe exactly what the Forum was, Greenfield finally described it as a "preconvention caucus" for Moderates hoping to regain control of the convention the next day.

Later that same evening ABC's Ted Koppel interviewed W. A. Criswell and Cecil Sherman live from Dallas on Nightline. During the broadcast Sherman reprised the dramatic citation of a "liberal commentator" from his Forum address earlier that day. The scholar he quoted had concluded that, in the story of the plagues of Egypt, the waters of the Nile River had not actually been turned to blood; they had only appeared to be blood because the red clay lining the river banks had darkened the water. The commentary in question, which Sherman held up for millions to see, was the *Criswell Study Bible*!

To this point SBC Forum was still a meeting with only an informal organization behind it. In Dallas, initial steps were taken toward providing some organizational continuity for the Forum with the election of Charles Wade, Kenneth Chafin, Henry Crouch, Kenny Cooper, and Pete Hill to serve as a program committee for the 1986 meeting, to be held in Atlanta.

Total expenses for the Dallas Forum, the largest of all the eight meetings, came to $20,566.

1986

The third SBC Forum met Monday, June 9, 1986, in Atlanta's Omni Coliseum, adjacent to the Georgia World Congress Center, site of the Southern Baptist Convention. Gene Garrison presided. The theme for the meeting was "The Hallmarks of Baptist Heritage."

Featured speakers included Norman Cavender, layperson from First Baptist Church, Claxton, Georgia; Carolyn Weatherford, executive director, Woman's Missionary Union, Birmingham, Alabama; Bill Sherman, pastor,

Woodmont Baptist Church, Nashville, Tennessee; R. Keith Parks, president, SBC Foreign Mission Board, Richmond, Virginia; and Peter James Flamming, pastor, First Baptist Church, Richmond, Virginia, who had been scheduled to speak the year before in Dallas but had to withdraw.

Scripture readings and prayers were led by Kenny Cooper of Georgia, Pete Hill of Florida, and Bill Bruster of Texas. Joe Morrell of Tennessee was music director for the meeting.

The Atlanta Forum cost $19,909.00. After all bills were paid, organizers reported a balance of $4,000 as seed money for the St. Louis meeting in 1987.[22]

Participants at the Atlanta meeting elected a steering committee of six pastors: Charles Wade of Texas, Henry Crouch of North Carolina, Pete Hill of Florida, Ken Chafin of Kentucky, Kenny Cooper of Tennessee, and George Steincross of Missouri. They were charged with recommending a purpose and structure for the Forum to the 1987 meeting in St. Louis.

On January 12, 1987, this committee established SBC Forum, Inc. as a Texas nonprofit corporation. Officers of record were Charles Wade, president; George Steincross, vice-president; Kenneth Cooper, secretary; and Henry Crouch, treasurer. Stanley Wilkes, a layperson in Wade's church (First Baptist Church, Arlington, Texas) was the attorney of record.

1987

The fourth SBC Forum, and the first two-day meeting, was held at Kiel Auditorium opera House in downtown St. Louis, June 14–15, 1987. Gene Garrison presided. The theme was "Uniting All Things in Christ."

Featured speakers at that first Sunday evening session were Roy Honeycutt, president of The Southern Baptist Theological seminary, Louisville, Kentucky; Don Aderhold, pastor, Columbia Drive Baptist Church, Decatur, Georgia; and former First Lady Rosalyn Smith Carter of Plains, Georgia. A fellowship was held following the evening session.

Participants in the Monday morning session heard James Slatton, pastor, River Road Church, Richmond, Virginia; Nancy Hastings Sehested, associate pastor, Oakhurst Baptist Church, Decatur, Georgia; and Dan Yeary, pastor, University Baptist Church, Coral Gables, Florida.

That afternoon Fisher Humphries, professor, New Orleans Baptist Theological Seminary, New Orleans, Louisiana; Lavonn Brown, pastor, First

---

[22]Minutes of SBC Forum steering committee meeting, 13 June 1987, St. Louis.

Baptist Church, Norman, Oklahoma; and I, now pastor of First Baptist Church, Asheville, North Carolina, spoke to the gathering.

Soloists for the meeting were Jim Davis, Jim Woodward, and Jeri Graham Edmonds, all of Oklahoma, and Cynthia Clawson of Kentucky.

Expenses for the St. Louis Forum totaled $15,019. Offerings were received totaling $15,235, leaving the Steering Committee with working capital of $6,937 for the next meeting.

Among the many non-Southern Baptist observers attending SBC Forum that year was Michael D'Antonio, Pulitzer Prize-winning religion editor for *Newsday* who was working on a book about the "Christian Right." In that volume D'Antonio discusses the Forum at length, yet misinterprets it as a "counterconvention . . . running opposite SBC sessions since the beginning of the conservative power push."[23]

The Steering Committee elected in Atlanta brought four recommendations to the St. Louis gathering, all of which were adopted with only minor revisions:

1. That the SBC Forum has as its purpose: To be a gathering of Southern Baptists where, on the Sunday and Monday before the annual meeting of the Southern Baptist Convention, a loyal witness to historic Baptist principles can be sounded and where the leadership of our churches, boards, agencies, and institutions can be encouraged.
2. That we delegate to a steering committee of nine persons, who are to be rotated on a three-year term, the task of implementing the purpose of the Forum.
3. That the steering committee be nominated by a three-member nominating committee appointed by the chair of the steering committee and elected by those present at the annual SBC Forum business session.
4. That the steering committee elect its own officers, which shall be chair, chair-elect, treasurer, and secretary.[24]

The following persons were elected to serve on the new steering committee.

---

[23]Michael D'Antonio, *Fall From Grace: The Failed Crusade of the Christian Right* (New York: Farrar/Strauss/Giroux, 1989) 203. D'Antonio interviewed several persons attending the St. Louis Forum and commented at length on some of the sermons.

[24]Minutes of the Forum steering committee meeting, 13 June 1987, St. Louis.

1987–1990	1987–1989	1987–1988
Kenneth Chafin	Kenny Cooper	Nathan Stone
Henry Crouch	Pete Hill	Jon Stubblefield
Charles Wade	George Steincross	Sarah Frances Anders

George Steincross was elected to chair the committee, and Sarah Frances Anders was chosen chair-elect. Henry Crouch of North Carolina was named treasurer, and Kenny Cooper of Tennessee was elected secretary. Kenneth Chafin was assigned responsibility for the 1988 program in San Antonio. Charles Wade was placed in charge of publicity.

The St. Louis convention had witnessed the hasty and uncritical adoption of the long-awaited report of the Peace Committee. Included in the Peace Committee's report was a recommendation specifically directed toward the Forum and the Pastor's Conference (recommendation 9):

> We recommend that the leadership of the Pastor's Conference and the SBC Forum take immediate steps to explore the possibility of 'getting together' in ways that will enhance and promote our mutually strong beliefs as expressed in the Baptist Faith and Message statement.[25]

The Forum Steering Committee made several good-faith efforts to implement the Peace Committee recommendation. George Steincross, pastor, Second Baptist Church, Liberty, Missouri, and Forum steering committee chair, wrote Stan Coffey, pastor, San Jacinto Baptist Church, Amarillo, Texas, and Pastor's Conference president, on August 18, 1987. The letter included an invitation to explore the possibility of "getting together," as called for in the Peace Committee Report. Steincross wrote:

> I am . . . taking the initiative . . . because of the Southern Baptist Convention action and as evidence of our willingness to comply. . . . The entire Baptist Faith and Message statement incorporates a balance of our "mutually strong beliefs" and a preconvention meeting of varied expressions of faith should be fruitful.[26]

Coffey waited two months to reply. In his letter of October 22 he ignored Steincross's invitation, choosing instead to "welcome back" all previous Forum participants to the Pastor's Conference. Coffey concluded:

---

[25]"Report of the Peace Committee," published as a separate pamphlet and mailed to all SBC pastors.

[26]Letter from George W. Steincross (pastor, Second Baptist Church, Liberty, Missouri) 18 Aug 1987.

It would seem that from the overwhelming response we have had to the Pastor's Conference in the last four or five years and the decline in attendance at the Forum meeting in St. Louis last year that the merger of our two groups is already in progress. . . . This will be the historic 53rd such annual meeting of Southern Baptist Pastors and I believe it would be in keeping with the spirit of the Peace Committee recommendation for all of us to gather in one great convocation.[27]

Steincross responded on November 6, 1987. "You have misunderstood the intent of my letter," he wrote. "It was not requesting permission to come 'back' to the Pastor's Conference. Rather, it was for us to comply with the Peace Committee's adopted recommendation that we get together and explore possibilities."[28] Steincross again requested a joint meeting of Pastor's Conference officers and the Forum Steering Committee. Coffey did not respond to the second letter.

On January 8, 1988, Steincross wrote Peace Committee Chairman Charles Fuller:

I am enclosing my correspondence on behalf of the SBC Forum steering committee with Stan Coffey and the Southern Baptist Pastor's Conference. This is for your files in documenting the SBC Forum's futile attempt to fulfill recommendation nine of the adopted Peace Committee recommendations. A perceptive reading of this correspondence indicates a rather accurate reflection of the dilemma of our denomination.[29]

Steincross asked Fuller for advice and counsel as the Forum steering committee prepared to make a specific proposal. Fuller did not respond.

The Forum steering committee met February 1, 1988, and proposed a specific plan for fulfilling recommendation number 9. They suggested a combined program with the Pastor's Conference in 1989, with program leadership representing segments of the SBC as reflected in the vote for convention president at the 1988 meeting to be held in San Antonio. Program speakers would be requested to refrain from negative comments about activities in SBC life. The effort would be to have "high moments of biblical preaching and inspiration applying God's Holy Word to Southern

---

[27]Letter from Stan Coffey (pastor, San Jacinto Baptist Church, Amarillo, Texas) 22 Oct 1987.

[28]Letter from George W. Steincross, 6 Nov 1987.

[29]Letter from George W. Steincross, 8 Jan 1988.

Baptist life."[30] Steincross wrote Coffey on February 4 detailing this proposal.
He concluded:

> If I do not hear from you by March 1, 1988, I will assume you do not
> desire to accept the above proposal or fulfillment of recommendation #9
> of the adopted report of the Peace Committee.[31]

Coffey never replied. On March 10, 1988, the Forum steering committee
announced that its "peace initiatives" had been disregarded by the Pastor's
Conference."[32] In a second letter to Peace Committee chairman Charles
Fuller, dated March 10, 1988, Steincross stated:

> I regret that the Pastor's Conference has sensed no need to do what the
> Southern Baptist Convention recommended. It seems to me that such
> arrogance has caused our denomination to experience the dilemma we now
> face. I'm referring to the fact that the *Pastor's Conference took no
> initiative at all to fulfill recommendation #9 nor was the Pastor's Confer-
> ence willing to have conversation in general terms or reply to a specific
> proposal toward fulfilling recommendation #9.*[33]

Fuller, like Coffey, had never responded to Steincross, for Steincross wrote
him again an May 17 as follows:

> It is a mystery to me and the SBC Forum steering committee the reasons
> you have for not responding to any of the correspondence. . . . It is now
> apparent the Peace Committee has not placed on its agenda any consider-
> ation of the Pastors' Conference being unwilling to fulfill recommendation
> #9.[34]

Fuller telephoned Steincross after receiving the May 17 letter. He assured
Steincross that the Forum/Pastor's Conference situation would be addressed
by the Peace Committee, although he declined to say what the outcome
would be.[35]

As late as April of that year, the Forum Steering Committee was still
hopeful that Texas pastor Paul Powell might be elected president of the

---

[30]Letter from George W. Steincross, 4 Feb 1988.

[31]Ibid.

[32]Press release issued by George W. Steincross, 10 March 1988.

[33]Letter from George W. Steincross, 10 March 1988.

[34]Letter from George W. Steincross, 17 May 1988.

[35]Memorandum from George W. Steincross to SBC Forum steering committee,
dated between 17 May and 11 June 1988.

Pastor's Conference in San Antonio, greatly improving the chances for the two groups to get together in one meeting in 1989.[36]

1988

The fifth SBC Forum was held June 12–13, 1988, at Trinity Baptist Church, San Antonio, Texas. The theme was "Contending For An Authentic Faith." Gene Garrison again presided.

Featured speakers at the Sunday evening session included Bill Leonard, professor of church history, Southern Baptist Theological Seminary, Louisville, Kentucky; Libby Bellinger, chaplain, Inner City Ministry, Waco, Texas; and Anthony Campolo, professor, Eastern College, St. Davids, Pennsylvania.

Monday morning participants heard Alan Neely, professor, Southeastern Baptist Theological Seminary, Wake Forest, North Carolina; Mildred McWhorter, director of Baptist Centers, Houston, Texas; and Winfred Moore, pastor, First Baptist Church, Amarillo, Texas.

The soloist was Billy Crockett. Choral music was provided by the sanctuary choir of Trinity Baptist Church.

Scripture readings and prayers were offered by Stephen Graham of Oklahoma, Timothy Norman of Virginia, Douglas Watterson of Tennessee, George Mason of Alabama, Eugene Bolin of New York, and Lee Berg of Texas.

In San Antonio the Steering Committee began a new annual tradition—honoring individual denominational leaders and local congregations with "Statesperson of the Year" and "Church of the Year" awards. That year Charles Wade announced the first recipient of the Church of the Year Award—the North Phoenix Baptist Church of North Phoenix, Arizona, where Moderate presidential candidate Richard Jackson was pastor. Wade presented the award to Bill Williams, president of Arizona's Grand Canyon College and a deacon of the church.

Cecil Sherman presented the Denominational Statesperson Award to W. Randall Lolley, the former president of Southeastern Baptist Theological Seminary who had resigned in protest of actions taken by his Fundamentalist trustee board.

---

[36]Minutes of SBC Forum steering committee, 11 June 1988, San Antonio, Texas, 1.

Three new members were elected to three-year terms on the steering committee: Glenda Fontenot of Texas, Bill Self of Georgia, and Cecil Sherman of Texas. Peter Rhea Jones of Georgia was elected to complete the unexpired term of Sarah Frances Anders, who resigned. Jones was also elected to chair the steering committee. Jon Stubblefield of Louisiana was chosen as chair-elect. Cecil Sherman was named treasurer. Bill Self was elected secretary.

No Monday evening reception was held in San Antonio, a disappointment to many Moderates in town for the convention. Expenses for the San Antonio meeting totaled $8,593, but offerings were received in excess of $10,000, leaving the Steering Committee with a cash balance of $15,038. Members voted to donate $3,000 to *SBC Today* as an expression of support for their current subscription campaign.[37]

1989

The 1989 Forum convened June 12, 1989, at the Theatre of the Cashman Field Complex in Las Vegas, Nevada. The theme was "The Priesthood of the Believer, the Preaching of the Gospel." Peter Rhea Jones presided.

Though the Steering Committee decided against a Sunday evening session, choosing instead to throw its full energies into the two Monday sessions, attendance was disappointing. This was due most likely to the lack of advance publicity, the remote location of the meeting several miles north of downtown, and the unfamiliarity of messengers with the city. The Monday evening reception drew fewer than 200 people.

Featured speakers included Molly Marshall-Green, professor, The Southern Baptist Theological Seminary, Louisville, Kentucky; Brian Harbour, pastor, Immanuel Baptist Church, Little Rock, Arkansas; Fred Craddock, professor, candler school of Theology, Atlanta, Georgia; Clyde Fant, dean of the chapel and professor, Stetson University, DeLand, Florida; and Robert Schuller, pastor, Crystal Cathedral, Garden Grove, California.

Bob Bailey and Cynthia Clawson were soloists. The Southern Seminary Vocal Ensemble also sang. Al Staggs, pastor of First Baptist Church, Portales, New Mexico, presented a dramatization of the testimony of Dietrich Bonhoeffer. Prayers and scripture readings were offered by Tom Starkes of Nevada, Michael Fuhrman of Missouri, Ches Smith of Georgia, Phil Line-

---

[37]Minutes of annual meeting, SBC Forum, Inc. board of directors, 13 June 1988, San Antonio, Texas.

berger of Texas, and Jon Stubblefield of Louisiana. The evening reception featured a concert by Bailey and Clawson.

The Church of the Year Award was presented to the Uptown Baptist Church in Chicago, Illinois, pastored by Jim Queen. WMU Executive Director Carolyn Weatherford was honored as recipient of the Denominational Statesperson Award.

Three new members were elected to three-year terms on the Steering Committee: Gene Garrison of Oklahoma, Molly Marshall-Green of Kentucky, and Ray Spence of Virginia. Jon M. Stubblefield of Louisiana was elected chairperson. Cecil Sherman was named treasurer.

Expenses for the Las Vegas Forum totaled $13,117, leaving the Steering Committee with a working balance of $6,338.38.[38]

1990

The seventh annual meeting of SBC Forum convened at the historic Saenger Theater in New Orleans on Monday, June 11, 1990, under the theme, "Recapturing the Future." Jon Stubblefield presided. Thomas Stoker, minister of music at Broadway Baptist Church, Fort Worth, Texas, designed and led the worship segments. Lynda Poston-Smith and Robert C. Smith provided sacred music.

Preliminary conversations had been held the previous summer with Bill Moyers about debating Paul Pressler at the New Orleans meeting. Pressler had delivered a tirade against Moyers at the SBC Executive Committee; the Executive Committee then refused Moyers's request to respond. Jerry Vardaman, an archaeology professor at Mississippi State University, wrote Moyers and Forum steering committee members about the idea. The idea was short-lived, since Moyers quickly declined the invitation:

> I've thought about it and decided not to press the issue at a public forum. The issues are larger than Moyers vs. Pressler and I think it's best to fight on another front. But I'm grateful for your spirited support of the idea.[39]

Featured speakers in New Orleans included Gene Garrison, pastor, First Baptist Church, Oklahoma City, Oklahoma; John Killinger, professor, Samford University, Birmingham, Alabama; Herbert Reynolds, president, Baylor University, Waco, Texas; Randall Lolley, pastor, First Baptist Church, Greensboro, North Carolina; Carolyn Weatherford Crumpler, former

---

[38]Summary of account, Summit National Bank, Fort Worth, 1 Oct 1989.
[39]Letter from Bill Moyers to Jerry Vardaman, 1 Aug 1989.

executive director, Woman's Missionary Union; and Frank Pollard, pastor, First Baptist Church, Jackson, Mississippi.

Prayers and scripture readings were led by David Allen Farmer of Louisiana, H. Stephen Shoemaker of Kentucky, Bobby Guffey of Louisiana and Randall O'Brien of Arkansas.

Pollard's congregation was recognized as recipient of the Church of the Year award. Since no denominational leaders remaining in the employ of the SBC were thought to possess sufficiently statespersonlike qualities, Cecil Sherman, pastor of Broadway Baptist Church, Fort Worth, was honored with the first (and last) "Prophet of the Year" Award. As Sherman's successor at First Baptist Church, Asheville, North Carolina, I made the presentation.[40]

David Montoya, a student at Southwestern Seminary and former Arkansas pastor, brought a brief word of testimony to the Forum about his experiences as a "field worker" in the Fundamentalist movement and his pilgrimage beyond Fundamentalism. The meeting adjourned with an invitation to the 1991 Forum in Atlanta.

Three new members were elected to the Steering Committee: Jann Clanton of Texas, and Richard Groves and I of North Carolina. I was elected chairperson. Cecil Sherman was again named treasurer.

Expenses for the 1990 Forum totaled approximately $10,000.00.

The next day Moderates suffered a series of resounding defeats on the convention floor. Fundamentalist candidate Morris Chapman was overwhelmingly elected convention president. Jerry Vines taunted Moderates in his presidential address, ridiculing their pastors and churches. When Moderates gathered Wednesday morning at the Baptists Committed breakfast, their mood had changed. No longer were their leaders urging the troops to "charge up the hill one more time" the following year in Atlanta. The emerging consensus was that the organized political resistance which had claimed their time, energy, and money since 1981 had failed. Many of those present vowed never again to attend a Southern Baptist Convention. It was time for a new approach.

At that breakfast Moderate presidential candidate Daniel Vestal of Georgia asked the various Moderate groups who had supported his candidacy to call a meeting for the purpose of considering future options for non-Funda-

---

[40]The Forum steering committee had wanted to present the award to Sherman at the Las Vegas meeting the year before. To their disappointment, Sherman did not attend the Las Vegas convention or any of its ancillary meetings.

mentalist Southern Baptists. Leaders left New Orleans expecting to gather later that summer to sort out options and devise some plan for the future.

Thirty days later the SBC Executive Committee gathered in Nashville and fired Baptist Press editors Alvin Shackleford and Dan Martin. The meeting of 200–300 Moderate leaders planned for August in Atlanta rapidly grew to become a national gathering for much of the Moderate movement.

In August 1990, 3,000 Moderates packed Atlanta's downtown Inforum for the "Consultation of Concerned Baptists." Participants elected an interim steering committee, chaired by Daniel Vestal, to guide the new organization, loosely identified as "The Fellowship," in the months between the August meeting and the organizing convocation planned for the following May in Atlanta.

As Forum steering committee chairperson I presided at one of the Inforum sessions, was elected a member of the interim steering committee, and later was named cochair of the committee planning the May convocation. I make this point to underscore the fact that the SBC Forum was considered a vital part of the Moderate Movement. As news spread about that May meeting of Moderates, I and others on the Forum Steering Committee concluded that most Moderates were coming to Atlanta in May, not June. We felt the new Fellowship Convocation would best fulfill the purpose and function for which SBC Forum had been originally founded.

After much discussion, the Steering committee voted to dissolve SBC Forum, Inc., cancel the annual meeting, and transfer any remaining assets to the fledgling Fellowship for the expense of its annual convocation.

However, since the Forum had been incorporated in 1987, any dissolution of the corporation legally had to be enacted by the "membership," that is, whoever showed up at the 1991 meeting. Therefore, on the advice of counsel, I issued public announcements in April that one last meeting of SBC Forum would be held the day before the Southern Baptist Convention in Atlanta, for the express purpose of dissolving the organization.

1991

The eighth and final SBC Forum convened Monday afternoon, June 4, 1991, in the chapel at Wieuca Road Baptist Church, Atlanta. Worship leaders included Carolyn Cole Bucy of Texas, past president of Southern Baptist Women in Ministry, and I as music director. Approximately 250 participants heard Dan Martin, former news editor of Baptist Press, tell the story of his dismissal by the Executive Committee the summer before. Having been elected as the moderator of the newly constituted Cooperative Baptist Fellowship three weeks earlier, I presented an overview of the birth of CBF.

I then presented the resolution of dissolution to the membership. After lengthy discussion, the resolution was adopted along with the request that the Fellowship continue a "presence" at future Southern Baptist Conventions for Moderates still obligated to attend.

Thus, in the summer of 1991, the corporation of SBC Forum was legally dissolved. All remaining funds were transferred to CBF as a designated gift for the 1992 general assembly in Fort Worth. SBC Forum was no more.

What did SBC Forum accomplish? Three things, at least.

First, the Forum did provide SBC messengers a clear and distinct alternative to other preconvention meetings, particularly the Pastor's Conference. It was "our kind of program," they said. It offered preaching and worship of a different style and substance than that showcased at the Pastor's Conference and on the convention platform. It clearly met a need.

Second, the Forum gave Moderate messengers unexcited about another Fundamentalist-dominated convention at least one good reason to come to the convention city. Though it never stooped to the level of the Pastor's Conference in using its program to anoint presidential candidates, the Forum did provide the Moderate political network a point of contact with messengers coming to vote. It became the public face of the Moderate political movement at the annual convention.

Third, SBC Forum spoke a consistent word of hope and promise to dispirited people during dark days. Among the reasons Moderates kept finding strength to "run up the hill one more time" was the good news echoed at each year's Forum. Moderates found free and faithful Baptists at the Forum, who shared their own commitments to historic Baptist distinctives and were committed to the restoration of those ideas within the life of the Southern Baptist Convention. SBC Forum helped to keep free Baptist hopes alive.

In reality, SBC Forum was the precursor to the General Assembly of the new Cooperative Baptist Fellowship. It provided a meeting place for Baptist people, a platform for Baptist ideas, and hopeful structure for a Baptist future. It was, therefore, most appropriate that SBC Forum die that the Cooperative Baptist Fellowship might live.

The History
of Baptists Committed

Jimmy R. Allen

At the height of the cold war, Senator William Fulbright made a classic foreign policy speech which he called "Old Myths and New Realities." When one examines the Southern Baptist experience during the years 1979–1990 from any of the perspectives of the Moderate Movement, that title fits us. As captives of old myths, we have had to move to new realities. This may be the common denominator of all the various Moderate Baptist responses to the Fundamentalist takeover. Baptists Committed in its various stages and forms was born out of this painful adjustment of facing these new realities.

1980–1984: Preludes of Awakening

The Old Myth of "Family Style Politics"

Before the 1979 Southern Baptist Convention in Houston, Texas, Southern Baptist politics were those of a family of faith centering on personalities rather than precinct organization with a narrow exclusive agenda of divisiveness. Shortly after concluding my term as president of the Southern Baptist Convention in 1979, I assumed agency leadership of the Radio and Television Commission. In the first Inter-Agency Retreat in the spring of 1980, I took it on myself to describe this changing strategy to the heads of all the agencies and point out that such a precinct activity by the Paul Pressler faction was directly threatening to all we were doing.

Something needed to be done in concert by agency leaders to alert our people to the threat. The Retreat was at Stone Mountain, Georgia, in May before the St. Louis convention of 1980 at which Bailey Smith was elected president of the convention. Carolyn Weatherford, head of the Woman's Missionary Union, happened to be presiding at that session. When I finished my description of these events, it was so unthinkable for agency heads to enter into partisan political activity that there was a dead silence, and then a closing prayer.

In that atmosphere the idea of organized and open political structure was hard to come by among us. This was true of the Fundamentalists who kept loudly and consistently denying the nature of their precinct enlistment activities. It was true as the Gatlinburg meeting began its political networking group.[1] It was true in the activities that preceded the going-public of the Moderate effort in the structure of Baptists Committed.

From 1981 through 1984, Moderates kept at their failed vision of the nature of politics, searched for an adequate terminology to call themselves, and failed again and again to win. Some knew hard work and time were needed. For instance, Clifford Johnston of Arlington, Texas, a former pastor, agreed in 1984 to work full-time on the issue through telephone and travel. Money was secured by private gifts through Foy Valentine and several others (including myself) to pay Johnston's expenses for work in favor of the candidacy of Grady Cothen in the Kansas City convention. It was too little, too late, too filled with old family-style political competition, and it failed dramatically.

The Old Myth of Simple Changing of the Guard

The complacency factor faced by all of us centered in the idea that there is always an adjustment to be made in the changing of the guard. We were told by our political pundits that this too would pass. Responsibility would temper the extremist goals of exclusion. It would right itself. The pernicious and persistent commitment of Fundamentalists living up to the nature of their worldview was ignored because few could really believe that secular political methods had been adopted and applied.

1984–1988: New Realities

The 1984 Convention created an awareness that sparked action. One of these was a new energy of the political networks which had been functioning beneath the surface to secure the candidacy of Winfred Moore for the SBC presidency. The informal meetings and telephone consultations took on new energy. Some agency heads became more vocal. The announced formation of a political action organization publicly was still rejected but an intense

---

[1][Editor's note: Regarding the Gatlinburg meeting, see Sherman's paper, "An Overview of the Moderate Movement," above.]

activity was engendered in the loose coalitions that had been formed. Larry McSwain of Southern Baptist Seminary was performing good work in this process. Cecil Sherman had energized the considerable network with which he was in touch. Every state was enlisted with the genuine hope of victory. The Dallas convention was both a high moment and a killing blow to those hopes.

The Formation of the *Baptist Laity Journal* in 1985

This was the time when public activity became more a part of the Moderate reality. The *Baptist Laity Journal* was formed by John Baugh with a board of interested Baptist laymen. It had Owen Cooper of Mississippi, a former president of the Southern Baptist Convention, as chairman of the board. John Jeter Hurt, then editor of the *Baptist Standard*, the state Baptist paper of Texas, was its editorial consultant. The editor was Neal Rodgers.

From its inception the journal had a national edition as it sought to interest laity in the issues. It also published a Texas edition.

This publication represented one aspect of the Moderate response to the takeover challenge. It went through several name changes for its body of participants. They were called "Laymen for the Cooperative Program" with a steering committee formed in an Atlanta meeting on January 23, 1986. This name was changed to "Laity for the Baptist Faith and Message" in the fall of 1986.

Board members of this organization were national in scope. Included in addition to Baugh and Cooper of Texas and Mississippi were James E. Carter, Phoenix, Arizona; Shad Medlin, El Dorado, Arkansas; C. Vaughan Pippen, Baltimore, Maryland; E. R. Brown, Deridder, Louisiana; Norman Cavender, Claxton, Georgia; J. Nixon Daniel II, Pensacola, Florida; Christine Gregory, Danville, Virginia; George Miller, Oklahoma City, Oklahoma; J. T. Luther, Jr., Fort Worth, Texas; Anita Seay Bass, Lubbock, Texas; and Milton Morales, Independence, Missouri. Attorney for the group and secretary of the board was P. Oswin Chrisman of Dallas.

In September 1986 an open appeal was made by laymen Maston Courtney, Judge Connally McKay, Dewey Presley, and John Baugh to meet in a series of public meetings for the purpose of restoring fellowship. This invitation was given to Drs. Criswell, Draper, Rogers, Smith, and Stanley.

Spurned in that attempt, they held public meetings in Dallas February 3, and in Fort Worth November 9, 1987. Following the convention in San Antonio in 1988, this organization was transformed into the nucleus of "Baptists Committed to the Southern Baptist Convention," popularly known as "Baptists Committed." This was formally done in a meeting in December

1988 at the Dallas-Fort Worth Airport. Participants included Winfred Moore, Norman Cavender, and James Slatton. Winfred Moore was named chair of "Baptists Committed to the SBC."

"Laity for the Baptist Faith and Message" was absorbed in the Baptists Committed organization. Publication of the *Baptist Laity Journal* was suspended. A national office was opened in Houston in January 1989. The 501(c)3 [eleemosynary] status was transferred to Baptists Committed.

The first state chapter of Baptists Committed was formed in Atlanta, Georgia, on April 7, 1989. The next week, April 13, the Texas chapter was organized. Chairman Winfred Moore stated on March 28, 1989:

> Baptists Committed to the SBC is an organization committed to returning our convention to its historic basis of cooperation in missions, evangelism, and education, thus ending this ten-year period of disunity.

The new organization had David Currie of San Angelo as its first staff person. His title was field coordinator. Oeita Bottorff of Houston was project director.

The structure of the organization consisted of an executive committee, board of directors, and advisory board. Included on its executive board were Marion Aldridge, South Carolina; Alfred Ayscue, North Carolina; John F. Baugh, Texas; Norman Cavender, Georgia; Stephen D. Graham, Oklahoma; Charles Horton, Florida; John E. Hughes, Missouri; Randall Lolley, North Carolina; Donald Mantooth, Kentucky; Winfred Moore, Texas; Howard G. Olive, Tennessee; David Sapp, Georgia; Cecil Sherman, Texas; James H. Slatton, Virginia; Clifton R. Tennison, Louisiana; Steve Tondera, Alabama; Charles Wade, Texas; and James F. Yates, Mississippi.

1989–1990: The Ultimate Reality

The defeat of the candidacy of Daniel Vestal in Las Vegas was one on which I have only secondhand information. After failing to persuade the Radio and Television Commission board to sell the ACTS network to a group of private investors and thus free it from Fundamentalist control, I resigned and was not in Las Vegas. I was so impressed, however, that the Moderate candidacy did so much better than I had predicted that I called Dan Vestal and told him I was willing to help in any way I could if he decided to run again. Freed of the yoke of agency limitations on public behavior, I could do more openly what I had been working at for ten years in the Fundamentalist takeover struggle.

In November 1989 Winfred Moore decided he could no longer be chair of Baptists Committed. Jim Slatton, vice-chair, called to ask me to take that responsibility. I agreed and was elected in a meeting at DFW Airport, November 16, 1989. Winfred Moore became honorary chairman and continued on the board.

The organization was structured into four committees: Finance and Budget, Operations, Legal Affairs, and Editorial. Task forces were implemented: WMU, seminaries, universities. Six field coordinators were made responsible for statewide organizations. A speakers bureau was formed. The candidacy of Daniel Vestal in New Orleans became the major objective. At the end of 1989 Baptists Committed had revenue totaling $239,884 and expenses totaling $235,380. Revenues came from gifts and memberships. A fund-raising meeting in Dallas on November 15, 1989 was hosted by Vester Hughes, Dallas attorney. Speakers were John Baugh, Daniel Vestal, Phil Strickland, and Winfred Moore.

In April 1989 Baptists Committed sponsored Baptist Heritage Rallies. In May 1989 Baptists Committed sponsored a symposium in Nashville with 150 leaders from over the nation. Messages were delivered by Daniel Vestal, Winfred Moore, Bill Sherman, John Baugh, David Sapp, Leon Smith, James Dunn, Russell Dilday, and Marion Aldridge.

In June we were to discover how vain these efforts were with the overwhelming defeat of Daniel Vestal in the New Orleans convention. The ultimate reality had arrived. There was to be no political solution to the problem faced by Baptists who valued their heritage, believed in unity in the midst of diversity, and wanted to do missions in the manner God had blessed with one of the foremost mission programs in the world.

1990–1991: New Reality in New Direction

The night of Vestal's defeat in New Orleans, Daniel Vestal and Jim Dennison, pastor of First Baptist Church, Midland, Texas, came to my hotel room. We had now had hours to absorb the fact of defeat. A Baptists Committed breakfast was scheduled for the next morning.

As Daniel Vestal was searching for direction along with all of us, I told him I knew of nothing else to do except to call Southern Baptist leaders to a consultation on the future. I offered to put the resources of Baptists Committed into that effort if he chose to issue the call. Since I had considerable experience in building meetings in the Astrodome, I knew it would be a major task to make the meeting a meaningful one in three months, between June and August. The suggestion was that we convene SBC leaders, perhaps three hundred. Upon discussion, the idea was to make it an open call. The next morning, Daniel did an excellent job of placing the challenge before us at a Baptists Committed breakfast meeting on June 13, 1990. Attendance at the breakfast exceeded 800. We set to work.

Oeita Bottorff is a masterful organizer. Our Baptists Committed board voted to support the effort wholeheartedly. We put in long hours and days in creating the meeting over which I was to preside. Between June and the August 1990 meeting of three thousand and the May 1991 meeting of eight thousand, the Baptists Committed network worked. We put more than $150,000 into the effort. However, the money was not the important element. Hundreds worked to make it work. Jack Harwell and *Baptists Today* worked hard and well in this effort. Each of the Moderate groups of Southern Baptists saw it as a meeting worthy of promotion and participation. Few will ever imagine the gratitude we should feel for the skills and energy of Oeita Bottorff in enlisting and organizing the meeting. Much has been said about three thousand showing up for a meeting designed to draw three hundred. But it was no accident. In the providence of God, we had the right people in the right place for Him to perform His healing and empowering to create the birth of the most positive development in Southern Baptist life in a decade.

Shortly after my return home from New Orleans, the telephone rang and Duke McCall was saying, "Jimmy, if we come to Atlanta and don't have a positive structure legally in place to put at the disposal of the people, we'll stumble and talk and not create." Of course, he was right. He had already conferred with his attorney son and others about the steps to take. Then he gave the news: "I'm leaving for China and don't have time to put this together. Could you do it?"[2]

Over the next few weeks by telephone and conference, I found what the depth of commitment was in a group of people in whom we could have confidence. They were ready to form the Baptist Cooperative Mission Program, Inc. They were like a Who's Who of Southern Baptist leadership: Grady Cothen, Florida (chairman); Duke McCall, North Carolina (vice-chair); Frances Prince, Tennessee (secretary), John Baugh, Texas; Raymond Boswell, Louisiana; Lavonn Brown, Oklahoma; Harold Cole, South Carolina; Carolyn Weatherford Crumpler, Ohio; Drew Gunnells, Alabama; Ophelia Humphrey, Texas; Randall Lolley, North Carolina; Esther G.

---

[2][Editor's note: McCall had reference to the formation of what came to be know as the BCMP, the legal funding mechanism for what came to be the Cooperative Baptist Fellowship. See McCall's "The History of the Baptist Cooperative Missions Program," below.]

McCall, Missouri; John R. McCall, Kentucky; Darold Morgan, Texas; William E. Poe, North Carolina; Gene A. Triggs, Mississippi; and Brooks Wicker, Florida.

BCMP, Inc. began its work with the idea of merging with whatever organization was formed. It provided immediate access to a method of missions. It completed its work and became a part of the Cooperative Baptist Fellowship on April 1, 1992.

New Reality: The Future

Baptists Committed early on decided that its task was to assure the existence and usefulness of this new missions tool for Moderate Southern Baptists. In a September 1990 column for the Baptists Committed newsletter, I sought to describe our objective:

> Shortly after the Consultation, the Baptists Committed Executive Committee held a teleconference. The discussion of the "Fellowship" and its future led to a positive commitment to help support Dan Vestal's leadership in helping us discover God's leadership in the days ahead. Baptists Committed stands ready to dismantle itself or to accept any role of positive contribution which emerges in the process of restoring trust and accelerating the mission toward which God is guiding us.

The Fellowship became the Cooperative Baptist Fellowship. The structure was open and inclusive. The passion for Baptist principles had a place for development and expression. The channel for mission expression was made ready. Other aspects of the Christian fellowship including theological education, ethics and public policy, the laity, the production of religious education materials, and the opportunity for inclusive fellowship was in place. In short, the Baptists Committed structure had fulfilled its mission. The executive board of Baptists Committed acted on June 1, 1992, to merge Baptists Committed with the Cooperative Baptist Fellowship.

One aspect of merging Baptists Committed at the national level is the status of state organizations. In several of the states, the old Baptists Committed organizations have changed their names to Cooperative Baptist Fellowship organizations. They continue to do political activities because a great deal is at stake for Moderate Southern Baptists in their state programs and institutions. In some states such as North Carolina, the organization cooperating with Baptists Committed never was called by that name. It has always been Friends of Missions. It remains so. It functions just as Baptists Committed in other states. It has also become the center of Cooperative Baptist Fellowship activities.

In Texas, the Baptists Committed organization is the functioning unit of Cooperative Baptist Fellowship. Many of the churches who have not yet declared themselves through Cooperative Baptist Fellowship funding channels are committed to Moderate control of their state convention. They work hard on that issue and are a part of the Baptists Committed organization. Baylor University president Herbert Reynolds has been an active leader in Baptists Committed from its beginning. There is considerable force in Baylor University alumni and friends. These cooperate with other Moderate Southern Baptists for the sake of common cause. The Baptists Committed network in Texas with its committed workers and activities centered on the decision to support Baylor University's altered relationship with the Baptist General Convention of Texas. David Currie, formerly field director for national Baptists Committed, serves as coordinator for Texas Baptists Committed. He assists in organizing Moderates to resist the Fundamentalist takeover at the state convention of Texas. Issues such as the level of Baylor funding and methods of missions are under constant attack by the Fundamentalist faction in Texas. The 60/40 vote in favor of the Moderate cause at the 1991 Texas convention was assured and predicted by Baptists Committed zone leaders at the annual session of the convention. The Moderate cause nationally has been greatly served by Herbert Reynolds as president of Baylor University. This relationship demonstrates a model for our colleges and universities as they resist the Fundamentalist takeover. The challenge is now for Moderate Southern Baptists to maintain a close working partnership within these institutions of higher learning as part of the strategy of the new reality.

Conclusion

The new realities are welcomed. Baptists Committed members have been merging gladly into the new process. We are glad to see attitudes changing, positive purposes emerging, and hurts and angers being set aside. The call is to the future. It is time for us to "forget those things that are behind and press forward to those things that are ahead." The new realities are welcomed. We are coming back to our future.

The History
of the Alliance of Baptists

Alan Neely

Francis Parkman once wrote that being truthful in the writing of history "involves far more than a research, however patient and scrupulous, into special facts. Such facts may be detailed with the most minute exactness," Parkman said, "and yet the narrative, taken as a whole, may be unmeaning or untrue."[1] Those who have read much of what has been written about the Southern Baptist Convention during the past dozen years know the accuracy and validity of Parkman's observation.

Writing history, however, is not just *reproducing* what happened. Writing history rather is trying to *reconstruct* what happened. This means that in the process of trying to recover and tell the story, some things that happened inevitably fall between the cracks while other gaps that appear important to the historian are filled in—not always correctly. Although there is no surefire formula for avoiding mistakes, the best means available is for the historian to consult with those who were firsthand witnesses, examine any written accounts they may have maintained (journals, letters, and notes), cross-check the sources, and peruse the official records or minutes, provided such documentation exists.

In writing this historical account I have tried to utilize all of these methods. On the one hand, I was amazed during my research by the abundance of many details of crucial conversations and events that I had

---

[1] [Editor's note: This observation is from Parkman's introduction to his *Pioneers of France in the New World* (1865). Francis Parkman (1823–1893) was an American historian whose *realistic* Indians no one liked because they did not look like James Fenimore Cooper's Indians.]

completely forgotten. On the other hand, I was equally surprised how quickly myths get started and how only by appealing to the records can misunderstandings be corrected.

Some readers may wonder if I have dredged up all these individual and composite recollections for less-than-noble reasons. This is not my intention, for I believe we are responsible *for* each other and *to* each other, and I have tried to represent what took place as best I can.

There is an old Talmudic anecdote about two men crossing a large body of water in a small boat. Suddenly one of them takes out his knife and begins to bore a hole in the bottom of the craft. The second man, shocked by what he is seeing, says, "What are you doing?"

"I'm boring a hole."

"Boring a hole? My heavens, don't do that!"

"Tend to your own business," the man with the knife replied. "I'm boring a hole under *my* seat, not yours."

Rightly or wrongly, in 1979 or shortly thereafter, many of us became convinced that some of our fellow travelers had began boring a hole in the SBC boat, the only denominational vessel in which most of us had ever traveled. We began to protest. This account of the beginnings and subsequent developments in the Alliance is simply the story of one group that organized to protest. We had hardly gotten together, however, when we realized we were being called to a mission far more comprehensive and possibly more significant than protesting. Discerning that mission has been a collective, not an individual pilgrimage.

Some Embarrassing History

During my last year in high school and shortly after I had told members of my family that I was planning to enter the ministry—"surrender to the call to preach" in Texas parlance—I received a letter from one of my uncles who lived in Nashville, Tennessee. Uncle Fancher was for years an active member and deacon in the Belmont Heights Baptist Church in that city. He wrote to congratulate me on the decision I had made, and he told me how proud my grandfather John Thomas Sargent (1855–1935) would have been were he still alive. Grandfather during his entire adult life was a Mississippi bivocational farmer and Baptist preacher. Along with his letter Uncle

Fancher enclosed a small booklet which he said he hoped I would read. It was entitled *The Trail of Blood* and was written by J. M. Carroll.[2]

I am sure Uncle Fancher meant well, but the reading of Carroll's "history" of Baptists messed up my mind for several years because I had no background for evaluating the historical validity of Carroll's claim to have traced our Baptist lineage back through the Reformation, the Middle Ages, and the first-century church to John *the Baptist.*

I mention the incident because *The Trail of Blood,* patently false as history, is—whether we like it or not—a part of our Southern Baptist heritage. This should not be forgotten because *The Trail of Blood* is indisputable evidence that some of our ancestors, in ignorance or knowingly, distorted the historical record. Also, and perhaps more important for this study, *The Trail of Blood* should be remembered because it was one of the principal documents used to support Landmarkism. No historical or doctrinal aberration, I believe, affected Southern Baptist thinking more during the nineteenth century—and still shapes Southern Baptist ecclesiology, especially in the Southwest—than that of Landmarkism.

What were the teachings of J. R. Graves, J. M. Pendleton, A. C. Dayton—a dentist converted from Presbyterianism to Baptist Landmarkism—and J. M. Carroll? Briefly, proponents of Landmarkism insisted: (1) There is no such entity as the "invisible church" or the "Church Universal." There are only *local churches.* (2) Only Baptist churches (and not all of them—for example, *not* Primitive, Northern, or independent Baptist congregations) bear the marks of a true New Testament church. (3) Only *Baptist* churches can trace their lineage in uninterrupted fashion back to the New Testament, and only Baptist churches therefore are true churches. (4) If you want to see the Kingdom of God at work, look at Baptist churches for they are the only visible signs of the Kingdom of God. In fact, Landmarkism insisted, Baptist churches and the Kingdom of God are really two sides of the same coin. (5) All other so-called churches are counterfeit, imitations, or "human societies" as the Landmarkers called them, and Baptists should have no dealings whatsoever with them. (6) Finally, only a true church—that is, a Baptist church—can legitimately celebrate the ordinances of baptism and the Lord's Supper. Any celebration of these

---

[2][Editor's note: James Milton Carroll (1852–1931), younger brother of the better-known B. H. Carroll, was a Texas Baptist historian, pastor, and college president (Oklahoma Baptist University and Howard Payne College). His *Trail of Blood* was published the year he died, 1931.]

ordinances by non-Baptists is invalid. Thus "closed communion" or—as Stewart Newman used to say—"closed baptism" was the logical conclusion of such a cockamamy ecclesiology.

Recalling our Southern Baptist Landmark roots is not a digression from the theme with which I am dealing. It is important because without this awareness, one cannot appreciate the significance of the third article in the Alliance Covenant which speaks of "the larger body of Jesus Christ" and of "cooperation with believers everywhere in giving full expression to the Gospel," and one cannot understand the attachment most Southern Baptists have to the Southern Baptist Convention. To one steeped in Landmarkism, "cooperation" with non-Baptists is unthinkable, for there is no larger body of Jesus Christ apart from Southern Baptist churches and the Southern Baptist Convention.

Why the Alliance?

Though developments in the Southern Baptist Convention from 1979 to 1985 were disturbing and indicative of what was an irreversible direction in which the Convention was moving, 1986 was pivotal for most of us who later became part of the Southern Baptist Alliance. For from the time of the Houston meeting of the SBC in 1979 when Adrian Rogers was first elected president of the Convention until his second election as president in Atlanta in 1986, a concerted attempt was made by Moderates to defeat the Pressler-Patterson-Rogers candidates. Moderates and some not-so-Moderate joined in the effort. Yet all these attempts failed, and they failed for seven successive years. The defeat of the Moderate candidate Winfred Moore in Atlanta in 1986 marked not only our eighth straight loss to the Pressler-Patterson-Rogers coalition, but it was clearly a watershed for the SBC and a bitter setback for those who opposed what was happening. The so-called Peace Committee named in Dallas a year earlier was beginning to encroach on the seminaries by announcing the initiation of doctrinal inquiries. It was also clear that the Fundamentalists on the Peace Committee would focus particularly on Southern and Southeastern seminaries.[3] Moreover, a growing

---

[3]Even though most of what was happening in the Peace Committee was not divulged officially, the inflexibility of the Pressler, Patterson, and Rogers representatives was generally known. An unsigned set of notes, five single-spaced pages, of a subcommittee meeting of the Peace Committee that took place in Dallas, 28 July 1986, was circulated among Moderates, and it confirmed the worst fears and

number of Moderates, especially in the East and Southeast, were losing heart and were ready to give up on electing a Moderate president.

Within a few weeks after the Atlanta convention in 1986 the word went out that Moderates would gather in Macon, Georgia, at Mercer University in late August to plan their future strategy. Several of us at Southeastern Seminary wanted to attend, but the Macon meeting was scheduled at the same time as our annual faculty workshop. President Randall Lolley, therefore, agreed to send W. Robert Spinks, assistant to the president for financial development, to represent us and to bring back firsthand information concerning what was being planned.

On August 28, a week after the Georgia meeting, five faculty members met with President Lolley to hear from Spinks what had happened in Macon.[4] He reported that "our friends were of two minds on what needed to be done." One group, he explained, insisted on mounting another "major political campaign" to elect a Moderate president in the next annual meeting of the SBC in St. Louis. Several, however, according to Spinks, spoke just as fervently against continuing the political efforts and counseled instead an alternative approach. Spinks also told us that several who were advocating a new approach would meet in Raleigh within a month to discuss possible alternatives.

Meanwhile, the Moderate political organization in North Carolina, the "Friends of Missions," convened in Greensboro on September 4, 1986. Most of those present were notably ambivalent about the future. A well-known layman tried to inject some ardor into the discussion and urged us to mount a campaign to rewrite the SBC Constitution in order to include amendments protecting minority rights. If the Convention rejects such a proposal, he reasoned, "a good many churches would be ready to join a new convention with the right kind of constitution." The idea of another "campaign," however, generated little enthusiasm because, as several countered, if we cannot elect a president, how can we muster support for rewriting the SBC constitution? "We have lost the SBC, and we should be thinking in other

---

suspicions of those who saw the Peace Committee more as legitimizing an inquisition than promoting peace.

[4]Meeting with President Lolley and Spinks were Dean Morris Ashcraft and Professors Glenn Miller, Malcolm Tolbert, Furman Hewitt, and myself. "Minutes: Task Force," 28 Aug 1986. Three months earlier, Lolley had named a Seminary Task Force composed of administrators and faculty. We met monthly or at the call of the president until Lolley resigned in Oct 1987.

terms." Despite this gloomy assessment, we agreed to encourage as many as possible to attend the St. Louis convention. "Otherwise," we were reminded, "the Fundamentalists could, with sixty-six percent of the vote, change the constitution" in ways even more onerous for us.

On September 23 the meeting Robert Spinks had mentioned convened at Meredith College in Raleigh. A wide range of topics was discussed, but the most significant development was the proposal for a new kind of organization, the specific suggestion made by Walter Shurden of Georgia and relayed to the group. Lawrence Coleman stated that "the initial gathering of Southern Baptists was around Mission, Education, and Evangelism," and he questioned the ability of any group to generate significant support if the "center were to be religious liberty, a place for fellowship, or a theological forum."[5]

My personal notes are sketchy, but I did record that the group seemed to agree that renewed efforts to elect a president of the SBC were futile. Someone said, "I am not going to sign on to another failed political campaign. John Baugh [the Texas layman] has put together a traveling road show, but it's not going anywhere."

James Strickland of Georgia then suggested that we "form the Southern Baptist Heritage Fellowship." He did not make an official motion, however, and we decided first to develop a purpose statement and then choose a name. The following statement of purpose was approved: the new organization would be

> An alliance of individuals and churches dedicated to the preservation of historic Southern Baptist principles, freedoms, and traditions, and the continuance of its ministry and mission.

The name selected for the new organization that September afternoon, however, was not "The Southern Baptist Heritage Fellowship," as Strickland had proposed, but rather "The Southern Baptist Alliance." In light of subsequent events, one cannot help wonder what the "Cooperative Baptist Fellowship" would now be called had we opted for Strickland's suggested name.

---

[5]"Minutes of Concerned Southern Baptists at Meredith College, Raleigh NC, Sept 23, 1986." Signing the attendance list were: James Strickland (GA), Larry Coleman (NY), Randolph Cloud (political advisor to Friends of Mission in NC), Norman Cavender (GA), Douglass Murray (MD), Timothy Norman (VA), Steven Teague (VA), Frank Gilreath (NC), Robert Spinks (NC), Karen Smith (NC), George McCotter (NC), Jeff Roberts (NC), William Puckett, Jr. (NC), Thomas Austin (GA), W. Henry Crouch (NC), and Alan Neely (NC).

Henry Crouch was asked to assume responsibility for convening a second meeting, and everyone else, with the exception of Spinks, McCotter, Cloud, and Gilreath, agreed to work as committees on several specific goals: identity, information, fellowship, education, and publications. Lawrence Coleman's "missions" goal, however, was not included.

Of the sixteen people present in Raleigh, three—Norman, Teague, and Cavender—did not continue and soon were identified with the second group that emerged from the Macon, Georgia, meeting, that is, with those who continued the effort to elect a "moderate" as SBC president.[6] Eight of the original sixteen, however, became founders of the SBA: William Puckett, Henry Crouch, James Strickland, Thomas Austin, Lawrence Coleman, George McCotter, Frank Gilreath, and Alan Neely.

Organization of the SBA

Soon after the Raleigh meeting a letter was sent to a number of people inviting them to come to Charlotte on December 1-2. Twenty-four individuals arrived, but only four of them were women, two of whom were among the six nonordained individuals present.[7] The intensity of the three sessions

---

[6]This political coalition came to be known as "Baptists Committed," and most of those who later came to be identified with beginning the Alliance supported financially and otherwise the "Baptists Committed" efforts. It is only fair to say that we in the Alliance nourished little hope that the Fundamentalists could be turned back. But our pessimism and sometimes privately voiced cynicism did not prevent us from going to the Convention meetings and voting for the Baptists Committed candidates, hoping somehow to break the stranglehold Pressler, Patterson, and Rogers had on the Convention.

[7]The four women were Edna S. Langley and Sarah Wilson, members of the Church of the Covenant in Birmingham, Nancy Hastings Sehested, then associate pastor of the Oakhurst Baptist Church in Atlanta, and Susan Lockwood, pastor of the Connell Baptist Church in Chicago. The five laypersons, including Ms Langley and Ms Wilson, were George McCotter (NC), Randolph Cloud (NC), and Joseph Wayne Thomason of the Covenant Church in Birmingham. The remaining seventeen were William Puckett, Henry Crouch, Mahan Siler, Jr., Walter Coleman, Luther Brewer, Richard Groves, William Treadwell, and Alan Neely of North Carolina; Thomas Austin, Thomas Conley, Welton Gaddy, Walter Shurden, and James Strickland of Georgia; Bruce Morgan of South Carolina; Daniel Ivins of Alabama; and Larry Coleman of New York. "Minutes of the Southern Baptist Alliance," Charlotte NC, 1-2 Dec 1986, 1.

was palpable. There were debates and disagreements, but a number of significant decisions were made.

Walter Shurden opened the first discussion by reviewing recent developments in the SBC. He gave his assessment of the national political scene, its relation to what was happening in the denomination, and then spoke of the overall weariness of many Southern Baptists with the struggle going on in the SBC. He concluded with the warning, "If they view us as pulling out of the Convention, we will be perceived as the enemy." Despite this risk, Shurden later said we needed to create a new organization, one with "a purpose and a passion."

Rumblings and threats within the SBC Executive Committee to reduce the annual contribution to the Baptist Joint Committee on Public Affairs or defund it altogether, as well as the recent controversial decision by the Home Mission Board not to give any financial assistance to a congregation that called a woman as pastor, prompted James Strickland, then a trustee of the Home Mission Board, to propose we offer financial assistance to churches who called women as pastors and that we become a channel for funds to help the BJCPA. These two causes, Strickland said, could generate both passion and financial support. Several spoke in favor of Strickland's idea, but Lawrence Coleman said that though he was deeply concerned personally about both of these issues, he doubted "the average Baptist back home cared a great deal about these matters."[8]

Susan Lockwood then stunned several of us by saying she would object to any attempt to use the women's issue "as a means to reach larger ends." The men were visibly unprepared for her comment, and our bewilderment revealed a need for and the beginning of a process of consciousness-raising that would continue for many months. "What was she talking about?" some wondered out loud. It sounded irrational. It was not irrational, but it was unconventional, and the discussion that followed nudged us toward a new kind of relationship and signaled a nontraditional role for women in the Alliance. The men progressively learned to accept the fact that the women were unwilling to be used as objects to achieve our ends, no matter how reasonable and commendable they appeared to us.

The discussion that followed was heated and prolonged, and once the point was made, Lockwood as well as the other women agreed that financial support for congregations wanting to call women as pastors should be

---

[8]Ibid.

provided, but not because it was politically astute. A Baptist congregation should be free to call whomever they choose as pastor without having to secure the approval of the local Baptist association, the state convention, the SBC, or any of its agencies.

Work groups then were assigned to discuss the following questions. (1) Should a new organization be formed? (2) If so, what should be "the glue" that could hold it together? (3) If a new organization were formed, when should it take place? (4) What should be the extent of the organization's structure? It was quickly evident that the first question had already been answered. An organization dedicated to something other than electing a president of the SBC was needed. The groups therefore turned to the last three questions.

Reconvening after dinner, we heard from each group, and the reports were remarkably similar. The purpose statement proposed by the group that met at Meredith College was amended slightly and approved. It read:

> The Southern Baptist Alliance is an alliance of individuals and churches dedicated to the preservation of historic ["Southern" deleted] Baptist principles, freedoms, and traditions and the continuance of our [in place of "its"] ministry and mission *within the Southern Baptist Convention.* [Italics and bracketed notes are mine.]

The last phrase, "within the Southern Baptist Convention," was a calculated addition, and not everyone was comfortable with it. It was accepted as a practical necessity in order to avoid being regarded as a splinter group bent on leading people and congregations out of the SBC. Given the subsequent interpretations of our action, however, I would now question whether this or any other assurance of our concern for and commitment to the SBC would have prevented us from being labeled as "the radical left" or as a confederation of denominational renegades.

During the next five years, the name and the stated desire to continue working within the Southern Baptist Convention became points of increasing contention within the Alliance, and proposals were regularly made to change our name. Curiously, however, it was not the name that was first changed, but rather the statement that we would continue in the SBC. This phrase was quietly dropped from the purpose statement in 1991, and in 1992, during the convocation in Charlotte, the "Southern Baptist Alliance" became the "Alliance of Baptists." Both changes were made virtually without dissent.[9]

---

[9]By 1991 few Alliance members appeared interested in continuing to feign

(One should note in this regard that breaking ties with the SBC did not and does not necessarily mean an inevitable break with state Baptist conventions and with local Baptist associations. The future of these relationships is yet to be determined.)

Two decisions made in Charlotte in 1986 therefore had long-lasting repercussions. Besides moving towards formal organization, a list of principles that later became the core of the Alliance Covenant was endorsed, and an ad hoc committee was named to take these principles and develop them into a statement of "Affirmations." The principles on which the statement was to be fashioned were (1) freedom or religious liberty, (2) the priesthood of the believer, (3) the autonomy of the local church, (4) a reverence for the Scriptures, (5) missions and evangelism, (6) an affirmation of God's call to women as well as men, (7) the role of the laity in the church, and (8) the servant model for ministers and congregations. Further, it was suggested by one of the groups that once we agreed and made public our principles, "churches and individuals participating" in the Alliance could be challenged to "covenant" to do ministry in keeping with these principles.[10] Not everyone agreed that such a declaration was needed, but the majority voted to approve the naming of the committee and wait for the committee to convene and report.

Nancy Hastings Sehested then asked if the Alliance could not be a kind of "Shiprah and Puah" society—a biblical reference obscure even to the theological professors present, and the secretary helpfully noted in the minutes that Nancy was referring to the two midwives who disobeyed the command of the Egyptian pharaoh by refusing to kill the male Hebrew babies (Exodus 1:15-21). The implication was, as can now be seen, prophetic. The role of the Alliance would be to protect and support individuals threatened and wounded by what was happening in the SBC, and be an incubator of ideas and a catalyst for needed projects that otherwise might never see the light of day.

---

loyalty to the SBC. Most believed the Convention was no longer Baptist. During the convocation in Richmond, the statement of purpose was therefore amended as follows: "The Southern Baptist Alliance is an alliance of individuals and churches dedicated to the preservation of historic Baptist principles, freedoms, and traditions, and to the expression of our ministry and mission through cooperative relations with other Baptist bodies and the larger Christian community."

[10]"Minutes of the Southern Baptist Alliance," Charlotte NC, Dec 1-2, 1986, 2.

On the morning of December 2 a formal motion was made and approved to organize and incorporate the Alliance. The purpose statement was also approved.[11] Other actions and activities for the immediate future were discussed, including public policy statements on the threat to the Baptist Joint Committee, and the Home Mission Board's action regarding women in pastoral ministry; communicating with Walker Knight, editor of *SBC Today*, to ascertain the possibility of obtaining a page in the journal for the SBA; establishing a fund to support churches desiring to call women as pastors; and sponsoring a national convocation—at a time other than that of the annual SBC—for worship and fellowship. Also, it was agreed that as long-term goals we should work to develop some means of placement for those in vocational ministry, consider the publication of Bible study materials and other kinds of literature, and commission someone to investigate the possibility for alternative theological education.

The committees assigned to work out the details of each of these tasks were as follows. To draft an Affirmation, Mahan Siler was asked to serve as chair with Richard Groves, Bill Treadwell, Alan Neely, Luther Brewer, and Walter Coleman. Matters of structure were assigned to William Puckett, chair, Henry Crouch, Bruce Morgan, James Strickland, Alan Neely, Lawrence Coleman, George McCotter, Edna Langley, Tom Conley, and Nancy Hastings Sehested. Future plans and programs were to be considered by Thomas Austin, chair, Welton Gaddy, Walter Shurden, Dan Ivins, and Susan Lockwood.

Finally, the group set the date for their next meeting, February 1-2, 1987, and agreed that a public announcement of the formation of the Alliance would follow on February 12.

A provisional steering committee met in Charlotte, January 11-12, 1987, and persons were suggested as possible members of a "pro-tem board" representing twelve geographical areas—mostly states—plus eight persons "at large."[12] Only fourteen of the forty-two persons nominated, however,

---

[11]The three officers selected to meet the requirements of incorporation were William Puckett, Jr., chair; W. Henry Crouch, vice chair and treasurer; and Lawrence B. Coleman, secretary. North Carolina was approved as the legal domicile.

[12]The geographical areas agreed upon and the persons to be nominated were as follows. Northeast: Lawrence Coleman, John Roberts, and Glenn Morrison. Virginia: Timothy Norman, Steven Teague, and Thomas Jackson. North Carolina: Mahan Siler, Jr., Mary Caldwell, Alton McEachern, William Puckett, Jr., and W. Henry

agreed to serve. We were beginning to encounter resistance to the idea of a nonpolitical alternative organization.

When the group reconvened in Charlotte, February 2-3, 1987, however, twenty-one individuals were present.[13] News of what we were doing was beginning to circulate. Richard Groves and Lawrence Coleman reported on a conversation with James Dunn, executive director of the Baptist Joint Committee on Public Affairs. Dunn, they said, was reluctant to openly accept financial help from the Alliance. He did not want the BJCPA "tied to issues like women in ministry or debates on inspiration," and he specifically stated, according to Groves and Coleman, that his goal was to maintain ties with the Southern Baptist Convention. If the BJCPA were to be "too closely identified with" a movement "perceived to be a splinter group . . . his objective could be endangered," Coleman said. Dunn requested therefore that his agency not publicly be identified as a beneficiary of the Alliance.[14]

If these were discouraging words for the group, there is no evidence of it. Dunn's position was understood and accepted. The report from the subcommittee working on the Affirmation, later called the Covenant, was approved, and there was lengthy discussion about the structure of the organization. The first officers were elected: Henry Crouch, president; Susan Lockwood, vice-president; Richard Groves, recording secretary; and Bruce

---

Crouch. South Carolina: Bruce Morgan, Harold Cole, Terry Wilson, and "the pastor of St. Andrews Church in Columbia." Georgia: James Strickland, Dorethea Gatlin, and Walter Shurden. Florida: Peter Hill, Clyde Fant, and "the pastor of the Stetson Church in DeLand." Alabama: Edna Langley, Todd Wilson, Ralph Langley, James Auchmuty. Mississippi: No names were listed. Kentucky: William Tuck, Spurgeon Hayes, Richard Bridges. Tennessee: Dillard Mynatt, Calvin Metcalf, Billy D. Sherman, and Earl Davis. Texas: Cecil Sherman, Bill G. Bruster, and Libby Bellinger. Oklahoma: Lavonn Brown. At large: Frank Gilreath, George McCotter. Norman Cavender, Mary Dalton, Thomas Austin, Alan Neely, Larry McSwain, and Marse Grant. "Minutes of the Southern Baptist Alliance Steering Committee Meeting," Providence Baptist Church, Charlotte NC, 11-12 Jan 1987, 2-3.

[13]William Puckett, Jr., Walter Coleman, Frank Gilreath, Randolph Cloud, Henry Crouch, Richard Groves, William Treadwell, Alan Neely, George McCotter, Dale Mullinix (NC), and Mahan Siler, Jr. (NC); John Roberts (MD); Susan Lockwood (IL); James Strickland, Thomas Austin, Walker Knight (GA); Bruce Morgan (SC); Sarah Wilson and Joseph Thomason (AL); and Lawrence Coleman (NY).

[14]"Minutes of the Southern Baptist Alliance Meeting on February 2-3, 1987," Providence Baptist Church, Charlotte NC, 1.

Morgan, treasurer. Plans for the first convocation were presented, and the date of May 14-15 was approved.

The Alliance Goes Public

As earlier agreed, simultaneous news conferences announcing the formation of the "Southern Baptist Alliance" were held in Raleigh, Charlotte, and Atlanta on February 12, and the reaction was immediate and passionate. Telephone calls, letters, and individuals came to Henry Crouch in growing numbers. Most were affirming. Some, however, wrote to express their concern that the SBA would divide the efforts being made to turn back the Fundamentalist tide in the SBC. Others were critical because the SBA Covenant failed to avow our faith in an inerrant Bible.

Some wrote that the SBA signaled an eventual split in the SBC, and some of these observers admonished us to leave the Convention immediately. "You are so few," we were told, "you will not be missed." Though the negative communications were painful, letters and telephone calls from "would-be-except-for" supporters were more difficult to handle.

The Alliance nonetheless was now a reality, and it was up to the officers and members to shape its image and try to guide it toward the future.

Growth and Development of the Alliance

I have devoted the bulk of this discussion to recounting the reasons for, the persons involved in, and the steps taken to bring the Alliance into being. In order merely to touch on the subsequent developments within the space allotted, I must from this point deal with the history thematically.

Growth of the Alliance. More than five years have passed, and the Alliance has grown steadily, though not as dramatically as some wished and others expected. From the twenty-one persons who met in Charlotte in February 1987, the membership has increased as follows.

YEAR	INDIVIDUAL MEMBERS	CHURCHES	TOTAL MEMBERSHIP
1987	21	0	21
1988	2,106	40	23,256
1989	2,874	73	43,611
1990	2,539	101	56,162
1991	2,497	131	71,989
1992	2,331[a]	133	73,496

a. Individual membership has been dropping for three years, likely for one or more reasons: (1) when a congregation begins supporting the Alliance, members of that congregation tend to drop their individual Alliance memberships; (2) some members have begun to look to the Cooperative Baptist Fellowship rather than the Alliance as their alternative national body;

and/or (3) maintaining individual members is a perpetual struggle for every volunteer
organization and national economic conditions have a visible impact on such organizations.

As of now, Alliance members reside in thirty-eight states and the District of
Columbia, with some forty members who live outside the United States.
Congregations supporting the Alliance are located in seventeen states and
the District of Columbia.

It is clear that since the formation of the Cooperative Baptist Fellowship
in 1990–1991, support for the Alliance has diminished, and many Moderates
are asking when the two groups will get together. This is a question
Alliance supporters cannot ignore.

Leadership. Since the early meetings, the Alliance has had competent
and dedicated leadership in the presidents selected: Henry Crouch
(1987–1988), John Thomason (1988), Anne Neil (1988–1990), Richard
Groves (1990–1992), and Ann Quattlebaum (1992–). Only John Thomason,
because of a personal misfortune, has not served two terms. All have led the
organization with incredible skill and dedication, and at no small personal
sacrifice.

Richard Groves who served as secretary for the first thirteen months and
who wrote the first year's history of the SBA tells of a conversation with
a professor of history who had been secretary of the faculty at a university.
"I could not believe," Richard wrote, "that this individual had been willing
to be secretary for so long. I asked him, 'In all those years, didn't you ever
want to hold some other office? Didn't you ever want to be president?'
'No,' he responded disdainfully. 'Presidents only make decisions. Secretaries
write history!'"[15] Lawrence Coleman, Richard Groves, Daniel Ivins, and
William Puckett have bequeathed to us their own unique and remarkably revealing histories.

In one of the preliminary meetings, before the public announcement of
the organization of the Alliance, consideration was given to the need for a
permanent executive director. But neither the money nor the person to serve
in such a capacity appeared available. Thus the load and responsibility for
the day-to-day administration fell on Henry Crouch, Frank Gilreath, and a
part-time secretary, Dawn O'Neil. Office space was provided at no cost by
the Myers Park Baptist Church in Charlotte, and things somehow "got

---

[15]Richard Groves, "The First Year in the Life of the Southern Baptist Alliance,"
n.d. [1988], 1.

done." These were exciting days, but demanding on Henry Crouch and those who were helping him in Charlotte.

When I agreed to be the provisional executive director in the Spring of 1988, Wendy Graves was employed to serve as office director, and she together with Dawn O'Neil and Frank Gilreath did the public relations, bookkeeping, and correspondence that were increasing in geometric proportions. This arrangement continued even after I moved to Princeton Seminary in July, until Stan Hastey was elected as the first permanent executive director and assumed the responsibility on January 1, 1989.[16]

Hastey, formerly assistant executive director of the Baptist Joint Committee and the bureau chief in Washington for Baptist Press, was soon joined by Jeanette Holt who also came to the Alliance from the BJCPA where she was administrative assistant. The office was moved from Charlotte to Washington, into space leased from the First Baptist Church located at 16th and O Streets NW. Hastey's and Holt's experience and competence have resulted in a far more stable organization with a much broader ministry and a membership that almost doubled from 1989 to 1991. It is not possible to record in this summary the immense contribution Hastey and Holt have made to the Alliance. Representing the organization in churches and associations, in ecumenical meetings and interdenominational dialogues, to pastors and church members, the scope and consistently high quality of their work is widely recognized and appreciated. Their contacts in the nation's capital and their ability to do many different things well have confirmed the wisdom of the search committee and board in electing them in 1988. Hastey was elected by the board of directors in their Fall 1988 meeting, and Holt was employed the following February.

Convocations. Early participants in the Alliance were bruised and disappointed individuals. Some had been pushed out of their jobs, and others longed for a less-fettered vocational environment. Some came from churches excluded from their local Baptist association, and nearly everyone testified of their increased feeling of being marginalized by the denomination they had considered their own. The hurt and disappointment that had increased with the repeated victories of the Fundamentalists led the Alliance board to plan for an alternative to the annual SBC keelhauling.

Five convocations have been celebrated. The years, places, and estimated attendance have been as follows. 1987. Meredith College, Raleigh, North

---

[16]*SBC Today* 6, Jan 1989, 1-2.

Carolina, 450. <u>1988.</u> Mercer University, Macon, Georgia, 400. <u>1989.</u> First Baptist Church, Greenville, South Carolina, 750. <u>1990.</u> Third Baptist Church, St. Louis, Missouri, 350. <u>1991.</u> Grace Baptist Church, Richmond, Virginia, 600. And for the fifth anniversary, <u>1992.</u> Providence Baptist Church, Charlotte, North Carolina, 650.

The fellowship, worship, and positive and affirming atmosphere of these gatherings have provided a renewed sense of excitement and belonging for participants, and there have been other significant benefits as well. Addresses given by Thomas Halbrooks, Cecil Sherman, Richard Groves, Rachel Richardson Smith, William L. Turner, Walter Shurden, Anne Thomas Neil, and Norman Cavender were the core of the first book published by the Alliance, *Being Baptist Means Freedom* (1988), which I edited. The decision to begin the Richmond Seminary was made during the Greenville Convocation in 1989. The following year in St. Louis, "The Call to Repentance" was unanimously approved. The "Call" was in reality a long-overdue public confession of sin and repentance. The sin was the complicity of our forebears in the institution of slavery and their self-righteous justification for the formation of the Southern Baptist Convention. The "Call to Repentance" was a symbolic act to be sure, but the result was an unexpected response from black Baptists as well as others. It enabled Alliance President Richard Groves and Executive Director Stan Hastey, for example, to be received with openness and appreciation in the 1991 annual session of the Progressive National Baptist Convention.

Invited as guests to the Richmond Convocation in 1991, a delegation from the Fraternity of Baptist Churches in Cuba sealed the evolving relationship between the Alliance and that Caribbean Baptist body, and in the 1992 Charlotte convocation the presence of spokespersons from the American Baptist Churches and the National Council of Churches were substantive reminders of our commitment "to the larger church."

Finances. Financially, the Alliance has operated from income that resembles the flour in the widow's jar described in 1 Kings 17:15, never any excess, but always enough—until this year. Annual receipts have increased from $46,902 in 1987 to $387,191 in 1991. Beyond the basic operating budget, there has been a growing amount available to assist in a wide range of needs. Total receipts during the five years since the Alliance was founded have been $1,185,818, with nearly $370,000 of that amount invested in various ministries and mission projects.

For example, the Alliance has regularly given significant amounts of its receipts to the Baptist Joint Committee on Public Affairs, Southern Baptist

Women in Ministry, the Baptist Peace Fellowship, Habitat for Humanity, the Baptist Theological Seminary at Richmond, the Missionary Counseling Center in Winston-Salem, North Carolina, as well as providing aid to a number of struggling churches and ministry projects for which funding was not available from any Southern Baptist agency. Most of the churches assisted have been unable to secure help from regular SBC sources because women were serving as pastors, and/or the churches have been engaged in the kinds ministries that the Alliance members have judged to be vital but un- or underfunded. A large number of additional requests have been met from the regular Alliance budget, such as Baptist students studying at Candler and Duke, the Fraternity of Baptist Churches in Cuba, and a grant in 1989 to assist the professors at Southeastern Baptist Seminary in their struggle to maintain a measure of academic freedom in that institution.

By mid-1992 signs of an approaching cash flow problem for the Alliance budget were evident, and Stan Hastey, the executive director, together with the board were being forced to reassess the import of this economic trend.

Global Mission Offerings. The first Global Mission Offering was announced in 1990, and more than $24,000 was given. The offering receipts increased to $52,524 in 1991, and will likely exceed $70,000 in 1992. Monies given through these offerings have been given for creative evangelism projects, theological education, "restored living" projects, and groups working for peace and justice. Specifically, grants have been made from the global missions offerings to three congregations in Cuba as well as the Fraternity of Baptist Churches in Cuba; the Baptist theological seminaries in Rüschlikon, Switzerland, and Richmond, Virginia; the Thomas J. Holmes House for terminated ministers in Georgia; a shelter for the homeless in Fayetteville, North Carolina; a small congregation in Alabama providing food regularly for the hungry; an inner-city program in Chicago; scholarships for seminarians; the Associated Baptist Press; the Baptist Convention of Nicaragua; shelter projects in Atlanta and Raleigh; a ministry of outreach in Providence, Rhode Island; an interracial association of Baptist churches in Charlotte; and a reconciliation ministry with the families of prison inmates in Nashville, Tennessee.

The recent announcement by the Cooperative Baptist Fellowship that it would be promoting a global missions offering in 1992 has induced the Alliance to propose a consolidation of the two appeals in 1993.

The Struggle for Inclusiveness. In his brief history of the first year of the Alliance, Richard Groves makes a crucial observation. He says that from the first meeting, many involved in the Alliance were "concerned with the serious imbalance between men and women and between clergy and laity" that existed "on most if not all Southern Baptist Convention committees and boards." A perusal of the minutes reveals the depth of the struggle to accord women their rightful place,[17] but the first year's Alliance board was hardly balanced itself, being composed of eighteen men and three women, thirteen of whom were ordained and seven unordained. The following year a dramatic change came with a board composed of eighteen men and fourteen women, nineteen of whom were ordained and thirteen unordained. A policy on the use of inclusive language in SBA meetings and communications was adopted by the board in November 1987,[18] a prelude to the decision to drop the use of titles such as "Reverend" and "Doctor." The intent to assure women an equal place in the organization was repeatedly reaffirmed.

The figures for the five years of the Alliance's existence, however, illustrate how difficult it is—without adhering to quotas—to maintain a real balance. A total of 107 persons have served on the board: sixty-eight men and thirty-nine women, fifty-one ordained men and twelve ordained women.

---

[17]E.g., "Minutes of the Board of Directors," 14-15 Sept 1987, 2-3, 5, 8; and for 19-20 Nov 1987, 3-4, 7-8.

[18]"Minutes of the Board of Directors," 19-20 Nov 1987, 7-8. The "Inclusive Language Policy for the Southern Baptist Alliance" reads as follows.

Language reflects, reinforces, and creates our perception of reality. Therefore, the Southern Baptist Alliance is committed to the use of inclusive, rather than exclusive language in our worship and communications. All members are encouraged to avoid the use of language that reflects racial, sexual, ethnic, or religious bias.

On Human References. The Southern Baptist Alliance is committed to the use of inclusive language for humanity in its worship and communications. The SBA discourages the use of the terms "man," "men," "clergymen," "brotherhood," "he," etc., as generic terms and encourages the use of inclusive terms such as "human," "humanity," "minister," "s/he" or "he and she," etc.

On Speaking of God. The Southern Baptist Alliance believes that the exclusive use of masculine titles, pronouns, and imagery in reference to God is inappropriate. This exclusive use of language in reference to God has perpetuated the subordination of women to men. The Southern Baptist Alliance encourages a balance in the use of masculine and feminine imagery, titles, and pronouns in reference to God in SBA worship and communications.

The current board of directors is composed of twenty-four men (eighteen ordained) and sixteen women, four of whom are ordained. Only in 1992 have two minority persons been added to the board.

Working to achieve balance on the Alliance board is, in my judgment, not the most important development in relation to the goal of inclusiveness. The lengthy and testy debates, the constant struggle, and the awkward attempts to regard women as peers soon passed, and though the goal of parity and mutual respect has not been completely achieved, the Alliance has served as a public proving ground for the lofty ideal articulated in the Covenant.

The Alliance Legacy

Whether the Alliance of Baptists continues as an autonomous entity is not the primary issue for most of us. The organization came into being to meet specific needs of some hurting and disillusioned people. Together they have made some visible contributions, initiated a number of projects, some of which will likely continue and flourish. I can mention only the most obvious of these.

The Alliance Covenant. It is my hope that one of the most long-lasting contributions of the Alliance to Baptist life will be the Covenant. It is a document that bears the fingerprints of a number of people. No single individual nor any identifiable group can claim credit for having written it. Soon after the Covenant was adopted, a story began to circulate that it had been written by four or five people in a one-day meeting in Winston-Salem in December 1987. Without detracting from the significance of what this ad hoc committee did, it should be remembered that they did not create the Covenant *de novo*. Several of the principles that became the core of the covenant statement were recorded in the Meredith College meeting in September 1986, and the "affirmations" approved in Charlotte the following December constituted the basic framework utilized by Mahan Siler, Walter Coleman, Luther Brewer, Richard Groves, and I when we drafted the Covenant later that same month. What was remarkable about their composition was not so much the content of it, but the fact that when it was presented in the plenary meeting in February 1987, only three words were deleted.[19]

---

[19]The original text of the first principle read: "The freedom of the individual, led by God's Spirit within the family of faith, to read and interpret the Scriptures

With the 1991 revision of the purpose statement and the change of name in 1992, the Alliance Covenant now reads as follows.

The Alliance of Baptists is an alliance of individuals and churches dedicated to the preservation of historic Baptist principles, freedoms, and traditions, and to the expression of our ministry and mission through cooperative relations with other Baptist bodies and the larger Christian community. As an alliance we commit ourselves to the following:

•First, *the freedom of the individual*, led by God's Spirit within the family of faith, to read and interpret the Scriptures, relying on the historical understanding by the church and on the best methods of modern biblical study;

•Second, *the freedom of the local church* under the authority of Jesus Christ to shape its own life and mission, call its own leadership, and ordain whom it perceives as gifted for ministry, male or female;

•Third, *the larger body of Jesus Christ*, expressed in various Christian traditions, and to the cooperation with believers everywhere in giving full expression to the Gospel;

•Fourth, *the servant role of leadership* within the church, following the model of our Servant Lord, and to full partnership of all of God's people in mission and ministry;

•Fifth, *theological education* in congregations, colleges, and seminaries characterized by reverence for biblical authority and respect for open inquiry and responsible scholarship;

•Sixth, *the proclamation* of the Good News of Jesus Christ and the calling of God to all peoples to repentance and faith, reconciliation and hope, social and economic justice;

•Seventh, the principle of *a free church in a free state* and to the opposition to any effort either by church or state to use the other for its own purposes.

As all such confessions or declarations, the Covenant reflects a particular historical context. It is not a confession of faith, for the doctrines of God, creation, Jesus Christ, salvation, sin, the church, the ordinances, and eschatology are not included. I cannot tell you what the writers of the Philadelphia or New Hampshire Confessions of faith meant in some of their articles, nor even what the authors of the two "Baptist Faith and Message" statements (1925 and 1963) had in mind (especially with regard to article 1,

---

for oneself." And the fifth principle read: "Theological education in congregations, colleges, and seminaries, *education* characterized. . . . " The three italicized words and a comma were deleted.

namely, "[The Bible] has . . . truth, without any mixture of error, for its matter"). But I do know what we were thinking and what we meant by the seven assertions that comprise the Alliance Covenant. We were explicitly rejecting the notion of "biblical inerrancy"; the Southern Baptist Fundamentalist hierarchical, connectional authoritarianism; the arrogance of professed Southern Baptist preachers who dismiss the doctrine of the priesthood of the believer as a misunderstood and misapplied frivolity in favor of the despotism and tyranny of the pastor; theological indoctrination masking as theological education; and the medieval, obscurantist, dogmatic Southern Baptist theologians and biblical interpreters who act as if Copernicus, Galileo, Isaac Newton, H. E. Dana, E. Y. Mullins, and W. T. Conner had never lived.

We were rejecting the distortion of the mission of Jesus Christ and his community to a narrow, deductive view of evangelism and "church planting." We were affirming that evangelism is a calling by God to all peoples to "repentance and faith." But likewise, we were asserting that evangelism is a calling to reconciliation and hope, to social and economic justice. Thus whether people have potable water and food to eat, whether they have access to education and health care, whether they are considered and treated with dignity and respect are as indispensable to the Christian mission as is "preaching the gospel." In fact, providing such things as potable water *is* in many cases preaching the gospel.

Finally, we were rejecting the crass self-interest of those who want to cozy up to the government in order to endow with public monies, that is, taxes, their private church institutions such as church schools, and feather their own ecclesiastical and denominational nests.

Publications. The small book *Being Baptist Means Freedom*[20] was the first substantial piece produced by the Alliance. It was followed by a larger volume on the ministries and place of women in the church, *The New Has Come*, edited by Anne Thomas Neil and Virginia Garrett Neely.[21] The Alliance's literature committee first chaired by Welton Seal began a partnership in January 1989 with *SBC Today* to publish a monthly Bible or Sunday School "Commentary" that has been written by a wide variety of biblical scholars, men and women, and included as a six-page insert in the periodical since that time.[22] Furthermore, the spadework regarding the kind

---

[20]Charlotte NC, 1988.
[21]Washington DC, 1989.
[22]*SBC Today* 6, Jan 1989, 10-15.

and scope of alternative literature needed, research that began in 1988 by the literature committee,[23] was passed on to Smyth & Helwys when they launched their publication venture two years ago.

Ministry of Placement. Baptist ministers are conditioned to think individually, and as a consequence, disagreements are commonplace. There is, however, almost perfect unanimity in the belief that the congregational system of church government is less than ideal when a minister wants or needs a call to another church or task. The system is inefficient and oftentimes unjust, and at least since 1979 it has been greatly complicated by the conflict within the SBC.

For this reason, in 1987 Peter Hill of Florida and later Kelley Belcher of Charlotte, North Carolina, were asked to assume responsibility for receiving resumés from ministers who wanted to move and channeling them to congregations who requested them. After the office was moved to Washington, Donald Retzer, then pastor of the First Baptist Church of Waynesboro, Virginia, chaired a committee that developed the structure and means by which this ministry began to flourish.

The Baptist Theological Seminary at Richmond. Given the fact that President Thomas Graves is presenting a paper on the Seminary,[24] my comments will be abbreviated. The decision at the Greenville convocation to launch the seminary was one the most controversial actions the Alliance has taken. But, as more than one has pointed out during the last several months, the Seminary may be the Alliance's most obvious legacy. It was an objective, however, that could never have been achieved by the Alliance alone, and it has not been an institution controlled by the Alliance. At the present time the majority of the trustees are associated with the Alliance, but that will likely change in the near future. The primary reason is that though the Alliance launched the seminary, it now prospers because others such as the Baptist General Association of Virginia, the Cooperative Baptist Fellowship, scores of churches, and hundreds of individuals now support it.

Relations Established with Other Baptist Groups. The first dialogue with representatives of the American Baptist Churches took place at their initiative[25] when John Sundquist, chair of a special ABC task force,

---

[23]See *SBC Today* 5, July 1988, 14.

[24][Editor's note: Graves's paper on the Seminary appears below—"The History of the Baptist Theological Seminary in Richmond."]

[25]John Sundquist, now executive director of the office of international mission for the ABC, was the chair of a task force named by the ABC in 1984 to relate to Southern Baptists as individuals and churches "amidst the theological and institu-

contacted Henry Crouch to inquire if the Alliance board would be interested in meeting with them. The meeting was arranged and took place in Raleigh, North Carolina, April 25, 1988. Since that initial encounter, dialogues between spokespersons of the Alliance and the ABC have met annually. In addition Stan Hastey was invited to address the General Board of the ABC in November 1990,[26] and representatives of the ABC have addressed Alliance convocations.

The same kind of meetings began in 1991 with representatives of the Progressive National Baptist Convention. The second dialogue session between the Alliance and the PNBC was scheduled for November 1992.

Though the relations between the Alliance and the Fraternity of Baptist Churches of Cuba are moving on a different track, a genuine partnership in mission is developing with their coming to the United States as missioners to us, and our sponsoring groups to go to Cuba as missioners to them. This kind of exchange is as enriching as it is new for most of us accustomed to the Southern Baptist way of doing missions.

Early in 1988 Henry Crouch received a letter from one of the leaders in the Atlantic Baptist Fellowship in Canada inviting the Alliance to send Walter Shurden to their Fall Assembly to interpret for them what was happening in the SBC and the reason for the Alliance. Shurden and his wife Kay were received with manifest appreciation, and both of them spoke to the assembly which convened September 30–October 1 in the First Baptist Church in Halifax, Nova Scotia.[27] The editor of the Fellowship's bulletin said of the visit, "The Shurdens did a great job of informing us of the origin and objectives of the SBA. It was very apparent that our ABF is trying to

---

tional crises in the Southern Baptist Convention." See "A Statement of Purpose and Direction of the General Staff Council Task Force on the Southern Baptist Convention," n.d., 1. It should be made clear that the purpose of the task force was *not* to encourage individual Southern Baptists nor their churches to leave the SBC and join the ABC. Rather, the task force was given a threefold commission: "to monitor the developing crisis within the Southern Baptist Convention, to interpret the crisis and the Southern Baptist Convention to the General Staff Council, and to appropriately express our concern for our hurting brothers and sisters within the Southern Baptist Convention." See "Summary of the December 1, 1988 Report to the General Board Executive Committee by John A. Sundquist on the Work of the GSC Task Force on the Southern Baptist Convention," 1.

[26]*SBC Today* 7, 11 Jan 1990, cover page of Alliance edition.

[27]*Bulletin of the Atlantic Baptist Fellowship* (Dec 1988): 3, 5, 8-11.

do much the same thing among Atlantic Baptists as your folk in the SBA are doing within the SBC."[28]

Surely the most scrutinized dialogue in which the Alliance is currently engaged is that with representatives of the Cooperative Baptist Fellowship. Two meetings have been held between representatives of the groups. The first conversations took place in Raleigh in July 1991, and a joint statement was issued expressing belief that the two organizations could "accomplish our goals and mission more effectively together than separately." Moreover, the participants committed themselves to working toward reaching a decision about the relationship between the Alliance and the CBF by the Spring of 1993.[29] A second session was held in early September 1992, and though substantive issues were raised that still must be resolved, no insurmountable obstacle appeared that would prevent a merger or at least a mutually supportive and cooperative relationship.

In discussing the convocations sponsored by the Alliance, I intentionally omitted any reference to an important meeting held in the Woodmont Baptist Church in Nashville, September 8-10, 1988. Though sponsored by the Alliance, it was labeled a "Dialogue Meeting" in an undisguised attempt to reach out to all Moderates and try to devise ways and means by which all could move together toward common goals. Representatives from all the Moderate organizations and several of the SBC agencies were invited to be a part of the program, and many accepted: Winfred Moore, Bill Sherman, Kirby Godsey, Helen Graves, Betty McGary, Ray Vickery, Buckner Fanning, Henry Crouch, James Strickland, A. C. Shackleford, James Dunn, Jack Harwell, Bobbie Sorrill, Keith Parks, and others.

Scheduled as soon as possible following the San Antonio Convention, more than 700 people were present.[30] No other meeting where Moderates spoke as openly about the future of the SBC and our place in it had involved as many people, and no gathering up to that time—other than the conclave at Mercer University in August 1986—so clearly revealed the conflict in thinking. The difference that divided Moderate energies after the Mercer meeting was not resolved in Nashville.

---

[28]Letter to Alan Neely from Morris R. B. Lovesey, 22 Nov 1988.

[29]*Biblical Recorder* 157 (5 Oct 1991): 8.

[30]"Southern Baptist Alliance Dialogue Meeting, Sept 1988." Two video cassettes of the meeting are available from the SBA.

Winfred Moore, for example, said any talk about a new denomination was premature. "I haven't heard the fat lady sing yet, and she's not singing in my part of the country," he declared.[31]

Keith Parks pled with us not to do anything to divert money from the Cooperative Program. "We must be very, very careful when we correct what we perceive to be Baptist deviations," Parks cautioned. "I am still convinced we can support what is going on with integrity, regardless of where you are in the political spectrum."[32]

Richard Groves and Thomas Graves, however, disagreed. It is a violation of our principles to continue to give money to agencies controlled by the Fundamentalists and closed to us, Groves insisted. "The worst thing you can say about any Southern Baptist church is that it isn't cooperative, that it isn't loyal—to Jesus Christ?—no, no, no—to an institution."[33]

"There has been a death *in* the family," Tom Graves declared. "No," he continued, there's been "a death *of* the family—and life will never be the same again." Moderates need to acknowledge the death of the SBC and move on, Graves insisted. "This can be the most creative period for Baptists in one hundred years on this continent. . . . We can dream of overcoming racial and regional differences that have divided Baptists since before the Civil War."[34]

Cecil Sherman was unconvinced. To use the "death" metaphor, he said, was inappropriate. The SBC is "not dead," Sherman declared, and then altering the metaphor he said the Southern Baptist family is still in the house, and they're having fun. The problem is "we've been put outside the house. You can get in if you say the magic words. If something inside you doesn't let you say the magic words, [you can't get in and] you can't play."[35]

The Nashville meeting, however, did produce two significant results that need to be remembered. The literature committee of the Alliance decided to begin the "Commentary" project with *SBC Today*, primarily the result of the intense interest expressed by the large number who attended the workshop led by Robert Fulbright—so many that the group had to move to a much larger space. Another important development was discussing several

---

[31] *The Tennessean* (Nashville) 9 Sept 1988, A1, 2.
[32] *The Nashville Banner*, 10 Sept 1988, C5.
[33] Ibid.
[34] *The Sunday Tennessean* (Nashville) 11 Sept 1988, A1, 8.
[35] Ibid.

alternate giving plans which had been proposed by a number of individuals, then collated and presented by the Alliance finance committee.

My own hope that in Nashville Moderates would begin a process of combining their efforts did not occur, and reflecting on that meeting has led me to conclude that we in the Alliance made at least two mistakes. First, we were—as we had been since 1986—simply "ahead of the curve." The vast majority of Southern Baptists, even those who later led in organizing the Cooperative Baptist Fellowship, were not yet convinced that the time had come to make any kind of break. Sherman, who I believe reflected the sentiment of many, asked, "Where are we going? We're feeling our way through a time. It takes patience. Gestation for larger animals takes a longer time. . . . But we need time for worship as well as strategy. Our task is neither to repossess the SBC nor replace it."[36] Precisely what the task was Sherman did not say, but he did concede that, given the present conditions, it was unclear whether Moderates could or would remain indefinitely in the Convention.

A second mistake the Alliance made, I believe, was moving ahead and sponsoring the Nashville meeting alone. The idea for the meeting surfaced in San Antonio the same day Richard Jackson was defeated for the presidency of the SBC. Cecil Sherman and I were sitting together in the lobby of the hotel waiting to go dinner. As we talked, one of us suggested some kind of Moderate convocation. Cecil said Nashville would be centrally located and that Woodmont Church would probably invite us. We both agreed the meeting should be convened as soon as possible. I was moving the next month from Wake Forest to Princeton, but I believed with Cecil that to wait beyond September would be a tactical error. We talked about how to involve representatives from all the Moderate groups, and we finally agreed that in light of the urgency, the Alliance should proceed. Neither I nor anyone else in the Alliance leadership was unwilling to cosponsor the meeting with Baptists Committed or any other group, and we did attempt to involve a representative number of people from the Alliance, Baptists Committed, and Southern Baptist Women in Ministry in the selection of the site, the structure of the program, and the stated goal of the meeting. But, like other efforts, differences in the rate at which people were moving[37] and

[36]Ibid., A8.

[37]I recall a statement by Cecil Sherman in our conversation in San Antonio. We were talking about the fact most people associated with the Alliance were ready to move on and not concern ourselves further with the SBC. The Saturday after the

the pressure to "do something" prevented the kind of joint effort that the Nashville meeting could have been.

Some Other Omissions and Miscalculations

Had I the space, I would mention a number of other failures and miscalculations which, could we reverse history, we might do differently. At times we have lacked patience and equanimity toward those who we felt were wedded to the SBC and unwilling to face reality.

Another shortcoming, not of will but of commitment, has been our inability to respond in concrete ways to the victims of the SBC battles. Nothing distresses me more than the fact that as a group we have not been able provide the support vocationally, financially, and spiritually which I believe we as Moderates should furnish those who have been forced to resign or have been fired because of Fundamentalist pressures and threats—individuals such as Richard Harman and George Sheridan (HMB), Michael Willett (FMB), Dan Martin (Baptist Press), Sam Balentine and Roy DeBrand (Southeastern Seminary), and a host of others whose names deserve to be mentioned. Some, such as Paul Simmons (Southern Seminary), even now hang by a thread and could be terminated at any moment.[38]

Doubtless, some would say our most glaring mistake—one that incites differences even among Alliance supporters—has been the attitude we have manifested toward persons marginalized and often ostracized in our society. The Alliance has consciously and intentionally tried to move toward authentic inclusiveness. We have made some progress, but we have also learned that racial, gender, and cultural prejudice are as widespread and

---

Dallas Convention in 1985 Cecil told me that he was ready to "move on." I was satisfied that he had not changed his mind, but it was evident that he did not want to act precipitously. He then used a fitting image. "The sun comes up at different times for different people." he said. "For you and me, it is four o'clock in the afternoon, but many moderates are just now beginning the see the first rays of the dawn."

[38][Editor's note: Paul Simmons, professor of Christian Ethics at The Southern Baptist Theological Seminary in Louisville for twenty-two years, had been the target of Fundamentalist attacks because he would not capitualte to their rigid views on abortion. Effective 31 Dec 1992, Simmons took early retirement from the seminary as a protest against the administration over disciplinary process and actions taken against him for a video he showed in a class on "The Church and Human Sexuality."]

pernicious today as it was when our forebears defended racism, legalized segregation, ignored the lynchings, and joined in the oppression of women. Despite knowing this history, we in the Alliance were not prepared for the viciousness and the impact of the prejudice that we now experience. Organizationally, our ingenuousness at this point may prove to have been a grievous miscalculation. If so, I would hope history will judge that we erred in love and out of a desire for justice and not out of timidity or a calculated yearning to play it safe.

To paraphrase the ancient writer (John 21:25), there are many other things that should be said, but if every one of them were written down it would take far more space than I am allowed in this condensed account. Understand that this is not the end of the story. History is still being written. In fact, we are not only writing history, those of us here this week are making history—which others, besides us, will undoubtedly write. I will be very interested in what they say.

More Hidden than Revealed: The History of Southern Baptist Women in Ministry

Libby Bellinger

Leon McBeth, chair of the church history department at Southwestern Seminary, once said that women have made significant contributions to Baptist life, but "from the angle of history, we have ignored you. We have hidden you or hidden from you, in recounting the stories of our heritage."[1]

Have you heard of Maeyken Wens? She was an Anabaptist woman of Antwerp who was arrested in 1573 for proclaiming the Gospel of Jesus as she understood it from her personal reading of the Scripture and from study and discussion with other Anabaptists.

Sister Maeyken withstood the church's inquisition and bodily torture by the civil authority. When she would not promise, after six months' imprisonment, to cease spreading the Word, she was sentenced to death. Included in the sentencing was the instruction that her tongue should be screwed fast to the roof of her mouth so that she might not testify on the way to her burning.

On the day of her death, her two young sons positioned themselves near the stakes so that they might be a presence at her execution. When it began, the eldest son Adriaen, only ten years old, fainted. But when the ashes had cooled, he sifted through them and found the screw with which her tongue

---

[1]H. Leon McBeth. "Perspectives On Women In Baptist Life," *Baptist History and Heritage* 22/3 (July 1987): 4.

had been stilled. Three other women and a man died that day for the same offense.[2]

Women in ministry have a rich heritage, but a heritage more hidden than revealed. Do you know that 139 years ago a Congregationalist woman, Antoinette Brown, was ordained in a Baptist church in Ohio? She was the first ordained clergywoman in America, not the first woman in ministry.

Many Southern Baptist women ministered without benefit of official ritual before Addie Davis became the first clergywoman ordained in a Southern Baptist church in 1964, only twenty-nine years ago. Thousands of them served in professional capacities through the local church, denominational work, and missions without benefit of a specific fellowship and support system.

The decade of the 1970s was important in the movement of the church toward a more visible recognition of women in ministry. In 1973 Norman Leitinger, a student at Southern Seminary, wrote his thesis on "The Women's Liberation Movement: Its Implications for the Southern Baptist Convention." Leitinger's research became part of the awakening of the consciences of women and men concerning the role of women in the SBC. In 1973 there were fewer than a dozen ordained women ministers, but the seeds of a movement were sown.[3]

In 1974 the Southern Baptist Convention Christian Life Commission sponsored a seminar at Glorieta Baptist Conference Center on the role of women in the church. Those lectures were published in the book, *Christian Freedom for Women—and Other Human Beings* (1974). Seminars based on this book were held across the Southern Baptist Convention.

The Winter 1975 issue of *Review and Expositor*, published by the Southern Seminary faculty, devoted an issue to "Women and the Church," and in 1976 the seminary offered a January-term course entitled "Women's Liberation Movement and Women in the Church."

In 1978 Frank Stagg and Evelyn Stagg published *Women in the World of Jesus*, which served as a scholarly base for a national consultation on women. At this consultation more than 300 Baptists met in Nashville to deal with issues of "Women in Church-Related Vocations." Although convened by leaders with no authority to take action in regard to issues discussed, the

---

[2]Will Campbell, "On Silencing Our Finest," *Folio* 3/3 (Winter 1985): 1.

[3]Sarah Frances Anders, "Pilgrimage toward Equity in Ministry, SBC," *Folio* 1/1 (June 1983): 1.

consultation was a catalyst for dialogue within the denomination. This meeting was held at the Baptist Sunday School Board in Nashville.

The Women's Missionary Union, responding to the growing need for an emphasis on women, held a "Women in Ministry Dinner" prior to the Southern Baptist Convention in New Orleans in June 1982. Sarah Frances Anders presented a white paper on the status of women in ministry, calling for a network of support and fellowship. The WMU responded with a pledge to help in such a venture. By this time there were reportedly 175 ordained clergywomen in the SBC, and about ten percent of local church staff members were women.

In October 1983, at the "Theology Is a Verb" conference on "Issues Affecting Women" in Charlotte, North Carolina, nine of the 150 women attending developed a rationale and plan for a support network. Nancy Hastings Sehested called for national/regional conferences for women and a regular newsletter. In less than two months a task force of nine men and women met at the Christian Life Commission to endorse and support such a denominational venture. The commission agreed to identify women in ministry as a special area of its work under a new woman staff member, Lela Hendrix. Nancy Hastings Sehested continued to establish a network of support for SBC women in ministry. She conferred with women and men around the convention and with leaders such as Foy Valentine (CLC) and Carolyn Weatherford (WMU) in an effort to develop a sense of the need for such a network. A consensus emerged that there should be a pre-SBC meeting of concerned women and men in Pittsburgh in 1983.

A meeting was called for March 20 and 21, 1983, prior to the annual CLC meeting in Louisville, Kentucky, to discuss the pre-SBC meeting and other related matters. Nancy Hastings Sehested consulted Anne Neil, Carolyn Weatherford, Sarah Frances Anders, and Reba Cobb in planning the Louisville meeting.

In March 1983, thirty-three women gathered to lay the foundations for a June pre-SBC session for women in ministry. The women who attended included: Becky Albritton (Ohio); Pat Ayres and Lela Hendrix (Tennessee); Harriet Clay (New York); Jeni Cook (Texas); Pearl DuVall, Nancy Hastings Sehested, and Susan Taylor (Georgia); Velma Ferrell, Linda Stack Morgan, Anne Thomas Neil, Brenda Paddleford, and Jenny Graves Weisz (North Carolina); Barbara McNeir (Virginia); Pat Bailey, Linda McKinnish Bridges, Reba Cobb, Anne Davis, Nancy Foil, Cindy Harp Johnson, Molly Marshall-Green, June McEwen, Karen Conn Mitcham, Carol Noffsinger, Betty McGary Pearce, Nina T. Pollard, and Lynda Weaver-Williams (Kentucky);

Verna Quirin (Iowa); Inez Register (South Carolina); Evelyn Stagg (Mississippi); and Carolyn Weatherford (Alabama).[4]

The meeting included fellowship, worship, and much discussion. Nancy Hastings Sehested gave an address entitled "Southern Baptist Women in Ministry: Vision, Goal, Strategy and Tactics." In her address Sehested called for a vision that would seek to transform the image of what it means—in biblical terms—to exercise power and authority. She suggested the following goals for Southern Baptist women in ministry: (1) to encourage women to fuller ministries in the life of our churches and denomination; (2) to provide an avenue for the sharing of the joys and struggles as disciples of Christ so women could gain courage, insight, strength, and challenge from each other; and (3) to explore, discuss, and form new paradigms of leadership in the Church, paradigms that empower, not control people.[5]

The business session resulted in the appointment of a task force to meet in Birmingham, Alabama, in April to plan for the preconvention meeting in Pittsburgh. The task force included Sarah Frances Anders, Reba Cobb, Anne Davis, Lela Hendrix, Anne Neil, Nancy Hastings Sehested, Carolyn Weatherford, and Jenny Weisz. At the same business session Reba Sloan Cobb and Betty McGary presented a proposal for the creation of a Center for Women in Ministry and a newsletter.

On May 5, 1983, in the WMU building in Birmingham, six of the eight members of the task force met to plan for the preconvention meeting. Anne Davis was elected moderator and Reba Cobb recorder. Davis led the group in developing a purpose statement and in planning for a pre-SBC meeting in Pittsburgh, June 11-12, 1983. Davis said the hope for the meeting was for women to get to know each other, to discover what they were about, and to decide who was supportive of women in ministry roles and who would affirm the call of women in church-related vocations. The program was to include worship, fellowship, and a business session. An additional group of women would be added to the task force. All women called and/or serving in professional ministries, ordained or not, would be welcome to participate.

The first meeting of Women in Ministry, SBC was held in Pittsburgh, prior to the 1983 meeting of the SBC. It was attended by seventy-five persons. The theme was based on 2 Corinthians 4:7-12. Speakers included

---

[4]Betty McGary, "A History of Women in Ministry, SBC," *Folio* 3/1 (Summer 1985): 9.

[5]Nancy Sehested, "Southern Baptist Women in Ministry: Vision, Goal, Strategy, and Tactics," unpublished paper presented March 1983 in Louisville.

Christine Gregory (Virginia), "Do We Dare Take the Risk?"; Debra Griffis-Woodberry, "Women in Ministry: Identifying the Issues"; Anne Neil, "The Servant Model." Nancy Hastings Sehested preached the Sunday morning sermon entitled "We Have This Treasure."[6]

In the business meeting convened by Anne Davis, the group adopted a statement of purpose saying that the organization should "provide support for the woman whose call from God defines her vocation as that of minister or that of woman in ministry within the SBC and affirm her call to be a servant of God."[7] The group decided to open its membership to all SBC women who feel called to the ministry and to their supporters, both male and female, as reflecting the "statement of purpose." Until a definite name could be selected, the working title of "Women in Ministry, SBC" was chosen.

Selecting a steering committee, the group agreed to hold the second annual meeting preceding the 1984 SBC in Kansas City. The original task force of eight was expanded to sixteen. The new members included Debra Griffis-Woodberry (NC); June McEwen (KY); Marilyn Mayse (AL); Linda Stack Morgan (NC); Inez Register (SC); Helen Lee Turner (SC); Lynda Weaver-Williams (KY); and Dianne Wisemuller (MD). This steering committee was empowered to elect its own officers. Lela Hendrix was asked to prepare a proceedings booklet and mail it to those in attendance.[8]

Volume 1 of *Folio*, a newsletter for Southern Baptist women in ministry, was distributed at the Pittsburgh meeting. One previous newsletter, *Called and Committed*, was published in 1978 and survived for three issues. *Folio* was published because of "an increased demand for more communication, support, and affirmation among Southern Baptist women ministers."[9] Edited by Reba Sloan Cobb and Betty McGary, *Folio* was published by the Center for Women in Ministry, located at Crescent Hill Baptist Church in Louisville. One hope of the editors was to provide space in each issue "to celebrate the ways in which Southern Baptist women are currently living out their vocations, to encourage the creation of new opportunities for service, and through our supportive applause for one another, praise the God who has called us to service."[10] This section known as "Ovations" has come to provide encouragement to women across the SBC as it lists information on

---

[6]Lela Hendrix, ed., "WIM, SBC Proceedings," 11-12 June 1983.
[7]Anne Davis, minutes, "WIM, SBC Proceedings," 11 June 1983.
[8]Steering committee "WIM, SBC Minutes," 1983.
[9]Reba Cobb and Betty McGary, eds., *Folio* 1/1 (June 1983): 1.
[10]Ibid., 3.

women's careers, service areas, awards, and ordinations not always available through the Baptist Press. The original volunteers of *Folio* sifted through state papers, seminary newsletters, and personal correspondence to gather the information that appeared in this section of *Folio*.

The first steering committee formed an ad hoc committee to make recommendations concerning *Folio* at the meeting in Kansas City. The committee reaffirmed the nature of the group to include SBC women in ministry, both ordained and unordained, and their supporters. The theme selected for the 1984 meeting was "Exercising Our Gifts." The Steering Committee held two planning meetings, both in Atlanta.

Women in Ministry, SBC, held its second annual meeting June 9-10, 1984, at the Raddison-Muehlbach Hotel, Kansas City, Missouri. The theme was based on Matthew 10:16-33. The convenor of this meeting was Anne Thomas Neil. Speakers included Lynda Weaver-Williams, "Exercising Our Gifts"; and Elizabeth Barnes (NC), "Into the Far Country." The preacher for the Sunday morning worship was Susan Lockwood (IL), whose sermon was entitled "Exercising Our Gifts: A Question of Obedience."[11]

At the business meeting the group expressed appreciation for *Folio* and other newsletters supporting women in ministry; however, they decided not to have *Folio* as the official voice of the organization at that time. The following new members were added to the steering committee: Sylvia Nadler (TX); Debbie Lastinger Pittman (MO); Anne Hickey (DC); Nancy Ellett (TX); Jane Medema (CA); Irene Bennett (TN); and Ashli Cartwright Peak (MO). They replaced the original task force members who had completed two-year terms. *Proceedings* were printed and mailed to registrants.

The support for women in ministry had been growing among Southern Baptists, as evidenced by the establishment of three regional resource centers for Southern Baptist women in ministry in the Southeast. The three centers were located in Wake Forest, North Carolina, Pineville, Louisiana, and Louisville, Kentucky. The centers were to serve as "clearing houses" for the gathering and dispensing of information, to provide communication and support, and to serve as a channel for networking. Women ministers also began to organize on the state level. The nationally organized group, Women in Ministry, SBC, appears to have energized women throughout the South to begin state and local support groups. In the Winter 1984 issue of

---

[11]Included in Libby Bellinger, ed., "Ears to Hear: Sermons by Southern Baptist Women" (unpublished manuscript).

Folio five state groups are listed: North Carolina, Texas, Alabama, Kentucky, and Tennessee. Four of the six Southern Baptist seminaries reported having women in ministry groups organized.[12]

In the fall of 1983 the ordination of women was a highly controversial issue at state Baptist conventions. Five state conventions debated resolutions concerning the ordination of women as ministers, and seven states had such resolutions introduced. At the initial meeting of the SBC Forum in 1984 one of the chief issues originally to be addressed was a pro and con discussion on the ordination of women. Addressing members of the Baptist Press Association at their 1984 meeting, Sarah Ann Hobbs, director of the mission division of the Baptist State Convention of North Carolina, said, "It is likely that the single most important issue among Southern Baptists today is women in ministry."[13] The 1984 Southern Baptist Convention was infamous for its "Women's Resolution" which stated that women should not be ordained as ministers.[14]

In its business meeting in Atlanta, the 1984–1985 steering committee sent letters of affirmation to Jewish rabbis, associations, and state conventions who supported the ordination of women and the positive role of women in Baptist churches and who expressed disapproval of the 1984 SBC resolution.[15]

Negative reactions to the SBC's "Women's Resolution" came at the state level as well. The Baptist General Association of Virginia was the first Baptist state convention to repudiate the SBC action and express approval of the ordination of women. The reactions of many individuals, churches, associations, and Baptist state conventions expressed disapproval and outrage at the 1984 SBC resolution. Many Southern Baptists obviously supported the resolution, however. For example, messengers from the First Baptist Church of Oklahoma City had difficulty being seated at the state convention because the church ordained women as deacons.

The WIM, SBC steering committee's work consisted of developing organizational guidelines; electing officers to take office in June 1985; the establishment of annual dues; the setting of guidelines for the control of usage of the mailing list; the acceptance of contributions, such as the one

---

[12]*Folio* 3/3 (Winter 1985): 2.
[13]As cited in *Folio* 1/4 (Spring 1984): 6.
[14][Editor's note: See excerpt from this resolution, above, xiii.]
[15]"WIM, SBC Minutes," 1984 and 1985.

made by the WMU, SBC; and the establishment of a program and theme development for the next meeting in Dallas.

Disdaining the controversy in the SBC and mocking the 1984 resolution against the ordination of women, WIM, SBC pressed forward towards their third meeting. The 1985 Women in Ministry, SBC meeting was held June 8-9, 1985, at the Wilshire Baptist Church in Dallas. The group conducted Sunday worship at the Adolphus Hotel in Dallas. The theme, "Voices of Hope from the Exile" (Col 3:12-17), had been selected because it captured the reality of the oppression felt by women in ministry in 1985, but it also acknowledged their will and determination to claim and hold on to hope.

The program itself was the most ambitious ever, with more than thirty leaders, two worship times, four major addresses and a concert by Cynthia Clawson and Ken Medema. The Sunday worship time began with a Bible study led by Carolyn Blevins (TN). Molly Marshall-Green preached on "Singing the Lord's Song" (Ps 137:1-4; Col 3:12-17). Attendance had grown from seventy-five in 1983 to 150 in 1984 to 350 in 1985. More than 500 people were present for the Sunday worship service. The highlight of the conference—as reported on evaluations—was hearing Addie Davis, the first Southern Baptist woman ordained to the clergy.

At the business session, eight women were elected to serve a two-year term on the WIM, SBC steering committee. They were Elizabeth Barnes (NC), Elizabeth Smith Bellinger (TX), Debra Harless (IN), Dianne Eubanks Hill (NC), Karen Conn Mitcham (KY), Meredith Neill (NC), Deborah Whisnand Stinson (TX), Susan Lockwood (IL), and Molly Marshall-Green (KY). Ashli Cartwright Peak was elected chair/convenor and Nancy Ellett was elected secretary/recorder. The membership accepted the recommendation on dues for the organization and adopted guidelines until a a constitution and bylaws could be drawn up. Registrants became voting members.

This was the first year the conference was recorded and made available on tape. The summer issue of *Folio*, which was distributed at the meeting, contained "A History of Women in Ministry, SBC" by Betty McGary in consultation with Nancy Hastings Sehested, Anne Thomas Neil, and Reba Sloan Cobb.[16]

Following the annual meeting, the steering committee held its first fall retreat at a conference center outside Atlanta. The retreat consisted of fellowship, the sharing of stories, planning meetings, and worship. Special

---

[16]"WIM, SBC Proceedings," 8 and 9 June 1985.

guest speaker for the retreat was Welton Gaddy of Macon, Georgia, who spoke on "The Status of the SBC." The committee received a report from Dorothy Proctor (GA), who was serving as Carolyn Weatherford's representative on the committee, that the WMU would help defray some costs and expenses to be incurred during the year. The WMU held an ex officio position on the steering committee.

Both the fall and spring meetings of the steering committee were busy ones. Under Ashli Peak's leadership, the committee worked on the following. New subcommittees were formed and appointed: a *Folio* committee, long-range planning, historical, membership/registration, public relations, program, finance, nominating, and resolutions. *Proceedings* were printed and mailed to registrants of the 1985 meeting. A Limited Cooperative Agreement between the Center for Women in Ministry, Inc. and WIM, SBC was recommended for a vote by the membership. The establishing of a tax-exempt status was begun. Officers were elected to begin serving in June 1986. A constitution and bylaws were developed and recommended. Two women were appointed to fill vacancies on the committee: Marilyn Prickett (DC) and Carolyn Whitehurst (LA).

The fourth meeting of WIM, SBC was in Atlanta, June 7-8, 1986, at Second Ponce de Leon Baptist Church and the ballroom of the Omni Hotel. The theme for the meeting was "We Preach Not Ourselves" (2 Cor 4:5).

The business session on Saturday focused on the adoption of the first constitution. The essence of the document established a structure and affirmed the purpose as a support group for women in ministry. Since 1983, WIM, SBC had existed without official membership or constitution.

With the approval of the constitution, the name of the organization was officially changed to Southern Baptist Women in Ministry (SBWIM). The designation of "officers" can officially be used from this point, as the constitution called for a president, vice-president, recorder, treasurer, and program coordinator. Ashli Cartwright Peak was reelected president (formerly convenor). The number of steering committee members was increased from sixteen to eighteen, with terms of service changing from two years to three. The six steering committee members elected at this meeting were: Isabel Decampo Austin (LA), Patricia Lawson Bailey (KY), Virginia C. Barfield (NC), Esther J. Nahm (NY), Anne Plunkett Rosser (VA), and Nancy Hastings Sehested (MO). Resolutions of gratitude were adopted and presented to WMU, SBC and to Second Ponce de Leon Baptist Church. The Radio and Television Commission, SBC taped and videotaped the meeting for the first time. This was the first meeting in which the program appeared in a booklet form.[17]

On Sunday, June 8, the morning began with a Bible study of 2 Corinthians 4 led by Virginia Barfield (NC). Jan Fuller Carruthers (TN) preached on "Abundant Grace, Much Thanksgiving." Ten percent of the offering was donated to a women's prison group in Atlanta.

Jan Fuller Carruthers (prior to her marriage) had been the focus of a controversy at the Home Mission Board, SBC, because of her status as clergy and because of a request that she be appointed as a missionary. At the 1985 spring meeting of the HMB, the issue of women's ordination was debated for about an hour, and then a special committee was asked to be appointed to develop guidelines concerning ordination for use in the appointment of missionaries.

At the October 1986 meeting of the HMB, this report was received. It recommended there be no change in the Board's policy concerning the appointment of chaplains nor in the Board's relationship to ordained women then serving; however, it was recommended that the Church Pastoral Aid Program (CPA) no longer be available to churches needing assistance if they employed a woman as pastor. At the time of this action, Broadneck Baptist Church in Arnold, Maryland, was the only church with a woman pastor (Debra Griffis-Woodberry, former WIM, SBC Steering Committee member) that was funded by the Home Mission Board's CPA program.

When the HMB action was revealed, the SBWIM's steering committee's resolutions committee took the unprecedented step of making an official statement publicly protesting the Home Mission Board's action. In an interview, Susan Lockwood, chair of the resolutions committee, responded:

> It's a very difficult time for every Southern Baptist woman minister I know. Politics and strategizing, confrontations and public criticism largely go against our grain. Not many Southern Baptist women relish this kind of battle. . . . We come at this from a pietistic, theological basis, and it's very painful to find ourselves having to be assertive. The situation is not one any of us would choose, but we find ourselves in the place in history; we've got to raise a prophetic voice.[18]

Besides responding to the Home Mission Board's action, the Steering Committee also conducted the following business: historical depositories were established at the WMU in Birmingham, at the SBC Historical

---

[17]"SBWIM Minutes," 1986.
[18]*Folio* 4/3 (Winter 1986): 3.

Commission in Nashville, and at the Women's Resource Center, Southeastern Seminary in Wake Forest, North Carolina, and an oral history project on women in ministry was begun by Baylor University's Oral History Institute in Waco, Texas; an official logo was chosen and printed; the Limited Cooperative Agreement with the Center for Women in Ministry was refined and revised; and representatives to the editorial board were selected. At this point Molly Marshall-Green began as interim editor of *Folio*.

The Southern Baptist Alliance was discussed at the meeting, and a statement of encouragement and support was sent to Henry Crouch, president of the Alliance. Several former and present steering committee members were active in forming the Alliance. Susan Lockwood was the first vice-president, and Anne Neil later became president of the Alliance.

Officers were elected; the WMU continued to have a representative present at meetings and provided financial and printing assistance; the program was set for the next annual meeting; SBWIM's first brochure was printed and distributed; and committee reports were given and future plans made.[19]

The fifth annual meeting was held June 13-14, 1987, at Kirkwood Baptist Church, Kirkwood, Missouri, and the Clarion Hotel, St. Louis. The theme for this year was "Living Toward a Vision of Shalom" (Eph 2:14). The meeting was marked by inclusiveness through the language, hymns, and program personalities. The musical theme that ran throughout the meeting was: "Come, let us walk in the light of the Lord, calling our enemies friends. Building a kingdom where justice reigns, and God's creatures walk hand in hand."[20]

In spite of the climate in the SBC, the SBWIM meeting turned its attention to the broader vision of God's kingdom and shifted its focus from the organization itself to the larger community. Catherine Meeks of Mercer University in Macon, Georgia, preached Saturday morning, "Then I Will Speak upon the Ashes." In the evening, testimonies were given by Vernon Davis (MO), his daughter Carol Davis Younger (IN), and Sally Murphy Morgan (IL). The Sunday morning sermon was "Visions of a New Humanity" (Luke 1), preached by Lynda Weaver-Williams (VA). This was the last meeting at which the WMU, SBC shared its meeting space for Sunday worship. Ten percent of the morning offering was given to a St. Louis women's group dealing with domestic violence.

---

[19]Libby Bellinger, "SBWIM President's Notes," 1986–1989.
[20]"SBWIM Program," 13-14 June 1987.

At the business session on Saturday, the following officers were presented: Libby Bellinger (TX), president; Anne Rosser (VA), vice-president; Diane Hill (NC), recording secretary; Deborah Whisnand Stinson (TX), treasurer; Marilyn Prickett (DC), program; and Pat Bailey (KY), membership. Five new steering committee members were elected to fill vacancies to serve three-year terms: Carol Causey (AL), Nancy Furgerson Cole (MO), Betty Winstead McGary (TX), Phyllis Rogerson Pleasants (KY), and Linda Bridges (KY).[21]

As in the past, the Steering Committee met twice after the St. Louis gathering. Donna Charlton Starkes (NV) was appointed to fill a vacancy on the committee. The committee's main function was to plan for the next annual meeting in 1988. The business conducted included the giving of input to the Southern Baptist Alliance on the needs of SBWIM. As a result of this input, the Alliance gave SBWIM a direct monetary gift, directed church giving to SBWIM, and added the amount of $5,000 to its budget in order to provide a student intern for *Folio.*

The president reported on a meeting with Carolyn Weatherford, head of the WMU. Weatherford shared some of the "heat" the WMU had been receiving because of its relationship with SBWIM; however, the visit solidified the supportive relationship of WMU. Weatherford and I jointly wrote a chronicle of the WMU/SBWIM relationship. Historical items were placed in the WMU archives, and the WMU printed and mailed the *Proceedings* of the St. Louis meeting. SBWIM was invited by the WMU to participate in their centennial celebration through a booth. At this booth, SBWIM distributed brochures, pins, labels, and the "chronicle of relationship." The Steering Committee was invited to have one of their 1988–1989 meetings in Birmingham at the WMU headquarters.[22]

The president also reported on two other items: (1) a joint press release issued by a group of Moderate Baptists on actions occurring in the SBC (this was the first such recognition of SBWIM as a Moderate voice in the SBC); and (2) a report on the latest statistics available from Sarah Frances Anders. These statistics included (as of June 1988): 460 confirmed clergy-women (of estimated 525 total); 18 pastors; 36+ associate pastors; 73+ chaplains; 4+ associational missionaries; and 20+ campus ministers. Almost

---

[21]"SBWIM Proceedings," 1987.
[22]"SBWIM Minutes/President's Notes," 1987–1988.

half were ordained in, and their present positions were in, Virginia, North Carolina, and Kentucky.[23]

The sixth annual meeting was held June 11-12, 1988, in San Antonio, Texas, at the Manor Baptist Church and the Arneson Theater on the River Walk. The theme for this meeting was, "Differing Gifts according to Grace" (Rom 12:6). As usual, the meeting focused on worship; however, Jann Aldredge Clanton preached the only sermon on Saturday morning ("Prophesy by Faith"). The Sunday morning service was rich in music and visuals. The highlight was "A Dialogue of Gifts," presented by Carolyn Cole Bucy, Ardell Clemens, Barry McCarty, Libby Potts, and Carmen Sharp. Ten percent of the offering from this service went to children's programs of the San Antonio Parks and Recreation Department.

The business meeting was held Saturday afternoon at Manor Baptist Church. The first order of business was the election of steering committee members. The following persons were elected: Sheila Black (NC), Carolyn Cole Bucy (TX), Nancy Campbell (TX), Cheryl Collins (VA), Cindy Johnson (MD), Elaine Henderson (AL), and Marsha A. Moore (NM). Officers for 1988–1989 were introduced as follows: Betty McGary, president; Phyllis Pleasants, vice-president; Ginger Barfield (NC), recorder/secretary; Donna Charlton-Starks (NV), treasurer; Pat Bailey (KY), membership; and Nancy Cole (MO), program.

An open discussion on the possibility of SBWIM conducting a retreat in the future led to the consensus that a regional retreat format in addition to the regular annual meeting would be desirable. A motion was passed that the steering committee take these sentiments under advisement, confer with state leadership of WIM chapters, and present a report at the business meeting in Las Vegas in 1989.

After considerable discussion, the members passed a bylaws change. Section V of the bylaws was amended to read: "Annual dues will be required of all members of SBWIM. The dues will include a subscription to *Folio*." It was also announced that the SBWIM logo was available for those state chapters that wished to identify themselves as an affiliate.

Molly Marshall-Green presented a report on *Folio* and offered appreciation to the Southern Baptist Alliance for a contribution of $5,000. A motion was also passed that SBWIM commend the CBS producers of "Designing Women" for one of the best efforts at televangelism ever. A motion was

---

[23]Sarah Frances Anders, "Statistics," 1988 (unpublished).

passed that the Steering Committee find sites for future meetings that are handicapped-accessible and that all materials be printed in large type on white paper. The business meeting was followed by a fiesta at La Villita on the River in downtown San Antonio.[24]

McLean Baptist Church, McLean, Virginia, was the setting for the fall meeting of the SBWIM steering committee. The Las Vegas meeting was the top-priority agenda item. It was decided that along with the usual business session, seminars, and worship, an opportunity would be provided for a "hands-on" ministry project in the community. The steering committee spent significant time processing the need for continuity and structure in SBWIM. Because of this discussion, a revised constitution was brought for consideration at the winter meeting. This meeting was held, at the invitation of Carolyn Weatherford, at WMU headquarters in Birmingham. The first male member of the steering committee, Edgar Tanner (TX), was appointed to fill a vacancy. The steering committee was informed that the executive board of the Southern Baptist Alliance voted an annual grant of $7,200 to SBWIM for a student intern to assist in the production of *Folio*. SBWIM was also included in the Global Missions budget of the SBA, and by action of the SBA board the SBWIM president was added as an ex officio member of the SBA board.[25]

The Steering Committee also sadly discussed the closing of the Women's Resource Center at Southeastern Seminary. The center had been on the campus for five years. Its purpose had been "to provide support, to foster understanding among men and women, to make available resources for women's pilgrimages and growth toward fulfillment in their Christianity."[26] The Southeastern Women in Ministry chapter had staffed the center since it had become an official student organization in 1986. After a protest of this closing, the Resource Center was reopened in January 1989 with a dedication service on the lower level of Binkley Chapel.[27]

During the fall of 1988, another group related to SBWIM was also meeting. The Board of Directors for the Center for Women in Ministry, Kentucky, took steps to reorganize its staff. Prompting this move was the resignation of Molly Marshall-Green as editor of *Folio*. The reorganization was designed to allow the Center to provide more services for SBWIM.

---

[24]"SBWIM Program and Minutes," 1988.

[25]*Folio* 6/4 (Spring 1989): 1.

[26]Women's Resource Center *Newsletter,* 1984.

[27]Ibid., 6/4 (Spring 1989): 2.

Reba Sloan Cobb, former coeditor of *Folio* for four years, volunteered to administer the work of the center.[28]

The seventh annual meeting of SBWIM was held June 10-11, 1989, at Alexis Park Resort, Las Vegas. For the first time the meeting took place entirely in one setting. The Alexis Park Resort was chosen because of its convenience and because of the absence of a casino. The program began with Saturday morning worship. Catherine Allen of the WMU in Birmingham preached. The theme was, "Stories of Faith: A Rich Tapestry" (Heb 12:1-2). The Sunday morning services had a separate title: "A Tapestry of Faith: Readings and Testimonies." The service was written by Marcia Moore (NM), a member of the steering committee. Testimonies were given by Jack U. Harwell (GA), Ken Sehested (MO), Phyllis Rodgerson Pleasants (KY), Cheryl Collins (VA), and Marsha A. Moore (NM).

At the business meeting the following were elected to the Steering Committee: Ruth Fowler (NY), Roger Paynter (TX, the first male to be *elected* to the steering committee), Christine Rowland (TX), Sue Skinner (CA), Pamela Tanner (TX), and Edgar Tanner (TX). The Steering Committee brought the following items for consideration and discussion by the membership: (1) adding the office of president-elect to the present SBWIM officers; (2) the appointing of a committee to study and revise the constitution; (3) the appointment of a committee to study the feasibility of a fiscal relationship between SBWIM and the Center for Women in Ministry, Kentucky. A rationale was distributed for taking such action; however, a vote was not taken at the meeting. Officers were presented: Betty McGary (TX), president; Nancy Cole (MO), vice-president; Carol Causey (AL), recorder; Carolyn Bucy (TX), program; and Sheila Black (NC), membership.[29]

The steering committee met three times during the interim between the Las Vegas and the New Orleans meetings. At these gatherings the committee and subcommittees were busy. They worked on plans for the annual meeting, which had always been the focus of these meetings. They worked on recommended constitutional changes that would extend the office of president to two years through the addition of a president-elect office, and—the most dramatic change—the merger of CWIM with SBWIM. The two organizations began in 1983 and had existed autonomously and cooperatively since that time.

---

[28]Ibid., 1.
[29]"SBWIM Program and Minutes," 1-11 June 1989.

The constitutional change also added new ex officio members to the board: the chair of the SBA Women in the Church Committee, the president of Baptists Committed, the president of the Southern Baptist Convention, the executive director of the WMU, and the pastor of Crescent Hill Baptist Church.[30]

The committee also considered altering the nomination process of new steering committee members. It was suggested that a nomination selection committee be implemented in order to provide a wider representation of SBWIM's diversity on the steering committee. Betty McGary, president, also reported on the naming of a committee to plan the celebration of the ten-year anniversary of SBWIM.[31]

The eighth annual meeting of SBWIM was held June 9-10, 1990, in New Orleans, at the Hotel Intercontinental. The theme for this conference was, "Welcoming the Stranger . . . Sojourners in the Fellowship of God" (Eph 2:19). A diverse offering of workshops and seminars was available along with business sessions. Worship started the day on Saturday, the highlight being the sermon by Carolyn Weatherford Crumpler of Ohio.

The Sunday morning session began with a Bible study led by Rosalie Beck of Waco, Texas. The Sunday worship, "An Invitation to the Table," was a communion service celebration of the inclusiveness of the Gospel. As a symbol of this inclusiveness, breads from around the world were offered at five tables. Meditations were offered by Greg and Katrina Pennington, Sarah Frances Anders, Donna Starkes, Betty McGary, and Edgar Tanner. The offering from this service was used for the Carver Center for tuition for camp fees for underprivileged children.[32]

Registration for this meeting was the largest in history, with more than 500 attending the Sunday morning worship service. In the business session, members approved constitutional revisions that merged the SBWIM steering committee with the board of the Center for Women in Ministry in Louisville. The name "Steering Committee" was changed to "Executive Board." This board was given the job of interim management of the affairs of SBWIM and CWIM between annual sessions. It would propose bylaws, fill vacancies, appoint committees, make necessary appropriations, prepare a

---

[30]"SBWIM Constitution," 1990.
[31]"SBWIM Steering Committee Minutes," 1989–1990.
[32]"SBWIM Program," 9-10 June 1990.

budget, set the date and place of the annual meeting, arrange the program, and propose plans for the future.[33]

The aim of these changes was to "provide for more membership involvement on the Board, more continuity of leadership, and add members of the CWIM to the SBWIM board."[34] A few voices of disapproval greeted these changes, but the new constitution was approved by a majority vote.

Six SBWIM members were elected to serve three-year terms. In addition, six members of the board of directors of CWIM were appointed by that board. Elected were Phil Christopher (KY), Nancy Foil (VA), Carolyn Sue Hale (KY), Michelle Cooper McClendon (SC), Geneva Nell Metzger (NC), and Katrina Pennington (OK). From the CWIM board the following agreed to serve: Sarah Frances Anders (LA), Reba Cobb (KY), Nancy Howard (TN), Andrew D. Lester (KY), Clara McCartt (KY), and Carmen Sharp (KY). New officers were Carolyn Cole Bucy (TX), president; Cheryl Collins (VA), vice-president; Nancy Campbell (TX), treasurer; Cindy Johnson (MD), recorder; Pam Tanner (TX), program; and Sheila Black (NC), membership.[35]

Meeting in Louisville in October 1990, the new SBWIM Board began planning the 1991 meeting for Atlanta. President Carolyn Bucy describes 1990–1991 as a transition year for SBWIM. To handle the changes, she appointed a transition committee composed of Edgar Tanner, Donna Charlton-Starkes, Nancy Howard, Nancy Campbell, and Clara McCartt. This committee recommended the establishment of an ad hoc constitution committee to address further changes required by the merger and by changes within the SBC. These changes were to be recommended for a vote at the Atlanta meeting.[36] It was announced that Mary Zimmer was the new editor of *Folio* and Nancy Morgan was the administrative assistant for CWIM.

Reports were heard on the first Cooperative Baptist Fellowship Convocation, which would be held in Atlanta in May 1991. President Bucy had been asked to speak as a representative of SBWIM. Several former steering committee members and current SBWIM members were involved in planning the Fellowship meeting.

---

[33]"SBWIM Constitution," June 1990, and *Folio* 7/4 (Spring 1990): 1.

[34]*Folio* 8/2 (Autumn 1990): 1.

[35]Cindy Harp Johnson, "SBWIM Memo," 1991, included with "Minutes," 1990–1991.

[36]"SBWIM Executive Board Minutes," 1990.

A letter was written by Recorder Cindy Johnson to the Fellowship worship committee following the spring 1991 Convocation, affirming their inclusiveness on the program and worship. In it she answered the oft-asked question, "Just what do you women want?" Her response:

> What SBWIM and our supporters want is an absence of reneging on our denominational heritage of the autonomy of the local church, and the right of those churches to ordain and call women as ministers, to be represented in those ministers who act as worship leaders at Southern Baptist meetings. What SBWIM and our supporters want is an absence of reneging on the denominational dream of celebration of diversity as a tool through which a lost world might be won to Christ. In short, our desires echo the longings of all who have been disenfranchised throughout the existence of the SBC, including the fundamentalists of recent history and the moderates of current times. We want to be recognized as valid and vital members of the Body. And this is not a request for a quota-system mentality. It is a challenge to capture a vision of all the components of our denomination, and to allow the leaders and the language of our gatherings to reflect that true identity.[37]

The ninth annual meeting of SBWIM was held June 1-2, 1991, at Oakhurst Baptist Church, Decatur, Georgia. The theme was, "Be Strong and Courageous" (Josh 1:9). The program for the meeting was reduced in size. The event started Saturday evening with a dinner at Stone Mountain, Georgia. The rationale for this was the expectation that the number of women participating would be reduced because of a drop in Moderate attendance at the SBC and because the organization was planning a retreat for the fall and needed to focus on that event.[38]

A new precedent was set at the Sunday morning worship: for the first time it was held during the eleven o'clock worship hour at a local church. The congregation of Oakhurst Baptist Church turned over its worship time to SBWIM. The congregation even set up an ad hoc committee to help with preparation and helped serve as worship leaders. Communion highlighted this service. It was led by Sharyn Dowd (KY), and an "Invitation to Courageous Living" was given by Nancy Ammerman (GA).[39]

The business session was held for the first time on Sunday, following a lunch at Oakhurst Baptist Church. Eight new board members were elected:

---

[37]Cindy Harp Johnson, "SBWIM Memo," 1991.
[38]"SBWIM Executive Board Minutes," 1990.
[39]"SBWIM Program," 2 June 1991.

Susan Coyle (KY), Terry Huneycutt (NC), Romelle Jones (MD), Bill Leonard (KY), Catherine Miller (NC), Dixie Petrey (TN), Sharlande Sledge (TX), and Cherie Smith (KY). It was announced that the SBA was continuing its grant of $5,000 to SBWIM. The first annual retreat was announced for November. The major constitutional change was to delete the need for the annual meeting to be held prior to the SBC.[40]

The officers for this year were: Pam Tanner (TX), president; Carolyn Hale (KY), vice-president; Reba Cobb (KY), treasurer; Michelle McClendon (SC), recorder; and Nancy Howard (TN), membership.

The main focus of the fall meeting of the executive board and SBWIM was the first retreat held November 7-9, 1991, at the Scarritt-Bennett Retreat Center in Nashville. "Proclamation: Our Lives as Living Word" was the theme for the weekend gathering. Fifty men and women came together to rest, renew, share, grow, fellowship, and worship. The retreat was led by Mary Zimmer (KY). She shared biblical stories from the perspective of five biblical women. Worship services were led by Sarah Frances Anders (LA), Carolyn Hale (KY), and Cindy Harp Johnson (MD).

At the November meeting prior to the retreat, the SBWIM board voted to hold the 1992 SBWIM annual meeting in April prior to the Cooperative Baptist Fellowship General Assembly in Ft. Worth, Texas. The board officers for 1992–1993 were Carolyn Hale (KY), president; Terry Huneycutt (NC), vice-president; Dixie Lee Petrey (TN), recording secretary; Phil Christopher (KY), treasurer; and Mary Zimmer (KY), membership.

Broadway Baptist Church, Fort Worth, was the setting for the 1992 annual meeting. Following a litany of fellowship and a review of the year by outgoing President Pam Tanner, there was a recognition of outgoing board members. Elected as new board members were Susan Cauley (LA), Sharon Kirkpatrick (TX), Donna McConnico (AL), Natalie Nicholas (GA), Karrie Oertli (TX), Judith Powell (NC), Ronda Steward-Wilcox (KY), David Waugh (RI), and Mary Zimmer (KY). Carolyn Plampin (CA) was previously elected by the board to fill a vacancy.[41]

The Alliance of Baptists continues to be the primary financial supporter of SBWIM through its annual grant of $5,000. In addition, SBWIM has been designated to receive up to $2,000 from the special annual Alliance offering which is received throughout the year. For the first time the

---

[40]Carolyn Cole Bucy, "President's Notes," 1991.
[41]*Folio* 10/1 (Summer 1992): 1.

Cooperative Baptist Fellowship, through its Ethics and Public Policy Committee, included SBWIM in the budget under all three contribution plans of the CBF.[42]

Southern Baptist Women in Ministry and *Folio* celebrate their tenth anniversary in 1993. In preparation for this event, a broadscale survey is being conducted seeking current information on women in ministry in Southern Baptist life (to be available in the spring of 1993). A Decade Committee has been formed under the leadership of Betty McGary, former SBWIM President. This committee is planning a theme that will be in effect for the entire year. The theme is Rev 3:8: "I know your work. Look, I have set before you an open door, which no one is able to shut. I know that you have but little power, and yet you have kept my word and have not denied my name" (NRSV). Under the new editorship of Amanda Hiley, *Folio* will be redesigned. The next annual meeting will occur May 1993, preceding the Cooperative Baptist Fellowship meeting in Birmingham.

It should be reported as part of the saga related to SBWIM that the Women's Resource Center begun at Southeastern Seminary nearly nine years ago was moved in 1992 to the Baptist Theological Seminary at Richmond. New Testament Professor Linda Bridges noted a symbolic significance of the move, saying, "As these resources have a new home at BTSR, so too do Baptist women who feel called to ministry. BTSR is becoming a place that welcomes with enthusiasm all who feel called to ministry, and this resource center coming to us is another sign of this hope."[43]

Summary

A decade has passed since SBWIM was formed. The group has moved from a loosely affiliated support system with a convenor to a highly structured nonprofit organization that employs a staff and publishes a newsletter.

SBWIM moved from a narrow purpose statement to a complex set of rules and regulations. The merger of CWIM and SBWIM has strengthened CWIM and has probably enabled both to stay "alive and healthy."[44] However, the original nature of the group included the ability to dissolve easily and simply because it was unencumbered by organizational structures.

---

[42]Ibid.

[43]Baptist Theological Seminary at Richmond *Newsletter* 1/3 (July 1992).

[44]Betty McGary, "President's Column," *Folio* 8/1 (Summer 1990): 2.

Perhaps all such groups become institutionalized, as have the Alliance of Baptists and the Cooperative Baptist Fellowship, but this does not seem to have been the intent of the original foremothers. The organization has not modeled new forms of leadership for the church but conformed to the white-male system of control and structure.

At the same time, SBWIM has encouraged women to fuller ministries in the church and has provided an avenue for the sharing of the joys and struggles of women in ministry. Its leadership has made visible the "invisible" in Southern Baptist life. The organization is frightening enough to some that "the women" must be dealt with; the organization has supporters enough that "the women" will be dealt with.

SBWIM is not what it was or what it can be in the future, but within Southern Baptist life, the organization has supported those women and men whose calling from God is to proclaim the Gospel; has supported those women and men who have felt as though they were to be burned at the stake; and has cried out against those in this century who would silence their tongues forever.

The cover of the Spring 1988 issue of *Folio* had a cartoon with the clarion call, "the Women are Coming . . . the Women are Coming." Well, gentlemen—and ladies—the women are here. Baptist women in ministry are in step with our courageous forebears, going against the tide of ecclesiastical disapproval. They choose instead to be accountable to God. They can do no other.

We have a rich heritage. Gladly is it revealed.

Cross Reference of Names

Nancy Hastings Sehested—Nancy Sehested
Carolyn Weatherford Crumpler—Carolyn Weatherford
Anne Neil—Anne Thomas Neil
Reba Cobb—Reba Sloan Cobb
Linda McKinnish Bridges—Linda Bridges
Cindy Johnson—Cindy Harp Johnson
Molly Marshall—Molly Marshall-Green—Molly Thurman Marshall
Betty McGary—Betty Winstead McGary—Betty McGary Pearce
Susan Lockwood—Susan Lockwood Wright
Libby Bellinger—Elizabeth Smith Bellinger
Nancy Ellett Allison—Nancy Ellett
Patricia Bailey—Patricia Lawson Bailey
Jan Fuller Carruthers—Jan Fuller
Anne Rosser—Anne Plunkett Rosser
Jann Aldredge-Clanton—Jann Clanton
Carolyn Bucy—Carolyn Cole Bucy
Phyllis Rogerson Pleasants—Phyllis Pleasants
Ginger Barfield—Virginia C. Barfield
Donna Charlton-Starkes—Donna Starkes

The History of
Baptists Today (1982–1992)

Walker L. Knight

In the fall of 1982 the takeover of the Southern Baptist Convention by Fundamentalists had manifested itself through the convention's last four presidential elections. Moderates, led primarily by a coalition of pastors united by Cecil Sherman of Asheville, North Carolina, and Kenneth Chafin of Houston, Texas, had garnered a sizeable vote for their candidates in the elections of 1981 and 1982, but they had failed to meet the challenge of the sharp shift to the right engulfing not only the SBC but the nation itself.

More and more Moderate leaders felt the need for a national publication to counterbalance the propaganda and bogus charges leveled against denominational employees, seminary faculty, and other longtime SBC leaders. In the fall of 1982 a group of Moderates meeting in Louisville determined to establish such a publication, provided someone with name recognition could be found as editor. Larry McSwain of Southern Baptist Theological Seminary, a member of the group, contacted me. At the time I was director of editorial services at the SBC Home Mission Board (HMB) in Atlanta. The group had learned I was dissatisfied with the direction the HMB was moving under President William Tanner.[1] Tanner frequently questioned the editorial direction of *Missions USA*, which I had edited for the past twenty-three years. Tanner recently had asked for the creation of an editorial policy, a move I felt would curtail the editorial freedom of the publication which he had used to deal openly and thoroughly with racial attitudes, other national ethical concerns, women's role in ministry, social justice, and an openness to new ideas. Then fifty-nine years old, I was

---

[1]"Journal," unpublished, by Walker L. Knight, 16 Sept 1982 to 26 Feb 1983.

considering alternative areas of work, including joining *Seeds*, a national hunger magazine, or buying a weekly newspaper.

When McSwain called me in October 1982, I was eager to explore possibilities of a national newspaper directed toward Southern Baptists. Along with other Baptist journalists, I had long nurtured a dream to create a national newspaper. We saw this as a vacuum in Southern Baptists' vast communication network which state newspapers were unable to fill and be faithful to their local assignments.

A National Newspaper

Larry McSwain asked me to present my vision of such a publication, including the start-up costs, to a meeting of Moderate leaders at the Atlanta airport the day after Thanksgiving, November 29, 1982. At the meeting I outlined a publication of news and opinion directed toward a national audience of church and denominational leaders, laity and clergy. I saw SBC periodicals as either narrow in focus, such as mission magazines, or narrow in circulation, such as state papers. The new publication would be a nonprofit institution, governed by a board of directors, and operating as an autonomous unit, thus avoiding the pressures to report less than the truth either by distortion or by avoidance of the unpleasant. The publication would start as a monthly and, when able, increase its frequency. Included in its pages would be a discussion of the controversial with both sides presented, articles concerning the religious life, opinion, letters from the readers, news from all available sources, reviews of books and movies, editorials and cartoons and columns. The scope would be national and international geographically and broad in subject treatment. I asked for an initial $45,000 from the group to finance the first six months of operation, and some continuing support afterward.

The group discussed the proposal at length, with major concerns over the role of the editor and the inclusion of the Moderate "political" message. Some of the fourteen pastors and lay leaders considered my presentation too neutral and wanted assurance their message would be presented. I explained that as editor I would determine the content of the issues, but I was as concerned as they were with the Fundamentalist message, tactics and unfounded charges. A strong effort would be made to present news as fair and objective and to label opinion as such. All of their concerns about the controversy would be addressed in the publication, but my vision extended beyond the current struggle. The group pledged to raise the $45,000 by January 15, 1983, and, when the funds were in hand, I would announce my early retirement from the mission agency to start the publication. The group also assured me they would back me for the next two years.

The timing of the publication was upset by a pastor who was raising some of the money but who had not attended the meeting. He announced publicly that I would be resigning my position at the Home Mission Board and would start a new publication. Fearful that a distorted version of what was to happen would spread by word of mouth, I announced on December 6 my early retirement from the HMB effective March 1, 1983, and my intention to start a national publication with the first issue dated April 1983.[2]

On December 12, during worship services at Oakhurst Baptist Church in Decatur, Georgia, I sounded the call for a mission group of volunteers to staff and to support the new publication, using the passage from Joel 2:28 on young men seeing visions and old men dreaming dreams. Forty-five persons, including twelve with journalism experience, responded to the call, and were the nucleus around which the publication was created. This group voted to name the paper *SBC Today*, a name suggested by Jim Newton, news editor at the HMB.[3]

The news stories in the secular and religious press generated support from others throughout the nation, including nationally known journalists such as Elaine Furlow, a recent staffer in the Carter White House, and Warner Ragsdale, Jr., on the staff of *U.S. News and World Report* in Washington, D.C., and Roddy Stinson, a columnist for the *Express-News* in San Antonio. Oakhurst Baptist Church offered office space and gave $5,000 for the purchase of typesetting equipment. Individuals gave typewriters, desks, a copy machine, and office equipment. Lynn Donham, a volunteer with publication design experience, created the format for the *SBC Today* tabloid. Rob Suggs volunteered his services as an editorial cartoonist.

Susan Taylor, a communications specialist with an Atlanta hospital who had attended The Southern Baptist Theological Seminary and had worked as an intern with the Kentucky state paper, *The Western Recorder*, volunteered to leave her position at the hospital and work part-time for *SBC Today* as associate editor. Aspiring journalist Andy Orr volunteered as a ten-hour-a-week intern.

By February the Moderate group had $21,000 on hand, with another $16,000 pledged. The publication eventually received slightly more than

---

[2]*The Christian Index* 161/47 (16 Dec 1982): 3.
[3]Knight, "Journal," Feb 1983.

$30,000 from this group. Subscription rates were set at $15 for one year and $25 for two years, and a special appeal was made to secure charter subscriptions of $25 for two years. I had agreed to work for half my salary at the Home Mission Board, a move made possible because my wife Nell continued to work as a secretary at the HMB.

SBC Today and *Seeds,* which also had offices at Oakhurst Baptist Church, met both publications' needs by purchasing a computer jointly for circulation services.

The Moderate group secured a mailing list of more than 40,000 clergy and laity in the SBC, and this was used for the first issue and for most of the first year. There was a healthy response to appeals for subscribers, and by the end of the first year, more than 3,000 were paying subscribers, many for two years. Dick Fuller, starting a business of services for magazines, became the advertising representative, working for a percentage of advertising revenue. Hettie Johnson, retired director of business services at the HMB, volunteered as business manager.

The First Issue

The twenty-eight-page first issue, April 1983, presented a national and international scope in its news reports, including a firsthand account of the annual SBC Christian Life Commission meeting in Louisville and a report of the first meeting of what would later be the Southern Baptist Women in Ministry.[4] Furlow had volunteered as Washington editor and her first report dealt with the strength of the New Right. Reporter John Long of Louisville provided an update on heresy charges by an Arkansas Fundamentalist against Professor Dale Moody of Southern Seminary that Moody was teaching apostasy. Other features included a story on Baptist involvement with the Shroud of Turin, a fight against pornography by Paul McCommon, extensive foreign reports, a survey of readers asking if the SBC would split, a photographic feature on building a home for a widow, a sermon by John Nichol of Decatur, Georgia, reviews of books and movies, the first of a series of humor columns by layman Roddy Stinson, and the first of a three-part historical look at the glue that holds Baptists together by historian Walter Shurden. The issue included a feature unique to Baptist publications, "Politics & Corridor Talk" (suggested by public relations consultant Floyd Craig, then of North Carolina), which dealt with the political process at

---

[4]*SBC Today* 1/1 (April 1983).

work in the SBC, reports of rumors, and behind-the-scenes activity. The first column dealt with the process of naming persons to SBC committees.

My first editorial, "Why SBC Today?", presented the framework for the publication's reason for being. I outlined my experience as a journalist and my thirty-four years with Southern Baptists, and said I was not breaking that relationship with the creation of this autonomous publication. I affirmed the publication's support for missions and the Cooperative Program. Then I affirmed my belief in a regenerate church membership and soul competency or priesthood of the believers, "the individual's ability and right to go to the Scriptures without a creedal straitjacket."

I also wrote, "We believe the scriptures have as much to say on the many justice issues . . . as on the equally important subjects of evangelism, worship, education, and missions." I contended that religious liberty and separation of church and state followed from these other principles, indicating they would be championed by the publication.

Reaction to the publication crossed the spectrum from elation to despair to charges of liberalism, slanted news, and a counterpoint to the Fundamentalist-sponsored *Southern Baptist Journal*, also started by a former staff member of the Home Mission Board, Bill Powell.[5] In 1983 *SBC Today* received from the Baptist Public Relations Association the first-place award for publications.

The masthead of the first issue published the members of its executive board; however, the board of directors was still in formation. The executive board was composed of David Sapp of Chamblee, Georgia, as chair; Dallas M. Lee of Avondale Estates, Georgia, as vice-chair; Jack U. Harwell of Tucker, Georgia; T. Melvin Williams of Decatur, Georgia; William Self of Atlanta, Georgia; Charlene W. Shucker of Atlanta, Georgia; Earl Davis of Memphis, Tennessee; and I as secretary-treasurer. Sapp, Williams, Self, and Davis were all pastors. Lee, Harwell, and Shucker were all journalists. Wanting the initial presentation of the publication to appeal to as broad a spectrum as possible, I asked that neither Sherman nor Chafin be on the executive committee or board, since both were seen as lightning rods in the political controversy.

The August-September issue announced the creation of the board of directors, which added the following to those on the executive committee: W. Oscar Brazil, Jr. of Asheville, North Carolina; J. Dan Cooper of Lexington,

---

[5]See "Today's Mail" in issues of *SBC Today, 1983.*

Kentucky; Vernon Davis of Kansas City, Missouri; Larry K. Dipboye of Louisville, Kentucky; Pope A. Duncan of Deland, Florida; Don B. Harbuck of Chattanooga, Tennessee; T. B. Maston of Fort Worth, Texas; Abner V. McCall of Waco, Texas; Duke K. McCall of Louisville, Kentucky; and Guy W. Rutland, Jr. of Decatur, Georgia. Brazil and Rutland were laymen. Cooper, Dipboye, and Harbuck were pastors. Davis, Duncan, Maston, and the two McCalls were educators. In January 1984, the board was completed with the addition of educators C. Welton Gaddy and R. Kirby Godsey of Macon, Georgia, and Eleanor Wilson Nutt of Louisville, Kentucky.

On May 5, 1983, the publication was incorporated in Georgia as SBC Today, Inc. I served as the registered agent with the executive board as the initial board of directors.[6] The articles of incorporation read:

> The corporation is a nonprofit corporation organized for the following general purposes: to foster and advance throughout the United States and elsewhere the religious, charitable, literary, and educational objective of disseminating information regarding the Southern Baptist Convention, and other information of import to Southern Baptists.

All powers and authority were invested in the board of directors.[7]

The August meeting also received a report of income and expenses through July 31, 1983, showing $104,303.54 income, mostly through subscriptions ($49,089) and donations ($41,393). Advertising and a $10,000 computer loan provided the balance. Directors, because of the SBC contro-

---

[6]Incorporation papers for SBC Today, Inc., filed at offices at 222 East Lake Drive, Decatur GA.

[7]The law firm of Sutherland, Asbill & Brennan of Atlanta, was employed to secure exemption for SBC Today, Inc. from the federal income tax under section 501(c)(3) of the Internal Revenue Code. After lengthy work with the Internal Revenue Service, the exemption was granted on 10 August 1983 (identification number 58-1522462). However, the delay was costly to the publication, as the U.S. Post Office would not grant nonprofit status until the IRS did. I estimated the delay cost more than $7,000 in mailing expenses. Documents submitted to the IRS indicated assets on 31 July 1983 to be $52,928.96. My salary was listed at $16,000 and Taylor's at $12,000.

Bylaws, circulated by mail to the newly formed board, were adopted by the executive committee at its 15 August 1983 meeting. The bylaws stated the purpose of the organization was "to provide a nationally circulated publication of religious news and opinion of, by, and to members of the Southern Baptist Convention and for other persons interested in news of the denomination."

versy, asked that director's liability insurance be secured by January at a cost of $1,000.

An ambitious budget of $157,200 was adopted for 1984, which included the production of twelve issues during the year circulated to more than 30,000, even though only slightly more than 3,000 paid subscriptions had been secured at the time. When the executive committee met March 5, 1984[8] it was apparent the ambitious free circulation could not be sustained, and directors approved a reduction to 10,000, including the 4,000 paid subscribers, plus a reduction in the number of pages per issue. Promotional copies would be rotated through the larger mailing list on a monthly basis. A direct-mail appeal for gifts had secured cash and pledges of $16,000. In addition Oakhurst Baptist Church gave the paper another $3,600, and First Baptist Church of Decatur, Georgia, gave $2,500. A revised budget for 1984 called for the expenditure of only $60,000 for the year.

The first meeting of the board of directors was held June 11, 1984, in Kansas City, Missouri, the city where the Southern Baptist Convention was meeting. Directors voted to adopt an open policy on advertising, restricting it to the integrity of the enterprise and accuracy of the ad. Board members indicated a general agreement with the thrust of the paper, and "they were not concerned about being labeled 'liberal'."[9] Directors were concerned with the low salaries and the chair was asked to study the possibility of increasing them.[10] David Sapp and I were reelected as chair and secretary/treasurer, and Earl Davis replaced Dallas Lee as vice-chair in order to shift some of the leadership outside Georgia.

Not All Moderates Pleased

While the directors had indicated they were in general agreement with the editorial direction of the paper, not all Moderates were as pleased. In the fall of 1984 a committee of Moderate leaders, composed of Don Harbuck, Bill Self, and Jim Strickland, visited me to ask that I take a stronger position attacking Fundamentalists. I told the group that I would have difficulty

---

[8]"Executive Committee Minutes," 5 March 1984; on file at 222 East Lake Drive, Decatur GA.

[9]"Minutes, Board of Directors, SBC Today," 11 June 1984; on file at 222 East Lake Drive, Decatur GA.

[10]Both Taylor and I were given $2,400 a year raises at the January 1985 executive board meeting.

making attacks on personalities, but that I would be willing to publish articles Moderates might write as long as accusations could be documented, that I saw my role as primarily that of a journalist and I felt the controversy would be lengthy, which meant that the publication had to meet greater needs than just the political battle in order to survive.

Moderates, wanting a publication that would better serve as a "call to arms" against Fundamentalists, financed another tabloid in 1985, edited by Larry Dipboye in Louisville, Kentucky, under the name of *The Call, Dallas '85*. The primary purpose of this publication was handling charges and countercharges with the Fundamentalists and producing a turnout of Moderates for the SBC meeting in Dallas in June. I cooperated with the new publication by providing the names and addresses on file at *SBC Today* and offered to help in other ways. Dipboye remained as a director of *SBC Today*, offering to resign if I saw any conflict of interest. The new publication did not accept advertising or solicit subscriptions. Also, it did not have a definite publication schedule. Consequently, I did not feel it was in direct competition with *SBC Today*, although I did realize it would take away energy and resources. *The Call* continued to publish some issues through 1986.

Lay leadership, including John Baugh of Houston, Texas, Owen Cooper of Yazoo City, Mississippi, and Dewey Presley of Dallas started another publication, *The Baptist Laity Journal*, in 1985 in Texas. *The Journal's* purpose was very similar to *The Call*, and also did not have a subscriber base or accept advertising and addressed only the SBC controversy. *The Journal* later was associated with the Moderate organization "Baptists Committed to the SBC," an outgrowth of the Sherman/Chafin group. *SBC Today* directors asked its executive committee to make overtures to both *The Call* and *The Journal* to see if all three might not be joined, since they were directed to the same audience and had similar purposes.[11] The overtures were made but no positive response came from those publishing the other publications. *The Journal* stopped publication in 1990.

Controversy Dominates

The pages of *SBC Today* following the SBC meeting in Kansas City in 1984 dealt more and more with the controversy through reporting and opinion articles, including a study sponsored by a concerned lay couple in Birming-

---

[11]"Minutes, SBC Today, Board of Directors," 10 June 1985; on file at 222 East Lake Drive, Decatur GA.

ham, Julia and Bob Crowder, on the low support of the Cooperative Program by persons being nominated to serve as directors for SBC agencies.[12] The study generated a strong reaction, and was repeated the next year.[13] Following the Dallas meeting of the SBC, the Crowders announced in September they intended to file suit against the denomination because their rights were denied when bylaws were violated by rulings of SBC President Charles Stanley.[14]

In the fall of 1985, Associate Editor Taylor resigned to pursue a doctorate in economics. The paper employed Michael Tutterow part-time as an associate editor. He was a student at Candler School of Theology at Emory University and a journalist who had worked with me at the Home Mission Board. In addition, other part-time personnel were hired: Dick Fuller for advertising and typesetting, and Karen Mitchell for layout and design.[15] At this time the circulation had become stationary around 5,000, and the publication was operating on an annual budget of $84,500.[16]

Nancy Ammerman, a sociologist of religion at Emory University, approached me in 1984 about the need for someone to study what was happening with Southern Baptists, explaining that no sociologists had studied a major denomination during the time of conflict, only after the fact. I challenged her to undertake the study, and offered to aid in the financing for rights to publish the findings in *SBC Today*. Thus encouraged, Ammerman approached other, more neutral, sources and secured complete financing for her extensive and unique study. In December 1985 the newspaper published its first article by Ammerman, "Organizational Conflict in a Divided Denomination."[17]

In 1986 a series of articles, under the theme "Confronting the Bible" was launched by *SBC Today* in cooperation with Professor Robison James of the University of Richmond, who enlisted the authors and edited the

---

[12]*SBC Today* 2/3 (June 1984): 11, 12, 13.

[13]*SBC Today* 3/3 (June 1985): 6-7.

[14]*SBC Today* 3/6 (Sept 1985): 3.

[15]*SBC Today* 3/7 (Oct 1985): 10.

[16]"Minutes, Board of Directors," 10 June 1985; on file at 222 East Lake Drive, Decatur GA.

[17]*SBC Today* 3/8 (Nov 1985): 12-14. Ammerman's book *Baptist Battles, Social Change and Religious Conflict in the Southern Baptist Convention* was published by Rutgers University Press in 1990. A four-part condensation was published that year in *SBC Today*.

manuscripts.[18] Following their serial appearance in *SBC Today*, the manuscripts were published in 1987 by Word, Inc. under the title *The Unfettered Word*. This project was the first of several between James and *SBC Today*, and led directly to the publication in 1989 by *SBC Today* of a small book titled *Takeover in the Southern Baptist Convention*, edited by James. Based on a report from the denominational affairs committee of River Road Church in Richmond, Virginia, *SBC Today* and James produced the book both in paperback and in a tabloid format.[19] By 1992 its total circulation had exceeded 60,000 and the paperback was in its seventh printing.

Formation of the Southern Baptist Alliance

The 1986 Atlanta meeting of the SBC proved to be a watershed for many Moderate Southern Baptists. Options to continue participation with a convention controlled more and more by Fundamentalists began to surface, including the formation of a new convention, the move to other denominations, the forming of dual alignments, and/or the creation of a shadow convention.[20] In November 1986, as editor I joined a group of twenty-two individuals from Southern states who wished to move beyond politics to preserve Baptist "principles, freedoms, and traditions."

Meeting at Providence Baptist Church in Charlotte, North Carolina, the group decided to form The Southern Baptist Alliance (SBA), operating within the SBC, "dedicated to the preservation of historic Baptist principles, freedoms, and traditions and the continuance of ministry and mission within the Southern Baptist Convention." A covenant was adopted stressing seven principles: the freedom to read and interpret the Scriptures, the autonomy of churches, cooperation with the larger Christian body, the servant role of leadership, theological education characterized by open inquiry and responsible scholarship, evangelism and social and economic justice, and a free church in a free state.[21] The public announcement of the formation of the SBA was made simultaneously on February 12 in Charlotte, Atlanta, and Raleigh. The SBA budget would be financed by annual $25 membership fees for individuals and $1 per resident member for churches.

---

[18]*SBC Today* 4/2 (May 1986): 4-5.

[19]See *The Takeover in the Southern Baptist Convention*, ed. Robison James (Decatur GA: SBC Today, 1989).

[20]"Moderates Explore Options," *SBC Today* 4/5 (Aug 1986): 1.

[21]*SBC Today* 4/11 (Feb 1987): 4.

The newly formed SBA and *SBC Today* immediately entered into a partnership which benefited both. The publication offered to provide a subscription to each SBA member at a cost of $5 (normal rate for groups was $7.50) for the first year of the SBA's existence, after that it increased to $7. The SBA promoted its membership fee to include the subscription.[22] *SBC Today* became a primary vehicle for the promotion of the SBA and for the dissemination of its message. In the August/September issue of 1987 the first of a series on Baptist heritage began, written by SBA members.[23] This series, edited by Alan Neely of Southeastern Baptist Theological Seminary, was published in book form by the SBA in 1988 under the title, *Being Baptist Means Freedom.*[24] *SBC Today* also provided a special edition of each issue for the SBA circulated to its members in which one page was devoted to material provided by the SBA.[25]

Creation of the SBA exposed differing stategies for dealing with SBC Fundamentalism by members of the Moderate Movement. One group—the old political network that became Baptists Committed to the SBC—was determined to continue the political battle, while SBA members, many of whom would continue to attend the SBC annual meetings and vote for the Moderate candidate, believed such political strategy was doomed to failure. SBA members, searching for fellowship within a fractured convention, began giving their energies to preserving the traditions and heritage of Baptists. I identified strongly with the SBA, but *SBC Today* did not abandon those determined to continue the political fight for the SBC presidency.

However, when *SBC Today* later made overtures to the *Baptist Laity Journal* to find ways of working together, a lukewarm response was received. Members of the *SBC Today* board of directors reported the grapevine had it that *SBC Today* was considered "too liberal" and a "tool of the SBA" for effective political work. Later the same grapevine reported that some within the Moderate Movement felt it politically smart to label the

---

[22]"Minutes, Board of Directors, SBC Today, Inc.," 15 June 1987.

[23]Richard Groves, "Threat to Church Autonomy," *SBC Today* 5/5 (Aug 1987): 8-9.

[24]See *Being Baptist Means Freedom*, ed. Alan Neely (Charlotte: Southern Baptist Alliance, 1988).

[25]"Minutes, Board of Directors, SBC Today, Inc.," 24 Sept 1987.

SBA as liberal in order to make Baptists Committed appear more middle-of-the-road.[26]

It was true that both the SBA and *SBC Today* had taken supportive positions on the role of women in ministry. The SBA also was open to discussions with the American Baptist Churches for cooperation in missions and education, and there were few inerrantists within the ranks of the SBA, in contrast to Baptists Committed. As a consequence of the liberal charges and the stands taken, both the SBA and *SBC Today* found many doors closed to them among the churches, especially those west of the Mississippi River. The rift would not begin to heal until the formation of the Fellowship in 1990, which came when most Moderates, following Daniel Vestal's defeat at the New Orleans SBC annual meeting, realized the Fundamentalists were in complete control of the SBC and the political fight was hopeless.

A New Editor

At the September 24, 1987, meeting of the board of directors for *SBC Today* board members discussed who should be my successor as editor. I had told the board in June that I wanted to retire or work part-time when sixty-five. Chappell Wilson of Augusta suggested as a possible editor Jack Harwell, who was under Fundamentalist pressure to resign or be fired as editor of *The Christian Index,* the Georgia Baptist state paper. The board was excited by the possibility and asked me to contact Harwell, a member of the board from 1983 until 1986, to see if he was interested, and, if so, to schedule a called meeting of the board.[27] Harwell was interested, and on December 15 he was ousted as editor of *The Index* by a vote of 57 to 54[28] by the Executive Committee of the Georgia Baptist Convention.[29] The March issue

---

[26][Editor's note: It is illustrative of the fact the Moderate Movement was never homogenous and uniform that there were varying attitudes toward *Baptists Today.* E.g., Knight recounts how some Moderates thought the paper was too conservative in its approach to the Fundamentalist agenda. After the paper identified so strongly with the SBA, some thought it too "liberal."]

[27]"Minutes, Board of Directors, SBC Today, Inc.," 24 Sept 1987.

[28]"Harwell Forced to Retire," *SBC Today* 5/9 (Dec 1987): 1.

[29]"Minutes, Board of Directors, SBC Today, Inc.," 3 Feb 1988. The discussion covered the purpose of the publication, the role of the editor, a possible merger of the publication with *The Baptist Laity Journal,* salary expectations, and fund raising. The board elected Knight as publisher, voted to match Harwell's salary and benefits at *The Index* ($60,000), and voted to undertake a campaign to raise $250,000 and

of *SBC Today* carried the story of Harwell's acceptance of the editorship, including the announcement that I would take partial retirement in February 1989.

Harwell, a native of Mobile, Alabama, was fifty-five when elected. He had earned a degree in journalism from Samford University in Birmingham, worked for newspapers in Mobile and Atlanta, served four years as a public relations specialist for the U.S. Army and Air Force, and had joined *The Christian Index* in 1957 as an associate editor, becoming editor in 1966.

At the time of his election Harwell said:

> There's a long-range purpose for *SBC Today*, far beyond our denominational controversy. We need a newspaper on down the road that articulates classic Baptist positions of freedom, separation of church and state, the elevation of the laity, divine calling to ministry, and classic issues around liberty. I think *SBC Today* is the best vehicle now going by which to do this.[30]

A national development drive to raise $250,000 was launched in April 1989, with Mrs. Owen Cooper of Yazoo City, Mississippi, as national director. Mrs. Cooper is the widow of Owen Cooper, the last layman to have served as president of the SBC.[31] By May the announcement was made that the drive had reached a third of its goal, and Mrs. Cooper announced that Guy Rutland III, a Georgia business executive and active lay leader in First Baptist Church of Decatur, would serve as the chair of the development fund drive for Georgia, a key state because of Harwell's contacts.[32] At the May meeting of the board of directors, I reported $105,490 had been received in gifts and pledges following a direct-mail appeal, fund-raising dinners, and appearances at churches and meetings. At the March 21-23 meeting of the SBA a strong show of support for Harwell and me was made, including the pledging of $32,000 by individuals, more than half of them from the SBA Executive Committee.[33] By October the development drive had secured a total of $188,277 in gifts and pledges, and the circulation had doubled to 9,100. Karen Cheponis had been added to the staff as

---

to increase the circulation. Harwell, if he accepted, would start June 1.

[30]*SBC Today* 5/11 (Feb 1988): 2.

[31]"*SBC Today* Development Drive: Mrs. Owen Cooper to Lead," *SBC Today* 6/1 (April 1988): 1.

[32]"Funding Reaches Third of Goal," *SBC Today* 6/2 (May 1988): 1.

[33]"SBA Clarifies Vision, Names Neely Director at Macon Convocation," *SBC Today* 6/1 (April 1988): 2.

business manager, but Tutterow had accepted the pastorate of Mars Hill Baptist Church in Mars Hill, North Carolina, and Fuller had resigned for a full-time position elsewhere.[34] Kathy Fogg Berry, a graduate of Southern Baptist Theological Seminary and a journalist who had worked at the Kentucky *Western Recorder* and the Baptist Sunday School Board, was employed three-quarter-time as associate editor to replace both Tutterow and Fuller.[35] Berry left the publication in May 1990 to work at the Foreign Mission Board in Richmond, and Michael Usey, a doctoral student at Emory University, replaced her.[36]

Sunday School Lessons

In January 1989 *SBC Today* and the SBA launched a project to provide alternative Sunday school commentary to the Baptist Sunday School Board's Life and Work Series to counterbalance the increasingly Fundamentalist tone of that agency's material. Under the title of "Commentary" four pages each month were devoted to the material. The SBA enlisted the writers and provided $1,000 a month toward the publication costs.[37]

Following the success of the publication of *The Takeover in the Southern Baptist Convention*, *SBC Today* decided to venture even further into the book-publishing arena, asking me as publisher to handle this phase of work during the one week a month I was working. Consequently, an agreement was reached in 1990 with Clayton Sullivan of the Department of Philosophy and Religion at the University of Southern Mississippi, to publish his volume, *Toward a Mature Faith: Does Biblical Inerrancy Make Sense?* And in 1991 *SBC Today* negotiated with Robert Seymour for the publication of *Whites Only: A Pastor's Retrospective on Signs of the New South*. After Seymour's manuscript was accepted for publication by *SBC Today*, the author received word that Judson Press wanted to publish the book. *SBC Today* deferred to Judson, sensing the book would receive stronger promotion and distribution through an established publisher, but entered into an agreement with Judson Press to promote the volume.[38] With

---

[34]"Minutes, Board of Directors, SBC Today, Inc.," 25 Oct 1988.

[35]*SBC Today* 6/10 (Jan 1989): 3.

[36]*SBC Today* 8/3 (June 1990): 2.

[37]"Minutes, Board of Directors, SBC Today, Inc.," 25 October 1988, and *SBC Today* 6/10 (Jan 1989).

[38]*Baptists Today* 9/22 (14 Nov 1991); 9/23 (28 Nov 1991): 1, 7.

the advent of Smyth & Helwys, a publishing house created to fill the vacuum in books for Southern Baptists of a Moderate persuasion, *SBC Today* decided in 1991 to withdraw from the book publishing field and devote its energy entirely to the newspaper.[39]

Smyth & Helwys also decided to publish *Formations*, a new line of Sunday School lessons more acceptable to Moderates than that being published by the Baptist Sunday School Board.[40] Smyth & Helwys entered into agreement with the SBA to use material already being prepared by the Alliance for the adult series, and the lessons produced jointly by SBA and *SBC Today* were shifted to support *Formations*.

Final Political Effort

In December 1989 Harwell attended a strategy meeting of Baptists Committed to the SBC in Dallas where Jimmy Allen was elected president and the organization geared up for support of Daniel Vestal as a candidate for SBC president at the New Orleans convention.[41] In the issues *SBC Today* to follow Harwell strongly supported Vestal's effort, but that, too, failed, and it marked a decisive turning point for Moderates. Vestal called for a national convocation of Moderates on August 23-25, 1990, in Atlanta. Initially, plans were for 300 leaders, but interest forced an open meeting and 3,000 attended. A new funding mechanism, Baptist Cooperative Missions program, Inc., was established and the group called itself "The Fellowship."[42] The entire spectrum of Moderates was represented. An interim steering committee was appointed to report to another assembly in May 1991 with organizational plans. The May 1991 meeting was also held in Atlanta and 6,000 people attended, giving birth to the Cooperative Baptist Fellowship.[43]

Sensing a new interest among Moderates for more information and news, in November 1990 *SBC Today* took a financial risk and shifted its frequency from once a month to bimonthly.[44] The move also reflected the increasing control of Baptist Press by SBC Fundamentalists. That Baptist Press was no longer free was clear when Fundamentalists fired Director Al

---

[39]"Minutes, Board of Directors, SBC Today, Inc.," 10 May 1991.
[40]*SBC Today* 9/7 (5 April 1991): 3.
[41]*SBC Today* 7/10 (Jan 1990): 11.
[42]*SBC Today* 8/6 (Sept 1990): 1.
[43]*SBC Today* 9/10 (31 May 1991): 1.
[44]*SBC Today* 8/8 (2 Nov 1990): 1.

Shackleford and Editor Dan Martin. The Associated Baptist Press was started as a counter to Baptist Press.[45] *SBC Today* helped launch the news service with a contribution of $2,000.[46]

In May 1991 directors voted to change the name of the publication to *Baptists Today*, reflecting

> an intention to broaden its coverage within the religious field to be more inclusive of all Baptists, and a closer tie to the newly formed Cooperative Baptist Fellowship.[47]

With the name change the paper added journalist Amy Greene to its staff as another part-time associate editor. Greene had worked with the *Atlanta Constitution* before leaving to secure a theology degree from Union Seminary in New York. With Greene as the principal writer, *Baptists Today* launched a series of articles on the Baptist World Alliance and Baptist groups within the U.S., reflecting its broader Baptist concerns.

Following the creation in August of 1990 of the Cooperative Baptist Fellowship, *Baptists Today* gave the new organization a page in each issue for six months, starting with the November 16, 1990, issue. The paper saw this as a crucial time for the CBF in reaching Moderate Southern Baptists, and *Baptists Today* wanted to establish a relationship with CBF as it had with the Alliance of Baptists.[48] The free page was provided to CBF for six months, then the CBF paid for a half-page once a month through 1991. When Cecil Sherman was elected coordinator of CBF,[49] Editor Harwell asked him to write a monthly column, "Sherman in Atlanta, Again," alternating with Stan Hastey who had been writing a column, "A View from Washington" since his election as executive director of the Alliance.

In its September 10-13, 1992, meeting in Atlanta, the coordinating committee of the CBF voted to pay for a page in each issue of *Baptists Today* on a six-month trial. In addition, the CBF voted to assume the Alliance's share of publishing commentary on the *Formations* adult series in *Baptists Today*, after learning that the Alliance would no longer continue to pay for this. The CBF also was considering a recommendation from its communications committee to provide a subsidy of $1,000 a month to *Baptists Today*,

---

[45]*SBC Today* 8/5 (Aug 1990): 1.
[46]"Minutes, Board of Directors, SBC Today, Inc.," 4 Oct 1990.
[47]*SBC Today* 9/10 (31 May 1991): 1.
[48]"Minutes, Board of Directors, SBC Today, Inc.," 4 Oct 1990.
[49]*Baptists Today* 10/3 (6 Feb 1992): 1.

but this was delayed by the budget committee for future consideration.[50] Sherman told Editor Harwell he was committed to making *Baptists Today* the primary medium of communications for CBF to Moderates, and Harwell committed the paper to a strong circulation drive among Moderates.

The growth of the publication during its near-decade of operation was reflected in the print order for the September 24, 1992, issue—14,550 copies—and the budget for 1992 had been set at $260,800.[51] The next decade would build upon a strong foundation.

Summary

What role has *Baptists Today* played in the Moderate Movement in the SBC? *Baptists Today* has provided nearly ten years of consistent publication, never missing an established deadline, and in the process became the only publication available for all Moderates to disseminate their message(s).

On the negative side *Baptists Today* lost effectiveness on three counts: (1) the paper grew slowly because it faced a constant battle to survive financially, never having been adequately funded; (2) the circulation was thus limited after the first year of distributing free copies, but it generated a loyal and avid readership; and (3) it failed to secure backing from all the Moderate factions in the early years.

Nevertheless, *Baptists Today* became the only vehicle which carried a comprehensive range of news and opinion, as well as serving as a bulletin board for announcements about Moderates. In a unique way the publication became not only an educational tool, used widely by pastors who wanted to inform their churches of the nature of the controversy, but it became a public grieving vehicle, a "wailing wall," for a people who found themselves losing something they had long cherished.

Baptists Today also became a means for people to express opinions that could not be published elsewhere, and it provided a corrective to Baptist Press when that service gave only the official SBC version of an event. *Baptists Today* addressed not only the political nature of the SBC conflict, but presented series of articles dealing with biblical authority, inerrancy, Baptist history and traditions, as well as the sociological nature of religious conflict.

---

[50]"Minutes, Coordinating Committee, Cooperative Baptist Fellowship," 10-13 Sept 1992.

[51]"Minutes, Board of Directors, SBC Today, Inc.," 3 Oct 1991.

From the first, the publication established itself as one that would inform its readers concerning the broad spectrum of Baptist and other Christian activities and thought. In changing its name from *SBC Today* to *Baptists Today* it signaled an even stronger move in that direction for the future.

Appendix. Board of Directors

1983. Executive Board. David Sapp, Atlanta, chair; Dallas M. Lee, Atlanta, vice-chair; Jack U. Harwell, Tucker, Georgia; Melvin Williams, Decatur, Georgia; William Self, Atlanta, Georgia; Charlene W. Shucker, Atlanta; Earl Davis, Memphis; Walker L. Knight, Decatur, Georgia, secretary-treasurer.

1983. Board of Directors (in addition to executive committee). W. Oscar Brazil, Jr., Asheville, North Carolina; J. Dan Cooper, Lexington, Kentucky; Vernon Davis, Kansas City, Missouri; Larry K. Dipboye, Louisville; Pope A. Duncan, DeLand, Florida; Don B. Harbuck, Chattanooga, Tennessee; T. B. Maston, Fort Worth, Texas; Abner V. McCall, Waco, Texas; Duke K. McCall, Louisville, Kentucky; Guy W. Rutland, Jr., Decatur, Georgia.

1984. (added to board) C. Welton Gaddy, Macon, Georgia; R. Kirby Godsey, Macon, Georgia; Eleanor Wilson Nutt, Louisville, Kentucky.

1985. (deceased) Don Harbuck.

1986. (dropped) Pope Duncan, health; Vernon Davis, conflict with Midwestern Seminary policy; T. B. Maston, health; and Charlene Shucker (nonattendance).

1987. (resignations from board) William Self and Eleanor Nutt, overcommitments. Earl Davis, chair, and David Sapp, vice-chair.

1988. (board reduced to Georgia membership because of high cost—$3,000—of director's insurance) Mel Williams, chair; Dallas Lee, vice-chair; Welton Gaddy; Walker Knight, secretary-treasurer; Celeste Pennington of Atlanta; Jim Strickland of Cartersville, Georgia; Chappell Wilson, Gracewood, Georgia.

1989. (with Harwell as editor, board again expanded) Sarah Frances Anders, Pineville, Louisiana; Mrs. Elizabeth Cooper, Yazoo City, Mississippi; Buckner Fanning, San Antonio, Texas; C. Welton Gaddy of Macon, Georgia (chair); George McCotter of Lillington, North Carolina; Porter Roberts of Mobile, Alabama; Mrs. Ann Roebuck of Rome, Georgia (first vice-chair); Guy Rutland III of Atlanta; Harold Shirley of Monticello, Georgia; Jim Strickland of Cartersville, Georgia; T. Melvin Williams of Durham, North Carolina (second vice-chair); Chappell Wilson of Gracewood, Georgia; and Walker Knight, secretary-treasurer.

1991. Ann Roebuck, chair; Harold Shirley, first vice-chair; Mel Williams, second vice-chair.

1992. Ann Roebuck resigned, overcommitment; Harold Shirley, chair; Porter Roberts, first vice-chair; Mel Williams, second vice-chair. New members added in 1992: John Baugh of Houston, Texas; Louise Duke of St. Louis, Missouri; and Jack Snell of Jacksonville, Florida.

The History of
the Associated Baptist Press

Stan Hastey

In his classic work *Democracy in America* (1835), Alexis de Tocqueville summarized the perpetual dilemma faced by U.S. citizens concerning the essential nature yet inevitable excesses of a free press:

> In this question, therefore, there is no medium between servitude and license; in order to enjoy the inestimable benefits that the liberty of the press ensures, it is necessary to submit to the inevitable evils that it creates.[1]

Equally compelling, however, is the truth that the freedom tyrants seek first and foremost to obliterate upon assuming power is that of the press, to the end that the flow of information conveyed to the public about the new regime is controlled. My own mentor in journalism, W. Barry Garrett, repeatedly cautioned me at the beginning of my career that the reporter need not concern himself/herself with providing a certain slant on the news. Indeed, he contended, the strongest responses elicited from readers are those called forth by nothing more than telling the unvarnished facts of the matter at hand.

Tyrants understand this and act accordingly. In the matter of the takeover of the Southern Baptist Convention, one of the early objectives of the Fundamentalist party was to establish control over the convention's official news service, Baptist Press. Although the task of documenting this fact through the usual means of citing statements made—oral or written—is

---

[1]*Democracy in America*, pt. 1, ch. 9, as quoted in John Bartlett, *Familiar Quotations*, 13th and centennial ed. (Boston: Little, Brown and Company, 1955) 516. This quote is omitted in Richard D. Heffner's abridged edition of Alexis de Tocqueville, *Democracy in America* (New York: Mentor, 1956).

particularly difficult in this instance,[2] the results of a carefully orchestrated effort to change the direction of Baptist Press are painfully apparent.

Created in 1946 at the request of the Southern Baptist Press Association—whose primary membership consists of the editors of the Baptist state conventions' newspapers—Baptist Press was designed to provide a quasi-independent source of news coverage of significant events in Southern Baptist life. Baptist Press first was housed briefly in the Department of Survey, Statistics, and Information of the Sunday School Board. Its first director was the late Porter W. Routh, who for nearly thirty years was executive secretary-treasurer of the SBC Executive Committee.

In 1947 the Executive Committee assumed ownership and oversight of the news service. C. E. Bryant was elected publicity director for the Executive Committee and in that role became the first full-time director of Baptist Press. Four other directors have followed—Albert McClellan, 1949–1959; Wilmer C. Fields, 1959–1987; Alvin C. Shackleford, 1987–1990; and Herbert V. Hollinger, 1991–present.

Besides the home office at the Executive Committee in Nashville, Tennessee, Baptist Press has grown to include five bureaus, the first of which was set up in Washington in 1957 under terms of an agreement with the Baptist Joint Committee on Public Affairs. Creation of the other bureaus followed—in Richmond, at the Foreign Mission Board; in Atlanta, at the Home Mission Board; in Dallas, at the Baptist General Convention of Texas; and in a second Nashville-based office, at the Sunday School Board.[3]

From its beginnings, Baptist Press was operated under the journalistic philosophy that its primary task was to tell the Southern Baptist story and tell it straight, good news and bad—warts and all. Over the course of time,

---

[2]This is true due to restrictions placed on journalists in covering the meetings of subcommittees and work groups of the SBC Executive Committee. Under what are called "background rules," reporters may not quote or attribute statements made by participants. These rules provided cover for members of the Executive Committee, particularly Judge Paul Pressler, in their successful attempt to control Baptist Press. In fairness, it must be noted that these restrictions predated the takeover of the convention.

[3]For short histories of Baptist Press, see the unpub. 1979 document by C. E. Bryant, "The Beginnings of Baptist Press," in my file; and Jim Newton, "Baptist Press: Helping Inform Southern Baptists," *The Baptist Program* (Dec 1984): 11-12; see also Stan Hastey, "Baptist Press/Washington: A 25-Year Perspective and Analysis," address to the Southern Baptist Press Association, 17 Feb 1982.

pressure on the service came more from within the convention struc-ture—primarily from executives in agencies and institutions looking for their own spin on the news—than it did from critics outside the structure.

Yet until the consolidation of power in the mid-1980s by the prevailing Fundamentalist party, Baptist Press always had been able to rely on the Executive Committee itself for the necessary protection any news organiza-tion must enjoy to preserve its journalistic integrity. Despite the obvious liability of being a convention-owned-and-operated organization, it generally was able to resist undue pressure even from those in powerful positions of leadership precisely because the Executive Committee had made a deliberate choice of maintaining a legitimate news service. As de facto publisher, the Executive Committee itself saw to it that Baptist Press directors, editors, and writers remained essentially free to do their work.[4]

With the election of Judge Paul Pressler to the Executive Committee in June 1984, Baptist Press came under the severest internal scrutiny in its history, beginning at the September 1984 meeting. From that point forward, within the subcommittee and work group structure of the Executive Committee, Pressler repeatedly sought to air his charges of bias, lack of balance, and unfairness in Baptist Press coverage of the controversy in the convention. More often than not, his specific criticisms involved news stories in which he was a principal figure. His consistent contention was that Baptist Press writers displayed bias, if not outright hostility, toward him.

During the February 1985 Executive Committee meeting in Nashville, Pressler sought to bring public charges of unfairness against Baptist Press News Editor Dan Martin over coverage of an incident in Louisville, Kentucky, involving a student at Southern Baptist Theological Seminary and his charge that on September 1, 1984, Pressler had made an illegal tape recording of a telephone conversation between them. The student, J. Stafford Durham, filed a formal complaint with the Federal Communications Commission. The recorded conversation, he stated in the complaint, subsequently was used as the basis for a news story in the *Houston Chroni-*

---

[4]This was institutionalized within the Executive Committee in the Public Relations Work Group, the panel charged with direct oversight of Baptist Press. Most often, it functioned as an advocate for the news service and its needs within the Executive Committee. Also to be noted is the fact that prior to the dismissal of Alvin C. Shackleford on 17 July 1990, the director of Baptist Press was also Executive Committee Vice-President for Public Relations.

cle in which he and Southern Seminary President Roy L. Honeycutt were portrayed in an unfavorable light.

Pressler's specific complaint was that the September 17 Baptist Press story detailing Durham's allegations was printed in the September 17 issue of *Baptist and Reflector*—the weekly Tennessee Baptist newspaper—without any response from him. That response, in fact, appeared in the September 18 issue of Baptist Press. But because the *Baptist and Reflector*, alone among the Baptist state newspapers, faced a printing deadline on the evening of September 17, the story containing Pressler's response did not appear in that paper until the following week.[5]

Despite Pressler's complaint, the Executive Committee's Public Relations Work Group—whose assignment includes oversight of Baptist Press—refused to give Pressler the floor to present his grievances. He, in turn, went public with his complaint against Baptist Press and with criticism of the process that denied him a forum in comments made to Nashville's morning newspaper, *The Tennessean*, in which he was quoted as saying: "I think Baptist Press has been innately unfair. I think it should be censured. . . . I will keep on pressing to have the truth brought out."[6]

This episode has been chronicled in some detail, in part because it is one of the few thoroughly documented accounts of Pressler's charges against Baptist Press and because each of the principal players involved in it later became either a victor or casualty in the battle to control the news service. Louis Moore, religion editor of the *Houston Chronicle* and a personal friend of Pressler's, later was named to direct communications for the Southern Baptist Christian Life Commission by another Pressler protege, CLC executive director Richard Land. Al Shackleford, editor of the *Baptist and Reflector*, subsequently was elected director of Baptist Press. Shackleford and Martin were later to be dismissed from their posts by the Executive Committee.

---

[5]For many years, copies of the current issue of *Baptist and Reflector* have been available to members of the Executive Committee as they convene for their September and February meetings in Nashville. By coincidence, the Executive Committee convened on 17 Sept 1984, the very day the first of the two-part Durham/Pressler series appeared in the Tennessee Baptist newspaper, a fact that gave Pressler a ready-made weapon in his attack on Baptist Press.

[6]Quoted by Ray Waddle, "Baptist Panel Refuses to Give Conservative Leader Full Say," *The Tennessean*, 19 Feb 1985.

Largely because of the Stafford/Pressler/Martin/Shackleford incident, the Southern Baptist Press Association contracted with three respected professors of journalism—John Merrill of Louisiana State University, Clifford Christians of the University of Illinois, and John DeMott of Memphis State University—to investigate Pressler's charges. Their mandate was to look into Pressler's specific charges concerning the September 1984 coverage and the Houston judge's overall complaints against Baptist Press.

The journalism professors' conclusion was that "There is no evidence . . . of any kind of consistent bias against the SBC faction represented by Pressler and his associates." Their study also refuted charges that Baptist Press concentrated unduly on "negative" news, concluding, "BP's performance appears to be, generally, considerably above average for such news services, and meets the standards of professional practice in every way." The authors of the report, each of whom had served on the Professional Freedom and Responsibility Committee of the Association for Education in Journalism and Mass Communication, stated further:

> In arriving at the preceding conclusions . . . we did not use, as benchmarks, the norms of behavior that exist in professional news reporting generally around the country. On the contrary, we applied standards that, in our professional judgment, are those met by news organizations of high quality and ethics.[7]

Such evaluations also were confirmed by many members of the Religion Newswriters Association (RNA), the professional organization of religion writers and editors in the United States, each of whom receives Baptist Press. In letters solicited by Fields in the aftermath of the September 1984 coverage and the controversy provoked by Pressler's charges, numerous prominent religion writers gave Baptist Press high marks. One of these, George W. Cornell of the Associated Press, called Baptist Press "the finest example in the church world of straight, dependable journalism" and credited the service "as a model . . . in getting Catholic and Methodist bishops to open their meetings to the press and in other efforts for more open information in the church realm generally."[8]

Virginia Culver, religion editor of the *Denver Post,* wrote:

---

[7]Clifford Christians, John DeMott, and John Merrill, "Report of Special Inquiry," 5 Feb 1985.

[8]George W. Cornell, letter to W. C. Fields, 31 Jan 1985.

> Baptist Press is, without a doubt, the best press agency of any religious organization I can name. . . . I have sometimes covered the same stories your staff members are covering, and have found them fair, honest, accurate reporters.

She concluded:

> Such standards don't come easy, but are even more difficult in a religious institution, many of which are bent on self-preservation and want their press offices to print only the fluff and good news. [Baptist Press] reporters . . . seem determined to cover the Southern Baptist Convention honestly, even if that reporting shows some blemishes.[9]

Another example of such positive evaluations came from Kenneth L. Woodward, senior writer for *Newsweek* magazine who, like Cornell and Culver, is among the senior members of the RNA. Baptist Press, he wrote,

> stands out in its coverage of difficult—and, I'm sure, painful—controversies within the denomination itself. . . . the really useful thing is the service's reliable coverage of the tough issues. . . . Both sides in the current controversies within the SBC should be proud of the service you perform.[10]

Nearly four years later, following the 1988 SBC session in San Antonio, Texas, and another round of attacks on the news service by Pressler, RNA President Ed Briggs took a random survey of RNA members and concluded that Baptist Press "enjoys high credibility, if not the highest, when compared to news operations of other American denominations." Briggs, religion editor of the *Richmond Times-Dispatch*, stated further:

> RNA members told me they believe BP's coverage of the Southern Baptist Convention is impartial and fair. Coupled with its attention to detail, they say BP has a reputation of being a first-class operation with integrity.

Briggs further expressed his conviction that Baptist Press "will lose credibility if restricted or censored in any manner. Such a loss of credibility would place Baptist Press in disrepute and force secular newspapers to seek other sources of information" about SBC events.[11]

Indeed, editors and writers in the Baptist Press network came to realize as early as September 1984 that the service's credibility was at stake because of Pressler's initial attack. Following the raucous 1985 and 1986 annual sessions of the Convention in Dallas and Atlanta, respectively,

---

[9]Virginia Culver, letter to W. C. Fields, 31 Dec 1984.

[10]Kenneth L. Woodward, letter to W. C. Fields, 18 Dec 1984.

[11]Ed Briggs, letter to Charles Sullivan, *RNA Newsletter* (Sept/Oct 1988): 6.

former Baptist Press director Fields was asked about the possibility that the news service could be captured for partisan purposes. He responded,

> If Baptist Press were twisted to be a propaganda arm for any group, then a group would be invented to replace it and the editors of the state Baptist papers would be in the forefront of it.[12]

Pressler's effort so to use Baptist Press was documented during the Atlanta Convention in a newsroom incident during which the Houston judge angrily confronted me with a complaint about a single paragraph in a story about an organizational meeting of the Executive Committee on Wednesday, June 11, 1986. He accused me of misrepresenting a motion he had made to exclude visitors from speaking to motions on the floor during Executive Committee meetings unless they were granted permission by the body on a case-by-case basis.

Pressler's motion stemmed from a heated debate during a preconvention meeting of the Executive Committee two days earlier during which some nonmembers objected to a Pressler move, approved by the Administrative and Convention Arrangements Subcommittee, to ask the SBC Peace Committee to investigate what he called "inflammatory" reports of alleged voting irregularities during the Dallas convention the previous year. During the debate on his motion, which eventually failed in a 17-27 vote, Pressler sought to have visitors prohibited from speaking, despite longstanding Executive Committee policy permitting the practice.

In the newsroom confrontation, which came on the final day of the convention, Thursday, June 12, Pressler stated that unless a correction to the story was printed immediately, he would take to the floor to air his grievance against Baptist Press at the scheduled time for Fields's convention report. The disputed story, he said, was only the latest in a long series of Baptist Press stories which cast him in an unfavorable light. Pressler said he had received prior clearance from SBC president Charles F. Stanley to present his charges to messengers.

Fields, in his dual role as Executive Committee vice-president for public relations and director of Baptist Press, found himself in an unusually difficult position. While wishing on the one hand to protect the integrity of the news service, he faced the prospect of an angry platform scene in which he and Pressler would directly confront one another over a relatively

---

[12]Quoted by Ed Briggs, "Baptist Press Director's Job Part of Factional Fray," *Richmond Times-Dispatch*, 14 June 1986.

insignificant news story. Furthermore, Fields had announced his retirement months earlier; this was to be his final report as the convention's chief communications officer.

With scarcely half an hour to sort out the situation and with Pressler following Fields and me about the newsroom repeating his threat, I set out to issue a clarification of the disputed paragraph. Fields assigned me an isolated cubby where I might work quickly. But Pressler followed me into the work area and hovered over me, all the while reminding me of how quickly I had to work in order to meet the deadline. For the next fifteen to twenty minutes, Pressler returned frequently with an announcement of the countdown. With only minutes to spare, the clarification was sent to the copy editor and then distributed for reporters covering the convention.[13]

Fields was succeeded by Shackleford, who was elected to the dual post in February 1987 on a vote of 32-26. Previously, as noted, Shackleford had been editor of the *Baptist and Reflector* and, earlier, of the *Indiana Baptist*. Pressler, who vigorously opposed Shackleford's election, set out from the beginning to put pressure on him. In retrospect, what is surprising about Shackleford's tenure is that he managed to keep his post for more than three years.

Although Pressler kept up a constant stream of attack on both Shackleford and Martin, the beginning of the end for the pair came in the spring of 1988 with the airing on the Public Broadcasting System of a documentary series produced and narrated by Bill Moyers. The series, "God and Politics," included three segments, the middle of which focused attention on the takeover of the Southern Baptist Convention.

Titled "The Battle for the Bible," the program included a memorable interview sequence during which Pressler, on camera, became visibly agitated with Moyers over his line of questioning, namely, about Pressler's national political activities. Pressed by Moyers, Pressler declared the interview ended and stormed out of the room.

For the next several months, Pressler used the Moyers episode and Baptist Press coverage of it as further evidence of what he continued to claim was the news service's bias and unfairness toward him. In February 1989, he succeeded in having the Executive Committee issue a resolution

---

[13]See Stan Hastey, "Executive Committee Organization," SBC Newsroom Release, 11 June 1986; "Correction to SBC Newsroom Story of June 11, 'Executive Committee Organization,'" 12 June 1986; Briggs, "Baptist Press Director's Job Part of Factional Fray," *Richmond Times-Dispatch*, 14 June 1986.

protesting the Moyers program and what it termed the "use of federal tax dollars to support one faction in the Southern Baptist Convention controversy through the use of the Public Broadcasting System."[14]

Moyers then asked the Executive Committee for time to respond to the protest during its preconvention meeting in Las Vegas in June 1989. But the Executive Committee refused, countering with an offer that Moyers go to Nashville instead for the September 1989 meeting. Moyers later refused the counteroffer. The Moyers/Pressler episode, according to Don McGregor, then the editor of Mississippi's *Baptist Record*, "became the key factor in the entire struggle" over control of Baptist Press.[15]

At the Las Vegas convention in 1989, however, the issue surfaced in another of Pressler's newsroom confrontations with Baptist Press personnel. Pressler was particularly galled that Shackleford and Martin wrote a story about a letter from Moyers to Executive Committee Chairperson Charles W. Sullivan requesting the Las Vegas showdown. For his part, Sullivan complained the letter was private and should not be reported. However, because Moyers had sent a copy to Baptist Press, Shackleford and Martin believed they had no choice but to release it to the assembled media covering the Las Vegas session.

Once the Moyers story had been released, Pressler stormed into the newsroom, demanding from Martin an explanation. Martin responded, "I did what I had to do." Pressler then replied, "Then I'll go do what I have to do."[16] From that moment forward, Martin's and Shackleford's days were numbered, although they managed to survive through two more rancorous Executive Committee meetings in September 1989 and February 1990.

Yet the die had been cast. During the 1990 session of the Convention in New Orleans, the officers of the Executive Committee privately ordered Executive Committee President Harold C. Bennett to demand Shackleford's and Martin's resignations. Rather than informing them in New Orleans, Bennett waited until the Tuesday following the convention to confer with the pair in Nashville and convey the demand. When they refused to comply, the full Executive Committee was convened on July 17, 1990, for the sole purpose of considering dismissal actions. On identical votes of 45-15, the two top editors of Baptist Press were dismissed.

---

[14]See "Pressler, Executive Committee Criticize TV Series," Baptist Press article as printed in *Florida Baptist Witness*, 9 March 1989.

[15]Personal interview with Don McGregor, 1 Oct 1992.

[16]Ibid.

Although Shackleford and Martin had made formal requests through Nashville attorney and former Executive Committee member Frank C. Ingraham to have the complaints against them presented in an open meeting of the full Executive Committee, they were offered only five minutes each before the Administrative and Convention Arrangements Subcommittee. They declined, submitting written statements instead. According to Martin, the subcommittee "functioned as a grand jury," bringing the charges to the full Executive Committee, which met in closed session with armed, off-duty, Nashville police officers guarding the doors to the meeting room in the SBC Building. The specific charges against Shackleford and Martin never were released.[17]

Immediately following the firing actions, Shackleford, Martin, and Ingraham held a news conference, at the conclusion of which another Nashville attorney, Jeff Mobley, announced he had just filed incorporation papers with the Tennessee secretary of state creating a new news service to be known as Associated Baptist Press.[18]

Behind the announcement of the creation of an alternative news service lay the longstanding concern of several of the editors of Baptist state newspapers that the days of Baptist Press as a credible news operation were dwindling. Indeed, according to McGregor, the editors' concern over creating more distance between Baptist Press and the Executive Committee goes back some twenty-five years, when the idea of creating a news service

---

[17]Personal interview with Dan Martin, 5 Oct 1992; personal interview with Don McGregor, 1 Oct 1992; see also "Shackleford, Martin Told to Resign at BP," *Baptist Press*, 26 June 1990; "BP Editors Instructed to Resign: Must Keep Silent to Retain 6 Months' Salary," *Religious Herald*, 5 July 1990; Marv Knox, "Editors Affirm 'Right to Know,' Support Baptist Press Staffers," *Baptist Press*, 9 July 1990; Jim Jones, "Baptist Editors Reject 2nd Resignation Request," *Fort Worth Star-Telegram*, 11 July 1990; Frank C. Ingraham, letters of 2, 5, and 11 July 1990 to Sam W. Pace and Charles Sullivan; report of the Administrative and Convention Arrangements Subcommittee, 17 July 1990: (1) "Consideration of the Termination of the Employment of Alvin C. Shackleford, Vice-President for Public Relations" and (2) "Consideration of the Termination of the Employment of Daniel B. Martin, Jr., Editor, Baptist Press."

[18]Jeffrey Mobley, "Statement Announcing Associated Baptist Press," 17 July 1990.

of their own first surfaced. The notion had not been translated into reality, however, largely because of financial constraints.[19]

During his tenure as president of the Southern Baptist Press Association (SBPA), McGregor in 1982 suggested a "networking operation" that would designate an editor or associate editor of a state paper to provide Baptist Press coverage of meetings of SBC agencies and institutions. Such an endeavor, set up two years later by another SBPA president, Lynn P. Clayton of Louisiana, was an attempt to respond to one of the persistent criticisms of Baptist Press as a less-than-credible source of news about agency and institutional life.[20]

Yet, according to McGregor, the effort was less than successful. More often than not, he has said, editors assigned to provide such coverage simply reviewed news copy written by the agencies' and institutions' own reporters, signed off on it, and sent it on to Baptist Press in Nashville for release.[21]

With the pressure on Baptist Press steadily increasing, particularly during and following the Moyers/Pressler episode, a special meeting of the editors was held July 6-7, 1990, at Dallas-Fort Worth International Airport. In McGregor's words, "All we did was to pass a resolution enhancing our network committee, which really didn't amount to anything."[22]

At the meeting's conclusion, however, Bob S. Terry, editor of Missouri's *Word and Way*, convened a smaller, informal meeting of those editors particularly concerned with the future of Baptist Press. It was this group—consisting of Terry, McGregor, Julian Pentecost (editor of Virginia's *Religious Herald*), R. G. Puckett (editor of North Carolina's *Biblical Recorder*), Robert Allen (editor of Maryland/Delaware's *Baptist True Union*), E. Marvin Knox (editor of Kentucky's *Western Recorder*), and Jack Brymer (editor of the *Florida Baptist Witness*)—that conceived Associated Baptist Press (ABP). Two other editors, J. B. Fowler, of the *Baptist New Mexican*, and the late J. Everett Sneed, of the *Arkansas Baptist*, were present for portions of the meeting and participated in the discussions as well.[23]

Initially, Terry engaged the services of Floyd A. Craig, founder of Craig and Associates of Nashville, to produce the new service and handle all day-to-day matters. During the earliest days, in July–August 1990, however,

---

[19]Personal interview, 1 Oct 1992.
[20]Ibid.
[21]Ibid.
[22]Ibid.
[23]Ibid.

others of the founding editors questioned the decision, claiming insufficient funds had been committed to the project. At an initial meeting of the board of directors in September, McGregor has said, Craig essentially "ran the meeting" and shortly thereafter engaged the services of Dan Martin as interim news director. Actual production began in mid-September, with the first news story being that of Martin's employment.[24]

By the next board meeting, held in Nashville in January 1991, the decision was made to drop Craig and Associates. By McGregor's account, severing the relationship with Craig was accompanied by the unintended breaking of ties with Martin as well, in spite of the fact that directors voted at the same meeting to remove the "interim" from Martin's title in clear anticipation he would remain.[25]

Although initially Martin was not inclined to take the position, as reflected in his move from Nashville to Penland, North Carolina, only days before ABP's first board meeting, he accepted the position of interim news director following several conversations with Terry and Craig. Despite the latter's short-term arrangement with the board of directors, Martin has high praise for the significance of Craig's role:

> In my opinion, the fact that ABP was born at all is a testimonial to the fact that Floyd Craig picked up the ball and ran with it, assuming he had the support of the editors (and) not knowing what a mixed crowd they are.[26]

Reaction to the new service was mixed from the beginning, Martin has said, including the editors' willingness to pay for it. "It was because of my friendship with and loyalty to Floyd [Craig] that I agreed to take the job," after having first declined it, Martin elaborated.

> [Craig] virtually put his business on the line in his commitment to bring ABP into existence. . . . He virtually put everything else on hold to get ABP going. . . . We wrote off some of the bills. . . . For all intents and purposes Floyd and I were doing ABP full-time and billing for about half our time.[27]

During this initial phase of the operation, ABP was issued weekly, with occasional second and/or special issues in a given week. Martin is of the view that the fact he and Craig were distant from each other became

---

[24]Ibid.
[25]Ibid.
[26]Personal interview, 5 Oct 1992.
[27]Ibid.

"something of an issue" with the ABP board of directors. Some directors, Martin has said, apparently thought Craig "was gouging them" with exorbitant fees. Yet he has emphasized he never heard any of the directors complain about the service's contents.

For Martin, the growing discontent came to a head in January 1991 when the ABP board held an executive session, a development that, Martin said, "offended me because ABP's purpose statement was for openness," and especially because he and Shackleford had been fired behind closed doors.[28]

With Martin as primary writer, Craig and Associates produced ABP between September 1990 and January 1991. Martin's last story as interim news editor was of the called meeting of the Sunday School Board in which Lloyd Elder, SSB president, resigned. It was while covering that event that Martin came to a conscious realization that "I probably should not be covering SBC developments" any longer. His story came across as "bitter and angry," Martin recalls, especially in his characterization of Elder's early retirement package as a "golden parachute" accompanied by a "golden gag," two phrases used in the story.

Unable to make contact with ABP board of directors chair Charles Overby to talk things out concerning his future, Martin wrote what he has described as "a very angry letter" to the board resigning his position.[29]

Overby and McGregor, designated by other directors to function as a two-person search committee before Martin's resignation, approached their task with the assumption Martin would stay on. Already the board had voted to remove the "interim" designation from his title, assuming Martin would be named permanent news editor. McGregor, who has called this period "the worst time of my life," first tried to set up a meeting involving the three principals in Atlanta, "but Charles [Overby] couldn't make it." A second meeting was to have been held in Nashville but Martin and Overby could not agree on the length of time needed. While Martin wanted a thoroughgoing discussion of ABP's present and future operations, Overby said his schedule would accommodate only a brief meeting. In the process of trying to negotiate their differences over the meeting, according to McGregor, Martin essentially terminated the discussions.[30]

---

[28]Ibid.
[29]Ibid.
[30]Personal interview, 1 Oct 1992.

Between January and June 1991, McGregor—designated by other directors as interim executive director—produced ABP from Jackson, Mississippi. During this period, he and Overby interviewed Greg Warner, associate editor of the *Florida Baptist Witness*, for the vacant position.[31]

Warner was elected executive editor of ABP in April 1991 and began his work May 1. With his election, the headquarters for ABP was moved to Jacksonville, Florida. Among his early actions was to employ Franceen Cornelius, formerly of the staff of the *Florida Baptist Witness*, as administrative assistant.

Warner, who was present when ABP's formation was announced on July 17, 1990, said following his election he had a keen desire to be a part of the new service from the beginning:

> The Baptist Press firings made it clear . . . that freedom of the press, which had been such an important part of our denominational heritage, had been seriously compromised. The Executive Committee proved itself an unfit guardian of that freedom, which made establishment of ABP as an independent, nonaligned news service a moral and practical necessity.[32]

An award-winning writer during his years as associate editor of the *Witness*, Warner moved quickly to help repair relationships with both Craig and Martin. Noting that he was among those who favored paying Craig in full those billed charges incurred during the start-up phase, Warner has said the Nashville-based public relations executive "has been supportive since then in a number of instances." And early in his tenure Warner asked for and received consent from ABP directors to contract with Martin for coverage of events he deemed appropriate. Martin has undertaken several such assignments.[33]

Since March 1992, ABP has been issued twice weekly, marking a decided improvement in the timeliness of its stories. Among the Baptist state papers, twenty-three have used ABP in varying degrees. Warner's assessment places these newspapers' usage of the service into three categories: (1) those papers, ten to twelve in number, that carry ABP stories "frequently if not preferentially"; (2) those that seem to be trying for a rough balance in usage of both Baptist Press and ABP; and (3) those that

---

[31]Ibid.

[32]"Associated Baptist Press Names Floridian Editor," *Florida Baptist Witness*, 18 April 1991, 2-3.

[33]Personal interview with Greg Warner, 5 Oct 1992.

show preference for Baptist Press but carry those ABP stories "that can't be ignored." Even Hollinger, Shackleford's successor as director of Baptist Press, has said that "ABP is helping BP do a better job," specifically by causing state paper editors to request Baptist Press coverage of events they have learned ABP is to cover.[34]

Besides its clientele among the Baptist state papers, from its inception ABP has been sent to many of the major daily newspapers, newsmagazines, and news services, free of charge. By October 1992, forty-three such news organizations were on ABP's list of clients. Many of the religion editors of these news outlets appear to be using ABP routinely in the way they previously used Baptist Press, namely, as their primary source of news about Southern Baptist life.

Warner cites as an important example the use made of an ABP exclusive on the churchmanship of Democratic Party presidential nominee Bill Clinton and vice-presidential nominee Al Gore by George Cornell, religion editor of the Associated Press in New York. Cornell's story on the first all-Baptist ticket in the nation's history was printed widely in daily newspapers. And Warner has stated that on average he receives one or two calls a week from reporters in the secular media.[35]

Although ABP is transmitted free of charge to secular news organizations, the Baptist state papers are billed $1,200 annually for the service. Some have paid this amount, while others have made partial payments. At least one, Oklahoma's *Baptist Messenger*, has been instructed by its governing body not to accept the service at all.

Receipts from these newspapers amount to only a small percentage of ABP's income. During 1991, income sources included Baptist state conventions, principally Virginia, North Carolina, and Texas (forty-five percent); the Cooperative Baptist Fellowship (nineteen percent); other contributions, including the Alliance of Baptists, congregations, and individuals (nineteen percent); and service fees (seventeen percent).[36]

Of special note have been two grants from the Freedom Forum, formerly the Gannett Foundation, of $5,000 and $20,000, both made in 1992. Created primarily to champion freedom of the press, the Freedom Forum is headed by former ABP board of directors chairperson Charles Overby. The initial

---

[34]Ibid.

[35]Ibid.

[36]"Associated Baptist Press Fact Sheet," undated.

grant of $5,000, presented in April 1992, was the very first to a religious organization made by the Arlington, Virginia-based foundation.[37]

Of ABP's financial base, Warner has said, "I'm convinced we're here to stay." He anticipated ABP's 1992 income to exceed its $132,000 budget.[38]

The service's financial health, according to Warner, "has mirrored the growth of the Cooperative Baptist Fellowship." Receipts from CBF for 1992 were expected to cover twenty-seven percent of the budget—up from nineteen percent in 1991—with higher percentages anticipated in succeeding years. Such a hopeful appraisal rests in large measure on the fact that ABP is listed in all three CBF funding tracks. Warner has said that ideally he would like to see the percentage of receipts from CBF limited to about one-third of ABP's total income. At the same time, should they exceed that proportion, Warner has expressed his expectation that CBF will respect ABP's editorial freedom. Thus far, he has said, "there hasn't been a hint of any intention to control ABP—either its content or its governance—from the Fellowship."[39]

Another substantial contribution to the early success ABP has enjoyed has been made by the Baptist Joint Committee on Public Affairs through its two newswriters Larry Chesser and Pam Parry, who provide regular coverage of national events and other stories from Washington. For ABP, this connection with the Baptist Joint Committee, as Warner has put it, amounts to having a "national desk we wouldn't have otherwise."[40]

Associated Baptist Press is governed by a self-perpetuating board of directors of no fewer than ten and no more than twenty, each elected to a three-year term. Directors may be elected to successive terms indefinitely. Although several of the earliest directors have made substantial contributions to the early development of ABP, the role of Jeff Mobley of Nashville, Tennessee, merits special mention. An attorney in the Nashville firm of Gullett, Sanford, Robinson, and Martin, Mobley also serves as legal counsel for ABP, a service he renders without charge. It was he who registered ABP's incorporation papers on July 17, 1990, prepared the official statement announcing the formation of the service that same day, and wrote the bylaws.

---

[37]Ibid.
[38]Ibid.
[39]Ibid.
[40]Ibid.

In the words of its Mission Statement, adopted by the board of directors in September 1990, the purpose of Associated Baptist Press "is to serve as a trusted source of Baptist information" and is dedicated to reporting news fairly and accurately to Baptists in particular and the larger religious community in general.[41]

In the judgment of many observers—professional journalists and laypeople alike—ABP has succeeded admirably in meeting these objectives. The need for the kind of news coverage provided by ABP in the present climate of controlled news within the Southern Baptist Convention is indisputable. Particularly during a time of transition for "free and faithful Baptists," its value truly is immeasurable.

Yet because freedom is fragile and freedom of the press so often is subverted, even by some who claim to champion it, the eventual success of Associated Baptist Press most assuredly will depend upon the determination of freedom-loving Baptists to leave it alone so that it may fulfill its high calling.

---

[41]Associated Baptist Press, "Mission Statement," adopted 11-12 Sept 1990.

The History
of Baptist Theological Seminary
at Richmond

Thomas H. Graves

Theological education has been at the center of most of the major controversies in the history of the Southern Baptist Convention. That was true in the case of Crawford Toy, the Whitsitt dispute, and more recently the Elliott Controversy.[1] Without question the key ingredient in the current denominational debate is the fight over the proper role of theological education within the denomination. The Peace Committee's discussions and investigations were focused on issues pertaining to seminary life. A crucial turning point in the controversy was the Glorieta Statement of the six seminary presidents.[2] It is not unimportant that one of the key architects of the Fundamentalist camp, Paige Patterson, has been rewarded with the presidency of Southeastern Seminary.

Why the seminary classroom is the flash point of denominational disagreements can be traced to many sources. The anti-intellectualism of

---

[1][Editor's note: Professor Crawford Howell Toy (1836–1919) resigned from Southern Seminary in 1879; Professor and President William Heth Whitsitt (1841–1911) resigned from Southern in 1899; Professor Ralph H. Elliott (1925–) was "dismissed" from Midwestern Seminary on 25 Oct 1962. These three controversies are briefly treated in "The Background of the Moderate Movement," above. These three are only representative of controversies over the years involving Baptists, the Bible, and education.]

[2][Editor's note: Regarding the Glorieta Statement (Oct 1986), see esp. Sherman's "An Overview of the Moderate Movement," above.]

Southern Baptist life and Southern culture has a part to play. Despite their high level of funding for seminaries, Southern Baptists have historically relied heavily on the unschooled preacher for leadership. That has led many in the denomination to be suspect of one who is seminary trained. The fact that, relative to other major denominations, Southern Baptists as a whole are less educated, makes fertile ground for attacks on educational institutions. Add to these ingredients the gap that has developed between seminary classroom and parish pew in all major American denominations and one understands that the problem is simply exacerbated because of the particularities of Southern Baptist life.

Financial factors also influence the central role played by theological education in Convention disputes. The combined assets of the six Convention seminaries now total $283,342,629.[3] Additionally, the Southern Baptist funding mechanism for theological education offers an almost free seminary education to any aspiring minister. Consequently, Southern Baptist theological institutions have grown to be some of the largest in the world, enrolling twenty percent of American seminarians. In addition to any doctrinal disputes, seminaries have been on the firing line in Southern Baptist life for financial reasons as well.

The search for alternatives in theological education was related to pressures brought to bear on each of the six convention seminaries. However, the one event that served as the chief motivating force prompting the birth of the seminary in Richmond was the demise of Southeastern Seminary in Wake Forest, North Carolina. Southeastern was one of the clear and early targets of the Fundamentalist attack. The forced resignations of the school's president and dean resulted in a torrent of creative energies seldom unleashed at any point in the current denominational crisis. Faculty, friends, and alumni of Southeastern responded in an organized and forceful fashion to repudiate the forces undermining their school and to investigate in a constructive manner how theological education for Baptists in the South could be preserved in a free and scholarly fashion.

The earliest alternatives to emerge were the expansion of the program for Baptist students at Duke University Divinity School and the establishment of a new divinity school on the campus of Wake Forest University. The connection to Duke was natural due to its geographical proximity and the congenial relationship that already existed with the faculty at Southeast-

---

[3]Executive Committee, Southern Baptist Convention, *Annual of the Southern Baptist Convention* (1991): 319-54; and *Annual of the SBC* (1990): 309-13.

ern. Initial inquiries were made by Max Rogers, a Durham resident who taught on the faculty of Southeastern. Official contacts were then established between Dennis Campbell, dean of the Duke Divinity School and members of the Theological Education Committee of the Alliance of Baptists (formerly the Southern Baptist Alliance). At first the discussions were quite expansive, envisioning a program in which a House of Baptist Studies would supervise the teaching of as much as a third of the curriculum for Baptist students. Dean Campbell was very encouraging in these early meetings, but as the plans were discussed by the faculty of the Duke Divinity School, they were drastically cut in scope and size. The Divinity School library was seen as too small to accommodate a large number of new students and the faculty seemed unwilling to give up control of such a large portion of its course supervision. Disappointed, one of the participants in the discussion, Alan Neely, responded in a letter to Campbell:

> [A] small "Baptist House of Studies" . . . would not be a program of sufficient magnitude to enable us to provide balanced theological education for those students who would be attracted to a Duke-Baptist program, nor would it be the kind of program for which we could raise the necessary funds.[4]

From these discussions was born the currently operating House of Baptist Studies at Duke Divinity School, a much smaller program than originally envisioned.

Another alternative was initiated by Michael Queen, pastor of First Baptist Church, Wilmington, North Carolina, who also served as the president of the Wake Forest University Ministerial Alliance. On December 17, 1987, Queen convened a meeting on the campus of Wake Forest, attended by the university president Tom Hearn, other key administrative personnel, and several others interested in the establishment of a new school for Baptist ministerial education in the region. From that meeting came a commitment from Hearn to investigate the feasibility of adding a divinity school to the academic programs of Wake Forest University. At first, Hearn appeared positive in the consideration of a new school. Robert Spinks was hired as development officer for the effort and more than two and a half million dollars was raised. Five years after its inception, the effort seems to have lost momentum and to be greatly reduced in scope.

---

[4]Alan Neely (Charlotte NC) to Dennis M. Campbell (Durham NC) 17 Sept 1988; transcript in my possession.

Other investigations were being carried on in the state of Virginia, particularly at Averett College, where a written plan for the establishment of a Master of Divinity program was proposed in March 1988. The drive for an option in Virginia was strong enough that the Baptist General Association established a committee to investigate the feasibility of Virginia Baptist institutions expanding their programs to provide theological education. The committee, chaired by Michael Clingenpeel, reported that such a course was not feasible.

There were other efforts, at Emory University and elsewhere. The Theological Education Committee of the Alliance of Baptists was eagerly pursuing and supporting all such alternatives and desirous of establishing other options as well. There were repeated resolutions of affirmation adopted by the Alliance supporting this search for new options such as the report of the Theological Education Committee in March 1989 stating, "we affirm all those institutions that are seeking to provide new avenues of theological education reflecting our Baptist heritage and expressing the ideals of the Southern Baptist Alliance."[5] It was clear that a more aggressive posture had to be adopted if significant alternatives were to be established.

The roots of the possibility for a new school in Richmond can be traced to a meeting of the Alliance of Baptists in November 1988. From earlier discussions between representatives of the American Baptist Churches (ABC) and the Alliance, it was learned that the ABC might have an interest in supporting a joint effort with the Alliance to provide theological education, particularly if it could be tied to attempts to undergird the program at the ABC-sponsored School of Theology at Virginia Union University. In the fall of 1988 the board of the Alliance took action supporting the beginning of a new school in conjunction with ABC seminaries. On November 30, 1988 in Charlotte, North Carolina, a meeting was held to discuss the establishment of a cooperative arrangement between the Alliance and American Baptist seminaries. Present at the meeting were members of the Alliance Theological Education Committee, now chaired by me, ABC denominational executives John Sundquist and Harold Germer, Allix James and John Kinney of the School of Theology at Virginia Union University, and ABC seminary presidents Larry Greenfield of Colgate-Rochester and George Peck of Andover-Newton.

---

[5]Southern Baptist Alliance, *Information Packet*, 1-3 March 1989, 6.

In discussing the core values envisioned for the new school in Richmond, the group listed several items: adherence to the Alliance Covenant, continuity with the tradition of Southeastern Seminary, ecumenical in outlook, globally focused, racially inclusive, intellectually honest, congregational focused theological learning, emphasis on quality not quantity, open to innovation, stress on the development of the spiritual life, and prophetic.[6] The meeting was characterized by a desire to develop a cooperative agreement, and, as stated by John Sundquist, "there is no little self-interest in this discussion because it provides the ABC people with the opportunity to make good the claims that 'we are open to something new being created'."[7]

Various models for the joint effort were put forth as Peck mentioned the relation of Regent's Park College to Oxford, James spoke of two institutions within one, and others referred to the structure of the Interdenominational Theological Center in Atlanta. Throughout the discussion both Kinney and James were attentive to the need to maintain the distinctive character and mission of their program at Virginia Union, saying, "a complete merger would change the character and nature of what Virginia Union University School of Theology is, whereas a cooperative relationship would enhance what they are doing."[8] The meeting concluded with the appointment of a task force to convene in Richmond, charged with the responsibility of developing a precise proposal for the establishment of a new theological center of study.

On January 3, 1989, the Seminary Task Force, convened by Alan Neely, met at the Northminster Baptist Church in Richmond. In attendance were Allix James, John Kinney, Harold Germer, Larry Greenfield, Alan Neely, Morris Ashcraft, and myself. To those persons who had attended the Charlotte meeting in November were added Heath Rada of the Presbyterian School of Christian Education, Bill Arnold of Union Theological Seminary, Stan Hastey of the Alliance of Baptists, and Sammy and Lynda Weaver-Williams of Northminster Baptist Church. The end result of the day's deliberations was the formulation of a recommendation that

> the Southern Baptist Alliance (SBA) move toward establishment of a
> school for the preparation of ministers in Richmond, Virginia, in the hope

---

[6]Minutes of the Special Meeting in Charlotte Regarding Possible New Seminary in Richmond, 30 Nov 1988.

[7]Ibid., 4.

[8]Ibid., 6.

that it will be a cooperative venture between SBA and theological institutions in Richmond and elsewhere.[9]

The task force proceeded with some very specific recommendations including that the Alliance Board "approve a provisional board of directors," that Morris Ashcraft be asked "to draw up the necessary documents relating to the school's founding," and that this new school "apply for admission into the Richmond Theological Center as an independent, self-standing institution."[10] A meeting was held for Richmond area pastors on January 4 and the task force made the first public presentation of a proposal for a new seminary in Richmond.

The report of the January task force meeting became the basis for the recommendation to be presented to the third annual convocation of the Southern Baptist Alliance meeting at the First Baptist Church in Greenville, South Carolina, March 1-3, 1989. The proposal was presented to the theological education committee and then to the board of directors of the Alliance. Even within the committee itself there was strong opposition to the plan. Some objection was also raised by members of the board, but the report of the Theological Education Committee was approved for presentation to the persons attending the convocation.

The recommendation of the theological education committee reflected precisely the suggestions of the seminary task force report of January 3 calling for the establishment of a new school in Richmond. The report met with immediate and vociferous opposition, much of it stemming from those associated with Southern Baptist Seminary in Louisville, who argued that there were in Baptist life resources adequate for dealing with the demise of Southeastern Seminary. The debate was so strong that persons involved in drafting the recommendation caucused to consider withdrawing the proposal altogether. The recommendation seemed to be headed for sure defeat and the feeling among that group was that it would be better to delay for a year's time the consideration of this new venture than to have it voted down at Greenville. The participants in the discussion included Morris Ashcraft, Tom Graves, Mahan Siler, Alan Neely, and others. It would not have been surprising had any of those persons moved to table the motion being considered. The larger debate raged longer than the allotted time and the chair ruled that discussion would be temporarily terminated in order to hear

[9]Report on Seminary Task Force Meeting, Richmond, 3 Jan 1989, 1.
[10]Ibid.

a scheduled address by Catherine Allen. It was planned to reconvene after lunch at which time the seminary issue would be considered again.

Two key events occurred to change the mood and outcome of the day's deliberations. First was the speech by Catherine Allen. She spoke with great caution, warning the participants at the SBA meeting to remain in the "middle of the stream" of Southern Baptist life. Speaking of the fear of offending what she perceived to be the mainstream of the denomination, Catherine Allen, in fact, offended many of the Alliance members who by their very presence in Greenville were voicing dissatisfaction with business as usual in convention life. Second was a brief plea voiced by Elizabeth Barnes of the Southeastern faculty when the recommendation from the theological education committee was taken up again in the afternoon session. Among the few others that spoke, Barnes delivered a precise and eloquent appeal that options in theological education must be established for the sake of women in Southern Baptist life. The vote was taken and the seminary received the approval of more than ninety percent of those in attendance at the Greenville meeting. This newest seminary was officially begun in the same church that had given birth to the oldest of Southern Baptist theological schools.[11]

Before leaving the 1989 SBA meeting in Greenville, the Alliance board of directors met in order to name the members of a provisional board of trustees for the Richmond seminary. The provisional board held its first meeting in Richmond on April 24-25, 1989. Members present at the meeting included Sue Fitzgerald, Basil Manly, Alan Neely, Ross Shearer, Mary Strauss, Lynda Weaver-Williams, and Elmer West. Mary Strauss of Hagerstown, Maryland, was elected as chairperson of the board. Basil Manly introduced a motion "to engage Morris Ashcraft immediately for such a time until the board of directors moves to employ a permanent CEO."[12]

Ashcraft's decision to serve as acting president brought to the seminary the leadership of the former dean who had been at the center of controversy in theological education not only at Southeastern, but also as Ralph Elliott's colleague at Midwestern Seminary, and at Southern Seminary as one of thirteen professors choosing to leave in 1958. As a scholar, administrator,

---

[11][Editor's note: In 1859, First Baptist Church, Greenville, moved into new facilities, and the newly established Southern Baptist Theological Seminary rented and then purchased the vacated buildings.]

[12]Minutes of the Southern Baptist Alliance Richmond Theological Project Provisional Board of Directors, 24-25 April 1989, 3.

and one schooled in the Convention's denominational turmoil, Ashcraft brought a wealth of experience to the fledgling institution. He moved temporarily to Richmond, working out of facilities provided by the Presbyterian School of Christian Education.

The immediate tasks confronting Ashcraft were those of raising funds and securing facilities for the seminary's operation. By the fall of 1989 progress was being made on both fronts. Calvary Baptist Church of Richmond, in merging with a sister congregation, decided to give a percentage of its assets to the seminary. Elmer West was instrumental in arranging for this gift amounting to more than $100,000, the largest gift thus far received by the school. In September 1989 Frank Goare, formerly on the staff of Southeastern Seminary, was hired as director of development. Ashcraft also began negotiations with Northminster Baptist Church to provide a temporary home for the seminary offices. By January 1990 an agreement had been formalized allowing the seminary limited use of the church facilities.

In his March 5, 1990 report to directors, Ashcraft summarized the progress made during the initial months of the seminary's existence by noting its financial support of $481,000 in receipts and pledges, and its legal status with the approval of its incorporation papers and bylaws. Ashcraft went on to list for the directors the liabilities and weaknesses faced by the young institution, including a lack of widespread financial support, the continued ambivalence of the Alliance of Baptists, the lack of church and denominational support, and a prevailing attitude of "wait and see" on the part of so many potential supporters.

Of particular concern to Ashcraft was the lack of support from the Alliance of Baptists. Of the ninety-seven churches belonging to the Alliance, only seventeen offered financial support to the young school. Within the Alliance itself there remained a strong voice of opposition to the seminary. At a meeting of the Alliance board on November 30, 1989, a motion was proposed to restrict the seminary's support from the annual offering of the Alliance because there are those who "do not wish to contribute substantially to the seminary, and in some cases also may not wish to be identified with it as a major . . . SBA venture."[13] The motion was approved by the Alliance board of directors by a vote of 16-14.

Recognizing both the prospects and the pitfalls, Ashcraft detailed three options now confronting the seminary board members:

---

[13]Rob James (Richmond) to the board of directors of the Southern Baptist Alliance, 11 Dec 1989, 2; transcript in my possession.

1. Open in the fall of 1990 on a limited basis by faith, hoping for the funding to come.
2. Abandon the effort altogether, fulfill the obligations made, and notify the SBA that we do not think that now is the time nor Richmond the place for such an effort. . . .
3. Extend the time of development and preparation until funding for the seminary is more secure, leaving the opening date undetermined.[14]

Though a great deal of progress had been made, the future of the school remained in doubt.

The board of directors met on April 17 and in effect recommitted itself to the opening of the seminary by naming a search committee to seek a president. Ashcraft had earlier expressed his intent to step down as acting president by stating "my wife and I have concluded . . . that we are not able to make the necessary move to Richmond for me to be able to continue in this role."[15] Ashcraft continued to meet with the seminary board and offered extensive help while his successor was being sought. The trustees adopted a description for the job of seminary president in the wording of an advertisement circulated for the position:

> Baptist Theological Seminary at Richmond seeks applications and nominations for Chief Academic Officer. The preferred candidate, man or woman, must be a Baptist with an earned doctorate in a recognized theological discipline and a committed church person who desires to work in an ecumenical and interracial consortium dedicated to the training of persons for ministry.[16]

A Search Committee composed of eight trustees was elected, with Alan Neely serving as chairperson. The committee had its initial meeting on June 18, 1990, and by that time had already received several nominations for the position. The committee quickly began to narrow the list of names to be considered but also extended the date for further nominations. Six characteristics were listed by the committee as being desirable in any nominee: (1) a recognized name/credibility; (2) some academic experience; (3) practical experience; (4) the ability to work in an ecumenical setting; (5) leadership

---

[14]Acting President's Report to Directors, 5 March 1990, 4.

[15]Morris Ashcraft (Richmond VA) to Mary Strauss (Richmond VA), 16 April 1990; transcript attached to the Minutes of the Board of Directors' Officers Meeting, Baptist Theological Seminary at Richmond, 17 April 1990.

[16]Minutes of the Board of Directors' Officers Meeting, Baptist Theological Seminary at Richmond, 17 April 1990.

style; and (6) track record.[17] The committee determined to ask nominees for essay answers to questions concerning commitment to the principles of the Alliance and how a faculty, staff, and curriculum would be fashioned in light of those principles.

By August 20 the search committee narrowed the twenty-three names that had been submitted to three persons who were subsequently interviewed. The search committee came to a decision that was announced in a September 19 memo to all trustees:

> The committee was in unanimity in its decision to issue the invitation to M. Vernon Davis. Dr. Davis has enthusiastically agreed to serve as the next president of Baptist Theological Seminary at Richmond.[18]

Vernon Davis, vice-president for academic affairs at Midwestern Seminary and a former Virginia pastor, seemed to be the proper choice for the new Richmond seminary. His respected leadership among Virginia Baptists while serving as pastor of First Baptist Church, Alexandria, provided a clear linkage between Virginia Baptists and the seminary that was so necessary if the school were to succeed. The date of October 8, 1990, was set for a public announcement of Davis's acceptance.

In the last week of September, just a few days before the scheduled announcement, Vernon Davis wrote a letter of withdrawal. Having made the decision to move, he now found the actuality of leaving Midwestern too difficult and burdensome. Davis wrote to each member of the search committee:

> Several people . . . have likened us to a sinking ship. Perhaps that observation is correct, although I . . . hope not. If it is, however, I still cannot escape the conviction . . . that the officers are not to jump first.[19]

Davis concluded that he was no longer confident that it was the right choice for him to come to Richmond. Expressing the sentiments of trustees, Strauss wrote later to Davis that "there was no anger or resentment or animosity directed toward you or your decision. We could all empathize with the extremely difficult choice we had asked you to make."[20]

---

[17]Minutes of the Search Committee Meeting, Baptist Theological Seminary at Richmond, 18 June 1990.

[18]Mary M. Strauss (Richmond VA) to BTSR Trustees, 19 Sept 1990.

[19]M. Vernon Davis (Kansas City MO) to Alan Neely (Princeton NJ) 27 Sept 1990, 2; transcript in my possession.

[20]Mary M. Strauss (Richmond VA) to M. Vernon Davis (Kansas City MO), 18

The news of the withdrawal came to Alan Neely while attending a board meeting of the Alliance in Washington, D.C. As other members of the search committee were also present, a caucus was held and the decision was made to move on immediately with the process of locating a new president.

I was in attendance at the Alliance board meeting. In discussing the situation at Richmond, Neely asked if my name could now be considered by the search committee. Having only recently gone as pastor to St. John's Baptist Church in Charlotte (in 1987), I had asked previously that my name not be considered by the committee and as a result I was not a part of any of the committee's prior deliberations. My answer to Neely at the time was that I did not see how I could consider such a move. On the trip returning from the Alliance board meeting, I flew with Henry Crouch who had been a party to the conversation with Alan Neely. Crouch, also a Charlotte pastor, finally said in the course of the lengthy discussion, "If you go to Richmond, I will resign and go with you to raise money for the school." Though still hesitant and unsure, I called Neely and said I was willing to talk with representatives of the search committee.

Of prime consideration was the financial condition of the school. I had arrived at the same conclusion as Ashcraft months earlier: the financial viability of the school had to be assured prior to asking anyone to serve as president. Without increased budgetary stability, any new president would be faced with an overwhelming job of fund raising, leaving no time for the many other tasks needing to be accomplished. Understanding this, the members of the search committee pledged to seek a $100,000 increase in the seminary's reserves by year's end. The goal was exceeded as $108,000 was raised in a matter of weeks, a promising sign of the seminary's potential.

By the end of the year, I had consulted with family, close friends, and staff at St. John's and felt comfortable with the decision to accept the position of president of the Baptist Theological Seminary at Richmond. On January 7, 1991, the board of trustees voted unanimously to elect me as president of the Seminary.

The most pressing task facing me as the school's president was the selection of faculty. The board of trustees were to meet March 15-16, to approve faculty positions and to determine if the school would begin classes in the fall. The first contact was with Linda McKinnish Bridges. Bridges,

---

Oct 1990; attached to Minutes of the Board of Trustees Meeting, Baptist Theological Seminary at Richmond, 18 Oct 1990.

who had been highly recommended by trustees acquainted with her work, had taught previously at both Union Seminary in Richmond and at Southern Seminary. She had proven herself to be a splendid teacher of Greek and also one well aware of issues being debated in Southern Baptist life. Her biography was in many ways a microcosm of the convention struggles with issues of women in ministry and theological openness. Bridges agreed to serve as assistant professor of Greek and New Testament and she then helped in locating adjunctive faculty resources to round out the biblical studies area. Jerome Creach, a Ph.D. candidate at Union Seminary, agreed to teach the Old Testament survey classes and James Luther Mays, recently retired from Union, accepted with great enthusiasm the offer to teach elective courses in Old Testament.

In searching for a dean of the school, no name surfaced more often than Tom Halbrooks. He taught in the area of church history, one of the basic areas of the curriculum. More importantly, Halbrooks had extensive exposure to academic administration as assistant to Morris Ashcraft at Southeastern and from his experience working in the community college system of Virginia. It was most helpful that Halbrooks had been a leader among the Southeastern faculty's AAUP chapter, thus acquainting him fully with accreditation expectations and legal guidelines. He agreed to accept the gargantuan task of writing a catalog, developing a curriculum and selecting the remainder of the adjunctive faculty.

Chevis Horne, longtime Virginia pastor who was completing his work as visiting professor of preaching at Southeastern, agreed to come and teach preaching at Richmond. Horne and his wife Helen became a key ingredient in the seminary's community life during the first year. No one could have been more loved. Robert Dale, on the staff of the Baptist General Association of Virginia was added to the adjunctive faculty in practical theology while Henry Mugabe, of the Baptist Theological Seminary of Zimbabwe, agreed to teach a course in theology during the first winter term. With the faculty now assured, the proposal was taken to the trustees that the school open for classes in the fall of 1991 and that Bridges and Halbrooks be elected to the faculty.

The press of time and the masterful work of Halbrooks cannot be overestimated. Although a catalog had to be prepared for recruiting purposes within a matter of a few weeks' time, a curriculum plan, school schedule, and administrative policies were established with due regard for accreditation standards and academic respectability. The early faculty meetings in which these decisions were hammered out were frank but always collegial.

Bridges's influence was seen from the central role played by the biblical languages in the seminary course work. By May the new catalog was ready and the school was earnestly seeking its first students.

The congregation of Northminster Baptist Church had been extremely generous and gracious in making facilities available to the seminary. It soon became apparent that a larger amount of office space would be needed. Discussions were held with Presbyterian School of Christian Education (PSCE) that resulted in their offer to lease facilities to the seminary that would provide for all the staff, faculty, classroom, dorm, and chapel space needed the first year. On August 1, 1991, Baptist Theological Seminary at Richmond moved to its expanded space in Paisley Hall on the PSCE campus.

With faculty and facilities in place there was now time to turn full administrative attention to the seminary's financial development. From its inception the seminary had consciously tied its fund-raising efforts to the life of the Alliance of Baptists. Individuals and congregations supportive of the Alliance were the pool of potential supporters being targeted by the young seminary. It was clear that a much broader base of support was needed for the school's future success. Contacts were initiated with Virginia Baptists through Ron Crawford who served both as a seminary trustee and as vice-president of the Baptist General Association of Virginia (BGAV). At a meeting in Charlottesville on April 30, the seminary presented its story to a group of Moderate leaders from throughout the state. The support of that group proved contagious as the school gained an open and friendly access to Virginia Baptists. In May a presentation was made to the denominational relations committee of the BGAV which resulted in a resolution adopted by the 1991 meeting of the BGAV. The committee's resolution read in part:

> [Be] it resolved that the messengers . . . affirm, in principle, the vision of the founders of the Baptist Theological Seminary at Richmond by praying for its ministry, by endorsing it as an appropriate place for ministerial candidates to study, and by establishing internships for students to serve.[21]

During the same time a formal request was made of the BGAV budget committee that the seminary be placed in the state convention's budget. Ernest Boyd, chair of the budget committee, presented a recommendation to the 1991 annual meeting that the seminary be included in the BGAV's alternative budget for 1992.

---

[21]The Baptist General Association of Virginia, *Book of Reports* (1991) 49.

The support of Virginia Baptists opened the door for the seminary to gain the significant support of the Keesee Educational Foundation of Martinsville, Virginia. The Keesee Fund is a $30,000,000 trust used to support persons from Virginia and North Carolina who are preparing for ministry in Baptist churches. Until this time the fund had only supported the six SBC seminaries and institutions related to the BGAV. Now the request was placed in front of them to lend their support to students at the Richmond seminary. Following the decision of seminary trustees to invite the BGAV to nominate a member of the seminary's board, the directors of the Keesee Fund voted to include students at the Richmond seminary in the awarding of its substantial scholarships. As two-thirds of the students at the seminary were either from Virginia or North Carolina, the support of the Keesee Fund was the most important step in development achieved in the early history of the school. In this process, Chevis Horne, a Keesee trustee and adjunctive teacher at the seminary played no small role.

Another avenue of support became the quickly growing Cooperative Baptist Fellowship. From the beginning, the Richmond seminary was placed in two of the Fellowship's three budget options and later was added to the third. Linda McKinnish Bridges of the seminary faculty served as a member of the Fellowship's coordinating council, providing a liaison between the two organizations. By 1992 the Fellowship was the largest single contributor to the seminary and ready to discuss the strengthening of its ties. With growing financial aid from the BGAV, the Cooperative Baptist Fellowship, and many churches and individuals, the seminary's financial situation became more and more secure.

In the summer of 1991 the seminary staff grew with the addition of Beth McMahon as director of communications and student services and Nell Summerlin as director of administrative services. On August 1, 1991, the same day as it took possession of its new facilities on the campus of PSCE, the seminary held an open house for prospective students. Fifty persons were in attendance as the dreams of several years took concrete shape. On September 10 the opening convocation was held and the seminary began its first semester with thirty-two students enrolled.

The History
of the Baptist Center for Ethics

Robert Parham

In the 1940s, two Baptist ministers had a vision of an interracial, agrarian community that would empower impoverished farmers. They gave their vision a fancy name—Koinonia Farm.

It was hardly a real community in the earliest days, just two men. It was hardly a real farm, just 400 acres in southwest Georgia. They were hardly real farmers, just two preachers.

Since they had no mules, Clarence Jordan and Martin England took turns being the mules. One hitched up to the plow and pulled. The other pushed and steered. Then, they switched places.[1]

Like Koinonia Farm, Baptist Center for Ethics is a fancy name for another vision. It is hardly pan-Baptist, just a group of thoughtful Southern Baptists. It is hardly a real center, just a network. But like Koinonia, BCE is breaking the soil of a new ethics frontier with mulish determination.

Four Southern Baptist Ethics Paths in the Twentieth Century

Four understudied paths carry the Southern Baptist ethics tradition in the twentieth century. In the 1990s, ethics is the term for study of values, moral issues, and social involvement. Southern Baptists have given the concept different names: "the social gospel," "social service," "social Christianity," "applied Christianity," and "the Christian life."

---

[1]P. Joel Snider, *The "Cotton Patch" Gospel: The Proclamation of Clarence Jordan* (Landham MD: University Press of America, 1985) 14.

The Soul-Winning Path. One tradition of Southern Baptist Christian ethics is the soul-winning path. In this view, the church's primary task is evangelism. The way to change society is to change individuals. The cure for societal wrong is spiritual salvation. The vehicle for change is white-hot preaching and fervent witnessing. The early Billy Graham and contemporary state convention evangelism conferences reflect this tradition.

The soul-winning tradition takes for granted that moral growth, sanctification, and discipleship automatically follow from conversion. It does not recognize the crippling nature of social forces on saved individuals and overestimates the individual's ability to change social systems. It also focuses almost exclusively on the spiritual over the physical.

The Prophetic Path. The second tradition is more like a trail than a path. It contains individual Baptist prophets. Clarence Jordan stands tallest in this tradition. Another forgotten representative is J. J. Taylor, who was dismissed in 1917 from the pastorate of Savannah's First Baptist Church over his pacifist views and later wrote *The God of War.*[2] Edwin McNeill Poteat, Jr., author of *Jesus and the Liberal Mind,* and Will Campbell wear the prophetic mantle.

The prophets bear two distinguishing marks. First, they are Christocentric. Jesus' followers speak to social issues because Jesus was in and spoke to the world, but Christians never try to manage the world.

Second, the thoughts and actions of Baptist prophets are generally so distant from the thoughts and actions of rank-and-file Baptists that the prophets are often mistaken for the enemy and are summarily dismissed. Some prophets form countercommunities. Others preach to the intelligentsia. Either way, Baptist prophets witness *against* the prevailing culture.

The Transformationist Path. The third tradition is the transformationist path. Well-known Baptists have walked this way: C. S. Gardner, J. B. Weatherspoon, A. C. Miller, Henlee Barnette, T. B. Maston, J. M. Dawson, Brooks Hays, and Jimmy Carter.

Baptist transformers are Christocentric. Jesus provides moral principles and stories rather than a model to emulate. Unlike the prophets, the transformers' objective is gradual change, not radical change. Their vehicle for social change is moral teaching, ethical preaching, and legislative initiatives, rather than the formation of an alternative community and cut-

---

[2]Robert Parham, "Taylor: 'Only One, But a Lion'," *Light* (July/august 1986): 4-6.

ting-edge social commentary. Transformers press with a cautious awareness about their context and a profound sense of human sinfulness.

The Conquest Path. The conquest path branches off the soul-winning path. Men like J. Frank Norris, W. A. Criswell, Ed McAteer, and Pat Robertson were originally opponents of "social Christianity" and preservers of the pillars of culture. While some of them came late to the field of social action, they came to conquer. The conquest tradition lacks the Christocentric core of the prophets and transformers.

Conquerors speak about the saving power of Jesus from personal sin, overlooking the social implications of love for neighbor. They ignore the Sermon on the Mount with its admonition to turn the other cheek and to walk the second mile.

Transformers and conquerors differ at two major points. First, transformers critique culture and seek its transformation. Conquerors attack culture at points which do not threaten the social order—the lack of state-written school prayer. The conquerors crusade to preserve culture at its core: white supremacy, male dominance, economic Darwinism, and militant nationalism.

Not surprisingly, transformers and conquerors differ on social issues. Transformers pursue an agenda of change: human rights, integration, foreign aid, welfare, women's rights, and peacemaking. Conquerors fight to preserve the status quo: *anti*liberation efforts, *anti*-integration, *anti*foreign aid, *anti*welfare, *anti*women's rights, and *anti*peacemaking.

The second difference between these two traditions is their Calvinistic approach to government. Transformers seek influence through the translation of Christian values into public policy and legislation. Conquerors yearn for control. Their vehicle is the religious right dominating the Republican Party, the Republican Party controlling the White House and then the White House establishing a Christian America.

These differences result from stubborn disagreement about sin. Transformers recognize human beings are sinful and reside in a fallen social order. Conquerors ignore the damnation of the social order. Failing to recognize their own cultural captivity, they cannot see that a Christian order is beyond their theocratic grasp.

The transformers and the conquerors are pitted against one another in the contest over which moral vision will prevail. The transformers attempt to manage the prophets, an utterly impossible task. The conquerors forge an easier alliance with the soul winners. The SBC Christian Life Commission has been the battle ground between the transformers, who bear the Moderate label, and the conquerors, who wield the Fundamentalist's sword of the Lord.

The Conquest of the Christian Life Commission

The First Wave. With hindsight, the Fundamentalist takeover of the CLC can be seen in three waves. The first wave flooded the CLC's board of directors with individuals driven by an ideological social agenda. Political right-wing orthopraxis replaced traditional Southern Baptist orthodoxy as the chief qualification for fellowship.

Historically, CLC board members were nominated and elected based upon their church leadership, educational accomplishment and vocational success. But all that changed in the early 1980s.

Membership in right-wing organizations distinguished the agency's new directors more than leadership in Baptist life. One member belonged to the John Birch Society. One pastor was a devotee of Operation Rescue. Another pastor noted that his support for Senator Jeremiah Denton (R-AL) qualified him for service on the CLC board. A stockbroker and recent member of the Baptist fold founded Southern Baptists for Life. A professor claimed he was a consultant on pro-life issues to Senator Gordon Humphrey (R-NH) and boasted that he lobbied for Supreme Court nominee Robert Bork. A state representative had provided the Baptist State Convention of North Carolina mailing list to Senator Jesse Helms (R-NC). Three women worked at local crisis pregnancy centers. Four other women were state leaders in Phyllis Schafley's Eagle Forum. All new directors were first and foremost antiabortionists.

While it had been clear all along that the Fundamentalist agenda included far more than the inerrancy approach to the Bible, Paige Patterson made this fact abundantly clear after the Fundamentalist victories at the SBC meeting in Atlanta in 1986. Patterson said the future hiring of denominational employees would be tied to the social as well as theological agenda of Fundamentalists. This included the Fundamentalist position on abortion, euthanasia, school prayer, and federal budget reduction. Saying that Southern Baptists would have more and more in common with the New Religious Right, Patterson said of the SBC acceptance of the social and moral agenda, "I think it'll go over nearly as well as the inerrancy thing."[3]

---

[3]Brad Owens, "Patterson Thrusts Social Agenda into Fray," *The Baptist Messenger*, 26 June 1986, 3.

The Second Wave. The second wave was the election of an executive director. During the 1985 CLC board meeting, a Fundamentalist asked if the CLC's abortion material would reflect the stance in SBC resolutions. "It will not reflect your view or the convention vote," Foy Valentine, the agency's executive director, shot back. "Your view has not prevailed and if it does, you need a new executive director."[4] The following April, Valentine announced his retirement plans.[5] A search committee was appointed a month prior to the 1986 SBC where eight Moderate CLC directors rotated off the board and eight new directors were elected. Fundamentalists were moving from a vocal minority to a voting majority.

Three flash points disclosed the division at the 1986 board meeting. One was the recommendation that the WMU's executive director, Carolyn Weatherford, probably the best-known female name in Southern Baptist circles, receive the CLC's service award. That motion passed by a 16-13 vote, after two new Fundamentalist directors acknowledged that they did not know who she was.

The second flash point was abortion. During a subcommittee meeting, a motion was made that the CLC material be "consistent with the 1980, 1982, and 1984 SBC resolutions on abortion." The motion prevailed on a six to four vote, but it was reversed during the general session by a 14-13 vote with two abstentions.[6]

The third flash point was the election of a Moderate chairman on a 15-13 vote.

With a clearly divided house, the CLC search committee struggled to find a candidate. Three individuals declined nomination before Larry Baker, vice-president for academic affairs at Midwestern Baptist Theological Seminary, was elected in January 1987 on a 16-13 vote.[7]

The September 1987 CLC board meeting was awash in rumors that the Fundamentalists would dismiss Baker.[8] Soon after the meeting began, Fun-

----

[4]My meeting notes, 10-11 Sept 1985.

[5]David Wilkinson, "Commission Initiates Search for Executive Director-Elect," Christian Life Commission news release, 5 May 1986.

[6]My meeting notes, 16-17 Sept 1986.

[7]David Wilkinson, "Larry Baker Elected CLC Executive Director," Christian Life Commission news release. 16 Jan 1987.

[8]Greg Warner, "Will CLC fire Baker?" *Florida Baptist Witness*, 10 Sept 1987, 5. CLC director Rudy Yakym said, "We'd have the votes" to fire Baker. He added, "If he's dismissed, it might be the thing that makes left-leaning churches leave the

damentalist Joe Atchison moved to remove Baker. Hal Lane, a South Carolina pastor, said "I do not feel responsible for it [the motion to dismiss Baker]. The responsibility lies with the search committee that did not listen to us."[9]

Two issues were at the heart of the Fundamentalists' effort. They believed the search process was flawed.[10] The more emotive issue was abortion. The Fundamentalists were furious that Baker's antiabortion position was not their antiabortion position. They wanted a leader who made only one exception. Baker made four. "You cannot carry the flag if you do not believe what the flag stands for," charged Nolan Phillips, an Ohio pastor.[11]

While the motion to dismiss Baker ended in a 15-15 vote,[12] the Fundamentalists dominated the remainder of the meeting. They adopted a policy position that allowed for abortion only "when the developing child represents a clear and present danger to the physical life of the mother." They withdrew two pamphlets "Issues and Answers: Changing Roles of Women" and "Critical Issues: Women in Church and Society." They commended President Ronald Reagan for his leadership on abortion.[13]

Baker left the leadership of the CLC and went to a pastorate in the spring of 1988.

During the summer of 1988, Richard Land was rumored to be the next executive director. He had served as an advisor for seventeen months on the staff of Governor Bill Clements (R-TX) and was a professor at Criswell College, where Paige Patterson was president. Some CLC directors and

---

convention. If we don't excise him, conservatives may feel nothing's going to change even though we have a majority on the board."

[9]Ray Waddle, "Conservatives Fail to Oust Baptist Leader," *The Tennessean*, 16 Sept 1987, A1-2.

[10]"Baker Keeps Post with 15-15 Vote," Baptist Press news release (BP), 18 Sept 1987. Fred Lackey, an Alabama Fundamentalist, had criticized the search process in January: "The [search] committee is monolithic. I feel that my point of view at least was not represented." See David Wilkinson, "Larry Baker Elected CLC Executive Director," BP, 16 Jan 1987.

[11]Waddle, "Conservatives Fail," 2.

[12]Cledith Campbell made a substitute motion to give Baker another six months. His fellow Fundamentalists opposed his motion. But in the process they had lost Campbell's vote and the attempt to fire Baker.

[13]"Conservatives Sweep CLC Officer Election," BP, 18 Sept 1987; and "CLC Tightens Abortion Rule," BP, 18 Sept 1987.

other Fundamentalist leaders opposed Land's candidacy, however. "Land is too political," said CLC chairman Fred Lackey. "I'll vote against him."[14]

Widespread rumors persisted that Fundamentalist Home Mission Board president Larry Lewis actually worked to block Land's candidacy. He believed Land was "too political." Lewis allegedly found a candidate who had the right position on abortion, was concerned about pornography and was seen as nonpolitical.[15] But Land, Paige Patterson's and Paul Pressler's protege, was not to be denied.

The search committee's stalemate was broken with a recommendation from Joel Gregory, pastor of Travis Avenue Baptist Church, Fort Worth, Texas. Gregory wrote that Land "is a personal friend."[16] Search committee chairman Joe Atchison admitted that Gregory's two-page, recommendation letter "carried lot of weight."[17] Land was elected executive director at the agency's September board meeting on a 23-2 vote. The Fundamentalists had their own man.

Land immediately asserted a commitment to parity on the CLC staff and in conference programming.[18] He promised to address all the issues and to work with all Baptists.[19] He justified hiring two Fundamentalist program staff people as counterbalances to the remaining two Moderates, a move toward parity.

The Third Wave. The third wave was the change in the Southern Baptist ethos. The 1988, 1989, and 1990 defeats of Moderate candidates trans-

---

[14]My notes of conversation with Fred Lackey, 21 June 1988.

[15]My notes of conversation with Jim Newton, public relations director for the Home Mission Board, 20 July 1988.

[16]Joel Gregory letter, 27 July 1988. Bobbie Patry, the Tennessee leader of Eagle Forum, also wrote a recommendation letter on 27 July. CLC director Gary Crum endorsed Land the previous day.

[17]Dan Martin, "CLC Search Committee Selects Richard Land," BP, 7 Sept 1988. Atchison said Gregory and Ralph Smith, pastor of Hyde Park Baptist Church, Austin, Texas, "made very strong recommendations, and neither of them have been in the quote political unquote arena in the past years, so we felt these recommendations were objective and very credible."

[18]In his first meeting with state ethics workers, Land said the present CLC staff represented diversity and the CLC does "need [a] pluralistic staff"; my meeting notes, 3-4 Dec 1988. Later, Land said, "we will reach a new equilibrium that will be very inclusive." Michael Duduit, "Consensus Challenges '90s, Scholars Say," BP, 16 Feb 1990.

[19]Dan Martin, "Land Says Position 'in line' with SBC," BP, 7 Sept 1988.

formed the environment within SBC entities. Fundamentalists moved from half-listening to ignoring Moderate concerns altogether. Nowhere was the adverse change in ethos more apparent than at the CLC. As the SBC ethos changed, Land changed course. In September 1989, he employed a young man whose entire adult experience was in right-wing, secular politics.[20] In September 1990, Land hired the staff journalist for Bellevue Baptist Church who for four years had coedited an Arkansas newsletter named *Flag* (which stood for family, life, America, God). Land also added an attorney who belonged to Lawyers for Life and the Christian Legal Society. The concept of staff parity had perished.

Land also replaced the cornerstone of the agency's staff philosophy. Historically, almost all CLC program staffers held Ph.D. degrees in ethics. Now, the CLC is without a program staff member with a Ph.D. in Christian ethics. Political ideology has replaced educational preparation as the chief qualification for employment.

Social Issues

Fundamentalists historically opposed "social Christianity" and racial integration. They feared the former detracted from evangelism and the latter led to race mixing. Over time this opposition rallied enemies of the CLC. When the takeover began, little effort was needed to stir opposition to the CLC. However, their wedge issue was abortion.[21]

Abortion. During the 1970s, SBC resolutions reflected a qualified antiabortion position.[22] Fundamentalist leaders agreed with these resolutions. Criswell said in 1977, "There are times, such as in the case of rape, incest or when the attending physicians determine that there will be abnormality,

---

[20]Ray Waddle, "Southern Baptists hire full-time Lobbyist," *The Tennessean*, 13 Sept 1989, B5. Smith said, "Land hired me in spite of my party identity." Smith had served as an intern on the staff of Congressman Newt Gingrich (R-GA).

[21]Nancy Ammerman notes that "the most volatile issue was abortion," in *Baptist Battles: Social Change and Religious Conflict in the Southern Baptist Convention* (New Brunswick NJ: Rutgers University Press, 1990) 100.

[22]The first SBC abortion resolution was adopted in 1971, making exceptions for "rape, incest, clear evidence of severe fetal deformity, and carefully ascertained evidence of the likelihood of damage to the emotional, mental, and physical health of the mother." See Robert Parham, "Where Do Southern Baptists Stand on the Issue of Abortion?" in *CLC Seminar Proceedings. Choosing Life: Southern Baptists and Abortion* (31 Aug–1 Sept 1987): 27-29.

that abortion is imminently acceptable."[23] Adrian Rogers, pastor of Bellevue Baptist Church, wrote that he "basically agreed with" Valentine's position.[24]

Beginning in 1980, SBC resolutions became more rigid. The 1980 SBC resolution called for "a constitutional amendment prohibiting abortion except to save the life of the mother." The language of resolutions shifted from the concept of "fetal life" to "pre-born life."[25] The tone for other SBC resolutions and actions was set.

Abortion became the litmus test for orthopraxis. Larry Baker was one of the first to fail this test. His position was not narrow enough to satisfy CLC directors. He made too many exceptions: rape, incest, threat to the mother's life, and severe deformity. Yet he moved swiftly to address the issue.[26]

Even with Land at the helm, abortion was the measure for fellowship. At the September 1989 board meeting, directors balked at Land's recommendation to give the agency's service award to foreign missionary physician Richard Goodgame. They feared his "liberal" education at Johns Hopkins University School of Medicine meant he was proabortion. Goodgame eventually passed the test.[27]

At the March 1990 board meeting, a motion was made to withdraw Land's speaking invitation to Southern Seminary ethicist Glen Stassen who was accused of being proabortion. Land rose to a point of personal privilege, saying that "if the board decided to pass the motion on pro-life, the members needed to give the staff a detailed definition of pro-life." He pointed out that fifty percent of Southern Baptists allowed abortion in the cases of rape, incest, and threat to life of the mother. Directors quickly

---

[23] Jonathan Pedersen, "Criswell Meets the Press at New Orleans Seminary," BP, 1 Dec 1977.

[24] Adrian Rogers and Foy Valentine's correspondence. Valentine answered Rogers's 8 Nov 1977 letter: "My own convictions about abortion are reasonably well reflected in the 1971 action of the Southern Baptist Convention." Adrian replied on 28 Nov: "your answer is clear and one that I basically agree with." Rogers changed his position, however, calling abortion the slaughter of unborn babies. His remarks were made during a 1985 SBC debate over a recommendation to add an antiabortion Sunday to the SBC calendar. See *SBC Annual* (1985): 88, 233.

[25] Parham, "Where Do Southern Baptists Stand?" 27-28.

[26] Ammerman, *Baptist Battles*, 237.

[27] Ray Waddle, "Missionary Honored after Views Examined," *The Tennessean*, 15 Sept 1989, A1, 4.

reminded him the CLC's policy did not allow for the exceptions of rape and incest.[28]

All new CLC program staff members pledged their antiabortion loyalty. Antiabortion resolutions were adopted at many of the seminaries. Southern Seminary trustees sought to silence ethicist Paul Simmons for his stance on abortion. The Sunday School Board made an antiabortion lesson part of Sunday school curriculum.

Race. "The battles between integrationists and segregationists in the South were fought in thousands of public and private arenas."[29] One battle-ground was the Supreme Court's 1954 decision against school segregation. Support for that decision by Southern Seminary professor and CLC chairper-son J. B. Weatherspoon and CLC director A. C. Miller ensured an opposition party to the CLC.[30]

Ironically, racism erupted decades later at the meeting when Land was elected. CLC director Curtis Caine called Martin Luther King a "fraud." He claimed apartheid "doesn't exist [any more] and wasn't bad when it did exist because it meant separate development."[31] Many CLC directors nodded in agreement. No director challenged Caine's statement.[32]

---

[28]CLC Minutes, 1-2 March 1990, 4-9. Also see Ray Waddle, "S. Baptists Ban Speakers Holding 'Pro-Choice' Views," *The Tennessean,* 9 March 1990, A1, 4; and Helen Parmley, "Baptist Speakers Face Screening on Abortion," *Dallas Morning News,* 24 March 1990, A40.

[29]Ammerman, *Baptist Battles,* 65.

[30]Robert Parham, "A. C. Miller: The Bible Speaks on Race," *Baptist History and Heritage* 27 (Jan 1992): 32-43.

[31]Ray Waddle, "Baptist's Tirade about King Embarrasses Panel," *The Tennessean,* 15 Sept 1988, B1.

[32]CLC director Marilyn Simmons said, "I don't feel he is a racist. King was a controversial man. Many people feel he helped blacks, but many feel he caused a whole lot of trouble." Ray Waddle, "Baptists Denounce SBC Official's Racial Remarks," *The Tennessean,* 30 Sept 1988, A4. The CLC of the Baptist General Convention of Texas called Caine's remarks "disturbing." The CLC's interim executive director denounced the remarks. African-American Southern Baptists asked how Caine could be removed from the CLC's board. A Mississippi Baptist Convention resolution said, "we in no way endorse these positions espoused by the trustee from Mississippi" on the CLC. See Ken Camp, "Texas CLC Opposes Comments Made by Southern Baptist CLC Member," BP, 26 Sept 1988; Marv Knox, "Racial Statements Distort SBC Stand, Ethicists Says," BP, 29 Sept 1988; and Marv Knox, "Priesthood Doctrine Attracts Most Southern Baptist Attention," BP, 23 Nov 1988.

Reaction to Caine's remarks forced Land to hold a race relations conference in January 1989. The event was praised as a model of how the two SBC factions could work together. Land's inclusive leadership was commended. Optimism was short-lived, however. A motion to remove Caine from the CLC at the 1989 SBC was referred to the SBC executive committee. The 1990 committee on nominations renominated him and he was reelected to another four-year term. Evidently Caine's position did not morally disqualify him for service.[33] Additionally, Land scaled back his second race conference to a private consultation.[34]

Hunger. Fundamentalist directors only blinked at the hunger issue. They virtually ignored staff reports on hunger concerning the stagnant level of giving to denominational hunger ministries. One director opposed hunger funds for Ethiopian famine relief, saying that such efforts kept the Marxist government in power.[35]

War and Peace. Peacemaking never interested Fundamentalists. Their Manichaean worldview demanded the arms race to stop the "evil empire." Arms control and peacemaking were viewed as deterrents to militant nationalism.[36]

Soon after his election, Land accepted an invitation to serve as an ex officio board member of the Baptist Peace Fellowship of North America. His involvement was seen as an inclusive step. Two years later, after the

---

[33]Ray Waddle, "Critic of King Should Resign, Baptists Urge," *The Tennessean*, 18 Jan 1989, B1, 3; and Ray Waddle, "Southern Baptists Brave Heat to Hand Out Bibles along Strip," *The Tennessean*, 15 June 1989, A6.

[34]Louis Moore, "CLC Plans Consultation on Race Relations Efforts," CLC news release, 2 Aug 1990; and Richard Land memorandum, 21 June 1990.

[35]James Hefley criticized hunger articles in *Light* as reflecting only "the liberal position on welfare," and failing to cite "conservative economists." James Hefley, *The Truth in Crisis: Bringing the Controversy Up-to-Date*, vol. 2 (Hannibal MO: Hannibal Books, 1987) 144-46. CLC director Alma Ruth Morgan complained repeatedly about the Foreign Mission Board's relief work in Ethiopia. Caine said that "world hunger is sometimes nothing more than systematic starvation of populations by communist regimes." Ray Waddle, *The Tennessean*, 15 Sept 1988.

[36]Hefley, *The Truth in Crisis*, 146-47. Hefley charged that the CLC's work on war and peace issues were "consonant with Soviet propaganda" and opposed the Nicaraguan contras.

U.S. had gone to war with Iraq, Land had his name removed from the list of board members.[37]

The CLC backed the Gulf War. Almost every other denominational public-policy agency reasoned that the war did not meet the standards of just-war theory. Land said it did. He claimed that the White House asked for his statement on the situation, that it was carried by helicopter to Camp David and influenced President Bush, although the two statements bear little resemblance. Land later went to the White House for an appreciation session.[38]

Partisan Politics. "Our agenda is not to storm the town this year. We have the potential to grow into that," said Michael Whitehead, a CLC staff member, about the CLC's role in the nation's capital.[39]

Some Fundamentalists dabbled for years in partisan Republican politics. W. A. Criswell had opposed Senator John Kennedy's presidential campaign in 1960. He endorsed President Gerald Ford on the steps of First Baptist Church, Dallas, in 1976.[40]

Beginning in 1980, however, Fundamentalist leaders launched an aggressive campaign to align rank-and-file church members with Republicans. Fundamentalists placed their blessing on presidential candidate Ronald Reagan at a rally in Dallas. Two years later Vice-President Bush spoke at the Pastors' Conference and the SBC adopted a resolution favoring a constitutional amendment on school prayer which the White House had sought.

The cross-fertilization increased. President Reagan sent a telegram to the 1985 SBC, thanking Southern Baptists for their role in the conservative re-

---

[37]Richard Land letter to Ken Sehested, 6 Feb 1991.

[38]Land denied he wrote the statement at the request of the White House: Land's letter, *SBC Today*, 22 March 1991, 10. Land did tell CLC directors, "the President invited me to come to Washington as part of a group of religious leaders that had been supportive of our effort in the Gulf and his leadership in the Gulf": Land, "Report of Meeting with President Bush," 7 March 1991.

[39]Larry Witham, "Southern Baptists Enter Fray," *The Washington Times*, 7 Dec 1990, B6. For additional discussion about the partisanship of Southern Baptist Fundamentalists, see Bill J. Leonard, *God's Last and Only Hope: The Fragmentation of the Southern Baptist Convention* (Grand Rapids: Eerdmans, 1990) 160-64; and Ammerman, *Baptist Battles*, 99-106.

[40]Lester Kinsolving, "Extremist May Lead Baptists," *San Francisco Chronicle*, 18 May 1968, 28. Criswell was quoted as having said, "If Senator John Kennedy is elected, it will sound the death knell of religious liberty in America." Richard Land told a pro-life legislators conference in Chicago that as a student in southeast Houston in 1964 he campaigned for Barry Goldwater.

surgence. Jimmy Draper hosted a reception at the 1987 SBC for Republican presidential candidate Pat Robertson. The SBC public affairs committee endorsed Supreme Court nominee Robert Bork later that year. In early 1988, three former SBC presidents denied that they were aligned with the "New Right."[41]

The relationship thickened in the 1990s. The SBC public affairs committee gave their religious liberty award to Jesse Helms (R-NC) who was locked in a bitter reelection campaign. Bush declined to speak at the 1990 SBC, but did address the 1991 SBC, following speeches by Oliver North and other right-wing notables at the SBC Pastors' Conference. Caught in a bitter Republican Party primary in Georgia in 1992, Bush changed his Sunday schedule from Atlanta's Peachtree Presbyterian Church to Fundamentalist First Baptist Church. Vice President Dan Quayle had SBC president Morris Chapman to travel with him prior to the Louisiana primary. In response to a question about what he hoped to gain from his appearance at the 1992 SBC, Quayle answered, "Support."[42]

Fundamentalists defended their partisan alignment, claiming that Moderates had aligned with the Democratic Party in the 1960s and 1970s. They reasoned that the perceived activities and sympathies of Moderates justified their activities. Their moral logic was that two wrongs make a right. They also failed to distinguish between individual involvement of Moderates and institutional alignment of SBC entities. Finally, they argued that it was not political alignment, but moral agreement over abortion.[43]

The Baptist Joint Committee on Public Affairs. While not institutionally related to the CLC, the Baptist Joint Committee on Public Affairs (BJC), the Baptist lobby for religious liberty in Washington, supported by several Baptist denominations in North America, had its own running battle with

---

[41]Ray Waddle, "Churchmen Reject 'New Right' Label," *The Tennessean*, 25 Feb 1988.

[42]John E. Yang and Thomas B. Edsall, "Bush Pushes Family Issues in Georgia," *Washington Post*, 1 March 1992, A1; Lynn P. Clayton, "Vice-President Quayle Worships at First Baptist, Shreveport," BP, 13 March 1992. Marv Knox, "Quayle Recruits SBC for Moral Campaign," Associated Baptist Press news release (ABP) 9 June 1992.

[43]Louis Moore, "Baptists Are Not Any 'Political Party at Prayer'," *The Tennessean*, 2 July 1990, A9; and Mark Coppenger's unpublished letter to Religious News Service, 23 July 1992. Also see Ray Waddle, "Are Southern Baptists the GOP in the Pulpit?", *The Tennessean*, 24 June 1990, G2.

SBC Fundamentalists. In 1984 at the SBC meeting in Kansas City, Ed Drake, a member of the First Baptist Church of Dallas, made a motion to amend the SBC budget eliminating funding for the Baptist Joint Committee. The motion was defeated by a slim margin of 51.65 percent to 48.35 percent, an omen of things to come.

Opposition to the BJC continued and was seen in speeches, "letters to the editor," and Fundamentalist publications. The BJC became a primary target for Fundamentalist attacks. The principal public complaints against the BJC were the committee's stand against govenment-prescribed public school religious exercises and the absence of any activity by the BJC in oppositon to legalized abortions.

The school prayer issue came into focus when the 1982 Southern Baptist Convention passed a resolution supporting President Reagan's proposal to amend the United States Constitution to allow government-sponsored prayer in public institutions. This resolution reversed the position of the SBC set out in nine Convention resolutions passed in the 1960s and 1970s. The BJC continued to oppose vigorously any public school religious activities.

When James M. Dunn became executive director of the BJC in October 1980, he insisted that the BJC adhere strictly to the program assignment guidelines for the BJC as set out by the 1975 Southern Baptist Convention. He and the full BJC, when it met in March 1981, interpreted the Committee's task as more exclusively focused on religious liberty and church-state separation, precluding any activity at all in the abortion debate. During Dunn's leadership, the BJC has not issued statements, joined organizations, participated in activities, debated, or in any other way engaged in the political struggle over abortion, pro or con. This did not satisfy the Fundamentalists. They continued to spread the rumor without one shred of evidence that the BJC is proabortion.

Another irritant to the Fundamentalists was Dunn's service on the board of the People for the American Way for one term, 1981–1983. Most of the furor about his identification with this group came after his refusal to accept a second term on the board.

A second motion to deny funding to the BJC was made at the Atlanta meeting of the SBC in 1986. This resulted in the formation of an SBC executive "fact finding committee" to study the relationship of the SBC to the BJC. The report of that committee to the SBC in 1987 restructured the membership of the SBC delegation to the BJC. The report eliminated most of the agency representation to the BJC and gave the SBC delegation known as the Public Affairs Committee (PAC) what the Fundamentalists on the PAC took to be a life of its own.

The PAC took up the full Religious Right agenda: supporting orgnaized public school prayers, endorsing Judge Robert Bork for the Supreme Court, demanding public school textbook reform, and attempting in other ways to bring the full Baptist Joint Committee in line with the Religious Right agenda.

All of the other members of the BJC, including most of the remaining SBC agency heads, resisted the Fundamentalist takeover of the BJC and repeatedly voted down evey PAC initiative. Among those initiatives in the October 1987 BJC meeting were demands for unilateral PAC evaluation of the BJC staff, a demand for all correspondence to or from the staff for the the last three years, and a call for detailed expense accounts for the past five years.

When the Fundamentalist faction discovered that they could not control the BJC as they had controlled the SBC, they determined once again to cut off SBC support of it. In the 1990 SBC meeting the budgeted support from the SBC was cut from $391,00 to $50,000. In 1991 the SBC dropped all financial support for the BJC. In 1992 the SBC ordered the Southern Baptist Foundation to reassign a capital needs fund designated for the Baptist Joint Committee by the 1967 Southern Baptist Convention. In a separate action the SBC severed all ties with the BJC, which it had helped form in 1936.

The Fundamentalist effort to destroy the BJC was unsuccessful. The BJC still enjoys strong support from Southern Baptists through the Cooperative Baptist Fellowship, the Baptist General Convention of Texas, the Baptist General Association of Virginia, and hundreds of local churches and thousands of individuals.

Trailblazing a New Ethics Venture

When the CLC fell to Fundamentalists, Moderates responded in a variety of ways. Moderate CLC staffers argued with the new Fundamentalist overlords. State CLC staffers distributed literature which the CLC board had banished and asserted their ownership of pamphlets to block wholesale revisions. Some ethics professors sought dialogue; others boycotted the agency. Too soon, however, Moderates found themselves totally excluded.

The Alliance. Ethics was a primary concern for Alliance Baptists. Their covenant, adopted in the spring of 1987, underscored the importance of "social and economic justice." In spring 1991, some Alliance Baptists formed a think tank on church and society, issuing a report that was thoroughly Christocentric and more concerned about a witnessing community than "managing society." The "praxis method" of mission trips and projects was advocated, rather than the CLC approach of "reports to educate and inform local churches." The Baptist Peace Fellowship of North America was suggested as the ethics group for Fellowship Baptists.[44]

Baptists Committed. In light of the Fundamentalist transformation of the CLC, a small group of mostly Texas Baptists met in Dallas in late November 1988 to discuss what new steps might be taken. These Baptists Committed-types talked about raising five to ten million dollars to start an organization. They discussed locating it at a Baptist university, what the Alliance Baptists might do and whether to take funds from the Alliance.[45]

Baptist Center for Ethics

In the late summer of 1990, Ray Higgins, assistant professor of Christian ethics at Southwestern Seminary, and I began exploring the ethics movement.[46] We discovered more than 300 ethics centers or programs in the U.S. We wondered about a new model of Christian ethics, unlike that of the CLC. Our discussions stalled, however, when a Texas Moderate argued that "the time was not right for such a venture."

Months later the conversation was renewed. Bill Tillman, associate professor of ethics at Southwestern Seminary, W. C. Fields, retired vice-president for public relations for the SBC's executive committee, Nashville attorney Jeff Mobley, and others joined the discussions.

One event and a series of conversations prompted more intense deliberations. The event was the May 1991 Fellowship meeting. At the 1990 meeting, Moderates repudiated the CLC by "defunding" it. Nine months

---

[44]Anne Thomas Neil, "The Freedom to Work for Global Justice," in *Being Baptist Means Freedom*, ed. Alan Neely (Charlotte NC: Southern Baptist Alliance, 1988) 69-81. T. Melvin Williams's letter to me, 25 Nov 1991. The Church and Society Group included Mel Williams, Kyle Childress, Susan Lockwood, Anne Neil, and Ken Sehested. Their study was titled "Living God's Shalom: Envisioning a New Structure in Baptist Life."

[45]Bill Tillman's meeting notes, 11 Nov 1988. Participants included Tillman, Jimmy Allen, Foy Valentine, David Sapp, and Phil Strickland. Jimmy Allen said toward the end of the meeting that an organization would need "to come out of a broad base, not Texas, not Valentine's living room."

[46]Ray Higgins's letter to me, 10 Sept 1990.

later, Moderates did not speak organizationally about ethics or offer public forums to discuss it.

Both Nancy Ammerman, a sociologist, and Carolyn Weatherford Crumpler encouraged a new ethics venture. Ammerman argued that the time was ripe for such efforts. Crumpler noted that Moderate Baptists were moving into a number of areas, except ethics where a vacuum existed. She concurred that "this is the time to begin."[47]

Several former CLC staffers and ethics professors underscored the need for "something new," rather than "rebuilding what was." They talked about a more inclusive and less centralized approach. Like Ammerman and Crumpler, they agreed that the time was right.

The Organizational Effort. Sensing a "fullness of time" moment, a meeting was held in May 1991 at Woodmont Baptist Church. Participants included Woodmont's pastor, Bill Sherman, Woodmont layman David Rogers, a public relations expert who had served as a senior advisor to Gov. Lamar Alexander (R-TN), W. C. Fields, Jeff Mobley, his brother Greg Mobley, a Ph.D. candidate at Harvard University, Gene Lovelace, minister of education at Nashville's Immanuel Baptist Church, Larry Dipboye, pastor of FBC Oak Ridge, Tennessee, and his wife Carolyn Dipboye who holds a Ph.D. in ethics from Southern Seminary and is a frequent writer for the Woman's Missionary Union, and myself. Joel Snider, pastor of Crievewood Baptist Church, chaired the meeting.

The first meeting explored the issue of timing. Everyone admitted Moderates had a mixed history of supporting needed efforts. Larry Dipboye noted that after working with Moderates for a decade, "We get a lot of voice but let things starve."[48]

The group also discussed a four-and-a-half-page draft document which affirmed that the lordship of Jesus Christ was essential for involvement with the Center. The document said the Bible was the treasure chest for ethical guidance and that the Center would seek "the best insights" from other disciplines. The document promised the Center would never speak for Baptists. It stated that the Center "remains rooted in the Baptist heritage of soul freedom, local church autonomy, personal and social responsibility, while it retains an ecumenical spirit."

---

[47]My conversation notes with Carolyn Weatherford Crumpler, 18 May 1991.

[48]My meeting notes, 30 May 1991. Jim Holliday, pastor of East Baptist Church, Louisville, attended subsequent meetings.

The Center's name was settled on at this meeting. The group rejected the name Southern Baptist Center for Ethics as too provincial. The long-term and larger vision was for the Center to be a resource for all Baptists. Either Sherman or Fields suggested the name Baptist Center for Ethics.

At subsequent meetings, the Center was constructed as a network, not a new bureaucracy. A key component was the associates who were professors and pastors with training in ethics and other disciplines. They were enlisted to write ethics commentaries for state papers, to respond to journalists' inquires about ethics, and to serve as resource people for ministers. The Center was designed to refer inquires on issues to the associates who were the experts.

The Public Announcement. The plans about BCE were leaked to Baptist Press four days before the scheduled press conference. James Sullivan, former president of the Sunday School Board, shared a confidential letter with a CLC Fundamentalist. He justified his actions, saying that Moderates were keeping the SBC from getting back together.

Press conference speakers promised to address a full range of issues, instead of just two issues as the CLC was doing (antiabortion and anti-National Endowment for the Arts). Furthermore, speakers articulated a new paradigm, pointing out that too often Christians take the *anti* side on issues: *anti*abortion, *anti*alcohol, *anti*gambling, *anti*hunger. BCE was committed to framing issues in a positive way instead of a negative and reactive way. Speakers noted that BCE would be prohealth, not antialcohol; profamily, not antipornography; prowomen and propeople of color, not antidiscrimination; propeacemaking, not antiwar; and pro-poor people, not antipoverty. One speaker said, "Some will perceive this as anti-CLC, but we want to transcend denominational politics and get on with the task of doing ethics."[49]

The Reaction. Land reacted defensively, saying that the abortion issue "is not one that preoccupies us to the exclusion of others."[50] Land added, "I don't think there is any confusion over who speaks for the majority of Southern Baptists in the year of our Lord 1991. It is not the Baptist Joint Committee. It is not the Baptist Center for Ethics. It is the Christian Life Commission."[51]

---

[49]Ray Waddle, "Moderate Baptists Form New Center for Ethics," *The Tennessean,* 29 July 1991, B1-2.

[50]Ibid., B2.

[51]Greg Warner, "Ethics Center Promises Comprehensive Approach," ABP, 1 Aug 1991.

Four state paper editors reacted to the formation of BCE. Al Mohler, editor of *The Christian Index*, cast BCE's formation as an opposition effort to the CLC's antiabortion position.[52] Another Fundamentalist, Gary Ledbetter, editor of the *Indiana Baptist*, said, "these brethren just don't like the way Baptists have expressed themselves on the subject of abortion." He added, "The BCE seems to be based on the assumption that our people are somehow nostalgic for the days of predictably leftist and mealymouthed statements and resources to moral issues."[53] Guy Henderson, editor of the *Baptist Record*, wondered why Baptists needed two ethics organizations, acknowledging that the CLC's agenda was too narrow and the exclusion of ethics professors was too limited.[54]

Marv Knox, editor of the *Western Recorder* studied the CLC's news stories between August 1, 1990 and July 31, 1991. He found that 71.42 percent of them dealt with just two topics: antihomosexuality/obscenity and antiabortion. Knox wrote, "we do not live in a two-issue world. Other ethical concerns need thorough treatment." He concluded, "The CLC will focus most of its energies on abortion and obscenity, and the BCE can help all of us deal constructively with a wide range of issues."[55]

A Year of Accomplishments

National Conference. The Center's first conference dealt with issues that had been ignored in Southern Baptist life, like the sexual activity of Baptist teenagers, the nation's health care crisis, the Human Genome Project, Christian reconstructionism, and the right-to-die. Will Campbell and Bobby Bowden were among two of the nationally known speakers. Unlike earlier CLC seminars, the program included traditional presentations and the case method. With only four months of planning, the Nashville conference at Immanuel Baptist Church attracted an estimated 275 participants from eighteen states.

---

[52]R. Albert Mohler, Jr., "Baptist Leaders Differ over Purpose and Need for New Ethics Center," *The Christian Index*, 8 Aug 1991, 4.

[53]Gary Ledbetter, "The Stealth Denomination," *Indiana Baptist*, 13 Aug 1991, 2.

[54]Guy Henderson, "Do We Really Need It?" *Baptist Recorder*, 29 Aug 1991, 2.

[55]Marv Knox, "We Need the Baptist Center for Ethics," *Western Recorder*, 13 Aug 1991, 2.

"McNugget Ethics." BCE has distributed a number of ethics commentaries on issues ranging from ministerial ethics to environmental ethics, from health care to racism. *Baptists Today* and many state papers have carried these short articles, nicknamed "mcnugget ethics."

News Stories. BCE has generated news stories carried by Associated Baptist Press. Commissioned free-lance writers Dan Martin and Kathy Palen have written stories on racism, sports ethics, world population, and profanity among elementary school children. Palen has written a four-part series on ministerial ethics which many Baptist state papers have carried.

Resources. The Center produces a regular newsletter, *Ethics Report.* A sixteen-part, audio cassette tape series on the Sermon on the Mount, *Loving Neighbors across Time: A Christian Guide to Protecting the Earth*, *Just Peacemaking: Transforming Initiates for Justice and Peace*, tapes from the first national conference, and a report on ministerial ethics represent some of the center's earliest resources.

Additionally, BCE and two ministry groups of the Cooperative Baptist Fellowship (ethics and public policy and curriculum development for Christian education) jointly produced an eight-page, global discipleship resource designed to encourage and to enable Baptist churches to observe a week of prayer for the hungry.

Credibility. BCE has gained credibility as a resource for moral reflection and social analysis. Newspaper religion editors call increasingly on the Center and its associates for direction on stories and interviews. *The Wall Street Journal, The Atlanta Constitution, The Tennessean, The Charlotte Observer,* and *Dallas Morning News* are some of papers that call the Center.

Financial Support. Within its first year, the Center has been included in the budgets of the Alliance of Baptists, the Cooperative Baptist Fellowship, and a growing number of local churches. Many individual Baptists have placed the Center in their personal giving plans.

The BCE and CLC offer Southern Baptists two competing moral visions and approaches. BCE addresses ethics issues from different perspectives, never speaking for Baptists but trusting Baptists to make up their own minds guided by the Word and led by the Spirit. The CLC is committed to ideological advancement, suspicious of diversity, and intolerant of substantive disagreement. BCE avoids the trend in some circles toward defining ethics solely as legislative lobbying and political involvement. BCE advances a proactive and proethics approach that breaks out of the reactive and negative cycle of both SBC politics and CLC pronouncements.

The CLC faces a stagnant future. The nation's shift away from the shores of right-wing politics does not bode well for an agency which has so clearly aligned itself with the right-wing of the Republican Party. A change in the White House may now cause Fundamentalists to become even more hypernegative and hyperreactive.

BCE's determination to reframe issues in light of the pro-ethics paradigm has captured the imagination and enthusiasm of free and faithful Baptists. Its decentralized structure, dependence on associates, descriptive approach to issues, and dedication to dealing positively with a host of issues ensures both growing support and unlimited opportunity. BCE faces a hopeful future.

The History
of Smyth & Helwys Publishing

Cecil P. Staton, Jr.

It seems strange to be writing the history of something still in its infancy. Officially Smyth & Helwys was not "born" until December 10, 1990 (date of incorporation). Yet the contribution of this small publishing venture has been so significant in its brief time in existence that it would be unthinkable to survey the history of the Moderate Baptist Movement without considering the birth and brief history of Smyth & Helwys. It is particularly awkward for me because of my personal involvement in the formation of Smyth & Helwys and in many of the events being described.

This brief history proceeds as follows. To understand the story of Smyth & Helwys Publishing one must first consider the broader background of the publishing struggle within the Southern Baptist Convention. This will be recounted first, though only briefly, given the limitations of this essay. Here the question is, "Why Smyth & Helwys, and why now?" The birthing process will then be considered and some detail given to significant persons, events, and dates. This will be followed by a survey of the rapid growth of Smyth & Helwys during the last two years. And finally attention will be given to the present state of Smyth & Helwys and the possible directions this new venture will take as it matures.

Antecedents

I often tell audiences that when you walk into the headquarters of Smyth & Helwys in Macon, Georgia, on the campus of Mercer University (in the basement of Penfield Hall, the Mercer University Press building) one of the first things you see are two ornamental busts (actually cut from black construction paper) of our founders. No, not John Smyth & Thomas Helwys, but Paige Patterson and Paul Pressler. I credit them with the founding of Smyth & Helwys.

I have often said—somewhat facetiously of course—that Smyth & Helwys is subsidized by the Southern Baptist Convention. The SBC completely covered the costs of our initial, and I would say, rather aggressive marketing campaign which sought to explain why an alternative press is needed. Some of their creative marketing was as follows: the forced "retirement" of Lloyd Elder, president of the Baptist Sunday School Board (BSSB) of the SBC; the refusal of BSSB to publish Leon McBeth's history of that agency; the firing of Al Shackleford and Dan Martin from Baptist Press; the hiring of Jimmy Draper to succeed Elder; and on and on. We could not have asked for better help.

Certainly the formation of Smyth & Helwys Publishing must be viewed against the broader background of the "publishing" struggle within the SBC. Limitations of time and space prevent a complete review of this long-standing battle. In passing, however, one must certainly mention key events, some long ago, which pointed toward the formation of an alternative press. The following events deserve mentioning.

Standing at the beginning is the controversy surrounding Ralph H. Elliott's *The Message of Genesis*, published July 1961.[1] To this one should add the crisis concerning and the eventual withdrawal from publication of G. Henton Davies' "Genesis" in the original volume one of *The Broadman Bible Commentary*. A brouhaha in the spring of 1969 erupted following the criticism by the then ABPR (Association of Baptist Professors of Religion) of the Sunday School Board's promotion of W. A. Criswell's *Why I Preach that the Bible is Literally True* as *the* Baptist view.

As recently as the mid-1980s, controversy surrounded Southeastern Professor John I Durham's five lessons on the book of Job. His first lesson suggested that "the satan" of the prologue does not represent Mephistopheles or a red devil with horns and tail, but rather an adversary, part of the heavenly council. He included a paragraph of explanation about this. The editor deleted the explanation, and inserted the statement that "The devil of the book of Job is not the devil of the New Testament." This obviously served as a red flag creating a furor with Fundamentalists who complained to the Baptist Sunday School Board and called for Durham's dismissal.

---

[1]See Elliott's *The "Genesis Controversy" and Continuity in Southern Baptist Chaos: A Eulogy for a Great Tradition* (Macon: Mercer University Press, 1992).

More recently one could point to the publication of the *New American Bible Commentary* based on the principle of inerrancy, an embarrassment to many Baptist scholars. Interestingly the word "inerrancy" has not been used in promotion of the series. In 1990 BSSB trustees refused to publish Leon McBeth's history of the Baptist Sunday School Board because, they believed, it portrayed the new Fundamentalist leadership in a bad light.

During the 1980s the board of trustees of the Baptist Sunday School Board, like all other agency boards, was being stacked with individuals who were committed to carrying out the Fundamentalist agenda. This culminated with the forced resignation of Lloyd Elder in 1990 and the election of Jimmy Draper on July 18, 1991, as president of the Sunday School Board. A final, if earlier, event should be mentioned. In 1988 a group of Moderate leaders met with representatives of the Sunday School Board. They requested that Christian education resources be produced for Moderates that would give attention to biblical scholarship and current educational philosophy. Max Caldwell represented the BSSB. The request was refused. Caldwell said the trustees would not support such a line of curriculum materials..

It is against such a background that the idea for an autonomous press for Baptists was born and nurtured. Even prior to the rise of the new Fundamentalism of Pressler-Patterson-Rogers, there was a long history of watering down scholarship in both books and Sunday School materials and the use of what Ralph Elliott calls "doublespeak" in Southern Baptist publishing. This long publishing struggle may lead one to question why in fact it took so long for an alternative press for progressive Baptists to be born. Perhaps the answer lies in the fact that Baptists have been loyal to the institutions they have founded. During the 1950s, 1960s, 1970s, and even much of the 1980s, it would have been thought a betrayal to suggest that an alternative publishing house be established for more progressive Southern Baptists. In fact every effort was made to brand any other ventures except those officially sanctioned and controlled by the SBC as suspect and outside "the family of Southern Baptists." Of course Smyth & Helwys is viewed by many in this way today. Indicative of the strong centraliziation which has occurred within the Southern Baptist structures, Smyth & Helwys cannot display at most State conventions because it is not an "SBC agency" or in the SBC or state conventions' budgets.

Beginnings

The idea of an alternative press to serve Baptists actually goes back farther than the late-1990 birthday of Smyth & Helwys. Sitting in the cafeteria of

Southeastern Baptist Theological Seminary, William Benton, now pastor of First Baptist Church, York, South Carolina, and I, now publisher of Smyth & Helwys, dreamed the idea of a new press as early as the spring of 1982. James M. Pitts, chaplain to Furman University, joined Benton and me, and Chanticleer Publishing of Wake Forest, North Carolina was born. Chanticleer's first book, a reprint of P. T. Forsyth's *The Cruciality of the Cross* was published in 1982. With only very modest resources available, by the spring of 1985 only eight books had been printed—mostly reprints of classics, some by Baptists like Carlyle Marney, H. Wheeler Robinson, and others.

In the summer of 1985, having nearly completed a Th.M. at Southeastern Baptist Theological Seminary, I was preparing to go to Oxford to do doctoral work. The others were busy with their own ministries. By this time David Helms, associate minister, First Baptist Church, Southern Pines, North Carolina, was also involved with Chanticleer. All of us realized it would be difficult to continue Chanticleer without someone giving it more attention. Chanticleer was disbanded and the stock of books was sold to Dick Stevens Book Shop, then in Wake Forest, North Carolina. This first simple experiment ended quietly.

Meanwhile I went to Oxford, enormously pleased to be 5,000 miles removed from the Southern Baptist controversy. Unfortunately it was difficult to let go of a feuding family back home. News that things grew worse reached England. It was becoming more and more obvious that there was no turning back the Fundamentalist tide which had swept in a new day for the SBC.[2]

I came back in the fall of 1988 and in January 1989 began teaching Old Testament at Brewton-Parker College, a Georgia Baptist institution, still hoping that common sense might prevail in the SBC. I joined in those final journeys to SBC conventions in Las Vegas and New Orleans to turn back the tide by electing Daniel Vestal. Those efforts failed. It became apparent to many, and I among them, that the political struggle for the Moderates in the SBC was over.

---

[2][Editor's note: It should be noted that much discussion about the need for new publishing ventures was going on among Moderates during the time Staton was in England. E.g., one of the earliest concerns of those who formed the Southern Baptist Alliance in 1986 was, as Alan Neely notes, "the publication of Bible-study materials and other kinds of literature" (above), 111.]

On the positive side, however, the Alliance was maturing and had come to terms with its mission and principles. The Fellowship was forming, following the Consultation on August 23-25, 1990, and the Convocation on May 9-11, 1991, both in Atlanta.

In the spring of 1990 the idea of an alternative press for Baptists once again became a dream of mine. The time seemed right. There was already an alternative, autonomous newspaper (*Baptists Today*). Avenues for alternative missions giving, support, and fellowship were developing or already available through the Alliance and the Fellowship. But what about publications? Where would Baptist scholars and authors turn who could no longer publish with Broadman? Many had already turned to other religious publishers. But that option was not available for every writer. And where would pastors and laypersons turn for books and devotional material with a Baptist flavor that could be trusted to be free from the Fundamentalist agenda now clearly in place at Broadman, Convention Press, and the Sunday School Board?

My earliest conversations were with three people. Scott Nash, a colleague at Brewton Parker, shared my personal interest in the need to interpret biblical scholarship for pastors and the people in the pew. Both were tired of all the attacks upon their professors and now upon themselves. Ron Jackson, longtime personal friend of mine, a pastor, saw the need for alternative materials and recognized the consequences for churches if no such materials were forthcoming, and thus joined the conversations. And Jim Pitts, another of my longtime friends, having served several churches and Furman University for nearly thirty years, brought additional enthusiasm for a free Baptist press. All agreed that such an outlet for free expression was essential to the future of the Moderate Baptist movement.

After numerous conversations among themselves, we four branched out to discuss their idea with other friends and colleagues, laity, pastors and church staff members, and other Baptist professors. After many conversations and encouragement from persons in several states, the commitment was made to begin the new press.

All involved were committed to the idea of a free press that would remain autonomous from any new or existing denominational entity. The new publishing house should not be subject to outside control or takeover. This new press would be committed to serving the publishing needs of the local church, to serving those who welcome open inquiry and scholarship, to bringing the best of Baptists to Baptists. But what should this new press be called?

During the summer of 1990 I started reading Leon McBeth's massive *The Baptist Heritage*. In the first chapter called "Baptist Beginnings" I found several times the linking together of two important early Baptist names: "Smyth and Helwys."

When I first suggested the potential name to Nash and Jackson, sitting around a conference table in the Salter Christianity Center at Brewton-Parker, Nash offered the suggestion that a better name for a Baptist press might be "Smith & Wesson." But it was decided at once. Smyth & Helwys it would be. What better name for a new autonomous Baptist press than Smyth & Helwys!

The name thus honors John Smyth and Thomas Helwys, two early pioneers of Baptist freedom, two individuals who stood for the separation of church and state and the freedom of the soul before God. Both John Smyth and Thomas Helwys published. In fact others said of these early Baptists that they kept the presses running, dripping with the ink of their "heresies." Helwys, the layperson, published his *A Short Declaration of the Mistery of Iniquity* in 1612. He presented a copy of the book to King James. The bluntness of Helwys's appeal for religious liberty obviously offended the monarch. Helwys, the layman, died in Newgate Prison in 1616 as a result of his published statement on the freedom of the individual in matters of religion.

A board of advising editors was set up in order to advise and guide Smyth & Helwys during these early days. Letters of invitation were sent and responses came quickly from some of the household names of the Baptist family. C. R. Daley, Bill J. Leonard, W. Randall Lolley, Alan Neely, Molly T. Marshall, Cecil E. Sherman, Frank Stagg, and Walter B. Shurden were among the first to serve on this advisory board. Cecil Sherman wrote, "I would be pleased to serve as an advising editor for the Smyth & Helwys Publishing Company. Thank you for asking me."[3] Frank Stagg replied, "As Baptists we must stand for an open Bible, open minds, and open discussion. The publishing venture which Smyth & Helwys is undertaking is a needed one. Channels once open to honest scholarship are now closed or closing. It is an honor to serve on the Board of Advising Editors."

A news release was issued on November 9, 1990, and was published in some state papers in December and mentioned in Walker Knight's column in *Baptists Today* in the December 1, 1990, edition. In the announcement the board of directors issued the following statement.

---

[3]Sherman to Staton, 20 Sept 1990.

The purpose of Smyth & Helwys is to offer supplemental and alternative materials for Baptists who have become increasingly concerned about the future direction of the Convention Press and Broadman. These channels for publishing will no longer be available, as is indicated by the recent action concerning Leon McBeth's work on the history of the Sunday School Board. Those involved in the formation of Smyth & Helwys feel it is time for a press committed to freedom of inquiry and reverent biblical scholarship, but which is at the same time autonomous and therefore free from denominational controversy.[4]

Concerning Smyth & Helwys, C. R. Daley, editor emeritus of *The Western Recorder*, said,

Smyth & Helwys Publishing promises to be a valuable addition to the supply of quality materials available for serious readers in today's world. The high standards set by the editors and advisory editors for its publications will be recognized by students, ministers, and laypersons.[5]

Alan Neely, Professor of Ecumenics and Mission at Princeton Theological Seminary, commented, "This is a sorely needed venture at this crucial time in Baptist history. We need it now more than ever."[6]

Smyth & Helwys Publishing was formally incorporated in the State of South Carolina on December 10, 1990, with Ronald D. Jackson serving as managing editor, Scott Nash as senior editor, James M. Pitts as chairman of the board, and myself serving as the first publisher.

Rapid Growth

Smyth & Helwys's first book was published in January 1991: *Studies in Acts* by T. C. Smith. Another book with twenty contributors, on Isaiah, the January Bible Study book for 1991, had been planned as the original volume.[7] Smith's book, however, unexpectedly became available following a series of lectures he gave at Brewton-Parker in the fall of 1990. It was rushed to press and used widely as a resource for the 1991 January Bible Study.

---

[4]Smyth & Helwys news release, 9 Nov 1990.
[5]Ibid.
[6]Ibid.
[7]*Interpreting Isaiah for Preaching and Teaching*, ed. Cecil P. Staton, Jr., Kerygma and Church series (Greenville SC: Smyth & Helwys, 1991).

Nine books were published during 1991. It should be remembered that Smyth & Helwys had no full-time employees during these very early days. And everyone involved had other full-time jobs. Nash and I, for example, were full-time professors and held interim pastorates. It was always assumed that it would be some time before anyone could venture out full-time, supported by revenues from the sale of books. Everyone pitched in, with Nash and Staton editing, Jackson marketing and promoting, and Pitts dealing with orders. As of October 1992, Smyth & Helwys has published fifteen books with another ten in various stages of production.

The initial ambition of Smyth & Helwys was simple. Smyth & Helwys would eventually publish as many as twenty books per year on a part-time basis until sales could support a full-time staff, perhaps three to five years down the road. However, those involved soon learned that the original vision was too limited. As early as January 1990 Smyth & Helwys began receiving letters asking, "When are you going to begin publishing Sunday School literature?" "We must have alternative Sunday School resources now. Don't wait!" In all honesty, the initial response to such requests was laughter. First, Smyth & Helwys's founders had little or no interest in publishing Sunday School resources. It was believed someone else would have to do this. With precious little time and financial resources it did not seem possible to undertake this enormous task. It did not cost that much to print a book. It would cost a fortune to develop and produce a new curriculum.

Members of the board of advising editors, however, encouraged us to take such suggestions seriously. At the encouragement of Bill Leonard, who had heard of some groups working on curriculum, Robbin B. Mundy, Minister to Children at First Baptist Church, Asheville, North Carolina, and Robert G. Fulbright, Minister of Christian Education at Kirkwood Baptist Church, Kirkwood, Missouri, and chair of the Alliance Curriculum Committee, were contacted.

Robbin Mundy was part of a growing number of children's educators long concerned about the direction of BSSB literature. Staton contacted Mundy in January 1991 and expressed Smyth & Helwys's desire to publish Christian education resources for children. Following a meeting of concerned educators convened by Mundy on January 28-29, 1991, a letter was sent to a larger group of children's educators. Mundy wrote,

> I want to share a historical moment with you. On January 28 and 29 a group of religious educators met to discuss optional curriculum to be used in Baptist churches for preschoolers and children. It was a wonderful and refreshing experience. The meeting was a result of many phone

conversations and letters from around the Convention. We were concerned about the changes at the Sunday School Board and the changes in the curriculum. . . . Ironically, the meeting was held just eleven days after the trustees met to determine the fate of Lloyd Elder. It was also held one week after the "Sanctity of Life" lesson in the Bible Searchers curriculum. . . . While those present expressed much respect and appreciation for the good people currently serving in the preschool and children's divisions of the Board, it seemed there were additional changes that needed to be made. After lengthy discussions and examination of other curriculum choices we felt the need to produce a new curriculum.

Robert G. Fulbright served as chair of the Alliance Curriculum Committee. Fulbright, author of seven books and more than seventy-five articles in denominational periodicals and professional journals, had previously served as supervisor of elementary education for the Baptist Sunday School Board (1965–1975), as manager of Broadman Press (1975–1977), and as Bible Teaching Division director for the Sunday School Board (1977–1980). Already, through the cooperation of several churches, a pilot project had been undertaken to produce a series of lessons used during the summer of 1990. More than twenty churches used these lessons and requested that additional lessons be produced. Following this success the committee took steps to produce lessons for Advent 1991 through Easter 1992. The original plan was to make the lessons available to churches on computer disks for printing and distribution to classes.

Fulbright was contacted by Staton in February 1991. Both agreed that without resources for printing and distribution, the Alliance lessons would be limited to a small audience. Smyth & Helwys offered to assume financial responsibility for the lessons, to produce them in printed form as a part of a new ongoing series of adult resources, and to promote the new materials to as many churches as possible. Staton wrote Fulbright on March 7,

In preparation for the meeting next week let me review what Smyth & Helwys has committed to do. Smyth & Helwys is now prepared to make the financial commitment to design, produce, market, and distribute a full line of Sunday School resources. If the Alliance agrees for us to use their material, then adult resources could be ready for the first quarter of the new church year [fall 1991], with materials for children and youth to follow in 1992.

The then Southern Baptist Alliance met in Richmond, March 14-16, 1991. A meeting of religious educators was arranged by Fulbright to discuss the possibilities of new Christian education resources. The announcement was met with guarded optimism. Many in the room had previously written or edited for the Board and knew better than the young publishers the tremendous undertaking being suggested. Could it be pulled off? Some obviously had their doubts and expressed them. The financial and human resources would be great. Nevertheless, the curriculum committee voted to recommend to the Alliance that the lessons commissioned for Advent 1991–Easter 1992 be turned over to the new Baptist publisher and that Smyth & Helwys's plan to produce continuing adult resources by the fall of 1991 and children and youth resources in 1992 be embraced.

Following the Richmond meeting, Smyth & Helwys was on the road toward publishing resources for Sunday School. The name "Formations" was chosen for the new literature series suggesting that Smyth & Helwys resources would take seriously the dynamics of faith formation for all age groups.

One major difficulty was limited financial resources. Full-time designers and editors could not be employed before the new resources generated revenue. It was necessary to adopt a decentralized approach which involved using many different advisors, writers, and editors from around the country who worked part-time. Many worked without pay. Most of those asked to help gladly gave of their energy because of a common commitment to alternative Christian education resources which would embrace and preserve the Baptist heritage. It is not too much to say that none of this would have been possible ten or more years ago. Computer technology and particularly developments in desktop publishing in recent years have drastically reduced the cost of necessary equipment.

Following the important Richmond meeting a curriculum design team was appointed to oversee the design stage and give general editorial oversight to the curriculum project. Bob Fulbright was immediately appointed chair of the curriculum design team. Other members were appointed in April: Dennis W. Foust, design editor for adult resources; David L. Cassady, design editor for youth resources; and Robbin B. Mundy, design editor for children's resources. Later in the year Leon W. Castle and Anne H. Smith joined the team as design editors for children's resources. Each design editor in turn named curriculum advisory groups for their respective age groups. On April 29 a press release was issued:

> Smyth & Helwys Publishing has announced that beginning this fall a new Sunday School Curriculum called *Formations* will be published. Continuous adult literature will be available from October 1991 with Children, Youth, and Preschool material to follow in the fall of 1992.

John Hewett, pastor of First Baptist Church of Asheville, North Carolina, and a member of the Adult Curriculum Advisory Group commented,

> Just when free Baptists were about to despair of finding Bible-study literature which would quicken the heart, stimulate the mind, and stir the soul, Smyth & Helwys stepped in with this new venture of faith. Written by Baptists for Baptists, the new literature is aimed at churches like yours and mine, churches where men and women, girls and boys are encouraged to "rightly divide the word of truth" for themselves in the context of mutual support and fellowship. The people at Smyth & Helwys are publishing for Baptists who actually still read. I commend them, people and product, and am glad to participate in the birthing of this new idea.[8]

Heading up the project for Smyth & Helwys, I remarked,

> We are extremely pleased with the initial response to *Formations*. More rapidly than we first imagined, the pieces have fallen into place and persons of vision and energy have joined with us to create the channels for meeting what is a growing need among us—Bible-study materials which reflect a healthy view of scripture and honor our cherished Baptist distinctives.[9]

The Curriculum Design Team met for the first time on April 12, 1991, at Buechel Park Baptist Church in Louisville with Fulbright, Mundy, Foust, and Cassady in attendance. Meetings were held approximately every two months during the design process and continue to be held on a regular basis.

In preparation for the fall, additional lessons were commissioned for October from Walter B. Shurden, noted Baptist historian and chair of the Department of Christianity at Mercer, on "Baptist Freedom." Lessons on stewardship entitled "Using God's Resources Wisely" were offered by John R. Tyler, a layperson and deacon at Kirkwood Baptist Church, Kirkwood, Missouri. Together with the Alliance Advent materials, the first Smyth & Helwys adult quarterly was coming together.

The next step was to prepare for the Fellowship Convocation May 9-11, 1991, in Atlanta. While the design team worked, a sixteen-page brochure was prepared with information about Smyth & Helwys, *Formations*, and a sample lesson and teaching procedure. Four additional books were quickly prepared for printing so as to be available for Atlanta. Smyth & Helwys was one of several displays at the Fellowship Convocation which attracted more

---

[8]Press release, 29 April 1991.
[9]Ibid.

than 6,000 persons. One of the most popular items was the free brochure on *Formations*, more than 4,000 of which were distributed. More than $6,000 worth of books were sold. The response of those attending clearly indicated that alternative resources for Christian education were needed and desired.

By this time the board of directors had realized that full-time help was necessary in order to take the next steps. Dozens of persons were now involved at different levels such as design, planning, writing, editing, shipping, and so forth. But all had full-time jobs, limiting how much could be accomplished. Calls and letters requesting information on *Formations* suggested the demand would be far greater than originally anticipated. Following the successful convocation of the Fellowship, the decision was taken to employ the first full-time publisher of Smyth & Helwys. On May 20, 1991, a press release was issued naming me, then assistant professor of Christianity at Brewton-Parker College, Mount Vernon, Georgia, as the first full-time publisher. My wife Catherine would serve as business manager. I commented upon my appointment as follows.

> Baptists have never been more ready for a press which is sensitive to the needs of the local church and yet free from denominational control. We are committed to providing quality works for ministers and laity. . . . I am thrilled by the commitment of the board of directors to proceed with the *Formations* curriculum line. Much of our energies in the coming months will be given to launching the Adult Sunday School literature this October and the materials for youth, children, and preschoolers in the fall of 1992. Baptists in Atlanta clearly signaled their desire for alternative Bible-study materials. We are responding with materials which will encourage an open and honest study of scripture while honoring our cherished Baptist principles.[10]

Throughout the summer, *Formations* interpretation workshops led by Robert G. Fulbright were held in nine churches in six states. More than 600 persons attended to learn more about *Formations*.

One of the most important events in the history of Smyth & Helwys occurred in June 1991 when I was contacted by R. Kirby Godsey, president of Mercer University. Following conversations with the chair of Mercer's Christianity Department, Walter B. Shurden, President Godsey initiated dialogue concerning the possibility of Smyth & Helwys and Mercer University Press cooperating and sharing key leadership. Mercer University Press (MUP), a scholarly press founded in 1979, publishes approximately

---

[10]Smyth & Helwys news release, 20 May 1991.

twenty books per year in the fields of religion, philosophy, and southern history. Mercer was looking for someone with scholarly credentials and publishing experience to assume the office of publisher of MUP.

After several meetings and the exchange of proposals, I was offered the position of publisher of Mercer University Press. Yet this would be an unusual agreement. I would remain as publisher of Smyth & Helwys while serving Mercer. Smyth & Helwys's editorial offices would come to Macon, rather than Greenville, South Carolina, where originally intended. Smyth & Helwys was given free rent and utilities for three years in the basement of Penfield Hall, the home of Mercer University Press. Smyth & Helwys received an important boost during these early critical days. Mercer received leadership for its press and the benefit of revenues from services purchased from Mercer by Smyth & Helwys. It seemed appropriate that the only university press on the campus of a Baptist-related school publishing scholarly works should cooperate with the new autonomous press for Baptists publishing books for pastors and laity, and church curriculum materials. The partnership would be to the mutual benefit of both presses.

A formal agreement of cooperation was reached on July 19, 1991, and I accepted the position of publisher of the Mercer University Press. An additional benefit was that Ronald D. Jackson, part-time managing editor of Smyth & Helwys, also came to Mercer as director of marketing and finance. Smyth & Helwys now had three employees: Ron Jackson, Catherine Staton, and me. Both Jackson and I, however, shared our time with Mercer. Our families moved to Macon in August and began work at Mercer Press on September 1, 1991.

The premier edition of *Formations* for adults was shipped to churches in September for use beginning October 1991. More than 400 churches in more than thirty states used the first edition of *Formations*. An original print run of 20,000 sold out, exceeding all expectations, and additional copies were printed. *Formations* was off to a great start.

Although only adult resources were available during the first year, preparations were under way for a fully graded line. The design team under the direction of Bob Fulbright continued to meet approximately every other month. It was obviously time to bring on additional staff in order to prepare for the following fall when the line would expand from two pieces to more than twenty pieces of literature. The decentralized operating procedure had served well for the first year. But additional staff was required for Smyth & Helwys to expand and produce the resources requested by the churches.

David L. Cassady was employed as managing editor of the Christian Education Division of Smyth & Helwys on January 1, 1992. Cassady, a Ed.D. candidate at the Southern Baptist Theological Seminary, was serving as associate pastor of Buechel Park Baptist Church, Louisville, and had served as design editor of youth resources on the curriculum design team from its inception. He had shown great energy, creativity, and commitment during his time on the design team. He now accepted the greatest challenge of his life. Cassady's job was to prepare to receive the materials for the fall of 1992 and prepare them for publication. Meanwhile he also assumed responsibility for preparing adult resources for press for the spring and summer quarters.

By this time the design team had made some significant decisions concerning the direction and shape of the new curriculum. Beginning in the fall of 1992 Smyth & Helwys would switch to a trimester system. Materials would be produced and ordered only three times per year, thus cutting costs. Resources for youth and children would be undated and reusable. Children's resources would follow a two-year cycle with updates afterwards, thus allowing churches to save after making the initial two years' investment.

Materials would be produced for infants to ones, toddlers to twos, threes to fives, kindergarten to first grade, second to third grade, fourth to fifth grade, with a special line for sixth grade. Both older and younger youth resources would be produced with a youth reflection guide for teenagers. A resource kit and commentary would be produced for adult teachers to supplement the teaching guide. Finally, a devotional guide for adults called *Reflections* was planned.

Adult resources would follow the life cycle of Jesus with special attention given to Advent through Easter each year. A core curriculum plan was adopted for all resources. Thus missions, theology, church history, and ethics would all be woven into the Bible-study materials. The design team sought to produce materials that were based upon the best educational theories, the best of biblical scholarship, and historic Baptist principles.

Additional staff was added throughout the spring and summer of 1992. Beverly Schaaf joined as accounts manager in April to handle the ever-increasing calls and requests for information and orders. A toll-free 800 number was introduced to make it easier for churches to contact Smyth & Helwys. David Adams, an Ed.D. candidate at Southern Seminary joined as projects editor in July. Donna Jackson joined as arts editor July 1. Plans were announced to produce Vacation Bible School resources for the summer of 1993 and a second adult line for younger adults in the fall of 1993.

Colorful brochures were prepared for the Fellowship meeting in Fort Worth in May 1992. Thousands were distributed during the general assembly. Throughout the summer, Formations Curriculum Worships were held in six states with more than 1,800 persons attending to learn about the full line of age-graded resources. A National Childlife Conference was held in Charlotte, North Carolina with more than 100 persons attending. Requests for information poured into Smyth & Helwys, suggesting that more churches were interested than originally anticipated.

Originally Smyth & Helwys hoped for 100 churches in the fall of 1991. More than 400 ordered. That number grew throughout the first year of adult resources to more than 550 in the summer of 1992. At this time (fall 1992) approximately 950 churches in forty-one states and four countries are using *Formations* during the 1992 fall trimester. During the fall trimester 1992 alone, adult resources grew by approximately forty-two percent. In one year the print run increased from 20,000 to 50,000. Such growth was and continues to be crucial, however, as production costs for the fully graded line easily exceed $500,000 per trimester when all costs are calculated.

One final event is indicative of the growth of Smyth & Helwys. On August 1, 1992, Scott Nash, formerly chair of the Division of Religious and Philosophical Studies at Brewton-Parker College, joined Smyth & Helwys as head of the Book Division. He also serves as Managing Editor of Mercer University Press. Although growth has taken place primarily in the area of Christian education resources, Smyth & Helwys is no less committed to books. During 1992 financial and human resources of necessity were focused on Sunday School literature. An ambitious publication plan for twenty books per year has been adopted and will be implemented under the direction of Nash.

The Future

In conclusion, some reflections concerning the future of Smyth & Helwys are in order. John Hewett, moderator of the CBF during 1991–1992, told many different audiences during his tenure, "I am hopeful, but I am not optimistic."

Perhaps those words also apply to the future of Smyth & Helwys. Friends of Smyth & Helwys are hopeful. Baptists need a Smyth & Helwys. Smyth & Helwys is of enormous importance to the Moderate Baptist Movement. A few persons have been bold enough to dream of a press that is committed to meet the needs of the local church, yet free from denominational control—a free press for Baptists. A review of the lessons learned during the takeover of the SBC suggests such freedom is imperative. Smyth & Helwys, the Baptist Theological Seminary at Richmond, *Baptists Today*, Associated Baptist Press, and the other new ventures should remain free. Some may worry about control, but needlessly. If Baptist sons and daughters are not sent to Richmond, the seminary will not survive. If churches do not use *Formations* literature, Smyth & Helwys will not survive. Free Baptists have a voice. Smyth & Helwys will remain sensitive to the needs of the local church.

Some have been bold enough to dream of a press which is not afraid of open and honest inquiry and the best of biblical scholarship. Smyth & Helwys is committed to bridging the gulf between biblical scholarship and the pew through the publication of twenty books per year as well as a full graded line of curriculum resources for Christian education.

But excessive optimism about this enterprise would be dangerous. Southern Baptists have grown accustomed to shopping at the company store. SBC churches have been franchises and have stocked their shelves with the recommended merchandise from the headquarters of the chain. All indications are that this will be difficult to change. But it is crucial that this change occur.

Many watched as the SBC institutions were taken over one by one. Every board is now controlled by members who are there to endorse the Fundamentalist agenda. For some, the great consolation was that at least the state conventions were safe. There Moderates would make their stand.

Although Virginia and, to some extent, North Carolina have not faced the same severe struggles as some other states, the battle lines have been drawn in many others. In some the battle has been won by the Fundamentalists and in others it continues with uncertain outcomes. At least, some still say, safety may be found in the local church, above and away from the fray of conflict. But the enormous influence of the Sunday School quarterly is forgotten or ignored at our peril. The fact of the matter is that the battle comes to the churches through the literature the people in the pew read. It is foolish to believe that churches will not be impacted and perhaps changed unless leadership within those churches is forthcoming to insure the availability of resources for Christian education which promote our rich Baptist heritage, repudiate the Fundamentalist agenda, and help our people to value open and honest inquiry and the diversity that makes us strong.

Smyth & Helwys faces tremendous financial challenges. To date, in 1992 the press has already incurred a $180,000 deficit. At current levels of usage 2,000 churches will be required to put the press on a solid financial footing. The Baptist Sunday School Board has approximately 1,400 employees. We have eleven, several part-time. I do not see a day when we will have more than twenty. It will continue to be a tremendous challenge to produce quality resources at reasonable prices with our small staff until revenues increase sufficiently to provide additional full-time resource persons.

The costs for this venture are enormous. The Baptist Sunday School Board prints hundreds of thousands and even millions of copies of certain pieces. Smyth & Helwys prints as few as a thousand copies of some children's pieces and sells even fewer. The challenge of pulling this off financially will probably not go away for a long time, if ever.

Other challenges include the relationship with the CBF. Smyth & Helwys is committed to remaining a free press for Baptists. Yet its base constituency is the same as the CBF and Alliance. How these organizations will relate in the future remains to be seen. Smyth & Helwys is committed to cooperation and will participate as fully as possible in the life of whatever new entity may arise for Moderate Baptists, but not at the cost of autonomy.

The brief history of Smyth & Helwys is remarkable. There is much to be hopeful about. More and more Baptists seem to be expressing a desire for alternative Christian education resources. Smyth & Helwys may make it. The task is enormous. The future of Smyth & Helwys is not assured. Optimism must be tempered by realism. Smyth & Helwys may never be a multistoried skyscraper with hundreds of employees and money to burn. But it may provide an invaluable service to Baptists who are searching for something different, refreshing, and challenging. Smyth & Helwys may signal a new day which many of us have hoped for, a new day which is coming. Smyth & Helwys is committed to being part of the revival of the authentic Baptist identity in this country. It is important that Smyth & Helwys survive.

In Will Campbell's parable *The Convention*, there is a fabulous scene in which the women have gathered to consider a potential candidate for the presidency of the Federal Baptist Convention. Miriam boldly preaches, "Someone has to care about this birthright filled with martyrs. Dissenting sisters, and brothers, too. These kinfolks were drowned in Lake Zurich, were burned to death in Geneva, were tortured with tongue screws in Holland. Not to mention Roger Williams who started all this in America. And why? All because they dared to think their own free thoughts, dared to ask questions and dared to defy those who exacted the right to franchise the tattered coat of Christ."

"For God's sake, Miriam, cut out the histrionics," Lilith moaned.

"But that is where we came from," Miriam rejoined.[11]

Change is difficult. I am hopeful, but not optimistic. We must preserve in our churches the history of where we came from. Smyth & Helwys must survive and contribute to that enterprise. It is unthinkable that there be no Smyth & Helwys. It is unlikely that the human and financial resources invested in Smyth & Helwys would be repeated in the near future should this grand experiment fail. A sixty-plus-year-old woman who teaches a class of seventy- and eighty-year-old ladies at a church in Fort Worth, Texas, recently reported that she walked into her class one Sunday and said, "Ladies, we are going to switch to *Formations*."

The reply was unanimous as the responses came quickly back: "Why are you doing this to us? You know we don't like change!"

To which she replied, "Well, if you don't like change, you're going to love *Formations*. Because it's *the other stuff* that's changing."

Amen, sister! Preach on!

---

[11]Will D. Campbell, *The Convention. A Parable* (Atlanta: Peachtree Publishers, 1988) 115.

The History of the Baptist Cooperative Missions Program

Duke K. McCall

The dismissal on October 25, 1962, of Midwestern Baptist Theological Seminary professor Ralph Elliott over his book *The Message of Genesis* sent shock waves through the six Southern Baptist Seminaries. Paul Pressler of Houston, Texas, was one of the vehement critics of Elliott. Faculty members girded for battle and started worrying about their long-term future. This battle was renewed over the Genesis volume of *The Broadman Bible Commentary* when it appeared in October 1969. In 1971 the Southern Baptist Convention by a narrow margin ordered the volume to be rewritten by new authors.

Convention controversies were augmented by faculty/administration quarrels within the seminaries. The rank and file of Southern Baptists lost much of their awe and respect for seminary personnel. Some extremely conservative Southern Baptists tasted blood, and Judge Paul Pressler, who would lead the SBC Fundamentalist movement of the 1980s, widened his battlefield from the Second Baptist Church of Houston, Texas, to the entire Southern Baptist Convention.

As president of the Southern Baptist Theological Seminary at the time, I read the situation as potentially disastrous. Other convention agency administrators were among those who, as late as 1982, thought I was an "alarmist." Having "knocked heads" with Pressler during the Elliott Controversy, I judged Pressler to be dangerous because of his intelligence, his intransigence, and his legal knowledge of the Achilles heel of the Southern Baptist Convention structure. Before Pressler, few Baptists ever studied or understood the legal documents that control convention procedures. In addition he was a successful politician who could use the political plan book of one of the national political parties. Simply put, he did not just rage against his opponents; he *organized* against them. And he had access to all the money necessary to run a successful political campaign.

This appraisal of the situation was put into one of the long-range planning scenarios for Southern Seminary. I asked myself what would happen if the Pressler party came into power? The SBC has two ways of demanding obedience of its agencies. The first is the election of members of the agency board. The second is the allocation of Cooperative Program funds for the agency budget.

Southern Seminary had bound itself to the convention by providing that its trustees would fill vacancies on the board from those nominated by the convention. After the Pressler-Patterson crusade began in 1979, many Southern Baptists were frightened by the ruthless manipulation of the election of the convention presidents who, in turn, ignored the convention bylaw requirement of consultation with the vice-presidents[1] in naming the Committee on Committees which, in turn, names the Committee on Boards to nominate the members for the agency boards. This hard-nosed fracturing of the way the SBC was supposed to work let the Pressler party focus its efforts on the election of the convention president—thereby to gain control of the boards of all of the agencies.

Legally, it was conceivable that Southern Seminary might insulate itself from the flood of "anti-intellectual" trustees by refusing to elect any new trustees for a decade or more. That would have maintained a balanced board of sixty-five Moderates and Fundamentalists. Attrition would have gradually reduced the board to better size. Alas, financially that course meant bankruptcy. Economic reprisal would have been immediate. How could eight million dollars annually from the Cooperative Program be replaced? Contingency plans included a structure for alternate funding in a rough version of the Baptist Cooperative Missions Program. I was scheduled to retire from the seminary presidency in 1980 and did so February 1982; so what I might have done was never tested.

When it became apparent in the mid-1980s that the Pressler party was firmly in control of the SBC, an updated version of this alternate funding plan was shared with the *SBC Today* newsmagazine as a way to give new options to unhappy churches. It was proposed that the corporate structure of

---

[1]Bylaw #13, *Southern Baptist Convention Annual* (1989): 13.

SBC Today be used as the channel for the gifts from individuals and church-es. This 1988 proposal was perceived as premature.

The Southern Baptist Convention in New Orleans in 1990 was the Waterloo for convention Moderates. Moderates agreed to support theological conservative Daniel Vestal of Dunwoody, Georgia, for the SBC presidency. With Vestal's resounding defeat even the optimists or politically naive could no longer dream of "throwing the rascals out." The revolution was over and a well-organized group of Fundamentalists were in control.

On May 21, 1990, a new call for the creation of an alternate funding plan was mailed to some forty convention leaders for their appraisal. In slightly different versions it read essentially as follows.

A Moderate Cooperative Program

The 1990 Southern Baptist Convention in New Orleans, Louisiana, provid-ed the last/best opportunity for the non-Fundamentalists to regain a toehold in the leadership of the convention. Now a different future must be faced.

The Problem. There are many issues: biblical inspiration, separation of church and state, abortion, role of women in ministry, priesthood of believers, authority of the pastor, purging of Moderates, peace, the home-less, the environment, etc. Issues are weighted differently by individual Moderates with some dissent at specific points. Every issue is important, but no single issue will unite a majority of Moderates *across the SBC territory* to the point of *action.*

After twelve years of effort the Fundamentalists have a solid majority of the votes and Moderates have 45–48 percent. That gives Fundamental-ists 100 percent *control* and Moderates have none—and almost no influ-ence. This has continued long enough for the Fundamentalists to get working control of the boards of all of the SBC agencies and organizations. They will have control of the agency staffs within the next five years.

Having lost a billion dollars worth of property and funds, and having no programs administered by compatible people, what will Moderate churches support? They will mount their horses and ride off in all direc-tions.

Principle. The basic principle is *the right of every donor to control his/her stewardship.* The Christian spirit requires action in concert with fellow Christians to seek to express the mind of Christ. All Moderates can act on this principle.

What to Do. Incorporate the Baptist Cooperative Program, Inc. as a Georgia corporation. Rent post office box 1845 in Atlanta, Georgia, in the name of Baptist Cooperative Program. Each church should take only one action different from the past. Ask the state convention office to send whatever portion of the gifts of the church that would have gone to Nashville to Baptist Cooperative Program, Box 1845, Atlanta.

Funds sent to Atlanta would be sent at least monthly to the SBC agencies or causes as instructed by the contributing churches, whose vote would reflect the amount contributed by each church.

The use of a title including the words "Cooperative Program" is essential to enable many churches to act. The Cooperative Program is the visible link for members of SBC churches, with its focus on missions, especially foreign missions. No wise pastor should ask his church to stop giving to the Cooperative Program, but it should not be hard to get people to vote to send their money to the version of the Cooperative Program their church has a voice in directing. [Note: The title "Cooperative Missions Program" was subsequently used to avoid legal conflict with the SBC over the name.]

It is also important not to threaten the state convention programs which thus far have fought off the Fundamentalists. It is important that state convention structures be safeguarded. If any state convention office finds problems in sending SBC portions of gifts to Atlanta, a suggestion that the church send all cooperative program funds to Atlanta first for return of the state portion from there, would probably solve the problems.

Churches making their Baptist Cooperative Program gifts as proposed here would continue to meet the current requirements for membership in the Southern Baptist Convention. Thus when the Southern Baptist Convention returns to normal operations (meaning without political party organizations) the closing of all breaches would be relatively simple. No new convention is envisioned or should be formed any time soon.

This proposal postpones important changes until mechanism for the donors to make them is in place. That avoids debate now about what, if any, changes should be made in funding. . . . not all members of the many Moderate churches are yet aware of the drastic redirection of the SBC. That will come with the elimination of all Moderate candidates for the mission fields and a few seminary dismissals under threat of budget cuts by the SBC Executive Committee in Nashville."

End of proposal.

A subsequent revision of this document added proposals about how the churches would control the Baptists Cooperative Missions Program. An effort was made to devise a voting procedure that would reflect the support by each church and would permit the church to vote in its own business meeting, if desired. Ballots could be cast by delegates from the church attending the annual meetings or could be cast in absentia through the use of fax, the mails, or other media. There were two dominant ideas. First, that every church would be able to participate in all decisions, to the end that all votes would represent all the churches, not just the opinion of those able to travel to the annual meeting. Second, that the men and women, not mainly the ministers, would debate and determine the position and vote of each church. The technology available in the 1990s, not the 1840s, would democratize the decisions of the body. The churches would become the voting units.

Obviously, the Baptist Cooperative Missions Program, as originally conceived, was the road not taken. It assumed that the problems with the Southern Baptist Convention were not primarily theological but rather systemic. The system was vulnerable to manipulation by a small group of determined and politically wise leaders. Such manipulation had occurred before for brief periods. Dominance by one or more strong leaders had occurred from time to time. The basic wrong to be cured was therefore conceived to be the processes of the Convention. The intention was to shift the focus of attention from "inerrancy" as a theological issue to the autonomy of the local church, not only in the election of officers of the Convention, but also in all other decisions including the adoption of Resolutions—and the distribution of funds.

The leaders of BCMP kept their promise to turn the organization over to whatever group of Baptists came out of the Fellowship meetings. They did so and stepped out of the limelight as soon as possible. They were and are supporters of the Baptist Fellowship, but policy making belongs to a younger generation.

The criticism of the Baptist Cooperative Missions Program leaders that surfaced in the Fellowship meeting in 1990 was that the directors represented "the good old boys network." The charge was legitimate. First, younger men and women had other agendas than creating a workable organization. Indeed, there was vocal opposition to *any* organization. This evoked the response, "Nobody wants a cup when they ask for a cup of coffee. But if the waiter squirts the coffee at you, it is hard to handle. Nobody wants an organization; but it is the way we handle things together." Second, the old friends who had worked together and trusted each other were the only ones willing to serve initially on the board of a new corporation with such political and economic risks in behalf of goals not yet commonly accepted. When asked to serve, young pastors uniformly proposed a layman for the job.

The former SBC agency head who was elected president of the board in its organizational meeting during the Atlanta Fellowship received such pressure from his old agency that he declined to serve. Grady Cothen, who wanted something done but was never enthusiastic about the BCMP idea, accepted the chairmanship on the spot. The enthusiasm generated in Atlanta swept some other younger men and women into accepting membership on the board. Mrs. Jack Prince, assistant secretary of education for Tennessee, became the secretary of the board. (See below for members of first board.)

When former Georgia Governor Carl Sanders was asked on June 22, 1990, to do the legal work to create a tax exempt Georgia corporation, he was supportive, but pointed out that his partners were not Baptists and should not be asked to invest in a potentially controversial project that might damage their practice. I then employed him personally with the request that he have a pro bono spirit when he sent the bill. This he did, most generously. I drafted the charter and bylaws at my home in North Carolina and faxed them to the Atlanta law office for translation into legal jargon and conformity to Georgia requirements.

Chairman Cothen and I, as vice-chairman, met in Atlanta September 21, 1990, three weeks after the Atlanta Consultation Fellowship adjourned. *SBC Today* offered to rent some of its office space for a small sum. Mrs. Hettie Johnson, former executive of the Home Missions Board, was recruited as volunteer office manager with the understanding that she would be elected treasurer of BCMP. She opened a bank account with First National Bank and rented a post office box. The latter cost sixty dollars which Grady Cothen paid out of his pocket. BCMP was in business with an Atlanta mailing address, an office and a staff member.

Baptist churches sent $258,428 through Baptist Cooperative Missions Program to SBC agencies and other objects before the end of the year. The Fellowship was without any legal organization or official name until after May 1991. The BCMP board refused to intrude upon the role of the Fellowship by inventing programs or promoting them. Except for work done for Baptists Committed by Jimmy Allen, almost nothing was done to enlist the support of churches or individuals. During that first full year of 1991 BCMP received $4,531,212. The total funds received during the life of BCMP was $6,380,048. This is a measure of the pressure built up within the Southern Baptist Convention for an alternate channel for distribution of the world outreach of the churches. During 1991, the only full year of operation by BCMP, fifty-nine percent of funds received were for SBC Agencies, seventeen percent for specifically Baptist Fellowship objects, and the remainder went to Baptist state convention institutions or other Baptist causes.

An unpleasant surprise was the discovery of the hardening of the arteries of the SBC Cooperative Program. With good intentions and little awareness of history or basic Baptist principles the Cooperative Program had gradually shifted from the best way for Baptists to work together in a variety of kingdom causes to being the only recognized way. The purpose of the changes was to combat designation of gifts either to or away from some official agencies of the SBC or state conventions. Some state conventions, such as Kentucky, link voting representation for a church to the amount of Cooperative Program gifts and connect the state and SBC Cooperative Program percentages to define qualifying gifts. In the first decade of the Cooperative Program a state Cooperative Program was so independent of the SBC that the state could and sometimes did set different percentage allocations to SBC agencies from those set by the SBC. Another illustration: on February 5, 1991, Troy L. Morrison, executive secretary-treasurer of the Alabama Baptist Convention, wrote to BCMP advising, "Our convention bylaws require that all funds received and disbursed by our convention must be for 'causes approved by the Alabama Baptist Convention or the Southern Baptist Convention'."

To provide a baseline to measure the shift from the beginning of the Cooperative Program at the Memphis Southern Baptist Convention in 1925, note the following quote from the 1958 edition of the *Encyclopedia of Southern Baptists*.

> As with anything which is a departure from the accustomed, the Coopera-tive Program at first met with vociferous objections from Baptists who (at least some of them) honestly felt that it was a violation of their dearly bought freedom of choice. These objectors and their objections have now come to be an almost negligible quantity by virtue of measures taken to safeguard their freedom of choice.[2]

The lockstep between the state conventions and the SBC effectively denies individuals and churches control over the objects of their giving unless they are willing to abandon their votes in the state convention. The autonomy of the local congregation was exposed as a state convention issue as much as an SBC issue. State conventions with whom churches had no complaint, lock the church into the SBC decisions on the use of church gifts. No one wanted to bell that cat, including editors of Baptist state papers.

Within weeks after the Baptist Cooperative Missions Program opened its doors the volume of gifts and communication required a larger organiza-

---

[2]J. W. Storer, "The Southern Baptist Convention," *Encyclopedia of Southern Baptists*, vol. 1 (Nashville: Broadman Press, 1958) 749.

tion. Sandra Davey, a former bank officer, was employed as office manager, the first paid staff member. Clarissa Strickland served as administrative secretary. Hettie Johnson continued to administer the office as treasurer. In the absence of staff for the Fellowship, Sandra Davey handled correspondence and phone calls for it. This was made possible by volunteers who stepped in from the beginning of BCMP. The offices were moved to larger quarters at 403 West Ponce de Leon Avenue, Decatur, Georgia. The office was largely furnished with Home Mission Board furniture that was being discarded.

In January 1991, Grady Cothen became immersed in a research project related to the Southern Baptist controversy, commissioned by the Lily Foundation. This project had forced him to turn over most of the chairman's role to the vice-chairman. In May I was elected chairman and Jim Lacey, chairman of the Fellowship's finance committee, was made vice-chairman. At the annual meeting of the board in September, all board members were asked to submit their resignations to permit the Fellowship to take over BCMP. Unfortunately, the tax-exempt ruling for the Fellowship was not yet available; so it could not take over BCMP. Instead the finance committee of nine from the Fellowship was added to the board, with ten old board members remaining. This majority of one provided continuity to satisfy IRS requirements to protect the tax-exempt status of BCMP. Hettie Johnson was elected chair of the board with the understanding that as soon as the Fellowship received tax exemption, the BCMP would be melded into the Fellowship and cease to exist as a separate corporation. This occurred on April 1, 1992.

The Baptist Cooperative Missions Program was available with tax-exempt structure to serve as an alternative funding mechanism until the diverse interests of the Baptist Fellowship could be structured and incorporated. The intentions of BCMP's founders were never on the table for serious consideration because more urgent and immediate concerns of other Baptists occupied the stage. Nevertheless, it served for a brief time to make possible the continuing cooperation of Baptists who could no longer stomach SBC aberrations. It transposed the concept of a united funding mechanism into the Fellowship, providing a convention rather than a society structure for the Fellowship.

Appendix

First Board of Directors
of Baptist Cooperative Missions Program, Ind.

John Baugh, Sysco Corporation, 1390 Enclave Parkway, Houston TX 77077-2027

Raymond T. Boswell, Boswell Insurance Agency, P.O. Box 5917, Shreveport LA 71105

Lavonn Brown, First Baptist Church, 211 West Comanche, Norman OK 73069

Harold Cole, 114 Stonehill, Chapin SC 29036

Grady Cothen, 8700 Royal Palm Blvd., Apt. E-153, Coral Springs FL 33065

Carolyn Crumpler, 5501 Donjoy Drive, Cincinnati OH 45242

Drew Gunnells, Spring Hill Baptist Church, 2 South McGregor Ave., Mobile AL 36608

Ophelia Humphrey, 1207 Florida, Amarillo TX 79102

Hettie Johnson, 113 Bruton St., Decatur GA 30033

Duke K. McCall, 3322 Casseekey Island Rd., Jupiter FL 33477

Esther McCall, 4607 Blue Ridge Blvd., Kansas City MO 64113

John R. McCall, Brown Todd & Heyburn, 1600 Citizens Plaza, Louisville KY 40202 [Lawyer son of Duke McCall, and legal consultant from the beginning.]

Darold Morgan, P.O. Box 830088, Richardson TX 75083

Bill Poe, 2600 Charlotte Plaza, Charlotte NC 28244

Frances Prince, Tennessee Department of Education, Career Ladder Division, 542 Cordell Hull Building, Nashville TN 37243-0376

Gene Triggs, Mississippi Chemical Co., P.O. Box 388, Yazoo City MS 39194

Brooks Wicker, 1553 Azalia Terrace, Jacksonville FL 32205

Daniel Vestal, Dunwoody Baptist Church, 1445 Mt. Vernon Rd., Dunwoody GA 303

Charter, Baptist Cooperative Missions Program

[Note: Legal sections mandated by Georgia Nonprofit Corporation Code are omitted.]

In affirmation of the Christian unity and freedom of those who believe in Jesus Christ as Savior and Lord, the Baptist Cooperative Missions Program is chartered for the purpose of eliciting, combining, and directing the energies of Baptist churches and individuals for the propagation of the gospel through out the world by Christian missions, Christian education, Christian social services, and benevolent enterprises, as may be deemed proper and advisable.

It shall provide means for Baptists to support any Southern Baptist Convention agency and/or other appropriate organization. It shall function to the best of its ability in friendly cooperation and support of Baptist associations, conventions (state and national), the Baptist World Alliance, and of other Christian enterprises.

A basic principle of the organization is that churches and individual donors have a right to direct their Christian stewardship. Such direction shall be in approximate proportion to the size of their gifts.

Representatives of supporting churches may give instructions to the directors of the corporation. The directors shall adopt such bylaws as are needed to direct its actions. The body shall seek Divine guidance in the conduct of its affairs and be guided by the teachings of the Bible and the leadership of the Holy Spirit.

Bylaws of Baptist Cooperative Missions Program as Revised 10 September 1990

[Note: Italics identify revisions.]

In order to carry out the purposes of the Baptist Cooperative Missions Program, Inc. the following bylaws are adopted.

1. The members of the Corporation shall be those Baptist churches and their members who distribute a portion of their gifts to national and worldwide Christian witness and ministry through this body.

(1) Meetings of the members may be held at the time and place chosen by them or the directors of the corporation.

(2) In case of necessity the directors of the corporation shall have power to reschedule such a meeting.

(3) Only representatives of qualified member churches shall be authorized to vote in such a meeting.

(4) The board of directors shall establish the procedure for determining the qualified member churches.

2. The officers of the corporation shall be a President, Vice- president, Secretary and Treasurer elected by the directors. One director may hold two offices.

3. Meetings of the directors may be held at the time and place called by the President or any three directors. Meetings may also be held by telephone conferences provided minutes shall record the names of those directors voting for and against each decision made in such a meeting. All decisions shall be made by a majority vote of the directors.

4. The Treasurer, in conformity with the Articles of Incorporation and these Bylaws, shall be required to carry out the instructions of any donor with reference to the distribution of funds sent to the Corporation by any church, Baptist organization, individual or corporation.

(1) The President or any *individual* officer named by him is authorized to advise or instruct *the Treasurer* as to the procedure to be used or action to be taken in the event that instructions accompanying any gift are unclear or in conflict with the purposes of the corporation.

(2) Any gift in conflict with (B) and/or (C) of the Articles of Incorporation shall be returned to the contributor.

5. The Board of Directors shall consist of not less than three nor more than *twenty-five* directors unless the Georgia Nonprofit Corporation Code is modified to require or permit a different number of directors.

6. The Directors constituting the initial Board of Directors of the Corporation shall be those named in the Articles of Incorporation. *Additional directors may be added to the initial Board of Directors by election of the directors present and voting at the organizational meeting of the Board.* The initial Board and any added directors shall hold office until the annual election of directors is held in accordance with these bylaws. The annual election of directors shall occur within eighteen (18) months of the incorporation date of the Corporation.

7. Any vacancy occurring on the Board of Directors may be filled by the affirmative vote of a majority of the remaining directors. A director elected to fill a vacancy shall be elected until the next annual meeting of the members.

8. The location and date for the annual election of the Board of Directors shall be determined by a majority vote of the members. At such election each director for the subsequent term of office shall be elected by a majority vote of the members. The term of office of a director shall be one year.

9. These bylaws may be amended at any regular or called meeting of the Board of Directors by a majority vote.

The History of the Cooperative Baptist Fellowship

Daniel Vestal

I was elected to the Peace Committee in 1985 because I was theologically conservative but politically nonaligned. I had resisted the Fundamentalist takeover both publicly and privately but had not engaged in any organized effort to stop it. If anyone came to the Peace Committee assignment with a sincere desire for reconciliation, it was I. And I honestly thought we could achieve that goal. I argued for theological renewal, and I argued for a cessation of the organized political efforts by the Fundamentalists to control the convention.

After a year of sincere effort at being a "man in the middle" reaching out to both sides, I realized that only one side really wanted reconciliation. I realized the Fundamentalists only desired control, total control, absolute control, and that they wanted no participation except with those who had that same desire.

In the 1987 SBC meeting in St. Louis I sat on the platform next to a trusted friend as the Peace Committee report was being given. I looked over at him and saw that he was crying. He said to me, "This is not the SBC I have always known." And indeed it wasn't. Shared decision making, open communication, acceptance of diversity were gone. In its place was a political machine that governed committee appointments, trustee selection, platform speeches, and even floor debate.

I left the 1987 Convention in a state of depression and grief. In August that year Bill Moyers contacted me about participating in the PBS documentary, "God and Politics." My appearance on that program in December 1987 thrust me into a public role I had not known. I received hundreds of responses by phone, mail, and personal visit. Everywhere I turned, people were saying to me, "Something must be done." I was aware of the previous

Moderate efforts, but now I was being urged and encouraged to get involved. In February 1989, I attended a press conference in Nashville sponsored by Baptists Committed, knowing full well what that meant. I knew it would now involve me politically in a way I had not been involved. When asked to be nominated for the SBC presidency in Las Vegas by several close friends and respected colleagues, I prayerfully consented.

From the beginning, my willingness to be nominated was motivated by the same desire that caused me to serve on the Peace Committee or appear in the Moyers's special. I genuinely wanted reconciliation. I had come to the conviction that there could be no reconciliation without political reconciliation, that is, there had to be inclusion of all Southern Baptists in the decision-making process. I made the open pledge that if elected I would purposely choose individuals from both sides of the controversy for the committee on committees. I promised inclusion instead of exclusion with the desire for genuine renewal. That was not enough, and I was defeated in Las Vegas.

During that summer, I weighed what I would do, and I decided to try again in New Orleans. I had decided to be nominated in Las Vegas only six weeks before the Convention. I felt that if I could have nine months to get out the message of hope, inclusivity, and cooperation, I could surely be elected in New Orleans in 1990. It was not to be so. I was defeated more decisively in New Orleans then in Las Vegas.

The Call for a Convocation

The night after the election, I attended a reception with friends from Dunwoody Baptist Church, Atlanta, and First Baptist Church, Midland, Texas. Afterwards, Jim Denison, pastor of FBC Midland, and I went to the hotel room of Jimmy Allen. We talked about the events of the day and the significance of those events in Baptist life. I felt the mantle of responsibility for the many who had voted for me and expressed their conscience in that vote. I sensed this defeat was an end to the Moderate political effort. It was the end for many reasons, the primary one being this was the twelfth straight defeat and the people were tired of the conflict. I realized that what I would say and do the next day would voice the feelings and concerns of a lot of disenfranchised and discouraged Southern Baptists. I felt accountability to them, but most of all I felt accountability to the convictions of my own conscience. Late in the evening I wrote the following words to be delivered the next day.

The election this year in New Orleans was not about who believes the Bible as the Word of God. I believe the Bible is the Word of God. Our presidents, administrators, professors, and denominational employees believe the Bible is the Word of God. Rather, the election this year was about our mission for the future—whether or not we will forge a united and inclusive denomination for world missions. On June 12, 1990 that vision failed. And to say that I am not disappointed would be dishonest. I am deeply disappointed.

Why did it fail? Why did we lose the election? I confess to you that I don't have all the answers. I've searched and questioned, but I am not emotionally or intellectually prepared at this time to offer an analysis. But this I do know: what we did was right. I will not say that everything we did was perfect, but it was right. We spoke to the issues that are crucial to our day: openness, fairness, missions, trust, and freedom. We resisted a political movement that excludes people from decision making, assassinates people's character, questions people's integrity and commitment to the Word of God. We resisted it, and we responded: "It's wrong, it's wrong, it's wrong." We called for a return to Baptist distinctives: the priesthood of the individual believer, religious liberty, separation of church and state. We called for a return to our Southern Baptist heritage: cooperative missions, unity in diversity.

The one overriding emotion I had on that Tuesday night was hope. Of course, I was sad and disappointed. But beyond that sadness and disappointment was a genuine conviction that God was at work. I honestly didn't know what ought to be done, but I felt that in the collective experience of Baptist people we could discern the will and work of God. I decided that the next morning at the Baptists Committed Breakfast I would call for a convocation of concerned Baptists. I determined to ask Baptists Committed to convene and plan the meeting. Its purpose would be renewal, and in it we would find ways to cooperate for the cause of Christ.

The next morning was a sober, but at the same time, a positive event. I remember the almost immediate response to the call for a convocation. It was a resounding affirmation that the time had come to move beyond political contest and theological debate. We somehow realized that the time had come to forge the future, to act instead of react, to find ways to cooperate without sacrificing our Baptist distinctives.

We all felt the need for a collective and corporate experience that would seek renewal. I was tired of the conflict. All of us were tired. We needed ways to be healed and to give healing. We needed a place to be accepted for who we are, true followers of Christ with a worldwide mission vision, Baptists who believe in the Bible but also believe in the freedom to interpret it. We needed a time to celebrate those distinctives and a time to deliberate together on how to implement those distinctives into action.

Words of Wisdom

The ten weeks prior to the consultation were weeks of anticipation and uncertainty. I received hundreds of letters with advice and counsel, condemnation and praise, anger and hope, fear and faith. Everybody had an opinion about what ought to happen, but no one knew what would happen. Following are some excerpts from letters that offered incisive counsel.

Ernest White from Kentucky wrote

> Options available to those who have supported and developed present SBC structures are limited. After twelve years of failed attempts to recover leadership and responsibility for the welfare of the organizations, continued investments of collective energy is highly problematic. The option of walking away and leaving the organizations to be plundered and destroyed has become increasingly reinforced on many who are tired of facing overwhelming odds created by Fundamentalists methods of false accusations, power politics and ruthless creedal enforcement. The Baptist Alliance option has provided some solace and mutual support for some Moderates but its level of structural life has not attracted wide following from churches and many committed to the well-being of the Southern Baptist Convention.
>
> An era that calls for creative and innovative approaches has come. It will be necessary to think differently, develop new perspectives and generate creative approaches to Southern Baptist life together if the better spirit of our corporate life is to survive and, once again, thrive. Concerned and committed Moderates in the SBC need not leave the convention.
>
> This immediate proposal is designed to stimulate the beginning and encouragement of the search and discussion which will lead to a future of intentionality and promise. In it I am inviting a look at our life together as Southern Baptists through a different frame than that to which we have become accustomed with the conventional Southern Baptist Convention. I will propose a structural approach to providing caring Southern Baptists and churches with vehicles which are beyond those presently available and captured by the Fundamentalists. I propose that Southern Baptists who want to accomplish the corporate missions, evangelism and educational goals long held as our shared purpose, develop a set of parallel organizations.

Jack and June McEwen from Tennessee wrote

As you and representatives of other groups in the SBC meet to prepare for a convocation to respond to the events in New Orleans please give some thought to these suggestions.

1. Churches need a quick, simple, easily grasped way to allocate Cooperative Program funds.

2. We need a plan for maintaining, bringing home, offering options to missionaries outside the USA.

3. We need literature.

4. We need, most of all, hope.

5. We need a plan for a transition from where we are to where we can be, both immediately and long range.

6. We need to concentrate on two or three things and not get side tracked by worthy but not basic (at the moment) issues.

7. Mostly we need some plan quick.

It seems to me that a small group of serious-minded, well-known, respected, knowledgeable people need to prepare an agenda before the general convocation. The agenda needs to be focussed so that the main issues are fully addressed. Other matters can be assigned to task forces to bring full reports at a subsequent meeting.

Please know that you are in our prayers. We desperately need leadership, a plan, hope.

Ervin Hastey from Virginia Wrote

I personally feel that an alternative program to what is now the Southern Baptist Convention must be worked out.

1. An alternative plan or program should be worked out as soon as possible with at least a skeleton organization. Many of our churches and people need an identification point where certain commonalities can be found.

2. A channel for missions giving should be established as soon as possible. This will avoid a lot of rambling designations.

3. Study commissions should be appointed in the following areas:

—The possibility of a new denominational organization.

—The possible provision for theological education.

—The possible establishment of a missions program.

—A possible general convocation of moderate/conservatives one year from now.

—The possibilities of financing a new denominational organization.

—The possible organization of State Support Groups for meetings of those who are really suffering now and need mutual support.

—The designation of certain works which need to be funded. An example is the Baptist Joint Committee on Public Affairs.

Stewart Newman from North Carolina wrote

It is reported here that you are planning to call a meeting of representative moderates in the near future. This is to urge that you do so.

By the experiences of the last several years you are strategically situated to render this service, a move that is very important to the Baptist cause at this time.

It would be difficult for moderates to continue to try to work within the limits that are being set by the Fundamentalists. If we should manage to win an election now and then it would be a sorry prospect for progressive Free Church folk to live under the constant pressures of what is being projected as the ultraconservatives agenda.

When we take a full step back and look at our organizational system there is nothing so very sacred about it. It is merely a vehicle that has been devised for the use of very sacred aspects of church life. It was begun under very questionable conditions in 1845 and could be duplicated for better reasons in the twentieth century.

Atlanta, Georgia Aug. 23-25, 1990 is not too far from Augusta in 1845 for us to *Dream the Southern Baptist Dream Again*—not a new convention new ways for our diversity to flow together as the Holy Spirit leads.

No church needs to leave the Southern Baptist Convention! I know all the complaints. I belong to the 40% minority too. But I still want to work with Southern Baptists and minister through my state Baptist Convention.

So I have dreamed of a way for "Moderate" Southern Baptists to keep on working together—supporting the missionaries and professors we all appointed—and following as God guides us. The instrument is the Baptist Cooperative Missions Program, Inc. in Atlanta which will use our Cooperative gifts forwarded from each state Baptist convention the way we vote in our churches.

Our Cooperative Program gifts beyond the Baptist state convention will go through Atlanta instead of Nashville, but the SBC agencies like the Foreign Mission Board and other causes such as the Joint Committee on Public Affairs will be supported by cooperating "Moderates." Whether our vote is important or not, we can use our Christian influence—wrapped in our stewardship.

I do not belong to Baptist Committed or the Southern Baptist Alliance, but I urge all "Moderates" to join Daniel Vestal in the "open" meeting he has called in Atlanta. Register to be there in person or in prayer. My proposal is one option. You may have a better one.

Let us "Moderates" stay together in our Christian witness, in the Southern Baptist Convention if conscience permits—and the majority allows. We ask only for space, not to fight against, but to bear witness to our convictions. Now it is time to dream that uniting dream again—in partial fulfillment of Jesus' prayer.

Cecil Sherman from Texas wrote:

I make an appeal to you.

1. You people have become leaders for us. Lead us. Leaders can cooperate when it is for a good cause. You can talk to each other and find some common way to pull the several strands of Moderates together. Please do this lest we fragment.

2. We will have a meeting. I hope all of you will help sponsor that meeting. Be present and a leader at the meeting.

3. We must have a plan to do missions to come out of the meeting. I cannot go back to my church and tell them I went to a meeting and wrung my hands with several hundred other handwringers. *We must have a plan.*

4. This plan must fund the parts of the SBC that are worth funding. It will defund the parts that do not represent our understanding of the gospel. It must be flexible enough to change as the SBC changes.

5. This fund must be willing to set up rival structures to SBC agencies. In a few years we will have no seminary worth funding. We will not have a foreign or home mission system that we have a part in building. So, we must be willing to live with the consequences of our actions.

The plan designed must be a shadow denomination. Whether it ever becomes full blown denomination, our children will decide. Our job is to do what is ours to do for now. We must tell the gospel and we must help people in Christ's name.

One last comment: we must not be afraid of what we are doing. If we try to hold onto the SBC, we deceive ourselves. It is not ours to hold. If we are afraid of what we are doing and the impact it will make on the SBC, we will be paralyzed. We must be free enough to move and to act.

Again, I appeal to you. Pull us together as you give leadership rather than shoring up your organization at the expense of a larger vision. This is an awful time. It is fraught with great opportunity. We are alive for this time. I know you will do well. I am praying for you.

The First Convocation

Baptists Committed, under the leadership of Jimmy Allen, began immediately to implement the daunting and awesome challenge of putting together a national Baptist meeting in a time of crises. What became apparent very soon was that the meeting was to be larger than we first anticipated. In my initial challenge I called for "a forum where representatives and interested individuals can meet for formal discussion." The plan was that it be for "invited participants, but open to the press and interested observers." Soon in the planning stage it was wisely decided to have an open meeting for any and all Baptists who wanted to attend.

The goal and intent of the intense planning was to devise a consultation that would provide opportunity for dialogue and discussion. For so long the closed and authoritarian environment of the SBC had stifled shared decision making. For so long people had been subjected to decrees, manipulation and criticism that many were wounded and hurt, but all the while longing for freedom, cooperation and unity.

So the desire in planning was a format that combined worship, work groups, state meetings and plenary sessions. The schedule was planned to balance large group and small group meetings, celebration and conversation, regional and nonregional fellowship. We sought diligently to have geographical, ethnic, gender and vocational balance in leadership. We structured a setting where Baptists could address themselves to the crucial concerns for future witness: funding, missions, evangelism, theological education, ethics, public policy and literature. We wanted to have genuine dialogue on legal issues, alternate information systems, local church and denominational relations. Hence, the idea was to have work group sessions and then reflections of those work groups in the plenary sessions. We realized people wanted to talk to each other and listen to each other, to hear and be heard. So the meeting was planned, not knowing the outcome, with an emphasis on process and participation.

Many people worked, planned and sacrificed to prepare for the meeting that would eventually give birth to the Cooperative Baptist Fellowship. But one person deserves special credit. Oeita Bottorff was the chief architect of that which would later be described as an "an event." She, more than any one else, anticipated the significance of the Consultation and labored to insure that the details and logistics were tended to so that the movement could express itself in concrete action.

The First Consultation

At 1:00 p.m. on August 23, 1990, Jimmy Allen convened the Consultation of Concerned Baptists at the Inforum in Atlanta, Georgia. The atmosphere was electric, and we sensed we were at an historic juncture. The theme for the Consultation was "For Such a Time as This." In my opening address I sought to interpret that theme.

> Why are we here? We're here to help, not hurt; to heal, not wound; to unify, not divide; to focus on the future, not the past. We're here to encourage each other, learn from each other, pray for each other and listen to the voice of God through each other. We're here as Southern Baptist Christians to find ways we can get on with the work of God's Kingdom,

to spread the Gospel of Jesus Christ, to minister to a hurting, hungry world, to be the people of God in our day.

In a sense we're here because we've been driven here, but also because we choose to be here. We've been driven here by a group of folks who have told us they don't want us to work with them in the cause of Christ. They call their movement, "the Conservative Resurgence," and they have said for 12 years that if you don't believe in that resurgence and won't work for it, you have no place among them.

They have not only maligned and libelled good and godly people, but they have caricatured and misrepresented others. They would take away our dignity and our freedom. I, for one, will not allow that to happen to me. I, for one, will not give that up. And so, in a sense I am driven here to find a people who will respect me even if they disagree with me, and will allow me to cooperate with them in the grand and glorious cause of Christ.

But do not pity me, for I also choose to be here. I choose because I believe in some principles and precepts that are foundational to my life: the priesthood of the individual believer, religious liberty and separation of church and state, cooperative missions based on the autonomy of every church, congregational polity and moral integrity in decision making. I am first and foremost committed to Jesus Christ. In that commitment, I believe in some principles and truths that are not only Baptist, but biblical and Christian as well. The reason I have been a Southern Baptist is because this denomination has represented and embodied those principles. But now, this denomination has not only abandoned those principles, but is acting in violation of them.

I am more committed to Christ and the principles of His Kingdom than any human institution. I do not believe I have left the Southern Baptist Convention, but rather the Southern Baptist Convention has left me. But even more significant, it has left these basic foundational truths. I still believe in much of our missionary enterprise. I still believe in many of our institutions and ministries. So I am also looking for ways to support that mission enterprise and those institutions and ministries without violating these basic foundational truths.

So why are we here? We're not here to form a new denomination. We're not here to plan political strategy. We're not here to wish anyone ill will or harm. But we are here to explore how we can cooperate with each other for the cause of Christ in ways that do not violate our conscience or the principles that inform our conscience.

During the three-day convocation 3,000 Baptist Christians from thirty states and the District of Columbia did indeed explore ways to cooperate with each other for the cause of Christ. We adopted an alternative funding plan, the Baptist Cooperative Missions Program, Inc. An inclusive fellowship organization was formed and a sixty-member interim steering committee was elected. That interim committee was charged with the following responsibilities.

1. Promote understanding, harmony, and community among those who choose to be a part of this fellowship.

2. Plan a spring convocation for common worship and for further planning and action of this body.

3. Develop proposals for the cooperative distribution of funds received by the Baptist Cooperative Missions Program, Inc. Also, approve interim distribution plans for contributions, consistent with designation of donors.

4. Develop a mission statement and necessary operating documents for consideration at the spring convocation and take any further interim actions necessary to function.

5. Receive, evaluate and develop specific strategies related to concerns expressed in the workshops.

6. Communicate to the churches, agencies of the SBC and other Christian bodies our sense of renewal and hope and our commitment to seek and do the will of God.

7. Develop a process for choosing a permanent steering committee to be elected in the spring convocation.

Prior to the Convocation the feeling was one of uncertainty. During the Convocation the prevailing atmosphere was one of joy and celebration. At the conclusion of the Convocation the general mood was positive and hopeful. Among many it was near euphoric. Ken Chafin reflected on his experience and captures the feeling of many:

> The Fellowship was the most inclusive Baptist meeting I've attended in my lifetime in terms of race, gender, age, size of church, background, interest, experience, theology, clergy, laity, or perspective. There was an intentionality to the push to see that every group which was created reflected our great diversity. In the midst of this diversity there was an underlying unity but it was based not on uniformity but on our common calling in Christ.

Interim Steering Committee

The Interim Steering Committee convened its first meeting in October, 1990. We divided ourselves into committees and began to fulfill the charge given us by the Convocation. We started with such basic decisions as voting to open a bank account and office as well as hire part time interim staff. We set the place and time for a second convocation and began immediately to plan and prepare for it. We accepted the offer of *SBC Today* to be a communication tool to churches and individuals. We heard regular reports from the Southern Baptist Alliance and Southern Baptist Women in Ministry and enjoyed open communication with these organizations. We were kept up to date with the actions and developments of the Baptist Cooperative Missions Program, Inc., all the while pursuing the goal of our own incorporation and tax exempt status. This could not be accomplished until our constitution and bylaws were adopted. In four meetings we prepared a Constitution and Bylaws, strategies for world missions, a multitrack funding plan and a working budget all to be presented to the second convocation.

We deliberated and discussed with intensity and sometimes sharp disagreements. We debated issues from diverse perspectives, because we were a diverse committee. Each of us had certain areas where we had strong convictions and deep feelings, so we tended to make speeches to one another. It was a way of dealing with our grief over what had happened to the SBC, and it was a way of learning to relate to each other. We respected each other, but we really didn't know each other. We had to learn, as we went along, how to build consensus and community. Some of us were still emotionally tied to the SBC, and some of us were not. All of us realized how very fragile was our fellowship, how very young was our organization and how very much we were dependent on God.

A telling moment in the work of the Committee came at its final meeting. Only a few hours prior to the second convocation the committee adopted a document prepared by Walter Shurden of Macon, Georgia.[1] Without alteration the committee agreed to offer the document as "An Address to the Public" stating historical, theological and practical reasons for the formation of our fellowship. The "Address" is as follows:

Introduction

Forming something as fragile as the Fellowship is not a move we make lightly. We are obligated to give some explanation for why we are doing what we are doing. Our children will know what we have done; they may

---

[1][Editor's note: Presented by Walter B. Shurden to the general assembly as "information" on behalf of the interim steering committee, the document is the work of two people, Cecil E. Sherman and Shurden. Sherman's is the primary hand. A brief history of the document is found in the archives of the Cooperative Baptist Fellowship at Mercer University in Macon, Georgia.]

not know why we have done what we have done. We have reasons for our actions. They are

I. Our Reasons are Larger Than Losing.

For twelve years the Southern Baptist Convention in annual session has voted to sustain the people who lead the Fundamentalist wing of the SBC. For twelve years the SBC in annual session has endorsed the arguments and the rationale of the Fundamentalists. What has happened is not a quirk or a flash or an accident. It has been done again and again.

If inclined, one could conclude that the losers have tired of losing. But the formation of The Fellowship does not spring from petty rivalry. If the old Moderate wing of the SBC were represented in making policy and were treated as welcomed representatives of competing ideas in the Baptist mission task, then we would coexist, as we did for years, alongside Fundamentalism and continue to argue our ideas before Southern Baptists.

But this is not the way things are. When Fundamentalists won in 1979, they immediately began a policy of exclusion. Non-Fundamentalists are not appointed to any denominational positions. Rarely are gentle Fundamentalists appointed. Usually only doctrinaire Fundamentalists, hostile to the purposes of the very institutions they control, are rewarded for service by appointment. Thus, the boards of SBC agencies are filled by only one kind of Baptist. And this is true whether the vote to elect was 60-40 or 52-48. It has been since 1979 a "winner take all." We have no voice.

In another day Pilgrims and Quakers and Baptists came to America for the same reason. As a minority, they had no way to get a hearing. They found a place where they would not be second-class citizens. All who attended the annual meeting of the SBC in New Orleans in June of 1990 will have an enlarged understanding of why our ancestors left their homes and dear ones and all that was familiar. So forming The Fellowship is not something we do lightly. Being Baptist should ensure that no one is ever excluded who confesses, "Jesus is Lord" (Phil 2:11).

II. Our Understandings Are Different.

Occasionally, someone accuses Baptists of being merely a contentious, controversial people. That may be. But the ideas that divide Baptists in the present "controversy" are the same ideas that have divided Presbyterians, Lutherans, and Episcopalians. These ideas are strong and they are central; these ideas will not be papered over. Here are some of these basic ideas:

1. Bible. Many of our differences come from a different understanding and interpretation of Holy Scripture. But the difference is not at the point of the inspiration or authority of the Bible. We interpret the Bible differently, as will be seen below in our treatment of the biblical understanding of women and pastors. We also, however, have a different understanding of the nature of the Bible. We want to be biblical— especially in our view of the Bible. That means that we dare not claim less for the Bible than the Bible claims for itself. The Bible neither claims nor reveals inerrancy as a Christian teaching. Bible claims must be based on the Bible, not on human interpretations of the Bible.

2. *Education.* What should happen in colleges and seminaries is a major bone of contention between Fundamentalists and Moderates.

Fundamentalists educate by indoctrination. They have the truth and all the truth. As they see it, their job is to pass along the truth they have. They must not change it. They are certain that their understandings of the truth are correct, complete and to be adopted by others.

Moderates, too, are concerned with truth, but we do not claim a monopoly. We seek to enlarge and build upon such truth as we have. The task of education is to take the past and review it, even criticize it. We work to give our children a larger understanding of spiritual and physical reality. We know we will always live in faith; our understandings will not be complete until we get to heaven and are loosed from the limitations of our mortality and sin.

3. *Mission.* What ought to be the task of the missionary is another difference between us. We think the mission task is to reach people for faith in Jesus Christ by preaching, teaching, healing and other ministries of mercy and justice. We believe this to be the model of Jesus in Galilee. That is the way he went about his mission task. Fundamentalists make the mission assignment narrower than Jesus did. They allow their emphasis on direct evangelism to undercut other biblical ministries of mercy and justice. This narrowed definition of what a missionary ought to be and do is a contention between us.

4. *Pastor.* What is the task of the pastor? They argue the pastor should be the ruler of a congregation. This smacks of the bishop's task in the Middle Ages. It also sounds much like the kind of church leadership Baptists revolted against in the seventeenth century.

Our understanding of the role of the pastor is to be a servant/shepherd. Respecting lay leadership is our assignment. Allowing the congregation to make real decisions is of the very nature of Baptist congregationalism. And using corporate business models to "get results" is building the Church by the rules of a secular world rather than witnessing to the secular world by way of a servant Church.

5. *Women.* The New Testament gives two signals about the role of women. A literal interpretation of Paul can build a case for making women submissive to men in the Church. But another body of scripture points toward another place for women. In Galatians 3:27-28 Paul wrote, "As many of you as are baptized into Christ have clothed yourselves with Christ. There is no longer Jew or Greek, there is not longer slave or free, there is no longer male and female; for all of you are one Christ Jesus" (NRSV).

We take Galatians as a clue to the way the Church should be ordered. We interpret the reference to women the same way we interpret the reference to slaves. If we have submissive roles for women, we must also have a place for slaves in the Church.

In Galatians Paul follows the spirit of Jesus who courageously challenged the conventional wisdom of his day. It was a wisdom with rigid boundaries between men and women in religion and in public life. Jesus deliberately broke those barriers. He called women to follow him; he treated women as equally capable of dealing with sacred issues. Our model for the role of women in matters of faith is the Lord Jesus.

6. Church. An ecumenical and inclusive attitude is basic to our fellowship. The great ideas of theology are the common property of all the Church. Baptists are only a part of that great and inclusive Church. So, we are eager to have fellowship with our brothers and sisters in the faith and to recognize their work for our Savior. We do not try to make them conform to us; we try to include them in our design for mission. Mending the torn fabric of both Baptist and Christian fellowship is important to us. God willing, we will bind together the broken parts into a new company in preview of the great fellowship we shall have with each other in heaven.

It should be apparent that the points of difference are critical. They are the stuff around which a fellowship such as the Southern Baptist Convention is made. We are different. It is regrettable, but we are different. And perhaps we are most different at the point of spirit. At no place have we been able to negotiate about these differences. Were our Fundamentalist brethren to negotiate, they would compromise. And that would be a sin by their understandings. So, we can either come to their position, or we can form a new fellowship.

III. We Are Called to Do More than Politic.

Some people would have us continue as we have over the last twelve years, and continue to work within the SBC with a point of view to change the SBC. On the face of it this argument sounds reasonable. Acting it out is more difficult.

To change the SBC requires a majority vote. To effect a majority in annual session requires massive, expensive, contentious activity. We have done this, and we have done it repeatedly.

But we have never enjoyed doing it. Something is wrong with a religious body that spends such energy in overt political activity. Our time is unwisely invested in beating people or trying to beat people. We have to define the other side as bad and we are good. There is division. The existence of The Fellowship is a simple confession of that division; it is not the cause of that division.

We can no longer devote our major energies to SBC politics. We would rejoice, however, to see the SBC return to its historic Baptist convictions. Our primary call is to be true to our understanding of the gospel. We are to advance the gospel in our time. When we get to heaven, God is not going to ask us, "Did you win in Atlanta in June of 1991?" If we understand the orders we are under, we will be asked larger questions. And to spend our time trying to reclaim a human institution (people made the SBC; it is not a scriptural entity) is to make more of that institution than we ought to make. A denomination is a missions delivery system; it is not meant to be an idol. When we make more of the SBC than we ought, we risk falling into idolatry. Twelve years is too long to engage in political activity. We are called to higher purposes.

Conclusion

- That we may have a voice in our Baptist mission, for that is our Baptist birthright . . .
- That we may work by ideas consistent with our understanding of the gospel rather than fund ideas than are not our gospel . . .
- That we may give our energies to the advancement of the Kingdom of God rather than in divisive, destructive politics . . .

For these reasons we form the Fellowship. This does not require that we sever ties with the old Southern Baptist Convention. It does give us another mission delivery system, one more like our understanding of what it means to be Baptist and what it means to do gospel. Therefore, we create a new instrument to further the Kingdom and enlarge the Body of Christ.

Second Convocation

On May 9-11, 1991, more than 6,000 participants representing 1,556 churches gathered in the Omni coliseum in Atlanta, Georgia. For less than nine months this fledgling organization had existed under the name "The Baptist Fellowship." The interim steering committee had acted in good faith to fulfill its responsibilities. It was prepared to challenge the participants to shape the future of the Baptist witness. Those participants showed that they were more than willing to accept that challenge.

Under the banner, "Behold I Do a New Thing," the second convocation followed much the same format as the first with a combination of worship, smaller discussion groups, plenary sessions for reports and business. The business sessions were lively but cordial. Substantive decisions were made in an environment of freedom and trust. A name was adopted: The Cooperative Baptist Fellowship. This was not the name recommended by the interim steering committee, but the participants overwhelmingly wanted it. A constitution was adopted with bylaws that made it a temporary document. It is to be replaced in 1993. A coordinating council was elected with John Hewett from Asheville, North Carolina as the first Moderator. A missions proposal calling for a missions center and new directions in world mission was enthusiastically approved and affirmed.

The following Tuesday, May 14, 1991, the *Atlanta Constitution* ran as its lead editorial the following:

> Last Saturday the Cooperative Baptist Fellowship was born in Atlanta. It is now the principal agency of the moderates who, for the past 12 years, have found themselves on the losing end of the Moderate-Fundamentalist struggle to control the Southern Baptist Convention (SBC). That struggle is now, more or less officially over.
>
> Is the Fellowship a new denomination?
>
> Its officials say no, but they also insist they have created a permanent organization. According to them, a denomination is too centralized, too bureaucratic, for what they have in mind.
>
> Historically, Baptists stood for religious freedom—the freedom of individual believers not to be bound to a specific creed, the freedom of congregations to govern their own affairs, the freedom of church from state. But in the course of this century, Southern Baptist churches have voluntarily surrendered more and more of this freedom to denominational headquarters in Nashville, Tenn.
>
> As Nancy Ammerman, director of Baptist studies of the Candler School of Theology, noted, "We had pledged never to get a pastor from anything but an official denominational seminary. We loyally accepted whatever doctrine came to us in Sunday School quarterlies from Nashville. And we promised to build our churches, plan our programs, train our leaders, educate our youth, robe our choirs, tag our visitors and pray our prayers according to calendars and programs and handbooks that came to us from Nashville."
>
> And since 1980, the SBC leadership has all but signed on as a wing of the national Republican Party.
>
> The Baptist Fellowship is animated, as much as anything else, by the desire to restore the Baptist freedom of old. This means it is to be commodious enough to accommodate doctrinal differences, inclusive enough to make a place for women and the laity in the ordering of Baptist life and scrupulous enough not to put its spiritual sword in the hands of any political party.
>
> It also recognized that many moderates may not yet be prepared to sunder all ties to the institutions of the SBC. Three different giving plans allow individuals and churches to disengage from the SBC to varying degrees. Already, however, a traditional Southern Baptist church can have access to global missions, seminarians, religious literature, a Baptist news service and political action solely through the Fellowship.

There have been times when the multiplicity of denominations has been seen as a cause of scandal in the Christian world. Why should the House of Christ require so many mansions? But spiritual needs, like spiritual gifts, are diverse, and it is clear that the SBC, as presently constituted, is no longer meeting the needs of a significant number of Southern Baptists.

The Cooperative Baptist Fellowship will have its headquarters in Atlanta. We should be grateful to have this pluralistic body in our midst.

The First Coordinating Council

Following the 1991 Convocation, the Cooperative Baptist Fellowship took shape with organization and purpose. Under the leadership of John Hewett as moderator, the Coordinating Council moved rapidly to consolidate the momentum gained in the first nine months. They accomplished a merger between the Baptist Cooperative Missions Program and the Cooperative Baptist Fellowship with the Fellowship. Gaining legal status as a nonprofit organization, they elected Cecil Sherman as the first Coordinator of the Coordinating Council. This was a most significant step because it represented the selection of a leader who combined pastoral, denominational and executive experience. Cecil Sherman, who had been pastor of First Baptist Church in Chamblee, Georgia, First Baptist Church, Asheville, North Carolina, and most recently Broadway Baptist Church in Fort Worth, Texas, had been vocal and active in the Moderate resistance to the Fundamentalist takeover. His understanding of and commitment to Baptist ideas, his courage, his ability to articulate who we are and where we are going as a movement, well qualified him to be the first leader of the fledgling and developing fellowship.

It would be difficult to say which was more important in the Fellowship's emerging identity—Baptist ideas or world missions? Both were essential ingredients in its reason for existence. The Coordinating Council approved a "Purpose and Strategy Statement for Global Missions." This "statement" was to the mission vision of the Fellowship what the "Address to the Public" was to the theological and practical reasons for its existence. It reads as follows:

I. Purpose

Our purpose is to lead people to a saving knowledge of Jesus Christ and to carry out the Great Commission through inclusive global mission in which all Baptists can participate.

II. Statement of Distinctives

Preamble

We start afresh in a world without borders, claiming the best from our free church heritage.

1. Ours will be one mission agency with no distinction between home and foreign missions.

2. Our concern is for all people who have not heard the gospel, and we regard as equally important all ministries that point people to Jesus Christ as Lord.

3. Our ministries will be open to all Baptists; our structure will be small and simple; and our work will be measured by quality.

4. In places where the church is already functioning, our missioners will work under the auspices of local and national church leaders, and decisions regarding the work will be made in concert with them.

5. Missioners will be asked to affirm their commitment to Jesus Christ, to the mission of the church and to their sense of God's leadership in their personal involvement, and they will be sent as servant facilitators to do work for which they are uniquely suited and for specified periods of time.

6. Baptists from other lands will be invited to join in the planning and doing of Christ's mission.

III. Statement on Relationships

Recognizing that the challenge of reaching the world with the Gospel belongs to the whole body of Christ, we are willing to communicate with, cooperate with, and joint venture with the mission agencies of the Southern Baptist Convention and other Baptist groups. We are also willing to work anywhere in the world with other Christian organizations with like objectives. In these cooperative relationships we will seek to maintain our principles and priorities.

IV. Five-Year Mission Strategy Statement

The major mission emphases of the Cooperative Baptist Fellowship for the next five years will be fourfold:

1. To strengthen Christian ministry in Eastern Europe and the former Soviet republics. Special emphasis will be placed on theological education and ministry training for church leaders.

2. To minister to internationals in the United States. Special emphasis will be placed on the development of such ministry within the context of local churches.

3. To sponsor and enable Christian witness within countries, cities, or people groups where there is no present access to the Gospel. Special emphasis will be given to lay involvement and nontraditional methodologies.

4. To target specific urban settings for the development of inner city ministries. Special emphasis will be placed on the homeless, the hungry, and the economically and educationally disadvantaged.

Specific implementation includes

1. Eastern Europe and the Former Soviet Republics

a. Increase support for Ruschlikon Seminary especially in the training of leaders for those areas.

b. Increase at their invitation our support of and involvement with Baptists of Eastern Europe and the former Soviet republics.

2. Ministry to internationals

a. Encourage and assist congregations to identify and minister to internationals in their community.

b. Provide models and enlist and train leadership to accomplish this ministry.

3. Unaccessed Areas and People Groups

a. Educate Baptists to the needs of the one-fourth of the world who have no access to the Gospel.

b. Target specific cities and peoples who have no Christian witness.

c. Develop means whereby people called to this task can be enabled to fulfill their mission.

4. Urban Ministry

a. Identify and communicate specific urban ministries that urgently need support.

b. Confer with church leadership and people in the inner city.

c. Direct personnel and financial resources.

d. Sensitize people to the continuing crisis of the hurting among us.

In addition to adopting the Mission Statement, the Coordinating Council made a bold offer to Southern Baptist Missionaries in Eastern Europe inviting them to work under the auspices of the Fellowship and approved exploring cooperative mission efforts with the European Baptist Federation. It was also concluded that a global missions offering be initiated to support such a mission effort as well as aggressive efforts to raise $2.5 for a 1993 mission budget. Such an offering and budget would support the missioners that would be available beginning in 1992.

By the time of the Third Convocation in Fort Worth, Texas, John David and Jo Ann Hopper as well as Charles and Kathy Thomas were indeed available. The Hoppers, Southern Baptist missionaries in Switzerland, and the Thomases, Southern Baptist missionaries in Romania, resigned from the Foreign Mission Board to become the first missioners supported by Cooperative Baptist Fellowship. Their appearance at the Convocation in Fort Worth was for many the highlight of that event.

The Third Convocation

April 30 to May 2, 1992, the General Assembly of the Cooperative Baptist
Fellowship convened in the Fort Worth Convention Center. The Fort Worth
assembly showed that the time had arrived when the Fellowship did not
need to define itself in terms of its detractors, or in terms of the past, or in
terms of the conflict in the SBC. This third meeting showed a growing
desire and commitment to define the Cooperative Baptist Fellowship in
terms of convictions and vision about the future. With 6,000 participants in
Fort Worth the spirit was one of renewal and hope. The theme was "Presence and Promise" and it aptly described the atmosphere of celebration and
the mood of anticipation. In business sessions the convocation approved
constitutional changes that put the selection of the coordinating council more
in the hands of the states. It installed Cecil Sherman as the first coordinator
and approved recommendations from each ministry group: global missions,
theological education, ethics and public policy and equipping the laity. It
also adopted a "statement of confession and repentance" rejecting racism in
the present and acknowledging our institutional and denominational sins of
the past. The opening address by John Hewett captured the feelings of so
many in Fort Worth. Hewett said:

> Brothers and sisters, a year ago we gathered in Atlanta to the beckon-
> ing whistle of a gospel train bound for glory. Now that train has returned
> to the station, as we promised, to pick up more free and faithful Baptists
> determined to journey onward by the power of the Spirit filled with the
> lively hope of the living God, under the control of no one save our Lord
> Jesus Christ. I'm happy to report tonight that thousands of you have said
> "Yes" to what God is doing among us. And God is at work! . . .
>
> A whole year has gone by, and we're back together—this time a little
> stronger, a bit wiser, and a whole lot happier. People ask me, will the
> Fellowship live? Does it have a future? I want you to know I am not
> optimistic about our future; I am hopeful. In the Eighties I learned that
> optimism is shallow and fragile; it always depends on what you can see.
> Hope, on the other hand, is deep and enduring. Hope encompasses the
> disappointments of the present by the promise of the future. Has anyone
> described it better than Augustine? "Hope has two beautiful daughters.
> Their names are anger and courage; anger at the way things are, and
> courage to see they do not remain that way." This hope is our watch-
> word—the wild hope that what God has started among us God will bring
> to completion.

Conclusion

The Cooperative Baptist Fellowship is a new association of Baptists Christians. In order for the Fellowship to function, it was necessary to adopt legal and organizational structure; hence, the name, constitution, coordinating council, budget and funding formulas. All these are important but more important is its intangible, spiritual nature and its primary purpose. Let me restate that purpose as written in the constitution: "The purpose of the Cooperative Baptist Fellowship is to enable the people of God to carry out the Great Commission under the Lordship of Jesus Christ, in a fellowship where every Christian exercises God's gifts and calling."

Historically, Baptists have associated themselves together for such a purpose. They have entered into covenants and communions. They have forged and formed partnerships in allegiance to Jesus Christ and His glorious Gospel. Such is the Cooperative Baptist Fellowship. It was born, to be sure, out of the fires of adversity, but even more than that, it was born out of a grand commitment to the Kingdom of God and a desire to extend that Kingdom and fellowship with other Christian believers.

This Fellowship is Baptist. Stewards of the historic Christian Gospel, this Fellowship is committed to the glory and goodness of God, the Lordship of Jesus Christ, the reality and power of the Holy Spirit. In summary, it is unashamedly and unapologetically a Christian Fellowship. But it seeks to be a Christian Fellowship that is distinctively Baptist. It seeks to function according to convictions that have been forged through the centuries that are described as Baptist convictions.

Among these are the conviction that each individual is a priest unto God, able to know and do the will of God. People are free to interpret and apply Scripture according to the dictates of their own conscience and not according to an ecclesiastical creed or a man-made document. The practice of believer's baptism is based on the conviction that each soul is able and responsible to accept Jesus Christ voluntarily as Savior and Lord. Baptists have fought and died for religious liberty and separation of church and state. Baptists have been champions of freedom, believing in a free church in a free state, resisting tyranny, whether ecclesiastical or governmental. Baptists have believed in the local church as a voluntary association of baptized believers. Each church is autonomous and self-governing, choosing its leadership, with that leadership functioning as servant leadership in the pattern of Christ Himself. For the Cooperative Baptist Fellowship these distinctives are not peripheral or tangential, but essential to being Baptist.

Finally, this Baptist Fellowship is Cooperative. We freely and voluntarily enter into cooperation. Our cooperation is in an environment of integrity, freedom and servanthood. We recognize the priesthood of each believer, the authority of each church, and the independence of each Baptist association. But we also recognize our need for each other, so we pledge to respect each other, be truthful and open with each and pray for each other. We recognize our diversity of gifts but our oneness in Christ. We are all ministers, some clergy and some laity, but we are one in Christ. We are male and female, but we are one in Christ. We have differences in interpretation, worship and practice, but we are one in Christ. Such is our cooperation.

We will be cooperative in decision making. Ours will be shared decision making. We will be cooperative in funding, each deciding in his heart what to give, "not reluctantly or under compulsion, for God loves a cheerful giver." We will be cooperative in spirit, showing love to each other and trust in each other. We will seek cooperation, not competition, among ourselves, other Baptists and other Christians as well.

Our cooperation is not an end in itself. It is for the sake of the Gospel that we cooperate. It is for the sake of those who need the Gospel that we cooperate. It is because we can accomplish more in cooperation that we can in isolation that we choose this way of ministry and this way of living.

The Struggle
for the Soul of the SBC:
Reflections and Interpretations

Walter B. Shurden

Somewhere I read this crazy story about an airplane that took off from London's Heathrow airport. A metallic, computerized voice came over the loudspeaker:

> Ladies and gentlemen, Vista Airlines would like to welcome you to the first transatlantic flight that is being controlled completely by computer. The possibility of human error has been eliminated because there is no pilot and no crew aboard. All of your needs will be taken care of by the very latest technology. Please, just sit back, relax, and enjoy your flight. Every contingency has been prepared for and nothing could possibly go wrong . . . possibly go wrong . . . possibly go wrong . . . possibly go wrong. . . .

Something went wrong!

What happens when you think something has gone wrong? You respond. The previous chapters describe the Moderate response to the Fundamentalist movement within the SBC from 1979 to 1990. Here are some reflections and interpretations.

What Fundamentalists Wanted and Got

The most poignant moment for me in the conference at Mercer where these papers were presented was when Daniel Vestal spoke his opening words. They were words about his experience on the Peace Committee in 1985, six years after the controversy had begun. Vestal said:

I was elected to the Peace Committee in 1985 because I was theologically conservative but politically nonaligned. I had resisted the Fundamentalist takeover both publicly and privately but had not engaged in any organized effort to stop it. If anyone came to the Peace Committee assignment with a sincere desire for reconciliation, it was I. And I honestly thought we could achieve that goal. I argued for theological renewal, and I argued for a cessation of the organized political efforts by the Fundamentalists to control the convention.

After a year of sincere effort at being a "man in the middle" reaching out to both sides, I realized that only one side really wanted reconciliation. I realized the Fundamentalists only desired control, total control, absolute control, and that they wanted no participation except with those who had that same desire.[1]

Vestal's last line is the important one:

I realized that the Fundamentalists only desired control, total control, absolute control. . . .

Vestal underlined my own interpretation of the entire controversy, an interpretation I alluded to in my introduction to this book where I contend that the basic issue is freedom versus control. Despite the final report of the Peace Committee, which highlights the "theological sources" of the conflict, I insist that theology can only be described as the source of the controversy if one is speaking in the broadest of terms.

If by "theological sources" one means "worldview" or "approach to life," then I agree. That was certainly *the* single, generic issue in the conflict. If by "theological sources," however, one means "liberalism which is destroying the denomination"—as Fundamentalists repeatedly claimed—I most certainly disagree. The line in the Peace Committee Report that best described the situation accurately is this one:

The question for the majority of the Peace Committee, however, remains not whether there is diversity in the Southern Baptist Convention, *but how broad that diversity can be while still continuing to cooperate.*[2]

The simple truth is that Fundamentalism cannot tolerate much diversity; it craves uniformity. It thrives on control, not freedom. It must dominate and restrict and curb.

---

[1]See above, 253.
[2]See below, appendix 1, p. 297; italics added.

To ask why this is so is to get at the heart of the Fundamentalist mind-set, a mind-set many Americans and many Moderate Southern Baptists really do not and did not believe existed. It is a mind-set described by Eric Hoffer as the "true believer." A true believer thinks he or she has the truth, the whole truth, and nothing but the truth, unhindered by human limitations.

Samuel Hill, a leading interpreter of religion in the American South, has a helpful analysis of Southern Evangelical Protestantism which is applicable at this point. Hill says there are four types of Evangelicalism in the South: (1) the truth oriented, rightly called "Fundamentalist"; (2) the conversion oriented who are "evangelistic"; (3) the spiritually oriented, "devotional" in nature; and (4) the service oriented, "ethical" in nature and concerned with justice issues.[3] While one may find all four types in a single denomination and certainly in the SBC, one should also note a very significant attitudinal difference among the four types. Types 2, 3, and 4 tend to be inclusive, relational, and nonabsolutist. Type 1, the truth oriented, tends to be exclusive, rationalistic, and dogmatic.

It is a descriptive not a derogatory statement to say that this is the very nature of the type of Fundamentalism that captured the Southern Baptist Convention. When a Christian believes he or she has a monopoly on the gospel and others err because they do not agree with a certain interpretation, trust is out the window, reconciliation, as Daniel Vestal said, is impossible, and Christians with a different point of view are labeled dangerous and heretical. The uncompromising, nonnegotiating aspect of Fundamentalism can only be understood in light of their passionate conviction that Fundamentalists and Fundamentalists alone are the truth-people. They think they *are* being "fair" when they do not appoint people to committees who disagree with them. They think they *are* being "fair" when they want people fired from faculties who do not agree with them. They think they *are* being "fair" when they want only their kind appointed to positions of leadership in the denomination.

Some among the Fundamentalists, to be sure, are small and petulant people. We all know of people who fall into this category. They are not alone in this moral shortfall, however. On the other hand, I would argue that some among them are people of conscience. More convicted by a particular

---

[3]Samuel S. Hill, Jr., "The Shape and Shapes of Popular Southern Piety," in *Varieties of Southern Evangelicalism,* ed. David Edwin Harrell, Jr. (Macon GA: Mercer University Press, 1981) 99.

understanding of truth than they are mean in spirit, their passionate and unbending and inflexible understanding of truth makes them appear mean in spirit. Their understanding of truth simply must exclude rather than include because for them truth is more important than love, a point most Moderates think they would have trouble reconciling with Jesus' understanding of authentic religious faith. It should come as no surprise that the multivolume, celebrated Fundamentalist interpretation of the controversy is entitled *The Truth in Crisis*.

Some have looked at this controversy from the outside with astonishment at the intensity of the debate. Most of American Christendom would view *all* Southern Baptists as belonging to a relatively conservative brand of the faith. These outsiders would have said of Southern Baptists in the 1980s what Gerald Cragg said of the various groups of competing Separatists who during the seventeenth century were so concerned about the intricacies of church order:

> At first sight it might seem that there was much to unite them. They held the same basic beliefs; they had come through similar experiences. They provide convincing proof that nothing divides so bitterly as common convictions held with a difference.[4]

This approach to the controversy, in my judgement, caused a number of Southern Baptists, laity and clergy, to sit out the fight. The translation as I heard it often was: "Don't worry about it; it's just a preachers' fuss." By which the speaker meant it did not amount to much and that it was not very serious. That was a very common and very wrong judgment.

To say that the Fundamentalist-Moderate Controversy focused on the nature and interpretation of the Bible is to fail to understand the heart of the conflict. As I said in the introduction to this volume, the Bible issue is only one manifestation of the real issue. At bottom the Fundamentalist-Moderate war was a clash of worldviews; it was a clash between Christians who approach modernity with much fear and those who approach it with less fear. It was a family struggle between spouses, one of whom wanted to give the kids reasonable freedom while the other thought the kids needed rigid boundaries. Putting it in theological terms, Glenn Hinson described this as the struggle for the freedom of the Word of God.

---

[4]Gerald R. Cragg, *Freedom and Authority* (Philadelphia: Westminster Press, 1975) 222.

In some lectures at Southeastern Seminary in 1980, shortly after the conflict began, I compared this with past Southern Baptist controversies. I said at that time that the unique and most dangerous thing about this controversy is

> that we now have for the first time in the Southern Baptist Convention a highly organized, apparently well-funded, partisan political party who are going not only for the minds of the Southern Baptist people but for the machinery of the Southern Baptist Convention.[5]

I meant that Fundamentalists aimed to *control* what Southern Baptists think by controlling the political apparatus.

One of the books about this conflict that has never received adequate attention is Joe Edward Barnhart's *The Southern Baptist Holy War.* At times as rough on Moderates as on Fundamentalists, Barnhart points out that Moderates often accused the Fundamentalists of wanting only raw power. Acknowledging that there was some truth to the charge, Barnhart went on to say that much more was involved:

> To say that the leaders of the Inerrancy Party are trying to grab power for its own sake is to misunderstand them entirely. What they truly want is the power to maintain their worldview against the threat of erosion and collapse.[6]

Politics for the Fundamentalists had purpose. It was a vehicle of control. If you control the seminaries, you can control what students hear. If you control the Baptist Sunday School Board, you can control what is read in Sunday School literature. If you control the mission boards, you can control who is appointed as a missionary. If you control the Baptist Joint Committee, you control the issues of church and state. If you cannot control, you defund. What Fundamentalists do not control, they will not support. Thus, the Baptist Joint Committee was abandoned and the WMU had better be on guard! Truth-oriented Fundamentalism—and there is no other kind—seeks power for a purpose. They do not want to open up the system. They want to narrow it. They go for the jugular.

---

[5]Walter B. Shurden, "The Inerrancy Debate: A Comparative Study of Southern Baptist Controversies," *Baptist History and Heritage* 16/2 (April 1981): 18.

[6]Joe Edward Barnhart, *The Southern Baptist Holy War* (Austin TX: Texas Monthly Press, Inc., 1986) 172.

Some Myths Moderates Spun

I was intrigued by Jimmy Allen's selection of language in his paper as he spoke about "Old Myths and New Realities."[7] At a retreat of East Tennessee Moderates in 1987 at Gatlinburg, I chose as my subject "Some Myths of Moderates." In hindsight those myths are even clearer and easier to see now. Here are some of those myths which, in my judgment, seriously handicapped Moderates in the conflict.

The Myth of Denial. This one is first because it came first chronologically. "Aw, don't worry about these Fundamentalists; it's the same ole stuff; it comes around every few years; we'll handle them." It was the denial syndrome that said, "It can't happen here." It reminds me of the last words of Civil War general John Sedgwick as he raised his head above the parapet at the Battle of the Wilderness: "Nonsense, they couldn't hit an elephant at this dist. . . . "[8] Cecil Sherman was told this by committed Southern Baptist leaders as insightful as Dotson Nelson and Porter Routh.

I first heard it verbalized in the hotel lobby in Houston, Texas, at the conclusion of the 1979 SBC. Adrian Rogers had just soared to victory on a first-ballot presidential vote, something unusual in Southern Baptist life. The person who uttered this myth was, in my judgment, one of the best Southern Baptist "watchers" and interpreters around. My point is that this myth didn't come only from starry-eyed optimists unacquainted with the rigors of Baptist life. The man who sought to calm apprehensions in the hotel lobby was a seasoned veteran. He was wrong, and he later said so in strong editorials. While some tried to point out that the 1980s Fundamentalism was not merely a J. R. Graves–J. Frank Norris redivivus, the myth stuck long enough to keep some good people from acting soon enough to temper the action of others.

In fact, as one looks back at the early months and years of the controversy, a lull does appear in the Fundamentalist momentum. Note three events. First, in early May 1980, Adrian Rogers announced he would not seek a second presidential term because of his church responsibilities in Memphis. While that may in fact have been the case, those responsibilities must have slackened in the mid-1980s when Rogers accepted the SBC presidency two more times. One wonders if Rogers genuinely believed the

---

[7]See above, 93-100.
[8]As cited by Martin E. Marty, Context (15 April 1989): 6.

takeover was a possibility early on. Maybe Rogers had second thoughts about the entire enterprise. Second, later in the same month, May 1980, Fundamentalist patriarch W. A. Criswell, Paige Patterson's pastor and "supervisor," announced Patterson would withdraw from the Fundamentalist effort at electing SBC presidents. The methods adopted by Patterson and others, Criswell said, are "those of a different world" that Baptists tradition- ally disdain. Everybody in the Southern Baptist Convention should have known something new was in the mix when Criswell could not rein in Patterson and Pressler. Third, in a speech in Georgia in May 1982, Rogers voiced grave doubt that the SBC would ever go back to what he called a "moderately narrow theology."[9]

My guess is the Fundamentalists were as surprised at their developing momentum around 1984 as those non-Fundamentalists who articulated the Myth of Denial. Regardless of what the Fundamentalists thought of their possibilities, Myth One retarded rather than rallied a strong and early Moderate defense.

The Myth of the Pendulum. "This thing will run its course in three or four years; things will swing back; this is just part of the pendulum syndrome; you just watch." Historical precedent supported this myth. The attack of J. Frank Norris on the SBC was a problem within the convention for about five years. The real heat came between 1921 and 1926. The Elliott Controversy lasted almost three years (1961–1963), as did the Broadman conflict (1969–1972). Some Moderates would not believe the promised persistence of Pressler-Patterson.

The pendulum never swung back; it got stuck in the far right corner. Waiting for it to return, some well-intentioned people did nothing to swing it back. In my judgment, they will not, cannot now swing it back. Only history, and great-grandchildren, can do that now.

The Myth of Fundamentalist Infighting. "You watch what I'm telling you. They will turn on each other and start fighting among themselves; they've got too many egotists among them." As we Moderates should have known and confessed, Fundamentalists have no monopoly on egotism. While I look forward to hearing the Fundamentalist side of this story to see if in fact there were ever any serious fissures in their ranks, my observation

---

[9]James C. Hefley, *The Conservative Resurgence* (Hannibal MO: Hannibal Books, 1991) 50. This is the fifth volume by Hefley on the controversy, written from the Fundamentalist perspective. The first four volumes were entitled *The Truth in Crisis* (see n. 11 below).

argues for more unity among them than among us. Our leadership rotated; theirs remained constant. As often pointed out, it did not take a Caribbean cruise ship to transport their decision makers. Cecil Sherman says they could have ridden in a minivan. I think they could have been comfortable in a pickup truck if it did not have bucket seats. They needed room for only three, and by the middle of the decade Adrian Rogers was driving.

In the paragraph above I said Fundamentalists had more unity than the Moderates. That is true, but I do not mean to suggest there were serious cracks in the Moderate movement, pasted together by runs at the SBC presidency. Much has been made in some of the papers about the Moderate meeting at Mercer University in August 1986, where first emerged the talk about a new organization, later to be the Southern Baptist Alliance. Buried in footnote four of Alan Neely's paper is an important and nuanced distinction between what came to be "Baptists Committed" and the earlier "Southern Baptist Alliance." Speaking of the emerging "Baptists Committed," Neely said:

> This political coalition came to be known as "Baptists Committed," and most of those who later came to be identified with beginning the Alliance supported financially and otherwise the "Baptists Committed" efforts. It is only fair to say that we in the Alliance nourished little hope that the Fundamentalists could be turned back. But our pessimism and sometimes privately voiced cynicism did not prevent us from going to the Convention meetings and voting for the Baptists Committed candidates, hoping somehow to break the stranglehold Pressler, Patterson, and Rogers had on the Convention.[10]

In the mid-1980s the major distinction within the Moderate ranks was between the pessimists and the hopers, but they were never at cross purposes in wanting to stop the onslaught.

The Myth of Culture. "When the general culture changes, Fundamentalists will be done in. They are just riding the crest of the cultural waves." SBC Fundamentalists elected their first SBC president in June 1979. That November the American people elected Ronald Reagan. From 1980 through 1992 the country was in the hands of Reagan-Bush and the religious and political right. Falwell and Bakker and Swaggart and Oral Roberts were big time. The eighties, as Martin Marty once observed, was a time when the world was moving away from toleration, not toward it. I do not believe the

---

[10]See above, 107n.6.

spirit of the times determines debates within religious groups, but it certainly contributes, enormously so.

The problem with this myth is that it was partly true. Fundamentalists were riding the crest of culture, but the culture lasted long enough for the Fundamentalists to accomplish their goals within the SBC. At this stage of Southern Baptist history, don't bet on a swing back during the Clinton years, no matter how long they last. Fundamentalism is just now getting its power in place with the executive leadership of the denomination. The boards and agencies are firmly stacked with Pressler-Patterson types, and the Moderates are no longer there to challenge. Bill Clinton is no John Kennedy and he will not take this country back into the 1960s. Even if he did, Southern Baptists won't budge. After all, the SBC was a conservative denomination in the 1960s. It has become a Fundamentalist denomination in the 1980s, and it will stalk into the next century stoutly resisting modernity.

The Myth of Money. "You watch what I am telling you; they are not going to support the convention financially; they are independent Fundamentalists." While that may be true of some of their leadership, some of whom "rule" over denominations in their own local churches and, therefore, have no need for denominational life, it is certainly not true of all. I have always thought Fundamentalists will pay for what they control. Watch some of the huge Fundamentalist churches whose pastors have been elected presidents of the SBC inch up their meager percentage contributions. Moreover, they will be happy to collect non-Fundamentalist monies for added support. The question for non-Fundamentalists in Southern Baptist life is: Will you pay for what they control and permit taxation without representation?

James Hefley is a nice guy who has written some very slanted books under the guise of neutrality and journalistic objectivity which the Baptist Bookstores once childishly refused to sell in the name of denominational peacekeeping. Hefley is the author of a five-volume set on the "history" of the controversy written from the Fundamentalist viewpoint. He has a wealth of information in those five books. And although we have been on different sides of the conflict, I found it easy to agree with some of his predictions about the outcome. In his first volume (1986) his closing chapter is entitled "Scenarios and Solutions." Discussing the fate of the Cooperative Program, the financial lifeline of the SBC, Hefley said,

> Exactly the opposite of what moderates have been predicting could happen. The Cooperative Program could take on new vigor as bellwether conservative churches up their percentages.[11]

In the margin of my copy of the book I wrote "True."

While it may not deal precisely with the myth at hand, it is appropriate at this point to say a word about the role of money in the controversy. The controversy cost money—lots of money on both sides. Money and the security it represented silenced some, probably caused others to speak out only to hush up later, but could not silence some others, such as Randall Lolley, courageous past-president of Southeastern Seminary. Moreover, the money trail will be the best index to the gradual split or splintering within the SBC. As with Fundamentalists before them, Moderate money will follow Moderate loyalties. If you want to know if and how much the SBC has cracked, ask people where they are sending their money and for what.

All of that notwithstanding, Fundamentalists will support what they control. Myth Five underestimates the significance of control for Fundamentalism. It also overestimated the loyalties of non-Fundamentalists to support, in the words of Adrian Rogers, what is "theologically repugnant" to them.

The Myth of Mellowing. "Fundamentalists will mellow when they get in power and be fairer; besides, there is so much pluralism in the SBC they will have to temper their extremism once they are in control." Tell that to Keith Parks, Al Shackleford, Dan Martin, Randall Lolley, James Dunn, Larry Baker, the former faculty members at Southeastern Seminary and all the women in ministry in the Southern Baptist Convention; but in the words of Carlyle Marney, a true Southern Baptist liberal, "Don't try to take up a collection!"

During some of the earliest years of the conflict Fundamentalists claimed that what they were after was "parity" in the denomination. Speaking for and of the Fundamentalists in 1985, Paige Patterson said,

> They do seek genuine parity in the faculties and administrations of the schools and insist that employees of the convention never, under any circumstances, call into question any statement of the Bible or say anything that might be construed as disbelief in the veracity of the Scriptures.[12]

---

[11]James C. Hefley, *The Truth in Crisis* (Dallas: Criterion Publications, 1986) 217.

[12]Paige Patterson, "Stalemate," *The Theological Educator,* Special Issue (1985): 10.

Note the two parts of the statement. First, said Patterson, Fundamentalists "seek genuine parity." "Parity" was the Fundamentalist buzzword in the early phases of the controversy. But since the overwhelming number of trustees on the various boards are now in the far-right camp, nothing more is heard of "parity." Parity has become "preeminence" and preeminence has been transformed into a theological cleansing.

In the second part of his statement, Patterson said, "that employees of the convention never under any circumstances, call into question any statement of the Bible or say anything that might be construed as disbelief in the veracity of the Scriptures." Candidly, this means one must toe the Fundamentalist line of biblical interpretation. Only a little more than a year after making that statement, Patterson indicated his group was tightening the noose and that it would tie the hiring of denominational employees to the Fundamentalist positions on abortion, euthanasia, school prayer, and federal budget reduction. Speaking of establishing the sociopolitical agenda in denominational life, Patterson said that he thought it would "go over nearly as well as the inerrancy thing."[13]

Parity was never the ultimate goal of the Pressler-Patterson coalition, although at one point it may have been what they thought they could realistically achieve. Ask any one of their leaders, now that they are ensconced in the seats of power, if that is still all they want. It really is not. It never was. And this is so because the Fundamentalist mindset is "truth-oriented." The inflexible component of Fundamentalism can only be understood in light of the Fundamentalist conviction that they are the truth-bearers. The history of this controversy verifies that the more power Fundamentalists get, the more rigid their posture becomes. Southern Baptists have experienced a growing hostility, not a growing civility, among its right wing. No one should be surprised at the tightening of the noose around the denominational neck. For a case study of the meaning of "parity" to Fundamentalists see Robert Parham's discussion ("The History of the Baptist Center for Ethics," above) of developments at the Christian Life Commission after Foy Valentine resigned.

The Myth of Isolation. "It won't affect our church; it doesn't matter what they do at the Southern Baptist Convention, we'll do what we want to do at the local church level." This was and is a blissful denial of the

---

[13]Brad Owens, "Patterson Thrusts Social Agenda into Fray," *The Baptist Messenger,* 26 June 1986, 4.

churchly nature of the SBC. Most Southern Baptists do not recognize how centralized an ecclesiastical organization the Southern Baptist Convention really is. To his credit, Paige Patterson does, and at one stage he insisted he wanted to do something about it. Now that he is a denominational executive, I hope he still does.

In recent years I have noticed that the phrase "The Southern Baptist Church" has appeared in print, especially in letters to editors. While that is a misinformed garbling of Baptist polity, I fear it represents something of the reality. Southern Baptists have "cooperated" themselves into a "super church." The connectionalism is so strong between the local church, the state convention and the national convention that one has great difficulty discerning the numerous points where local church autonomy has been sacrificed.

Paige Patterson is correct when he says there is "an unhealthy and subtle form of connectionalism in our ecclesiastical structure which must be resisted."[14] Local churches, not state conventions, should determine what portion of their funds should go to national causes and which ones.

Those who said, "It won't bother our local church" were not thinking. The controversy will "bother" the kind of ministry that is produced in the seminaries, the kind of literature that is produced at the Sunday School Board, the kind of books published at Broadman, the kind of missionaries appointed by the mission agencies, the kind of history written, the kind of music sung, the kind of family life portrayed, the kind of ethical issues tackled, and the kind of opportunities our daughters and granddaughters will have in the denomination. Local churches, affiliated with the SBC, do not live in blissful isolation.

Why Moderates Lost and Fundamentalists Won

Some of the contributing factors to the Moderate loss and the Funda-mentalist victory may be found in the discussion above on the Moderate myths. Most all those myths—the myth of denial, the myth of the pendulum, the myth of culture—and the attitudes behind them are to some degree responsible for the debacle of the SBC. I would, however, like to address more specifically the issue of why the controversy turned out the way it did even though I have little, if anything, new to add to what Ammerman,

---

[14]Paige Patterson, "My Vision of the Twenty-First Century SBC," *Review and Expositor* 88 (Winter 1991): 46.

Barnhart, Hefley, Leonard, and others have surmised at some length. I would like to echo some of what the contributors to this volume have said and offer a reflection or two.

Of course, there is a simple theological answer to explain the results: *God willed it.* Fundamentalists, unfortunately but not unsurprisingly, use this occasionally. Paige Patterson described the controversy euphemistically as "the goals of theological renewal and bureaucratic reduction which some of us attempted to facilitate" as having been "the commandment of God." Patterson knows, of course, that "winning" or "losing" are not signs of God's will.

There is also a simple pragmatic explanation for the Fundamentalist victory. *Fundamentalists persuaded more messengers to attend the annual conventions and vote for their presidential candidate than did the Moderates.* It is just that simple. It is easy now to say, "Moderates could never have won." As a matter of fact that is simply not the case. If Moderates had gone to the conventions in greater numbers, they would have won. More to the question at hand is why Moderates were unsuccessful in doing that.

If you read the previous chapters carefully you will find some interesting explanations of factors that contributed to the Moderate loss. John Hewett, while he certainly would not identify it as *the* cause of defeat, rightly identified the importance of the Fundamentalists' "ownership" of the SBC Pastor's Conference, the largest and most influential of all the pre-Convention meetings. The Pastor's Conference gave Fundamentalists a crucial platform immediately prior to the SBC presidential election, and they used it effectively.

James Slatton named money as an important factor, especially the Moderate need for more money to finance the political efforts. Cecil Sherman rattled off a litany of contributing causes: the Moderate ambivalence about being political, Moderates' changing leadership and reluctant followship, the inaccurate charge of liberalism, the silence of closet Moderates, and the betrayal of denominational leadership when it counted, the last being exceedingly important in Sherman's eyes.

The primary interpretation that runs through this and other studies regarding why Moderates lost is the one that ought to be most instructive to other denominations. It is found in the words of James Slatton:

> We always worked with the disadvantage that Moderates were, by defini-
> tion, *moderate*.[15]

Even when he singled out the monetary issue, Slatton went on to say, "This,
of course reflected an even more basic factor—Moderates in general lacked
the willingness to do what had to be done to prevail." I concur. Passion
won; moderation lost. Sherman may have said it best:

> Moderates did not have enough moral energy to win. We could not bring
> ourselves to use moral language to describe our cause. Truth was butch-
> ered. We said nothing. Good people were defamed. We were silent. Baptist
> principles were mangled and Baptist history was replaced, rewritten. All
> the while, teachers who could have written about the problems in calling
> the Bible inerrant, did not. And preachers who could have called us to
> arms said nothing. The want of moral energy was the undoing of the
> Moderate movement.[16]

I repeat, I doubt if there is a more important lesson for onlookers to learn
from this unholy Southern Baptist War.

Consequences: Centripetal and Centrifugal Motions

The results of the conflict, other than victory for Fundamentalists and defeat
for Moderates, are numerous. For example, the absolutely unspeakable
human pain on both sides is incalculable. At the first meeting of the interim
steering committee of what came to be the Cooperative Baptist Fellowship,
someone asked a room full of Moderates how many had ever dreamed about
the controversy in one way or another? I think I am correct when I say
every person present raised a hand. What some dismissed as a "preachers'
fuss" had gripped our unconscious; it had invaded the very depth of our
lives. In truth, the personal pain is absolutely impossible to quantify.

What one can observe today are two forces presently at work in the
SBC. Like so many of the revivals the SBC has promoted, these are
"simultaneous" forces; they work concurrently. These are forces of central-
ization and fragmentation. They both consolidate and separate, pull inward
and outward.

However one evaluates the conflict, this much is true: a constrictionism
has occurred within. The major centripetal force is, as one would expect,
theological. The tightening theology has expressed itself in a number of

---

[15]See above, 56.
[16]See above, 44.

ways. One is that the Southern Baptist Convention has become more creedalistic. This is a charge the Fundamentalists bristle at and deny, because they know they have stepped outside the Baptist heritage. While eschewing the word "creeds," they now speak of doctrinal "parameters." Yet the public statements of some of the Fundamentalist SBC presidents and the writings of Paige Patterson support the assessment that the SBC has become more creedalistic. In the interest of integrity and clarity, they would be better served to state this publicly. In addition to the 1963 "Baptist Faith and Message," Fundamentalists now call for compliance to the "Glorieta Statement," the "Peace Committee Report," and "The Chicago Statement on Biblical Inerrancy."

The constricting theology has also expressed itself in narrowing the role of women and in minimizing the prominence of the laity while maximizing the authority of the pastor. Likewise, no longer do all Southern Baptists have the opportunity to serve their denomination on boards and agencies. Only those who can pass the Fundamentalist litmus tests are now accepted. The narrowed theology has also witnessed an increasing restriction in SBC programming. The Baptist Joint Committee on Public Affairs has been defunded and is no longer an SBC enterprise, and something of the same now threatens the WMU. Diversity of points of view are no longer present in the Southern Baptist literature published by the Baptist Sunday School Board. These are only a few of the results of the centripetal forces at work within the SBC.

Centrifugal currents are swirling at the same time. Thinking that nothing much will come of the efforts of Moderates in the Cooperative Baptist Fellowship, Fundamentalists minimize the defection with the use of the term "splinter groups" and "splintering." Maybe so. The fact of the matter, however, is that some flagship Southern Baptist churches are saying "no" to the Fundamentalizing of the SBC. In a matter of two years the CBF has become the single largest financial contributor to the Rüschlikon Baptist Seminary, the Baptist Joint Committee on Public Affairs, and the new Baptist Theological Seminary at Richmond.

The "splintering" of SBC denominationalism is occurring on every front. Educationally it is easy to see. In addition to the independent Fundamentalist schools—Criswell, Mid-America Seminary, and Luther Rice Seminary, all of which the SBC could easily adopt—the six Southern Baptist seminaries now must compete for students with several other Baptist programs. These are Beeson Divinity School which tilts toward the new SBC establishment, the Baptist Theological Seminary at Richmond, clearly Moderate, the proposed seminaries at Baylor and Gardner-Webb College, and the increasingly popular Baptist Studies programs at Emory and Duke. Complicating the situation for the SBC schools is the fact that most of the Baptist religion faculties in the state Baptist colleges and universities are decidedly Moderate and will doubtless be more supportive of some of the new educational ventures.

Fragmentation has also occurred within the publishing realm. Smyth & Helwys Publishers are now producing books as well as Sunday School literature for the churches. Glad River Publications is also making itself known. Moderate Baptists have created a new ethics agency, a new historical society, a new Baptist press, and they have published since 1983 a national newspaper, _Baptists Today._ Loosening the SBC monopoly on itself, the WMU has acted to serve all Baptists with its powerful missionary education programs.

No one would argue that these activities of Moderates will bring down the powerful and influential SBC. We will all have to wait, however, to see how big the "splinter" becomes, for the "splintering" is in process.

Special Report:
SBC Peace Committee

Appendix I[1]

Introduction

During the 1985 annual meeting of the Southern Baptist Convention in Dallas, 11-13 June 1985, a special committee was created to attempt to determine the sources of the current controversy in the Southern Baptist Convention and to make findings and recommendations to resolve it. The motion, overwhelmingly adopted, says:

> With gratitude for God's bountiful blessings on us as Southern Baptists and with recognition of our unparalleled opportunity to confront every person on earth with the gospel of Christ by the year 2000 and with acknowledgment of divisions among us, which, if allowed to continue, inevitably will impede our progress, impair our fellowship, and imperil our future; and after much prayer, we offer the following motion:
>
> That a special committee be authorized by this Convention, in session, in Dallas, June 1985; and
>
> That this committee seek to determine the sources of the controversies in our Convention, and make findings and recommendations regarding these controversies, so that Southern Baptists might effect reconciliation and effectively discharge their responsibilities to God by cooperating

---

[1]The record of discussion and action regarding the special report of the Peace Committee is on pp. 54-55 (item #153) of the *Annual of the Southern Baptist Convention 1987*. The report was adopted at the Tuesday evening session (16 June 1987) of the SBC in St. Louis. The report as adopted—and as essentially reproduced here—appears on pp. 232-42 of the 1987 *Annual*.

together to accomplish evangelism, missions, Christian education, and other causes authorized by our Constitution, all to the glory of God. "By this shall all men know that ye are my disciples, if ye have love one to another" (John 13:35) (John 17:21); and

That this committee follow the 1963 Baptist Faith and Message Statement in regard to theological issues, and operate within the Constitution and Bylaws of the Southern Baptist Convention; and

That to accomplish its work, this committee shall recognize the role of trustees and shall work with and through appropriate boards, commissions, and agencies of the Southern Baptist Convention. This committee shall report on the progress of its work to each meeting of the Executive Committee. The trustees, boards, and agencies of the Southern Baptist Convention, and their officers and employees, shall fully cooperate with the committee to accomplish the purposes outlined in this motion; and

The staffing and professional advice for this committee shall be in accord with the Business and Financial Plan of the Southern Baptist Convention. Funding shall come from Cooperative Program funds received by the Executive Committee as a priority item before the percentage division and allocation of the Southern Baptist Convention Cooperative Program Allocation Budget; and

That the committee may conduct its business in open sessions, and may hold public hearings, but, the committee may also hold executive sessions to accomplish its work; and

That any vacancy, or vacancies, on the special committee be filled by the Executive Committee at its next meeting after such vacancy occurs. In the filling of any such vacancy, balance of representation shall be maintained; and

That the committee may make its final report and recommendation to the 1986 Southern Baptist Convention and request that it be discharged, or the committee may make a preliminary report to the 1986 Convention and may recommend that the special committee be continued in existence for an additional year, in which instance the committee shall make its final report and recommendation to the 1987 Southern Baptist Convention; and

That all Southern Baptists be urged to exercise restraint, to refrain from divisive action and comments, and to reflect Christian love while this committee is doing its work; and

That the following persons be designated to serve on the special committee: Charles G. Fuller, chairman; Harmon M. Born, Doyle E. Carlton, Jr., Mrs. Morris H. Chapman, *William O. Crews, Robert E. Cuttino, Mrs. A. Harrison Gregory, Jim Henry, William E. Hull, Herschel H. Hobbs, Albert McClellan, Charles W. Pickering, William E. Poe, Ray E. Roberts,

Adrian P. Rogers, *Cecil E. Sherman, John Sullivan, Daniel G. Vestal, Jerry Vines, Edwin H. Young, *Charles F. Stanley, *Winfred Moore.

*Note: William O. Crews was elected president of Golden Gate Baptist Theological Seminary 13 October 1986 but was asked to remain as a member; Cecil E. Sherman resigned from the special committee 22 October 1986 and was replaced by Peter James Flamming; Charles F. Stanley and W. Winfred Moore served by virtue of office as president and first vice-president of the Convention, and were asked to remain after their terms of office expired.

Since its creation, the Peace Committee has met fourteen times. Following each meeting, a report was given to Southern Baptists by Chairman Charles G. Fuller through the denominational news service Baptist Press.

In keeping with its assignment, the Peace Committee has determined what it believes to be the primary sources of the controversy, has made findings in reference to those sources, and, in this report, is making recommendations as to possible ways to effect reconciliation.

Sources of the Controversy

During its first meeting, the Peace Committee determined the primary source of the controversy is theological differences, but found there are political causes as well.

Theological Sources. In meeting after meeting of the Peace Committee, talk turned to the nature of inspiration of the Scriptures, often to the point of preempting the committee's established agenda. Gradually it became clear that while there might be other theological differences, the authority of the Word of God is the focus of differences. The primary source of the controversy in the Southern Baptist Convention is the Bible; more specifically, the ways in which the Bible is viewed.

All Baptists see the Bible as authoritative; the question is the extent and nature of its authority. The differences in recent years have developed around the phrase in Article I of the Baptist Faith and Message statement of 1963, that the Bible "has . . . truth without any mixture of error for its matter."

The action which created the Peace Committee instructed it to follow the Baptist Faith and Message statement of 1963 in regard to theological issues. Although the statement includes a preamble and seventeen articles, the committee has focused primarily on article 1, "The Scriptures":

> The Holy Bible was written by men divinely inspired and is the record of
> God's revelation of Himself to man. It is a perfect treasure of divine

instruction. It has God for its author, salvation for its end, and truth, without any mixture of error, for its matter. It reveals the principles by which God judges us; and therefore is, and will remain to the end of the world, the true center of Christian union, and the supreme standard by which all human conduct, creeds, and religious opinions should be tried. The criterion by which the Bible is to be interpreted in Jesus Christ.

Herschel H. Hobbs, a member of the Peace Committee and chairman of the committee which wrote the 1963 Baptist Faith and Message statement, explained the phrase "truth without any mixture of error for its matter" by reference to 2 Timothy 3:16 which says, "all Scripture is given by inspiration of God." He explained: "The Greek New Testament reads 'all'—without the definite article—and that means every single part of the whole is God-breathed. And a God of truth does not breathe error." Dr. Hobbs made the comments during the 1981 annual meeting of the Southern Baptist Convention in Los Angeles, California.

Using article 1 of the Baptist Faith and Message statement of 1963 as a yardstick, Peace Committee subcommittees visited each of the Southern Baptist seminaries and five other agencies: the Foreign Mission Board, the Home Mission Board, Baptist Sunday School Board, Historical Commission, and Christian Life Commission. Following those visits, the committee adopted a "Statement of Theological Diversity."

> The Peace Committee has completed a preliminary investigation of the theological situation in our SBC seminaries. We have found significant theological diversity within our seminaries, reflective of the diversity within our wider constituency. These divergences are found among those who claim to hold a high view of Scripture and to teach in accordance with, and not contrary to, the Baptist Faith and Message statement of 1963.
>
> Examples of this diversity include the following, which are intended to be illustrative but not exhaustive.
>
> (1) Some accept and affirm the direct creation and historicity of Adam and Eve while others view them instead as representative of the human race in its creation and fall.
>
> (2) Some understand the historicity of every event in Scripture as reported by the original source while others hold that the historicity can be clarified and revised by the findings of modern historical scholarship.
>
> (3) Some hold to the stated authorship of every book in the Bible while others hold that in some cases such attribution may not refer to the final author or may be pseudonymous.
>
> (4) Some hold that every miracle in the Bible is intended to be taken as a historical event while others hold that some miracles are intended to be taken as parabolic.

The Peace Committee is working earnestly to find ways to build bridges between those holding divergent views so that we may all legitimately coexist and work together in harmony to accomplish our common mission. Please pray that we may find ways to use our diversity to win the greatest number to faith in Christ as Savior and Lord.

Early in its second year, the Peace Committee continued to discuss theological concerns, including the fact that there are at least two separate and distinct interpretations of article 1 of the Baptist Faith and Message statement of 1963, reflective of the diversity present in the Convention. One view holds that when the article says the Bible has "truth without any mixture of error for its matter," it means *all* areas—historical, scientific, theological, and philosophical. The other holds the "truth" relates only to matters of faith and practice.

The Committee discussed whether the faculties of the SBC seminaries adequately reflect the views of many Southern Baptists who believe in the first interpretation. A Peace Committee subcommittee met with the six seminary presidents to communicate the need for the faculties to reflect the beliefs of these Southern Baptists.

In October 1986 the Peace Committee held a prayer retreat at Glorieta Baptist Conference Center near Santa Fe, New Mexico, attended by the Peace Committee and leaders of all national agencies. During that meeting, the seminary presidents presented a statement of their intentions which has become known as the "Glorieta Statement":

[The Glorieta Statement—22 October 1986][2]

We, the presidents of the six SBC seminaries,[3] through prayerful and careful reflection and dialogue, have unanimously agreed to declare these commitments regarding our lives and our work with Southern Baptists.

We believe that Christianity is supernatural in its origin and history. We repudiate every theory of religion which denies the supernatural elements in our faith. The miracles of the Old and New Testaments are historical evidences of God's judgment, love, and redemption.

---

[2]The subtitle—added here for convenience—does not appear in the *Annual*.
[3]Five presidents were at the Oct 1986 retreat: Milton Ferguson (Midwestern), Landrum P. Leavell II (New Orleans), W. Randall Lolley (Southeastern), Roy L. Honeycutt (Southern), and Russell H. Dilday (Southwestern). Coincidentally, William O. Crews, a member of the peace committee, had been elected on 13 Oct as the new president of Golden Gate, but did not assume the post until 1 Dec.

We believe that the Bible is fully inspired; it is "God-breathed" (2 Timothy 3:16), utterly unique. No other book or collection of books can justify that claim. The sixty-six books of the Bible are not errant in any area of reality. We hold to their infallible power and binding authority.

We believe that our six seminaries are fulfilling the purposes assigned to them by the Southern Baptist Convention. Nevertheless, we acknowledge that they are not perfect institutions. We recognize that there are legitimate concerns regarding them which we are addressing.

We commit ourselves therefore to the resolution of the problems which beset our beloved denomination. We are ready and eager to be partners in the peace process. Specifically

(1) We reaffirm our seminary confessional statements, and we will enforce compliance by the persons signing them.

(2) We will foster in our classrooms a balanced, scholarly frame of reference for presenting fairly the entire spectrum of scriptural interpretations represented by our constituencies. We perceive this to be both good education and good cooperation.

(3) We respect the convictions of all Southern Baptists and we repudiate the caricature and intimidation of persons for their theological beliefs.

(4) We commit ourselves to fairness in selecting faculty, lecturers, and chapel speakers across the theological spectrum of our Baptist constituency.

(5) We will lead our seminary communities in spiritual revival, personal discipleship, Christian lifestyle, and active churchmanship.

(6) We will deepen and strengthen the spirit of evangelism and missions on our campuses while emphasizing afresh the distinctive doctrines of our Baptist heritage.

(7) We have scheduled for Southern Baptists three national conferences.

A Conference on Biblical Inerrancy, 1987*

A Conference on Biblical Interpretation, 1988

A Conference on Biblical Imperatives, 1989

*Note: The first conference, focusing on biblical inerrancy, was held at Ridgecrest Baptist Conference Center 4-7 May 1987 with more than 1,000 in attendance.

We share these commitments with the hope that all Southern Baptists will join us in seeking "the wisdom from above" in our efforts toward reconciliation: "The wisdom from above is first pure, then peaceable, gentle, open to reason, full of mercy and good fruits, without uncertainty or insincerity." (James 3:17)

The Peace Committee affirmed the Glorieta Statement and ceased its official inquiry, referring unanswered questions and unresolved issues back to the administrators and trustees of Southern Baptist Theological Seminary,

Southeastern Baptist Theological Seminary, and Midwestern Baptist Theological Seminary, hoping the results of their actions would be satisfactory to the Convention at large.

During the committee's December 1986 meeting, additional questions arose as to the meaning and the implementation of the Glorieta Statement.

The seminary presidents report that their efforts to implement the Statement have included an effort to recruit conservative scholars to fill faculty vacancies, expansion of reading lists, invitations to conservative scholars to address chapel and other events, a commitment to treat all persons fairly, and expanded evangelistic and missions activities on campus.

The question for the majority of the Peace Committee, however, remains not whether there is diversity in the Southern Baptist Convention, but how broad that diversity can be while still continuing to cooperate.

Political Sources. In the opinion of the Peace Committee, the controversy of the last decade began as a theological concern. When people of good intention became frustrated because they felt their convictions on Scripture were not seriously dealt with, they organized politically to make themselves heard. Soon, another group formed to counter the first and the political process intensified.

The Peace Committee, primarily through its Political Activities Subcommittee, has studied charges and countercharges regarding political activity. It has looked at many issues, including

Restructuring the Constitution and Bylaws of the Southern Baptist Convention to limit the appointive powers of the president; restructuring the way in which the annual meeting is held, specifically shifting the pre-Convention meetings to post-Convention meetings; cooperation between the Pastors' Conference and the SBC Forum; discussing the coverage of personalities and issues in the controversy by the official and unofficial news media outlets; the use of descriptive terms and labels for the various groups; "de-politicizing" the Convention by asking the various groups to "stand down" from political activities; instituting stricter means of messenger registration and voting to prevent misuse of the registration and voting processes at annual meetings.

A primary area of discussion was changing the Constitution and Bylaws of the Convention to restrict the appointive powers of the president. However, the majority of the committee's members feel the basic Convention structure has served Southern Baptists well and should not now be changed.

The Committee investigated numerous charges of political malfeasance and voter irregularity. It heard a detailed report, complete with statistical analysis, on messenger participation at annual meetings, presented by the SBC registration secretary and Convention manager, as well as the chairman of a special study committee appointed by the SBC Executive Committee. Although the reports included isolated instances of registration and ballot abuse, there was no evidence of widespread or organized misuse of the ballot by any political group and no evidence of massive voter irregularities related to annual meetings.

The Political Activities Subcommittee, as well as a special ad hoc committee, dealt with the question of a parliamentarian for the annual meeting. The matter was deferred in 1986, because then SBC president Charles F. Stanley appointed a certified parliamentarian to assist him at the Atlanta annual meeting. The Committee is recommending a new bylaw be prepared concerning the appointment of a certified parliamentarian and two assistant parliamentarians for the annual meeting.

A special subcommittee also looked into the possibility of "negative designation" or "selective support" of agencies through the Cooperative Program, but concluded that a change in the basic structure of the unified giving plan would not provide significant help in resolving the crisis.

Some of the issues have been brought forward as recommendations from the Peace Committee. Others were not deemed sufficiently significant to warrant recommendations at this time.

Findings

The Peace Committee has made findings on Scripture and on politics.

On Theology. The Committee found there is significant diversity in the understanding of article 1 "On Scripture" of the Baptist Faith and Message statement of 1963. The Committee found there are at least two separate and distinct interpretations of the article. One holding "truth without any mixture of error for its matter" means *all* areas—historical, scientific, theological, and philosophical. The other holds "truth" relates only to matters of faith and practice.

The Committee, discussing whether the faculties of the SBC seminaries adequately reflect the views of many Southern Baptists who believe in the first interpretation, found there was not a theological balance represented in the faculties at Southern Baptist Theological Seminary or Southeastern Baptist Theological Seminary.

The Committee adopted two statements concerning its findings on theology, one a "foundational" statement, and the other a more elaborate statement.

1. *The Foundational Statement on Theology.* The Committee agreed the following Scripture references should be read as an introduction to the "Foundational Statement on Theology": Deuteronomy 4:2; Joshua 1:7; Psalm 119:160; Matthew 5:18; 2 Timothy 3:16; Revelation 22:10.

It is the conclusion of the majority of the Peace Committee that the cause of peace within the Southern Baptist Convention will be greatly enhanced by the affirmation of the whole Bible as being "not errant in any area of reality."

Therefore, we exhort the trustees and administrators of our seminaries and other agencies affiliated with or supported by the Southern Baptist Convention to faithfully discharge their responsibility to carefully preserve the doctrinal integrity of our institutions receiving our support, and only employ professional staff who believe in the divine inspiration of the whole Bible and that the Bible is "truth without any mixture of error."

The Committee also adopted the more elaborate statement on Scripture.

2. *The Statement on Scripture.* We, as a Peace Committee, affirm biblical authority for all of life and for all fields of knowledge. The Bible is a book of redemption, not a book of science, psychology, sociology, or economics. But, where the Bible speaks, the Bible speaks truth in all realms of reality and to all fields of knowledge. The Bible, when properly interpreted, is authoritative to all of life.

We, as a Peace Committee, reaffirm the Baptist commitment to the absolute authority of Scripture and to the historic Baptist position that the Bible has "truth without any mixture of error for its matter." We affirm that the narratives of Scripture are historically and factually accurate. We affirm that the historic accounts of the miraculous and the supernatural are truthful as given by God and recorded by the biblical writers.

We, as a Peace Committee, have found that most Southern Baptists see "truth without any mixture of error for its matter" as meaning, for example, that

(1) They believe in direct creation of mankind and therefore they believe Adam and Eve were real persons.

(2) They believe the named authors did indeed write the biblical books attributed to them by those books.

(3) They believe the miracles described in Scripture did indeed occur as supernatural events in history.

(4) They believe that the historical narratives given by biblical authors are indeed accurate and reliable as given by those authors.

We call upon Southern Baptist institutions to recognize the great number of Southern Baptists who believe this interpretation of our confessional statement and, in the future, to build their professional staffs and faculties from those who clearly reflect such dominant convictions and beliefs held by Southern Baptists at large.

However, some members of the Peace Committee differ from this viewpoint. They would hold that "truth without any mixture of error" relates only to faith and practice. They would also prefer a broader theological perspective. Yet, we have learned to live together on the Peace Committee in mutual charity and commitment to each other. We pledge our mutual efforts to fulfill the Great Commission, and we call on others within our Convention to make the same pledge.

On Politics. The Committee has found that the sources of the political aspect of the controversy are long-standing. Historically, informal political groups or coalitions have emerged in Southern Baptist life. Prior to the last decade, most of these groups operated informally by word of mouth among mutual acquaintances interested in selecting the leadership of the Southern Baptist Convention. More recently, these groups have developed organized coalitions centered around theological perceptions and committed to electing leadership committed to a particular viewpoint. The effort has been largely successful, but led to the formation of a countereffort which has increased hostility and turned up the heat on the controversy.

After its investigation, the Peace Committee found "that the extent of political activity . . . at the present time creates distrust, diminishes our ability to do missions and evangelism, is detrimental to our influence, and impedes our ability to serve our Lord."

The Committee adopted two statements, one a "foundational" statement and the other a more elaborate statement.

1. *The Foundational Statement on Politics.* It is the unanimous conclusion of the Peace Committee that fairness in the appointive process will contribute to peace.

Therefore, we exhort the present and future presidents of the Southern Baptist Convention, the Committee on Committees, and the Committee on Boards to select nominees who endorse the Baptist Faith and Message statement and are drawn in balanced fashion from the broad spectrum of loyal, cooperative Southern Baptists, representative of the diversity of our denomination.

The more elaborate statement on politics was also adopted.

2. *The Statement on Politics.* Politics are intrinsically a part of congregational polity, that is, voting, public and private discussions, influencing others to share one's view.

Historically, informal political groups or coalitions have emerged in Southern Baptist life. Prior to the last decade, most of these groups operated informally by word of mouth among mutual acquaintances interested in selecting the leadership of the Southern Baptist Convention. More recently, these groups have developed organized coalitions centered on theological perceptions and individual leaders committed to a defined viewpoint. These coalitions have adopted political strategies for electing officers of the Convention, appointing committees, and changing or preserving the character of accepted institutions. These strategies have included extensive travel, numerous informational and ideological meetings, mailouts, network of representatives who share in this common strategy, and sustained efforts to recruit messengers to attend the Convention.

We as a Peace Committee recognize that these political coalitions and strategies were born in part, at least, out of deep conviction and concern for theological issues.

But, we believe that the time has come for the Convention to move beyond this kind of politics. We find that the extent of political activity within the Southern Baptist Convention at the present time promotes a party spirit; creates discord, division, and distrust; diminishes our ability to do missions and evangelism; is detrimental to our influence; and impedes our ability to serve our Lord.

If allowed to continue unchecked, such political activity in the Convention can have disastrous consequences affecting our ability to serve our Lord and do His work.

Steps have been taken and additional steps are recommended in this report to resolve the theological issues involved in our present controversy. Because of our fear of the consequences of continued organized political activity within our Convention, and since steps have been and will continue to be taken to resolve theological issues, we feel that continued organized political activity within the Southern Baptist Convention is no longer necessary, desirable, or appropriate. We think the continuation of such political activity in the future would be unacceptable and could be disastrous.

We recommend that the Southern Baptist Convention request all organized political factions to discontinue the organized political activity in which they are now engaged. We think the following specific activities are out of place and request all groups to discontinue these specific political activities:

(1) Organized political activity;

(2) Political strategies developed by a group with central control;

(3) Holding information/ideological meetings;

(4) Extensive travel on behalf of political objectives within the Convention; and

(5) Extensive mailouts to promote political objectives in the Convention.

In 1986 the Southern Baptist Convention adopted the report of the Peace Committee which found:

(1) Some spokesmen on both sides of the political spectrum have used intemperate, inflammatory, and unguarded language, that is, "going for the jugular," "Holy War," "independent fundamentalists," "flaming liberal," and other pejorative terms.

(2) Some spokesmen on both sides of the political Spectrum and the autonomous independent journals on both sides of the issue have labeled and attributed improper motives to people with whom they disagree.

(3) Distribution of news is necessary in a democratic society. There have been instances when news releases have been altered, distorting the intent of the article and oftentimes creating confusion. In some denominational papers and in some autonomous independent journals, there has been prejudice against the conservative political activists and in some autonomous independent journals there has been prejudice against the moderate side.

The Convention in Atlanta [1986] adopted the recommendations of the Peace Committee as follows:

—That the Convention deplore the use of the type of intemperate, inflammatory, and unguarded language used by some spokesmen on both sides of the political spectrum.

—That the Convention urge Baptist Press, the state Baptist papers, and the autonomous independent journals to be especially careful to be fair and accurate in reporting events in the Convention and refrain from labeling and attributing improper motives.

Despite these recommendations approved by the Southern Baptist Convention, the Peace Committee finds that some of the state Baptist papers and the autonomous journal—the *Southern Baptist Advocate, SBC Today, Baptists United News,* and the *Baptist Laity Journal*—have continued to use intemperate, inflammatory language and have labeled individuals and impugned motives.

We renew again our request to these papers and journals to contribute to the process of reconciliation and the promotion of our cooperative work together as we seek to do the work of Christ. We again call upon all state Baptist papers and the independent autonomous journals to comply with the action taken at the Atlanta Convention and outlined above. We call upon individual Southern Baptists to use their influence to help stop these divisive actions.

We the Peace Committee ask Baptist Press, all Baptist state papers, Baptist publications, and independent autonomous journals to refrain from using terms and labels, specifically terms such as fundamentalist, liberal, fundamental-conservative, and moderate-conservative.

Conclusions

The enabling resolution of the Southern Baptist Convention at the 1985 Dallas Convention commissioned this special committee to determine the sources of the controversies within the Convention and to make findings and recommendations that would make it possible for Southern Baptists to effect reconciliation and to continue to cooperate in carrying out evangelism, missions, Christian education, and other causes.

Making peace among all Southern Baptists was not to be the work of the committee. *Reconciliation* was, and still is, the key word. Surely, there must be peace; that is, there must be an end to hostility among us, which is peace. Committed Christians must live in peace. No recommendation of the committee is needed to effect peace—it is found in the heart of the believer.

Reconciliation may be a first cousin to peace, but it rests on a different foundation. To reconcile is to harmonize, to cause to be friendly again, to reunite, to accept our differences, and to cooperate in all undertakings which enhance our mutual interests and goals. It was only through a subtle process of reconciliation, taking place over 142 years of history, that Southern Baptists have with God's blessing, and His help, achieved a preeminent position in missions, education, and evangelism. We have kept our differences from creating hostility, until recently, and not only have we lived in peace, but with remarkable harmony and cooperation.

We must never try to impose upon individual Southern Baptists nor local congregations a specific view of how Scripture must be interpreted. If such an attempt is made, then reconciliation is not the goal nor is it possible to achieve.

There is but one way for us to survive *intact* as a denomination. It involves recognition of some basic facts, among which are these:

(1) Changes are now taking place in the leadership of many Southern Baptist Convention boards.

(2) These changes will impact these boards and agencies for years to come.

(3) The role of many who have exercised leadership in the past will change as colleagues of different persuasions will fill leadership roles.

(4) This change will mean that some who have been in general agreement with Convention programs in the past will have less involvement, while those who previously have had difficulty in agreement with certain Convention programs will have more involvement.

(5) We have seen changes in Southern Baptist life in the past and we will see changes in the future. The important issue is that we must continue to be faithful stewards of the opportunities God has given Southern Baptists.

How then can we survive intact or substantially that way?

First, the hostility must cease within the heart of each of us. That brings peace.

Second, our leaders must have and must demonstrate a view of Baptist life that reaches beyond the limits of their own personal theology. No effort should be made or should be permitted to be made which would seek to eliminate from Baptist life theological beliefs or practices which are consistent with the Baptist Faith and Message statement and which have found traditional acceptance by substantial numbers of our people. Proponents of extreme positions at each end of the current Baptist theological spectrum should be encouraged to major on those things which lead to cooperative efforts and to minimize divisive issues and controversies.

Third, and most important, nothing must be allowed to stand in the way of genuine cooperation in missions, Christian education, evangelism, and our other traditional causes. While different leaders may arise, the nature and work of our Christian cooperative enterprise must continue unabated.

Finally, we should recognize and freely admit that the greatest source of our strength as a denomination lies in the thousands of local church congregations that support our cooperative undertakings. Through long years of experience, they have learned to trust our leaders, our agencies and institutions, and, because of that trust, they have provided magnificent support and responded to that leadership.

We have proclaimed this to be God's way of doing His work. Through continued cooperation in His enterprises, we can continue this mighty work. If we insist on having our way, drawing lines which exclude from places of leadership and responsibility those who do not hold our specific viewpoint, we can destroy what God has created in the Southern Baptist Convention. If, however, we can maintain a cooperative spirit and let our sense of Christian love bridge the gap of the diversity among us, we can continue to bear effective witness to His kingdom enterprise throughout all the world.

Recommendations

We make the following recommendations:

1. Although the Baptist Faith and Message statement of 1963 is a statement of basic belief, it is not a creed. Baptists are noncreedal in that they do not impose a man-made interpretation of Scripture on others. Baptists, however, declare their commitment to commonly held interpretations which then become parameters for cooperation. Therefore, we recommend that we

(1) Reaffirm the 1963 Baptist Faith and Message statement as the guideline by which all the agencies of the Southern Baptist Convention are to conduct their work.

(2) Request, respectfully, all Southern Baptists to continue their high view of Scripture as "given by inspiration of God" (2 Tim 3:16), and to diligently teach and proclaim the truthfulness, the reliability, and the authority of the Bible.

2. Although all Southern Baptists do not understand the Baptist Faith and Message statement on Scripture the same way, this diversity should not create hostility toward each other, stand in the way of genuine cooperation, or interfere with the rights and privileges of all Southern Baptists within the denomination to participate in its affairs.

Because fairness in the process of making committee and board appointments is essential to the process of reconciliation and peace, the committee recommends that the present and all future presidents of the Southern Baptist Convention, the Committee on Committees, and the Committee on Boards select nominees who endorse the Baptist Faith and Message statement, and are drawn in balanced fashion from the broad spectrum of loyal, cooperative Southern Baptists, representative of the diversity of our denomination.

Recognizing the nature of our diversity and the rightful place of biblical interpretation, we believe we can learn from each other and, in the long run, we can protect each other from unwanted extremes.

We, therefore, further recommend that the Southern Baptist Convention continue in every attempt to remain a unified fellowship, rejecting the notion of any official division of our body.

3. We recommend that the Southern Baptist Convention Executive Committee study and report to the Southern Baptist Convention in 1988 a Convention bylaw establishing an office of parliamentarian, and that the study include the following considerations:

(1) The president and two vice-presidents, acting together, shall annually appoint a chief parliamentarian and two assistant parliamentarians to advise the presiding officer of the Convention on matters of parliamentary procedure.

(2) The chief parliamentarian shall be a fully certified member of the American Institute of Parliamentarians who has the experience to serve effectively at annual sessions of the Southern Baptist Convention.

4. In view of the fact that the Cooperative Program is the lifeline of all that we are doing as Southern Baptists, we commend our churches and state conventions for their increased giving through the Cooperative Program and we recommend to our people that they continue their strong support of the Cooperative Program.

We recognize the historic right of each Southern Baptist church to give to the work of the agencies, in keeping with its deeply held convictions, without intimidation or criticism.

We recommend that the Cooperative Program be continued unchanged.

5. We recommend, in view of the intense public discussions of the last few years, that trustees determine the theological positions of the seminary administrators and faculty members in order to guide them in renewing their determination to stand by the Baptist Faith and Message statement of 1963, to the Glorieta Statement of their intention to work toward reconciliation of the conflict in the Convention, and to their own institutional declarations of faith as the guidelines by which they will teach their students in preparation for gospel ministry in the churches, mission fields, and service to the denomination.

The Bible is a book of redemption, not a book of science, psychology, sociology, or economics. But, where the Bible speaks, the Bible speaks truth in all realms of reality and to all fields of knowledge. The Bible, when properly interpreted, is authoritative to all of life.

We call upon Southern Baptist institutions to recognize the great number of Southern Baptists who believe this interpretation of article 1 of the Baptist Faith and Message statement of 1963, and, in the future, to build their professional staffs and faculties from those who clearly reflect such dominant convictions and beliefs held by Southern Baptists at large.

We, as a Peace Committee, recognize and respect those in Southern Baptist life whose view of Scripture differs from this one and pledge to continue to cooperate. We pledge the highest regard, charity, and commitment to them in our combined efforts to fulfill the Great Commission and we call upon them to make the same pledge.

6. We recommend that the Southern Baptist Convention request all organized political factions to discontinue the organized political activity in which they are now engaged. At this time, we think the following specific political activity is out of place and we request all groups to discontinue the following specific political activities:

(1) Organized political activity.

(2) Political strategies developed by a group with central control.

(3) Holding information/ideological meetings.

(4) Extensive travel on behalf of political objectives within the Convention.

(5) Extensive mailouts to promote political objectives in the Convention.

7. We recommend that Baptist Press, all state Baptist papers, independent autonomous journals, and individual Southern Baptist refrain from the use of intemperate and inflammatory language, labeling individuals and impugning motives.

Specifically, we request that all Baptist writers and individual Baptists refrain from characterizing fellow Southern Baptists in terms such as "fundamentalist," "liberal," "fundamental-conservative," "moderate-conservative."

We request all Southern Baptists to take a positive view of Southern Baptist life, to use their influence to help stop the above divisive actions, and to contribute to the process of reconciliation and the promotion of our cooperative endeavors as we seek to do the work of Christ.

8. We recommend that the Southern Baptist Convention request the SBC Committee on Resolutions to continue its policy of not presenting resolutions that are divisive in Southern Baptist life for at least the next three years.

9. We recommend that the leadership of the Pastors' Conference and the SBC Forum take immediate steps to explore the possibility of "getting together" in ways that will enhance and promote our mutually strong beliefs as expressed in the Baptist Faith and Message statement.

10. We recommend that the Southern Baptist Convention continue the present twenty-two members of the SBC Peace Committee to serve for up to, but not to exceed, three years for the purpose of observing the response of all agencies, officers, and other participants to the recommendations of

the Peace Committee in an effort to encourage compliance and foster harmonious working relationships among all segments of our Baptist family. The Peace Committee would meet once each year at a time of its own choosing and would make an appropriate report to each annual session of the Convention.

Acknowledgments

1. The Peace Committee wishes to acknowledge the assistance provided us by the office and staff of Harold C. Bennett, president-treasurer of the Executive Committee of the Southern Baptist Convention. Special appreciation is due Martha T. Gaddis, administrative assistant to Dr. Bennett, and to Dan Martin, news editor of Baptist Press.

2. The Peace Committee expresses gratitude to the host of Southern Baptists and to Christians of other denominations who have faithfully prayed for the work of the committee throughout its existence.

Charles G. Fuller, chairman
Southern Baptist Convention Peace Committee

SBC Peace Committee[4]

Charles G. Fuller, chairman
Harmon M. Born*
Doyle E. Carlton, Jr.*
Mrs. Morris H. Chapman (Jodi)*
William O. Crews
Robert E. Cuttino
P. James Flamming
Mrs. A. Harrison Gregory (Christine)*
Jim Henry
Herschel H. Hobbs
William E. Hull

Albert McClellan
Charles W. Pickering*
William E. Poe*
Ray E. Roberts
Adrian P. Rogers
Charles F. Stanley
John Sullivan
Daniel G. Vestal
Jerry Vines
Edwin H. Young
*Indicates non-church-related vocation.

[4]These persons comprised the Committee in 1987 when the report (above) was adopted. The list is as it appears in the 1987 *Annual*, 417. With this list compare the original-motion list as included in the report, above, 292-93.

An Address to the Public from the Interim Steering Committee of the Cooperative Baptist Fellowship

Appendix 2

[The Cooperative Baptist Fellowship is a group of Moderate Southern Baptists and ex-Southern Baptists. Born in August 1990 as a result of the Fundamentalist-Moderate Controversy, the name "Cooperative Baptist Fellowship" was adopted on 10 May 1991, after the adoption (on 9 May) of the following document. The originally proposed name of the organization was "United Baptist Fellowship," the term used in this document when presented to the Assembly. Here "United Baptist Fellowship" has been replaced by "Cooperative Baptist Fellowship," the present name of the organization.

Presented to the General Assembly on behalf of the Interim Steering Committee, the document is the work of two people, Cecil E. Sherman and Walter B. Shurden. Sherman's is the primary hand. A brief history of the document is found in the archives of the CBF at Mercer University in Macon, Georgia.

Designed primarily to distinguish Moderate from Fundamentalist Southern Baptists, "An Address to the Public" gives insight into what Moderate Southern Baptists believe to be consistent with the Baptist tradition of freedom and responsibility. Following a cursory background statement, the document lists some of the major issues in the conflict. It then commits Moderates to the building of a new organization that will embody Baptist principles and extend the missionary work of their people.]

Introduction

Forming something as fragile as the Cooperative Baptist Fellowship is not a move we make lightly. We are obligated to give some explanation for why we are doing what we are doing. Our children will know what we have done; they may not know why we have done what we have done. We have reasons for our actions. They are:

I. Our Reasons Are Larger than Losing

For twelve years the Southern Baptist Convention in annual session has voted to sustain the people who lead the Fundamentalist wing of the SBC. For twelve years the SBC in annual session has endorsed the arguments and the rationale of the Fundamentalists. What has happened is not a quirk or a flash or an accident. It has been done again and again.

If inclined, one could conclude that the losers have tired of losing. But the formation of the Cooperative Baptist Fellowship does not spring from petty rivalry. If the old Moderate wing of the SBC were represented in making policy and were treated as welcomed representatives of competing ideas in the Baptist mission task, then we would coexist, as we did for years, alongside fundamentalism and continue to argue our ideas before Southern Baptists.

But this is not the way things are. When Fundamentalists won in 1979, they immediately began a policy of exclusion. Nonfundamentalists are not appointed to any denominational positions. Rarely are gentle Fundamentalists appointed. Usually only doctrinaire Fundamentalists, hostile to the purposes of the very institutions they control, are rewarded for service by appointment. Thus, the boards of SBC agencies are filled by only one kind of Baptist. And this is true whether the vote to elect was 60–40 or 52–48. It has been since 1979 a "winner take all." We have no voice.

In another day Pilgrims and Quakers and Baptists came to America for the same reason. As a minority, they had no way to get a hearing. They found a place where they would not be second-class citizens. All who attended the annual meeting of the SBC in New Orleans in June 1990 will have an enlarged understanding of why our ancestors left their homes and dear ones and all that was familiar. So, forming the Cooperative Baptist Fellowship is not something we do lightly. Being Baptist should ensure that no one is ever excluded who confesses "Jesus is Lord" (Philippians 2:11).

II. Our Understandings Are Different

Occasionally, someone accuses Baptists of being merely a contentious, controversial people. That may be. But the ideas that divide Baptists in the present "controversy" are the same ideas that have divided Presbyterians, Lutherans, and Episcopalians. These ideas are strong and central; these ideas will not be papered over. Here are some of these basic ideas.

1. *Bible.* Many of our differences come from a different understanding and interpretation of Holy Scripture. But the difference is not at the point of the inspiration or authority of the Bible. We interpret the Bible differently, as will be seen below in our treatment of the biblical understanding of women and pastors. We also, however, have a different understanding of the nature of the Bible. We want to be biblical—especially in our view of the Bible. That means that we dare not claim less for the Bible than the Bible claims for itself. The Bible neither claims nor reveals inerrancy as a Christian teaching. Bible claims must be based on the Bible, not on human interpretations of the Bible.

2. *Education.* What should happen in colleges and seminaries is a major bone of contention between Fundamentalists and Moderates. Fundamentalists educate by indoctrination. They have the truth and all the truth. As they see it, their job is to pass along the truth they have. They must not change it. They are certain that their understandings of the truth are correct, complete, and to be adopted by others.

Moderates, too, are concerned with truth, but we do not claim a monopoly. We seek to enlarge and build upon such truth as we have. The task of education is to take the past and review it, even criticize it. We work to give our children a larger understanding of spiritual and physical reality. We know we will always live in faith; our understandings will not be complete until we get to heaven and are loosed from the limitations of our mortality and sin.

3. *Mission.* What ought to be the task of the missionary is another difference between us. We think the mission task is to reach people for faith in Jesus Christ by preaching, teaching, healing and other ministries of mercy and justice. We believe this to be the model of Jesus in Galilee. That is the way he went about his mission task. Fundamentalists make the mission assignment narrower than Jesus did. They allow their emphasis on direct evangelism to undercut other biblical ministries of mercy and justice. This narrowed definition of what a missionary ought to be and do is a contention between us.

4. *Pastor.* What is the task of the pastor? They argue the pastor should be the ruler of a congregation. This smacks of the bishop's task in the Middle Ages. It also sounds much like the kind of church leadership Baptists revolted against in the seventeenth century.

Our understanding of the role of the pastor is to be a servant/shepherd. Respecting lay leadership is our assignment. Allowing the congregation to make real decisions is of the very nature of Baptist congregationalism. And using corporate business models to "get results" is building the Church by the rules of a secular world rather than witnessing to the secular world by way of a servant Church.

5. *Women.* The New Testament gives two signals about the role of women. A literal interpretation of Paul can build a case for making women submissive to men in the Church. But another body of scripture points toward another place for women. In Galatians 3:27–28 Paul wrote, "As many of you as are baptized into Christ have clothed yourselves with Christ. There is no longer Jew or Greek, there is no longer slave or free, there is no longer male and female; for all of you are one in Christ Jesus." (NRSV)

We take Galatians as a clue to the way the Church should be ordered. We interpret the reference to women the same way we interpret the reference to slaves. If we have submissive roles for women, we must also have a place for the slaves in the Church.

In Galatians Paul follows the spirit of Jesus who courageously challenged the conventional wisdom of his day. It was a wisdom with rigid boundaries between men and women in religion and in public life. Jesus deliberately broke those barriers. He called women to follow him; he treated women as equally capable of dealing with sacred issues. Our model for the role of women in matters of faith is the Lord Jesus.

6. *Church.* An ecumenical and inclusive attitude is basic to our fellowship. The great ideas of theology are the common property of all the Church. Baptists are only a part of that great and inclusive Church. So, we are eager to have fellowship with our brothers and sisters in the faith and to recognize their work for our Savior. We do not try to make them conform to us; we try to include them in our design for mission. Mending the torn fabric of both Baptist and Christian fellowship is important to us. God willing, we will bind together the broken parts into a new company in preview of the great fellowship we shall have with each other in heaven.

It should be apparent that the points of difference are critical. They are the stuff around which a fellowship such as the Southern Baptist Convention is made. We are different. It is regrettable, but we are different. And perhaps we are most different at the point of spirit. At no place have we been able to negotiate about these differences. Were our fundamentalist brethren to negotiate, they would compromise. And that would be a sin by their understandings. So, we can either come to their position, or we can form a new fellowship.

III. We Are Called to Do More than Politic

Some people would have us continue as we have over the last twelve years, and continue to work within the SBC with a view to changing the SBC. On the face of it this argument sounds reasonable. Acting it out is more difficult.

To change the SBC requires a majority vote. To effect a majority in annual session requires massive, expensive, contentious activity. We have done this, and we have done it repeatedly.

But we have never enjoyed doing it. Something is wrong with a religious body that spends such energy in overt political activity. Our time is unwisely invested in beating people or trying to beat people. We have to define the other side as bad and we are good. There is division. The existence of the Cooperative Baptist Fellowship is a simple confession of that division; it is not the cause of that division.

We can no longer devote our major energies to SBC politics. We would rejoice, however, to see the SBC return to its historic Baptist convictions. Our primary call is to be true to our understanding of the gospel. We are to advance the gospel in our time. When we get to heaven, God is not going to ask us, "Did you win in Atlanta in June of 1991?" If we understand the orders we are under, we will be asked larger questions. And to spend our time trying to reclaim a human institution (people made the SBC; it is not a scriptural entity) is to make more of that institution than we ought to make. A denomination is a missions delivery system; it is not meant to be an idol. When we make more of the SBC than we ought, we risk falling into idolatry. Twelve years is too long to engage in political activity. We are called to higher purposes.

Conclusion

- That we may have a voice in our Baptist mission . . . for that is our Baptist birthright . . .
- That we may work by ideas consistent with our understanding of the gospel rather than fund ideas than are not our gospel . . .

- That we may give our energies to the advancement of the Kingdom of God rather than in divisive, destructive politics . . .

For these reasons we form the Cooperative Baptist Fellowship. This does not require that we sever ties with the old Southern Baptist Convention. It does give us another mission delivery system, one more like our understanding of what it means to be Baptist and what it means to do gospel. Therefore, we create a new instrument to further the Kingdom and enlarge the Body of Christ.

Contributors

Jimmy Allen has served in numerous leadership positions in Southern Baptist life. In 1978 he was elected president of the SBC and served in that office for two years. From 1980 to 1989 he served as president of the SBC Radio and Television Commission. In 1989 Allen became chairman of "Baptists Committed," the SBC Moderate political organization which sought to turn back the Fundamentalists. In August 1990 he presided at the Atlanta Convocation that led to the formation of the Cooperative Baptist Fellowship (CBF). Since the formation of CBF, he has been one of the group's major missionary strategists.

Libby Bellinger, a native of North Carolina, was in 1987–1988 president of Southern Baptist Women in Ministry. A graduate of Barton College and Southeastern Baptist Theological Seminary (M.Div and D.Min), she has served on the board of directors of the Alliance of Baptists. She preached at the SBC Forum in 1988 and at present serves as chaplain at the Central Texas Senior Ministries in Waco, Texas, where she has also served as president of the Waco Ministerial Alliance.

Thomas H. Graves is the first president of the Baptist Seminary at Richmond and is a former pastor of St. John's Baptist Church in Charlotte, North Carolina. Throughout the 1980s he was professor of philosophy of religion on the faculty of the Southeastern Baptist Theological Seminary, one of the targets of Southern Baptist Fundamentalists. While in North Carolina as professor and pastor, he helped spearhead the state Moderate movement.

Stan Hastey since 1989 has been executive-director of the Alliance of Baptists. Prior to accepting that position he served as associate with James Dunn at the Baptist Joint Committee on Public Affairs in Washington, D.C., and was the bureau chief of Baptist Press in Washington. The son of missionaries, he is a graduate of Oklahoma Baptist University and Southern Baptist Theological Seminary.

John H. Hewett, a graduate of Stetson University and Southern Baptist Theological Seminary, was pastor of the Kirkwood Baptist Church in St. Louis, Missouri, and subsequently First Baptist Church, Asheville, North Carolina, during the heart of the controversy. Active in the leadership of the SBC Forum, in 1991 Hewett succeeded Daniel Vestal as moderator of the Cooperative Baptist Fellowship.

E. Glenn Hinson joined the faculty of the Baptist Seminary at Richmond in 1992 as professor of spirituality, worship, and church history. Prior to that he taught for thirty years as professor of church history on the faculty of the Southern Baptist Theological Seminary. One of Southern Baptists' most prominent scholars, he has been an outspoken critic of and a prime target for SBC Fundamentalists. He has written twenty-three books, many of which have interpreted the Baptist tradition.

Walker L. Knight has been one of Southern Baptists' most acclaimed journalists for the last four decades. From 1950 to 1959 he served as associate editor of the *Baptist Standard*, the state Baptist newspaper of Texas. In 1959 he became director of editorial services of the Home Mission Board of the SBC and editor of *Home Missions* magazine, a position he held for twenty-four years. In 1983 he became the founding editor of *SBC Today* (now *Baptists Today*), and has served as publisher of that newspaper since 1988. He is the author of *Struggle for Integrity* and seven other books.

Duke K. McCall, one of the best-known Baptist leaders in the world, served as president of the Baptist World Alliance from 1980 to 1985. Remembered primarily for his thirty-year presidency of the Southern Baptist Theological Seminary in Louisville, Kentucky, he also previously served as executive-secretary of the SBC Executive Committee and as president of New Orleans Baptist Theological Seminary. He is primarily responsible for the creation of the Baptist Cooperative Missions Program, Inc., the funding mechanism of what came to be the Cooperative Baptist Fellowship.

Alan Neely, a former Southern Baptist missionary to Columbia, taught missions at Southeastern Baptist Theological Seminary from 1976 to 1988. One of the founders of the Alliance of Baptists in 1986 and the first executive of the Alliance, Neely became the Henry Winters Luce Professor of Ecumenics and Mission at Princeton Theological Seminary in Princeton, New Jersey, where he currently serves. He edited *Being Baptist Means Freedom*, a volume that focuses on the covenant of the Alliance of Baptists, and he has been a major voice on the CBF Missions Committee.

Robert Parham, a graduate of Baylor University and Southern Baptist Theological Seminary, served on the staff of the Christian Life Commission of the SBC from 1985 to 1991. He had a front-row seat to observe the transformation of that agency into a mouthpiece for SBC Fundamentalist leaders. Along with others, he led in the organization of the Baptist Center for Ethics (BCE), located in Nashville, Tennessee, and presently serves as its executive officer. Parham is the author of *What Shall We Do in a Hungry World?* and *Loving Neighbors across Time: A Christian Guide to Protecting the Earth.*

Cecil E. Sherman lives in Atlanta, Georgia, where he is the first person to serve as coordinator of the Cooperative Baptist Fellowship. He has been at the center of the Moderate resistance to SBC Fundamentalists since 1980. He was responsible for calling the famous Gatlinburg meeting in 1980 that launched the Moderate movement, and also served as the most outspoken Moderate on the SBC Peace Committee. During the years of the controversy he was pastor of First Baptist Church in Asheville, North Carolina, and then of Broadway Baptist Church in Ft. Worth, Texas.

Walter B. Shurden is Callaway Professor of Christianity and chair of the Department of Christianity at Mercer University in Macon, Georgia. Prior to coming to Mercer he was professor of church history and Dean of the School of Theology at the Southern Baptist Theological Seminary. The author and editor of eight books in Baptist studies, he has written and spoken widely on the controversy. He helped in forming the Alliance of Baptists in 1986 and led in the founding of the William H. Whitsitt Baptist Heritage Society in 1992.

James H. Slatton is pastor of the influential River Road Church in Richmond, Virginia, where he has served for twenty-one years. A graduate of Baylor University and Southwestern Baptist Theological Seminary, he was one of the major political strategists for Moderates during the controversy. Slatton's 1985 challenge to the report of the Committee on Committees and the resulting ruling of SBC president Charles Stanley was one of the most controversial moments in the entire Fundamentalist-Moderate controversy.

Cecil P. Staton, Jr., one of the founders of Smyth & Helwys Publishing, Inc., is publisher of both Smyth & Helwys and of Mercer University Press in Macon, Georgia. Before coming to Mercer in 1991, he was assistant professor of Christianity at Brewton-Parker College. A graduate of Furman University, Southeastern Baptist Theological Seminary, and Oxford University, he is the editor of *Interpreting Isaiah.*

Daniel Vestal, a graduate of Baylor University and Southwestern Seminary, was pastor of the First Baptist Church in Midland, Texas, when the Fundamentalist-Moderate controversy began. At that time First Church Midland led all Southern Baptist churches in giving through the SBC's Cooperative Program. Currently pastor of Tallowood Baptist Church in Houston, Texas, he also served as pastor of Dunwoody Baptist Church in Atlanta, Georgia. A member of the SBC Peace Committee and a two-time SBC presidential candidate during the controversy, Vestal issued the call for the Atlanta convocation in 1990. At the convocation he was elected the first moderator of the Cooperative Baptist Fellowship.